DUST CLOUDS
IN THE
MIDDLE EAST

DUST CLOUDS IN THE MIDDLE EAST

THE AIR WAR FOR EAST AFRICA, IRAQ, SYRIA, IRAN AND MADAGASCAR, 1940-42

Christopher Shores

GRUB STREET · LONDON

Published by
Grub Street
The Basement
10 Chivalry Road
London SW11 1HT

Maps by Jeff Jefford

British Library Cataloguing in Publication Data
Shores, Christopher
Dust Clouds in the Middle East: Air War for East Africa, Iraq, Syria, Iran and Madagascar, 1940-42
I. Title
940.5423

ISBN 1 898697 37 X

Edited by Daniel Balado-Lopez

Typeset by Pearl Graphics, Hemel Hempstead

Printed and bound in Great Britain by
Biddles Ltd, Guildford and King's Lynn

CONTENTS

EAST AFRICA

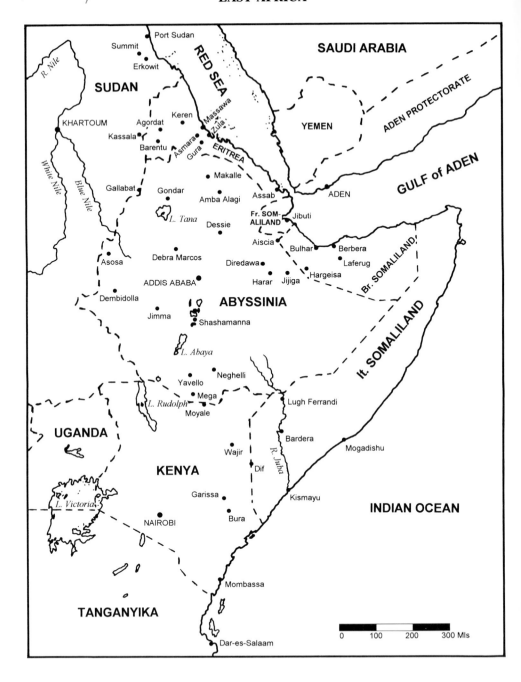

SAUDI ARABIA

Port Sudan
Summit
Erkowit

RED SEA

SUDAN

R. Nile

KHARTOUM
Agordat
Keren
Massawa
Zula
YEMEN
Kassala
Asmara
Barentu
Gura
ERITREA

ADEN PROTECTORATE

GULF of ADEN

White Nile
Blue Nile
Gallabat
Gondar
Makalle
Amba Alagi
Assab
ADEN
L. Tana
Dessie
Fr. SOM-
ALILAND
Jibuti

Aiscia
Bulhar
Berbera
Laferug
Asosa
Debra Marcos
Diredawa
Hargeisa
Br. SOMALILAND
ADDIS ABABA
Harar
Jijiga

Dembidolla
ABYSSINIA
Jimma
Shashamanna

It. SOMALILAND

L. Abaya

Neghelli
Yavello
Mega
Lugh Ferrandi
L. Rudolph
Moyale

UGANDA
Bardera
Wajir
R. Juba
Mogadishu

KENYA
Dif

L. Victoria
Garissa
Kismayu
NAIROBI
Bura
INDIAN OCEAN

Mombassa

TANGANYIKA

0   100   200   300 Mls

Dar-es-Salaam

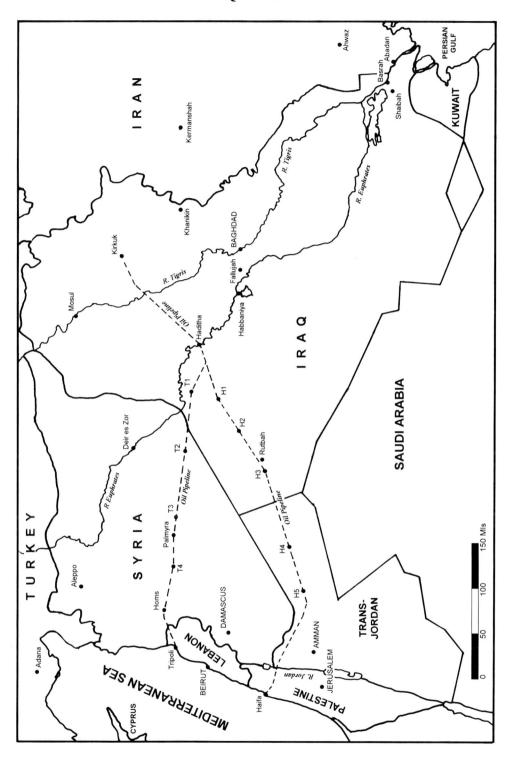

SYRIA

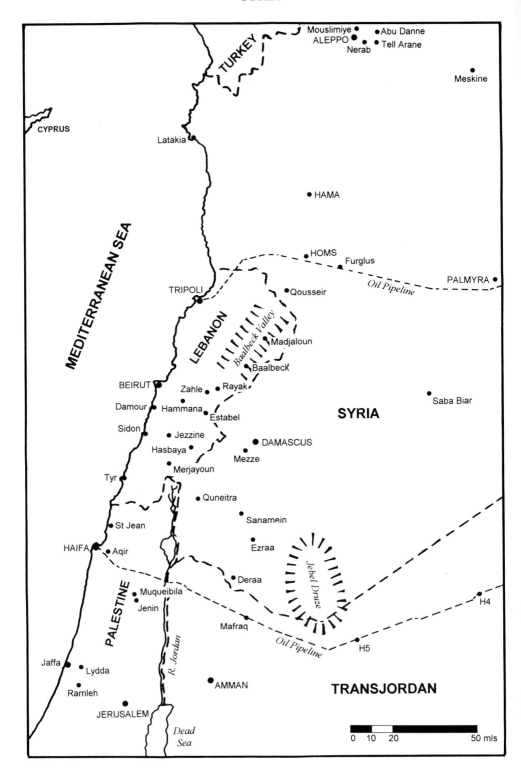

MADAGASCAR

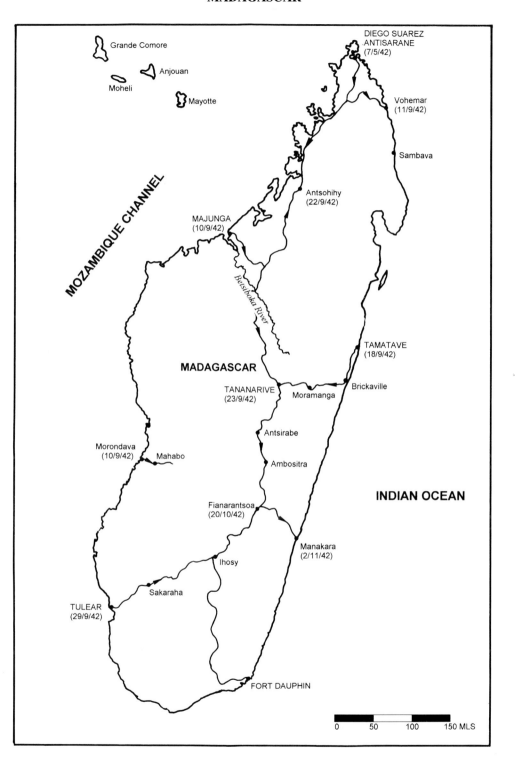

Grande Comore

Anjouan

Moheli

Mayotte

DIEGO SUAREZ
ANTISARANE
(7/5/42)

Vohemar
(11/9/42)

Sambava

MOZAMBIQUE CHANNEL

Antsohihy
(22/9/42)

MAJUNGA
(10/9/42)

Betsiboka River

MADAGASCAR

TAMATAVE
(18/9/42)

TANANARIVE
(23/9/42)

Moramanga

Brickaville

Antsirabe

Morondava
(10/9/42)

Mahabo

Ambositra

INDIAN OCEAN

Fianarantsoa
(20/10/42)

Manakara
(2/11/42)

Ihosy

Sakaraha

TULEAR
(29/9/42)

FORT DAUPHIN

0   50   100   150 MLS

INTRODUCTION AND ACKNOWLEDGEMENTS

This book began life as a variety of articles, some of which subsequently became books in their own right, although not in the English language. Brought up to date and linked appropriately, they fill the 'gaps' in the account of operations in the Middle East and Indian Ocean left by the other campaign histories in which I have been involved.

The East African Campaign occurred co-terminously with the events covered in *Malta: the Hurricane Years, 1940-1941, Air War for Yugoslavia, Greece and Crete, 1940-41*, and the first part of *Fighters over the Desert*.

The events in Iraq and Syria linked closely with those described in those same trio of books. The occupation of Madagascar followed the actions covered in the second volume of *Bloody Shambles*, just ahead of the reopening of the fighting in Burma in late 1942, and the invasion of French North-West Africa, dealt with in *Fighters over Tunisia*.

In the work involved in the writing of the East African chapters, I was originally greatly assisted by Generale Corrado Ricci of Rome, Italy. Indeed, in its original form he and I wrote the story for publication in 1979 as one of the Italian Stato Maggiore Aeronautica Ufficio Storico 'blue books', entitled *La Guerra Aerea in Africa Orientale, 1940-41*.

Most sadly, my dear friend Corrado died in late 1995, just before this new version appeared. Himself a fighter pilot and unit commander in East Africa, and subsequently a most dedicated researcher, he had been a career officer in the Regia Aeronautica, serving in Spain with the Aviacione Legionaria, where he flew Fiat CR 32s with the 16° Gruppo CT 'Cucaracha'. Posted to command the 410ª Squadriglia in Ethiopia, he continued to fly the CR 32. A stickler for accuracy, he would allow no claim to be submitted without full certainty as to its exactitude — and as a researcher I can confirm that his is the only unit I have ever come across where every claim can be verified, and some of the 'probables' as well! Invalided home to Italy by air shortly before the fall of Addis Ababa, Ricci later formed and commanded the first specialized night fighter unit in the Regia Aeronautica, the 300ª Squadriglia CN, flying Fiat CR 42s and Reggiane Re 2001s. Later in the war his unit was issued with a few ex-Armée de l'Air Dewoitine D 520s, and he was involved in some interceptions of USAAF B-24 Liberators in one of these French fighters during 1943.

Following the Armistice of September 1943, Ricci served with the Italian Co-Belligerent Air Force, and after the war remained in service, becoming Chief of Personnel. His Deputy, and subsequent successor following his retirement, was another ex-East African pilot, Romano Palmera, whose help with our original research was also of critical importance.

———

1

In later years, following the tragic deaths of several of his children in accidents, Corrado left Italy to start a new life in Gabon, where he set up a carpentry business. Subsequently he coupled that work with service as a missionary for the Roman Catholic Church. I pay tribute here to a truly kind and generous-spirited man, who is greatly missed.

By his good offices, this part of the account was aided substantially by a number of persons and agencies, to whom grateful thanks are due. Generali Romano Palmera, Michelangiolo Serafini, Corrado Santoro, Flavio Danieli, Nino Pasti, Antonio Raffi and Lucertini; Colonello Pierpaolo Leoni, Signori Ugo Zoino, Mario Di Trani and Parmeggiani all assisted in putting flesh on the skeletal details of the Regia Aeronautica operations, providing anecdotes, important names and dates, and illustrations from their personal collections.

Much assistance was received from Headquarters, South African Defence Force, and while the original work on the basic research was progressing, the spendid book *A Gathering of Eagles; the SAAF in Italian East Africa, 1940-41* by J.A. Brown (Purnell) was published. On the advice of the SADF, this was used so far as SAAF operations were concerned. Much later, considerable update information was provided by Michael Schoeman, who vetted the original text most carefully for me. He and another South African friend of many years, Ken Smy, also assisted with the collection of photographs, and both are due a great debt of gratitude.

Another work of great value was *South African Forces in WW II; Vol 1, East African and Abyssinian Campaigns* by Neil Orpen (Purnell). So far as the Army activities in Eritrea were concerned, *Eritrea, 1941* proved invaluable. Reference was also made to *The Mediterranean and Middle East, Vols I and II* in the HMSO History of the Second World War series, and to *Royal Air Force, 1939-1945, Vol 1, The Fight at Odds.*

A word is necessary also on certain shortcomings occasioned by lack of some basic reference material. Much Italian documentation was destroyed as the campaign progressed to that nation's detriment, and the main source of reference has been the daily wires telegraphed to Comando Supremo in Rome. Unfortunately these were not always as complete as could have been desired, and frequently reported events one or two days later than they had actually occurred. Undoubtedly the most successful Regia Aeronautica unit of the campaign was the 412ª Squadriglia, but sadly this was one of the least well documented.

On the British Commonwealth side, the records of 430 Flight and 'K' Flight for the latter months of the fighting were not available, and details of operations of some of the SAAF units were not always as complete as might have been wished.

Much assistance with illustrations was received, most notable from another old friend, Flt Lt Andy Thomas — who provided much support of this kind to all sections of the book — and from Nicola Malizia, Ian Simpson, Frank Smith and the late Air Marshal Sir Anthony Selway, Air Vice-Marshal L.H. Moulton, Grp Capt J. Pelly-Fry, and Flt Lt G. Whittard.

In more recent years I have also been aided by Ing Giovanni Massimello of Milan. As the manuscript was at proof stage, he was able to provide me with a nearly definitive listing of the victory totals claimed by the more successful Italian fighter pilots during the campaign, which is appended at the end of the Section dealing with East Africa.

Whilst the sections covering Iraq and Iran were researched and written by myself alone, much background information was again obtained from the HMSO's *The Mediterranean and Middle East, Vol I*. I was joined in the work on Syria and Madagascar by another valued friend of long standing, Christian J. Ehrengardt of Paris, France. Again, we initially prepared the accounts for publication in serialised article form for magazine publication in the UK, but both accounts, greatly increased in content insofar as the Syrian element was concerned, were included within a two-volume work published in France by Lavauzelle as *L'Aviation de Vichy au Combat*. Details of the Madagascar operations formed part of *Tome I; Les Campagnes Oubliees, 3 Juillet 1940 — 27 Novembre 1942*, while *Tome II* was given over entirely to *La Campagne de Syrie, 8 Juin — 14 Juillet 1941*. Published specifically for French readers, this section particularly, has been completely rewritten.

All sections have been enhanced by appropriate maps, for which thanks are due to another old friend, Wg Cdr C.G. 'Jeff' Jefford, who prepared these for us in his inimitable way.

Finally a word regarding my publisher, John Davies of Grub Street, who probably carries the main responsibility for this book appearing at all! Various friends and enthusiasts have suggested to me that such a volume ought to be produced, but I had never given much serious thought to such a possibility. Following some 30 years of 'spare time' research and writing, I was ready for a rest, and after the publication of *Aces High* in 1994, I had told John that I would write no more for at least a year.

Flatteringly unwilling to present Grub Street's new catalogue without a new title under my name included therein, he cajoled me — there is no other word for it — into producing this volume on the basis that most of the work was already done, and it would not involve a great deal more. I concurred. How wrong we both were! It has taken months of hard work, and considerable rewriting to achieve the finished product!

CFS
Hendon, January 1996

SECTION I · EAST AFRICA

Chapter One

WAR ON A SHOESTRING

June 1940 found the Mediterranean and Middle East in a state of tension, awaiting the inevitable spread of the war to this area as the German armoured columns swiftly overran northern France, driving the British Expeditionary Force from the continent of Europe at Dunkirk, and smashing the demoralised French armies with their unexpected *Blitzkrieg* tactics. The question was, how long would Benito Mussolini, Fascist dictator of Italy, keep his country out of the war now that rich pickings were available for apparently little effort?

The 'new Roman Empire' already existed, extending deep into East Africa. There Ethiopia (Abyssinia) had been added to the colonies of Eritrea and Italian Somaliland during 1935, the Italian dominion reaching as far as the northern borders of the British colony of Kenya. The small British and French holdings in Somaliland were surrounded on all sides but the sea by Italian territory.

Although most British strength was based in Egypt for the defence of the Suez Canal, East Africa had nonetheless a particular importance, as a hostile presence along the western coastline of the Red Sea could threaten all traffic en route to the Far Eastern colonies and the Antipodean Dominions. The imminent collapse of France greatly increased the importance of this area to the British; previously it had been taken for granted that the Allied naval bases in southern France, the French North African territories, and on the island of Malta would ensure the Mediterranean as an Anglo-French lake. Now, suddenly, there was every likelihood that should hostilities with Italy commence, the Mediterranean supply route would be closed, and all supplies for the British forces in the Middle East would have to be brought right round Africa, approaching Egypt from the south through the Red Sea.

Immediate efforts had been made to strengthen Imperial forces in the area, particularly so far as the Royal Air Force was concerned, but little could be spared from the already dangerously weak forces in Egypt. In the Sudan, Aden and British Somaliland, as in Kenya to the south, such forces as there were, were mainly for policing and garrison duties, and no adequate defence could be considered until substantial reinforcements could be sent. Much less could any offensive operations be planned, other than aggressive patrolling by small mobile columns.

For the Italians, however, the situation was not really so much better. Their empire in East Africa was about six times the size of the homeland, and was

---

basically an area of highlands about 6,000-8,000 feet above sea level, from which rose steep peaks, in many cases above 12,000 feet in height. These mountains gradually dropped away to the low-lying deserts of the Sudan and the arid Northern Frontier District of Kenya.

The area was affected twice a year by rainy seasons, the little rains coming in mid-winter, while the big rains fell from June to October. These rains, pouring down the many steep wild gorges, would quickly transform rivers and streams into raging torrents. Temperatures varied from sub-tropical in the semi-desert lowlands, to temperate in the hills and cold in the mountains. Vegetation was thick and lush in the highlands, but poor and sparse at lower levels.

The main problem, however, was the very poor communications system; a few good roads connected the major towns, but elsewhere only tracks existed, many of which became virtually impassable quagmires during the rains. There were two railway lines, one from Jibuti in French Somaliland to Addis Ababa, and one from Massawa, the main Eritrean port, to Asmara and Tessenei.

The area was almost totally isolated from Italy because its land and sea routes could be cut with ease by the British, leaving only a tenuous aerial route. For six years the Italian Army and Air Force had been fighting a colonial war, and both were basically equipped and trained for such operations. Indeed, the Army could muster but one division of regular Italian troops — the Granatieri di Savoia (Savoy Grenadiers) composed of two regiments each of two battalions; each regiment had a third battalion in reserve, one of Bersaglieri, the other of Alpini. These were crack units of northern Italians, and were to fight well. They were backed-up by the 'Blackshirt' battalions — virtually territorial units of volunteers known as the CCNN. As a practical way of reducing unemployment at home, people had been persuaded to apply for passage to East Africa, joining the CCNN to get there. Once there, they were intended to find work and settle for life, sending for their families. Most were middle-aged, and lacked both training and equipment, although some fought with spirit and determination when called upon to do so.

The greater part of the Army comprised native brigades, some of which were well manned and commanded, particularly those containing Eritrean personnel. There were many difficulties however; since many tribes were in a state of permanent hostilities, members of different tribes could not be put together in the same units. While usually good fighters in the attack when well trained and armed, they rarely stood up to artillery bombardment or air attack, and their morale was always a most variable factor. Their frequently stated view was 'We enlisted to fight men, not armoured cars or aircraft!' Their concept of war was the classic tribal one, and they had no understanding of the European way of fighting. Generally their training was inadequate for modern war — typified perhaps by the fact that all movement was undertaken on foot, led by officers mounted on horses.

Finally there were the 'banda' — companies of native skirmishers and scouts, some 'regulars', led by Italian officers. Others were 'irregulars' who were called to arms when necessary and supplied with arms held by the resident administrative commissioner. They were suitable only for local policing duties.

To support this force were the usual engineer, medical and administrative units, some elderly armoured cars and a few tanks, and the artillery. This latter comprised batteries equipped with 77/28 guns, or efficient 65/13 mountain guns; four batteries had ex-Austrian 75/27 guns, and there were ten 105/28 and

120/25 guns, several of them in fixed positions. In each case the first number related to the calibre of the weapon in millimetres and the second number to the length of the gun in calibres. There were also some really ancient pieces, some of which were used at Keren, and twenty-four 20mm Breda cannon, sent from Italy without sights. The anti-aircraft defences used 77/28 guns mounted on wooden platforms and traversed manually.

In total, the Italian ground forces could dispose sixteen national battalions, two armoured car companies with M/11 cars, two squadrons of light and medium tanks, and ten artillery groups; plus 123 native battalions or 'banda' groups, eight cavalry groups, two groups of mule-carried artillery and fifteen 'banda' — 280,000 men in all, subdivided into four theatres: North (Eritrea, Gondar); East (Scioa, Harar); South (Galla-Sidamo); Juba (Somaliland).

In June 1940 the reserves were called up, and the strength rose to 330,000, but the nationals who returned to the colours were mostly unfit for front-line duties, many being drivers or technicians, most others being too old or lacking in training. For the natives who were willing to enlist there was a great shortage even of relatively modern rifles, and many of those already in service, although considered as troops, had in fact been employed on road construction and were neither trained nor armed.

There was an almost total lack of intelligence information, native informers being the main source, and these of course could be bought by the British with ease, the information provided always being inconsistent and vague anyway. With the problems facing them, with very poor transport facilities, and with supply based on fixed depots, it was impossible for the Italians to consider any operations requiring rapid movement or advances over long distances.

More than 100,000 of the available troops were in the north, facing Port Sudan, Khartoum and Rosières, while 83,000 more were on the frontiers with British and French Somaliland. 20,000 formed the Army of the Juba, while light forces patrolled the rest of the frontiers with the Sudan, Kenya and Uganda. Over 40,000 men had to be retained in the central area because Ethiopian partisan activity in the Scioa area, and particularly around Ancober, was still far from subdued. Only the Northern and Eastern sectors were considered of importance, and in view of the general lack of mobility, main forces were held at suitable centres, patrols maintaining a watch on the frontiers.

The Italian Navy, based on Massawa and Assab mainly, was in little better shape. It possessed two squadriglie (squadrons) of destroyers of the *Tigre* and *Nullo* class, with top speeds of 28 and 30 knots respectively; all were old and in rather poor shape mechanically. There were eight submarines, but these remained unserviceable for months due to trouble with their refrigeration plants which suffered leakages of poisonous gas.

In 1939 the Italian government had looked at the possibility of building up the defences and supplies of the various parts of the empire so that they could remain self-sufficient for a period of one year, since it was considered that the main Italian forces would be in a position to maintain full war operations for only this period of time. The estimated cost of 900,000,000 lire was prohibitive however, and the idea was dropped. From East Africa there came a request for at least the supply of 10,000 lorry tyres and 100 fighter aircraft, the latter being urgently required to defend such a vast territory, and to cover any necessary troop movements. As to the former, for all available lorries there were just six tyres each, the two spares in most cases being the most worn. No replacements arrived, although eventually a single Japanese ship docked at Mogadishu in Somaliland and off-loaded a small supply; they were all of the wrong size! This ship also delivered a cargo of petroleum, but transport facilities were so bad that it could not be transferred to Ethiopia, and eventually it had to be burned to prevent it falling into British hands.

The one delivery that did continue was of new settlers, the last shipload of women and children arriving as late as 19 May 1940. These extra civilians were to cause many problems since they had all to be fed and protected with existing resources.

Late in December 1939 the Viceroy, the Duke of Aosta, sent the chief of the armed forces to Rome to report to Mussolini on the unpreparedness of East Africa. The latter assured him that Italy would not be involved in the war for at least a year, and then it would only be briefly, no long-drawn commitment being considered.

The sudden collapse of France in May 1940 caused Mussolini to change his plans and plunge Italy into the fighting before it was all over, but although large, East Africa was considered relatively unimportant at this stage, it being believed that the war would swiftly be finished.

Realising the weakness of his position, Aosta wished to undertake early offensive action before British reinforcements could arrive, and while his overwhelming numerical superiority lasted. Badoglio, the Italian Chief of the General Staff, would not have it however; forces in East Africa were to take up a completely defensive attitude on the borders, and any plans for offensive operations had to be submitted to Rome for approval, which would only be given in very special cases.

Possible targets for offensive action were Port Sudan or Khartoum in the Sudan, Mombasa in Kenya, or French and British Somaliland. Only the latter was practicable, as the former required strong forces, maintained over long lines of communication; ideally operations against the Sudan would be of greater strategic impact. Later, when Rome thought the British were about to capitulate, and it was considered desirable to bring some conquests to the victory table, a move into British Somaliland with all possible haste was to be ordered.

In the meantime, forbidden to undertake any offensive operations, the commanders in East Africa decided that from a defensive point of view it would be better to move all the forces to strong positions in the central highlands from where they could easily be despatched to any sector, and where it should prove possible to hold out until the end of the war. Having regard to the need to protect civilians from native partisans and brigands however, and to the political necessity to maintain frontiers as they existed, such a move was not acceptable.

The Regia Aeronautica in East Africa was quite substantial in size, and was backed up by more than seventy-five per cent reserves and aircraft undergoing repairs; the equipment, however, left much to be desired when the prospect of hostilities against an enemy possessing a sizeable air force of its own was contemplated. More than half of the squadriglie were equipped with Caproni Ca 133s, high-wing monoplanes powered by three engines, designed specifically for colonial operations — bombing and troop- or cargo-carrying, where the only opposition to be expected was small-arms fire from the ground. Consequently they were neither fast nor well armed, and were to prove easy prey for almost any opponent they were to meet. A substantial proportion of the remaining units flew Savoia S 81s; these were three-engined low-wing bomber-transport

Regia Aeronautica Savoia S 79 over Gondar's Azozo airfield. These fast bombers were able to outrun Gladiators and Blenheims on most occasions. *(Corrado Ricci)*

monoplanes with fixed undercarriages, possessing a performance somewhat superior to that of the Ca 133s but still far below standards pertaining for effective daylight bombing aircraft in 1940. They had performed creditably throughout the Spanish Civil War, but in East Africa, following early losses, were to be relegated to night bombing duties.

Two squadriglie operated Savoia S 79s, again three-engined low-wing monoplanes, but fitted with retractable undercarriages and a relatively heavy defensive armament of five machine guns, two of which were of the effective 12.7mm calibre. These were probably the most modern and potent aircraft available to either side throughout the campaign, and were undoubtedly the most effective weapon in the Italians' armoury. They were, however, somewhat underpowered, and due to the third engine in the nose, gave a very poor view forward for the bomb aimer, presenting him with his target very suddenly, and with little time to get the bomber accurately lined up. Like other Italian bombers, intercommunication between the crew in flight was very poor. There was also a considerable lack of spares, and when hostilities commenced many aircraft had to be cannibalised to keep others flying. The S 79s were nonetheless strong aircraft, very manoeuvrable for their size, and capable of sustaining much punishment; maintenance was also relatively simple.

Left: Fiat CR 32 fighter of the Regia Aeronautica's 410ª Squadriglia flown by the CO, Capitano Ricci, while the Squadron was based at Diredawa in 1940. *Right:* Close-up of the 410ª Squadriglia's insignia, a devil in a topi. *(Corrado Ricci)*

Insignia of the 412ª. *(Nicola Malizia)*

Four fighter squadriglie were also available, with a fifth forming, but two of these were flying elderly Fiat CR 32 biplanes, veterans of the Spanish Civil War. Although a splendid aircraft in its day, the CR 32 was well past its peak, and while it was to achieve some extremely creditable successes, it was frequently unable to catch the Allied bombers which it was supposed to intercept. The other three squadriglie, two of which arrived in East Africa just before the outbreak of hostilities, were equipped with Fiat CR 42 biplanes. These were not only one of the last fighter biplanes to be built, but also one of the best. Faster than the Gloster Gladiator, by which they would often be opposed, and more manoeuvrable than the Hawker Hurricane, they were to enjoy a number of successes, particularly during the early months of the campaign.

One CR 42 unit, the 412ª Squadriglia, was composed of experienced personnel and was to achieve very much more than the other, the 413ª, which was full of young and incompletely trained pilots, albeit with a determined and competent commanding officer. The 414ª Squadriglia had begun forming at Gura in 1939, commanded by Capitano Lucertini, who had previously led the 411ª Squadriglia. CR 42s were shipped from Italy and assembled at Massawa, but due to a shortage of pilots, another unit, the 409ª Squadriglia, had been disbanded and its CR 32s placed in store, the personnel being divided between the 412ª and

Fiat CR 42 of the 413ª Squadriglia over Ethiopia. *(Nicola Malizia)*

IMAM (Meridionali) Ro 37bis of the Regia Aeronautica's 110ᵃ Squadriglia. Designed mainly for reconnaissance and army co-operation duties, these biplanes were occasionally used as interceptors — a task in which they achieved no success whatsoever.

414ᵃ Squadriglie. By June 1940 the unit had six CR 42s on hand. At the opening of hostilities the 413ᵃ Squadriglia, which was also at Gura, was ordered to Assab. One other squadriglia, the 110ᵃ, operated Meridionali Ro 37bis two-seat observation and army co-operation biplanes, which were about as effective as any other aircraft designed for this particular set of duties during the 1930s.

A substantial element of this force, comprising three bomber gruppi with S 79s and S 81s, was immediately available to the air commander in East Africa, Generale Pietro Pinna, who could direct these units to whatever sector it was deemed required their striking power the most. The few available fighters were distributed for the defence of the most important centres — Massawa, Gura, Asmara, Assab, Diredawa and Addis Ababa — while the remainder of the units were at the disposal of the Air Sector Headquarters for operations in direct support of the ground forces.

The operational directive for the bomber units under Gen Pinna's immediate command on the outbreak of hostilities was to attack the most important British bases — ports and airfields — within range. Bombs of over 100kg were in short supply and aircraft were therefore normally to carry 50kg or 100kg bombs. Only against important concentrations of targets, especially ships in harbour, were 250kg bombs to be employed: because the difficulty of hitting ships under way was well known to the Italians, only 50kg bombs were to be used against these, the greater number carried giving a better chance of a hit of some sort being obtained.

The Regia Aeronautica's bomber squadriglia normally operated six aircraft, and was thus about the size of an RAF flight; in East Africa two squadriglie usually comprised a gruppo, which was thus roughly comparable to an RAF squadron, but some gruppi could include three squadriglie. Italian fighters and reconnaissance squadriglie operated nine aircraft each, somewhere between the strength of an RAF flight and a squadron. Dispositions of the Regia Aeronautica in East Africa in June 1940 are shown in the table.

ITALIAN AIR FORCE IN EAST AFRICA, JUNE 1940

Comando Settore Aeronautico Nord

(Air Sector Headquarters North), based on Asmara

26° Gruppo —11ª and 13ª Squadriglia	12 Ca 133s	Gondar and Bahar Dar
27° Gruppo —18ª and 52ª Squadriglia	12 Ca 133s	Assab (K14N strip)
118ª Squadriglia	6 S 81s	Assab (K14N strip)
28° Gruppo —10ª and 19ª Squadriglia	12 S 81s	Zula
29° Gruppo —62ª and 63ª Squadriglia	12 S 81s	Assab (K3N strip)
412ª Squadriglia	9 CR 42s	4 at Massawa, 5 at Gura
413ª Squadriglia	9 CR 42s	Assab
414ª Squadriglia	6 CR 42s	Gura
Gruppo Gasbarrini —41ª Squadriglia and Squadriglia dello Stato Maggiore del Settore Nord	12 Ca 133s	Agordat

Comando Settore Aeronautico Ouest

(West), based on Addis Ababa

4° Gruppo —14ª and 15ª Squadriglia	12 S 81s	Diredawa (K91, Scenele)
44° Gruppo — 6ª and 7ª Squadriglia	12 S 79s	Diredawa (K92, Chinele)
49° Gruppo —61ª and 64ª Squadriglia	12 Ca 133s	Jimma
110ª Squadriglia	9 Ro 37bis	Diredawa
410ª Squadriglia	9 CR 32s	Diredawa
411ª Squadriglia	9 CR 32s	Addis Ababa
65ª Squadriglia	6 Ca 133s	Neghelli
66ª Squadriglia	3 Ca 133s	Yavello
Squadriglia dello Stato Maggiore del Settore Centrale	6 Ca 133s	Addis Ababa

Comando Settore Aeronautico Sud

(South), based on Mogadishu

25° Gruppo — 8ª and 9ª Squadriglia	12 Ca 133s	6 at Gobwen, 6 at Lugh Ferrandi
Squadriglia dello Stato Maggiore del Settore	7 Ca 133s	Mogadishu

---

In addition to the above units was the transport force, comprising nine Savoia S 73s, nine Ca 133s, six Caproni Ca 148s, and a lone Fokker FVII. In reserve were 35 Ca 133s, one S 81, four S 79s, five CR 32s, six CR 42s and two Ro 37bis, while under repair were another 48 Ca 133s, 16 S 81s, two S 79s, 11 CR 32s, two CR 42s and two Ro 37bis.

Several big problems faced the Regia Aeronautica when considering the

Mainstay of the RAF in the Sudan in 1940 were three squadrons of Vickers Wellesley bombers. This is KU-N, K7775, of 47 Squadron. *(via A.S. Thomas)*

prospect of a full-scale war. Most airfields were situated around the periphery of the territory, for use by aircraft co-operating with ground forces on colonial duties, and as soon as any sort of invasion began, they would be lost to use. Additionally these, and a few available strips in the interior, had been prepared for use by Ca 133s and were uncomfortably short for both S 79s and CR 42s, which were thus virtually tied to a few fields at the main centres. For the bombers, maps of the area were not good, and the navigational skills of many of the newer crews left much to be desired; the almost total lack of radio communication either with the ground or between aircraft in flight was a most serious drawback.

At the start of 1940 the RAF had in the Sudan a small force of bombers, the Advanced Striking Force, under the control of 254 Wing which had its headquarters at Erkowit; all three squadrons were equipped with elderly single-engined Vickers Wellesleys, notable for their geodetic construction and very long range. These aircraft had been replaced in service everywhere else except in the Sudan, but here they were giving yeoman service. They were based as follows:

14 Squadron, commanded by Sqn Ldr A.D. Selway, at Port Sudan.
47 Squadron, commanded by Wg Cdr J.G. Elton, AFC, at Erkowit.
223 Squadron, commanded by Sqn Ldr J.C. Larking, at Summit.

47 Squadron had attached to it an additional flight, 'D' Flight, which operated seven Vickers Vincent general purpose biplanes in support of the Sudan Defence Force. The Wing was under the command of Grp Capt Macdonald. With the increase in tension in the Middle East, and the imminent possibility of Italy's entry into the war in mid-1940, the Wing was reinforced by the arrival of a detachment of nine Gloster Gladiator biplane fighters of 112 Squadron, which arrived at Summit on 3 June for the defence of the Sudanese bases and of Port Sudan. In August 203 Group would be formed to take overall control of the units in the Sudan; it would be commanded by Air Commodore L.H. Slatter.

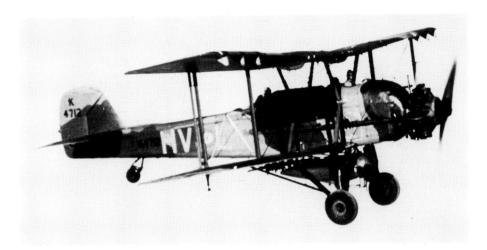

Vickers Vincent general purpose and army co-operation biplane HV-L, K4712, of 8 Squadron in Aden. In June 1940 this unit operated these aircraft and Bristol Blenheim Is side-by-side. *(8 Squadron via A.S. Thomas)*

In Aden was a further small force for the protection of supply convoys in the Red Sea and for punitive action against marauding tribesmen in the Aden Protectorate, under the command of Air Vice-Marshal G.R.M. Reid, who also commanded the garrison force.

The units here were: 8 Squadron, commanded by Sqn Ldr D.S. Radford, which was based at Khormaksar and operated one flight of Bristol Blenheim I bombers and one flight of Vincents; 94 Squadron, commanded by Sqn Ldr W.T.F. Wightman, which had recently been formed at Sheik Othman and still possessed only one flight of Gladiators; and 203 Squadron, commanded by Wg Cdr J.R.S. Streatfield, based at Khormaksar, and equipped with Blenheim IVs which had recently been converted to Mark IVF standard as long-range fighters, by the incorporation of a pack beneath the fuselage containing four forward-firing 0.303in Browning machine guns.

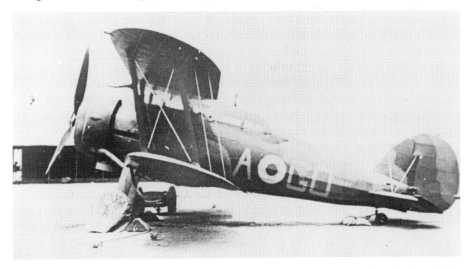

Gloster Gladiator II GO-A, N2288, of 94 Squadron at Sheik Othman, Aden, in June 1940. *(I. Simpson via A.S. Thomas)*

One of the first reinforcements to reach the RAF were the Blenheims Is of 39 Squadron from Singapore. This XZ-coded aircraft is seen shortly after arrival at Sheik Othman in June 1940. *(A. Dent via A.S. Thomas)*

Efforts were being made to reinforce Aden also, and the Blenheim Is of 39 Squadron were to arrive at Sheik Othman from India just as hostilities started. More Blenheim Is of 11 Squadron were en route from Singapore via India, but at the start of June no aircraft had yet arrived, although ground crew personnel were disembarking and moving to Sheik Othman.

In Kenya, to the south of the Italian territories, there were no RAF units at all at the start of 1940, and none was available. Fortunately for the British, the Empire was able to lend a hand and units were despatched from both the Dominion of South Africa and from Southern Rhodesia. 1 Squadron of the Southern Rhodesian Air Force, equipped with Hawker Hart, Hardy and Audax army co-operation biplanes, arrived at Nairobi in April where it came under British command and was incorporated into the RAF as 237 Squadron; the following month units of the South African Air Force began arriving.

In September 1939 the SAAF possessed four Hawker Hurricane Is, six Hawker Fury Is and one Blenheim IF for air fighting, sixty-three Hawker Hartbeestes* and eighteen Junkers Ju 86s for bombing and reconnaissance. The latter aircraft were converted airliners of South African Airways and were flown in the main by Airways crews who had been transferred to the SAAF overnight in 1939 with no formal military training. The numerically most important Hartbeestes were two-seat biplanes, developed from the Hart bomber and manufactured specially for South Africa.

By May 1940 a few additional aircraft had been received from the United Kingdom — notably Avro Ansons for maritime reconnaissance, and Vickers Valentia transports, while ten Junkers Ju 52/3m airliners had been taken over from South African Airways for military transport duties. At this stage three operational SAAF squadrons had been formed: 1 (F) with the Hurricanes and Furies, was commanded by Major N. G. Niblock-Stuart and was organised on

---

* Originally the 'Hartbeeste' was called 'Hartbees' by Hawker's who produced the first batch as new aircraft; existing Harts were later converted to the South African variant. 'Hartebeeste' is another spelling commonly used in RAF documents.

Designed as bombers by Junkers in Germany, but converted as airliners to South African Airways, these Ju 86s were converted back to the bomber configuration during 1939, and in June 1940 equipped 12 SAAF Squadron when it moved up to Kenya. *(SAAF Official)*

a three-flight basis, the flights being commanded by Capt S. van Schalkwyk, Lt B.J.L. Boyle and Lt S. van Breda Theron.

On 13 May 1940 twenty officers and fourteen other ranks of the first two flights went aboard three Valentias of 50 (Transport) Squadron, SAAF, (which had been formed in March) to be ferried from Zwartkop Air Station, Pretoria, to Abu Sueir, Egypt. There they were to be converted to Gloster Gladiators which they were then to ferry down to Nairobi. On arrival in Egypt the South Africans began their conversion training initially on Gloster Gauntlets, the Gladiator's predecessor.

Meanwhile on 19 May 11 (B) Squadron under Major R. Preller, with twenty-four Hartbeestes and a lone Fairey Battle, left for Kenya, arriving at Nairobi. While the move was under way the Ansons, which up to this point had equipped 12 (B) Squadron, were replaced by thirteen Ju 86s and took the place of the latter in four coastal reconnaissance flights; a few days later the Ju 86s, led by Major C. Martin, and the Hurricanes of 1 Squadron, led by Lt Theron, also left

Vickers Valentia I transport of 50 SAAF Squadron is seen here on an airfield in Southern Rhodesia, en route to Kenya. *(via A.S. Thomas)*

11 SAAF Squadron, arrived in Kenya even before 12 Squadron and five of the unit's Hawker Hartbeeste army co-operation biplanes are seen here with their engines running. The Hartbeestes were soon flying reconnaissance sorties near the front, seeking Italian airfields for the Ju 86s to bomb. *(MHAS)*

for Nairobi where they arrived on 25 May, 11 and 12 Squadrons then forming 1 Bomber Brigade under Lt Col S.A. Melville.

On 26 May 1 Squadron's Furies were crated and put aboard the SS *Takliwa*, arriving in Kenya on 1 June. There they were swiftly assembled, while from Nairobi two flights of 11 Squadron's Hartbeestes moved to Mombasa. By 10

Hawker biplanes were in a majority among SAAF aircraft in Kenya in June 1940. Here a section of three Fury fighters of 1 SAAF Squadron leads two sections each of three 11 SAAF Squadron Hartbeestes. *(SAAF via Ken F. Smy)*

June 46 South African aircraft in three squadrons had joined the single Rhodesian squadron and the hastily formed Kenya Auxiliary Air Unit of light aircraft for liaison duties, to provide a substantial if somewhat polyglot air component; Grp Capt W. Sowrey (soon to be promoted to Air Commodore) was posted to Kenya as Air Officer Commanding.

Early in June the Ju 86s of 12 Squadron were dispersed in flights, 'A' Flight under Capt Raubenheimer to Dar-es-Salaam on coastal patrol duties, 'B' Flight under Capt D. Meaker to Mombasa, while 'C' Flight under Capt D. du Toit remained at Nairobi.

In French Somaliland was based a small element of the Armée de l'Air comprising four Potez 631 reconnaissance-bombers, eleven Potez 25 TOE army co-operation biplanes, three Morane 406 fighters and two Potez 29 transport and general liaison biplanes.

These then were the dispositions on the evening of 10 June 1940 when Il Duce, Benito Mussolini, declared war on France and the United Kingdom.

Thursday, 11 June 1940

As in the Western Desert, the RAF reacted swiftly to the outbreak of war with Italy and at first light on 11 June 1940 eight Wellesleys of 47 Squadron from the Sudan took off to attack Asmara. The Italian anti-aircraft defences opened up and hit Wellesley K7730 piloted by Plt Off B.K.C. Fuge. The aircraft was last seen leaving the area trailing smoke and subsequently came down in Italian territory where the crew became prisoners.

However, the RAF was no quicker off the mark than the South African Air Force in the south. In the early hours of 11 June four Junkers Ju 86s from Eastleigh airfield, led by the newly promoted Maj du Toit in No 641, flew up to Bura where they were refuelled. Taking off again at 1000 they dropped 250lb bombs on a 'banda' camp at Moyale, this raid taking place some six hours before South Africa officially declared war on Italy in support of the mother country. Hawker biplanes of 237 Squadron (originally 1 Squadron, Southern Rhodesian AF) also made their first reconnaissance sorties over the northern Kenya border district, while from Aden the half-a-dozen Blenheim IVFs and a lone Blenheim I of 203 Squadron undertook photographic reconnaissance flights over Diredawa, Harar, Jijiga, Dessie, Assab and Massawa.

From the Sudan 14 Squadron's Wellesleys were delayed until 1600 in making their first attack due to difficulties with their underwing bomb containers. They finally took off to bomb Massawa where they claimed to have destroyed some 780 tons of petroleum.

Italian aerial activity on this first day was slight; one Savoia S 81 attacked Port Sudan, while a second reconnoitred the Red Sea. Three more set out on a night raid on Aden, but one had engine trouble and had to return almost at once. The other two completed their mission, but while returning to base one bomber struck a hill near Massawa and crashed in flames, the crew being killed.

Friday, 12 June 1940

Italian activity was stepped up considerably on the next day, Aden being the main target. Following the night attack, by day seven more S 81s from the 29° Gruppo at Assab bombed the port and airfield at Khormaksar without observed results. Another night attack followed by ten Caproni Ca 133s, while three more of these bombed the airfield at Kassala in the Sudan.

Bristol Blenheim I HV-Y, L6653, of 8 Squadron, based at Khormaksar, Aden. This aircraft took part in the unit's first bombing raid of the war against Macacca airfield, Assab, flown by Plt Off R.C. Young. *(8 Squadron via A.S. Thomas)*

In the south three Ca 133s of the 66ª Squadriglia from Yavello reconnoitred the Moyale and Dibbandibba area, bombing a column of about 200 men and half a score of vehicles. Other Ca 133s from the 65ª Squadriglia at Neghelli were also over Moyale during the day, two raids on the outpost itself being made, each by three aircraft, while others made reconnaissances over Buroli and down the coast south of Mogadishu. Small raids on outposts, columns and other targets near the front by formations of between one and three Ca 133s were to become almost daily occurrences, both in northern Kenya and along the whole of the Sudanese frontier with Eritrea and Ethiopia.

RAF attacks were also increased, and in the morning nine Blenheims from 8 Squadron at Aden made a combined high-level and dive-bombing attack on the airfield of Macaaca at Assab. On its return, L6654 belly-landed at Ras Ara landing ground and was damaged beyond repair. In the afternoon twelve more Blenheims from 39 Squadron, which had only arrived in Aden from India the previous day, made the first attack on the airfield at Diredawa. There a hangar was damaged and five Fiat CR 32 fighters slightly damaged, a small quantity of fuel also being set on fire and a few casualties caused.

From the Sudan nine 223 Squadron Wellesleys attacked Gura, while nine more from 47 Squadron raided Asmara. At Gura the Toselli aeronautical establishment was hit, two buildings and fifteen aero-engines being destroyed. A section of CR 42s of the 412ª Squadriglia were scrambled and attacked the bombers, shooting one up very badly (K7747) so that it crashed while landing on return to base; a second was hit by anti-aircraft fire, and returned in a 'write-off' condition.

The Italians claimed that the bomber attacked by them fell in the Keren area where the crew were taken prisoner, but it seems probable that this was in fact Plt Off Fuge's aircraft, shot down the previous day, and not seen to crash at the time by the defenders; the victory was credited to Ten Carlo Canella. Gunners in the Wellesleys reported that one CR 42 was seen to spin down apparently as a result of their fire, and a second was claimed as badly damaged; one fighter suffered engine trouble and had to make a force-landing without power, the pilot being slightly injured, while two more Fiats were slightly damaged. One of 47 Squadron's Wellesleys was also slightly damaged by a fighter during the Asmara raid.

In the south the first sorties were made by the Hartbeestes of 11 SAAF Squadron, Maj Preller leading three of these to refuel at Garissa and then make an offensive reconnaissance over the Kenyan border. This was part of a plan drawn up by Col Hector Daniel, DFC, Grp Capt Sowrey's Senior Air Staff Officer (SASO), for a concerted strike on the Italian Air Force and its bases in southern Ethiopia and Somaliland. With darkness, five Vincents of 8 Squadron from Aden set out to dive-bomb Macaaca airfield.

Saturday, 13 June 1940

In the early hours of 13 June four S 81s of the 4° Gruppo left Diredawa to bomb Aden. As they approached the area at 0440, four Gladiators from 94 Squadron were scrambled to intercept and Flg Off G.S.K. Haywood (in N2290) engaged one of the bombers flown by Sottotenente Temistocle Paolelli and Mario Laureati, shooting it down in flames off Ras Imran. Two members of the crew parachuted into the sea from where they were later retrieved by the Royal Navy.

A second S 81, flown by Colonello Mario Pezzi and Capitano Parmeggiani, was hit by anti-aircraft fire over the target, and after bombing, landed at the nearest friendly base, at Assab. A third aircraft force-landed due to engine trouble suffered before reaching the target, coming down within Italian territory. Fearing that they had landed in French Somaliland, the pilot and crew destroyed the aircraft and returned on foot. The final aircraft of the formation, flown by a very 'green' young pilot, apparently suffered some sort of technical trouble during the attack by the Gladiators, and landed at a British emergency landing ground at Husu Balid on the Arabian coast some miles east of Aden.

On 13 June 1940 four Savoia S 81 bombers of the 14ᵃ Squadriglia, 4° Gruppo, set off from Diredawa to raid Aden; none returned. This particular aircraft, '14-2', force-landed at Husu Balid, 150 miles east of Aden on the Arabian coast. RAF personnel made the aircraft airworthy again and flew it to Khormaksar, Aden, on 25 June. *(Imperial War Museum)*

Within three hours Gladiators were again scrambled as nine S 79s of the 44°
Gruppo from Diredawa also approached Aden. As they made for the target the
left-hand aircraft in the second vic of three, piloted by Sottotenente Ruffini,
was hit by an anti-aircraft shell from a warship, which was putting up an accurate
box barrage; several other bombers were hit and slightly damaged by splinters
as Ruffini's aircraft crashed. The remaining eight bombers passed over their
target twice, as on the first occasion the leader's bomb doors failed to open, and
this delay gave the fighters an opportunity to intercept.

As the bombers made their second run and headed for home, they were
attacked by two Gladiators, Sgt Price going after one pair of bombers while Plt
Off Stephenson attacked the other six.

Stephenson fired on the last of these at a point ten miles north of Sheik
Othman, following it to Khar Umera and noticing that the undercarriage had
dropped down and the port engine ceased to function. This aircraft, flown by
Capt Serafini, had in fact been hit by anti-aircraft splinters while on the first run
over Aden, and had made its second run with the undercarriage already fallen;
as it left the target leading the final vic, it was unable to keep up, and fell behind
the rest of the formation as the fighters attacked. The dorsal gunner reported
seeing large numbers of Gladiators and opened fire on Stephenson's aircraft,
hitting the centre-section of the top wing with a 12.7 mm bullet, which caused
considerable damage and punctured the oil cooler; Stephenson was at once
forced to land at Makhnuk.

The S 79, with some 100 bullet holes and other damage, returned to the
Eritrean coast and attempted to land at Assab, but as it did so the undercarriage
collapsed and it flicked over on its back, becoming a complete write-off. The
engineer and radio operator had both been wounded by shell splinters, as had
Serafini, whose flying helmet was pinned to his skull by small metal fragments.
During the fighter attack, which had stopped the starboard engine, three more
members of the crew had been wounded. Despite these wounds, all the crew
survived the crash. One other damaged S 79 also landed at Assab.

Flg Off Haywood in the third Gladiator had seen the S 79s, but had suffered
an engine failure before he could attack, and force-landed at Little Aden. S 79
gunners claimed to have shot down one Gladiator (Stephenson) and probably
a second.

During the time when the second attack was under way, a Blenheim IVF from
203 Squadron on a reconnaissance over Assab was attacked by CR 42s and
damaged. It was discovered when the aircraft was inspected upon landing that
the armour plate protecting the crew had withstood the penetration of the Italian
fighters' 12.7mm projectiles, but that the rivets attaching it to the fuselage hull
had pulled loose under the impact. Later in the day, and during the following
night, formations of Blenheims from 8 and 39 Squadrons attacked Macaaca
airfield at Assab and a new satellite landing ground there known as K14;
three Ca 133s of the 27° Gruppo were destroyed on the ground and one
damaged.

Plt Off Stephenson, the Gladiator pilot down at Makhnuk, was to be brought
back in a Vincent next day, but it was some time before the S 81 which had
landed at Husu Balid was found. On the 14th it was to radio its position to
Diredawa, but several searches by the Italians failed to find the aircraft.
Subsequently it was seen by a 8 Squadron Vincent on 19 June, but when another
Vincent attempted to land alongside on the 22nd, it crashed. The bomber was

eventually reached and made airworthy, and was flown to Khormaksar by an RAF crew on 25 June.

To return to 13 June, in the southern area Ju 86s of 12 SAAF Squadron carried out attacks on landing grounds at Kismayu, Jelib and Afmadu, all these having been spotted the previous day by 11 SAAF Squadron Hartbeestes, but no serious damage was caused at any of these targets.

Before dawn three Ca 133s of the 9ª Squadriglia took off from Lugh Ferrandi led by Capt Piva, arriving at dawn over Wajir where six aircraft of 237 Squadron were seen on the ground. They dived to attack from 1,500 feet in the face of fierce ground fire, and claimed to have destroyed three aircraft, damaged some buildings and caused a big fire; one Ca 133 was slightly damaged by machine gun bullets. In fact two Audaxes were hit, K7545 being badly damaged and K7531 slightly damaged; 5,000 gallons of aviation fuel were set alight and five personnel killed, four of them while attempting to fight the fire.

Sunday, 14 June 1940

Early on 14 June six Blenheims of 8 Squadron from Aden again attacked K14 landing ground at Assab, destroying the radio station; they were attacked from long range by two patrolling CR 42s of the 413ª Squadriglia but returned undamaged. Later in the day two Wellesleys of 14 Squadron attacked Massawa, but were intercepted and driven off. Wellesley K7743 flown by Plt Off Plunkett failed to return; the Italians claimed two shot down, one by a fighter of the 412ª Squadriglia and one by anti-aircraft — clearly a double claim on the same aircraft. For the 412ª Squadriglia, this was apparently the first victory for Ten Mario Visintini, soon to become the unit's leading pilot.

The Italians made a number of Ca 133 reconnaissances over the fronts, and S 81s reconnoitred the Red Sea. From Diredawa three S 79s bombed the port of Berbera in British Somaliland, one bomber being damaged by anti-aircraft fire. Following the incursion over Kenya by the Regia Aeronautica to attack Wajir on the previous day, three of 1 SAAF Squadron's precious Hurricanes were flown up to Port Reitz airfield near Mombasa in case an air attack on that port should now materialise.

Monday, 15 June 1940

On 15 June Blenheims from Aden were active again, six aircraft of 8 Squadron attacking Diredawa at low level and setting fire to an old dump of mustard gas bombs, also slightly damaging a CR 32. Three more Blenheims from 39 Squadron then dive-bombed the area and were engaged by fighters, one of the gunners — LAC Ford — claiming to have shot down a CR 42. In fact there were no CR 42s at Diredawa at this time; an attack on one Blenheim was however made by Sergente Maggiore Enzo Omiccioli of the 410ª Squadriglia in a CR 32, but no results were claimed and no damage suffered.

The usual series of reconnaissance missions were flown by the Italians, and three 9ª Squadriglia Ca 133s returned to attack Wajir again, claiming damage to three aircraft and a fuel dump; one bomber was slightly damaged by anti-aircraft fire. During the morning two S 81s bombed Erkowit airfield in the Sudan, where one Wellesley of 47 Squadron was damaged. As the evening drew on Wellesleys of 223 Squadron began taking off for night raids on Gura and Difein Island from Summit, but as one aircraft (L2711) was readied the flares which it was carrying ignited and it burnt out. Four aircraft finally took off at

1630 but at 2330 one Wellesley force-landed on a beach 60 miles north of Port Sudan, while a second crashed on landing at this airfield. A third Wellesley, L2654, flown by Plt Off Jenkins, failed to return; it was shot down over Difein Island by Italian anti-aircraft guns.

During the day the first five of 11 Squadron's Blenheim Is arrived at Sheik Othman, Aden, and were attached initially to 39 Squadron; nine had flown to Egypt, but two had been converted into fighters and handed to 30 Squadron there, and the other two were still undergoing inspection. The Italians now evacuated most units from Assab following the recent attacks there, the 27° Gruppo from K14 sending its 18ª and 52ª Squadriglie to Dessie and the 118ª Squadriglia to Sardo, while the 29° Gruppo moved from K3 to Mille; three of the 413ª Squadriglia's CR 42s moved to Addis Ababa where they were joined by five S 79s of the 44° Gruppo's 7ª Squadriglia. Three 414ª Squadriglia CR 42s flown by Sottotenente Provinciali and two sergenti now moved to Assab from Gura, to replace the 413ª Squadriglia aircraft.

Tuesday, 16 June 1940
During the night of 15/16 June two S 81s carried out a further attack on Erkowit, and when day broke three Gladiators of the 112 Squadron Detachment at Summit were despatched to this base for air defence duties; in the evening, however, Summit became the target for two more bombers. Two of the Gladiators still at this base were scrambled and drove them off.

In the south aircraft of 237 Squadron and 11 SAAF Squadron were busy strafing north of Moyale, while 'C' Flight of 12 SAAF Squadron despatched four Ju 86s on a raid. After refuelling at Wajir, Maj Martin's section of Ju 86s attacked Neghelli where ten Ca 133s and three CR 32s were identified on the ground, poorly dispersed; these were bombed and at least eight Capronis were claimed damaged, while the fighters were machine gunned. Italian records indicate that one Ca 133 of the 65ª Squadriglia was destroyed, a hangar damaged and several casualties suffered. The other pair of Ju 86s, led by Capt du Toit, refuelled at Lodwar, then attacked Yavello where six Ca 133s were bombed and strafed, one being claimed burnt out, one in flames and one probably burnt; the Italians reported that one Ca 133 and a hangar were damaged, two men were killed and three wounded.

Wednesday, 17 June 1940
On 17 June Maj Preller, CO of 11 SAAF Squadron, took off in the unit's lone Battle (No 901) to make a reconnaissance over the Mogadishu-Kismayu area. (This sortie has been reported in several accounts as having taken place on the 19th, but Italian contemporary records clearly report it as occurring two days earlier.) After taking photographs, Preller flew to Afmadu and dived down to attack a Ca 133 of the 8ª Squadriglia on the ground, making several passes during which the Italian aircraft was slightly damaged; during one pass however a bullet from the ground struck the Battle's radiator and the glycol rapidly drained away, causing the engine to seize as Preller left the airfield. He force-landed among some trees, and after setting fire to the aircraft, he and his crew, Air Corporals Petterson and Ackerman, set off to walk back to their own lines with only one waterbottle between the three of them.

An intensive air search was launched for the missing crew, but after a week hope of their return was abandoned. In fact, after leaving the two exhausted corporals at a waterhole, Preller had gone on alone. Finally, on 1 July, he was spotted by an aircraft of 237 Squadron, the crew of which saw him mounted on a camel on a track between Garissa and Liboi. An ambulance was sent out to pick him up, going on to collect the other two members of the crew and bring them all back. Preller was subsequently awarded a DFC, the first decoration of the war for the SAAF.

Border skirmishing in the Tessenei area had brought the Ca 133s out in strength meanwhile, at least sixteen sorties being made by these aircraft over various areas during 17 June. Three 18ª Squadriglia S 81s from Sardo bombed Aden where they caused a number of fires, but one aircraft was hit by anti-aircraft fire and landed near Debra Sina on return. Another S 81 bombed the port and airfield at Berbera claiming damage to a number of vessels, but this machine too was damaged by anti-aircraft fire. From the Sudan a Wellesley of 47 Squadron was attacked by Gladiators in error and forced down, fortunately with only slight damage.

The Italians had noted that a number of unexploded bombs were often found after British attacks, and these were inspected to ascertain why they had failed to operate. It was discovered that the safety pins had not been removed from the firing devices before they were dropped!

In France hostilities were now drawing to a close, but the position in the French colonies was still uncertain. A reconnaissance over Zeila and Jibuti by a Ro 37bis of the 110ª Squadriglia noted five or six warships in harbour and some twenty aircraft on the ground at an airfield in French Somaliland, close to the latter port. Next day the position became a little clearer when the local French commander, Général Legentilhomme, informed the British authorities that he intended to continue resistance.

Thursday, 18 June 1940

On 18 June forces from Italian Somaliland moved across the frontier into Kenya to capture the small defended locality of British El Wak. Aircraft of 237 Squadron attacked an Italian landing ground from which these forces were being supported, but Audax K7546 was hit in the radiator by a bullet and Flg Off Walmisley had to force-land at El Wak, finding the garrison just about to retire in the face of vastly superior forces. An attempt to tow the aircraft out was made, but the undercarriage collapsed and the Audax was then burnt to prevent it falling into enemy hands.

In the same general area Capt Piva of the 9ª Squadriglia from Lugh Ferrandi, while piloting a lone Ca 133, noticed a British camp at El Katulo and reported seeing a fighter aircraft on the ground and another in the air; he bombed the former and then escaped in cloud. He later returned for a second attack when two more aircraft dispersed on the edge of the airfield were claimed destroyed.

A number of other bombing raids were undertaken by Italian aircraft, three S 79s attacking Port Sudan where hits were claimed on hangars, a fuel dump and the railway; three S 81s of the 29° Gruppo bombed Aden, one being hit by anti-aircraft fire and force-landing at Dancalia on return. Three more S 81s from the 4° Gruppo raided the British airfield at Zeila, British Somaliland, but one of these aircraft, after 45 minutes in the air, suddenly crashed; two of the crew baled out but the other three were killed.

More reinforcements were on the way for the air component in Kenya: 40 SAAF Squadron had been formed on Hartbeestes under Maj J.T. Durrant in the Union as an army co-operation unit. Now, leaving all but four of its aircraft behind, its personnel were flown up to East Africa in Ju 52/3ms of the Airways Wing to take over the aircraft of 11 SAAF Squadron. This latter unit was now to re-equip fully with Fairey Battles which had just arrived in the Union from the United Kingdom.

During the day the Italian submarine *Galileo Galilei* was patrolling off Aden, having sunk the Norwegian tanker *James Stove* in this area on 16 June. On the 18th the submarine intercepted the Yugoslav merchant vessel *Drava* with gunfire, then boarded her, but after examination allowed the ship to continue on her way.

The gunfire was heard by coastwatchers, and the surfaced submarine was then spotted by Flg Off Haywood of 94 Squadron who was patrolling in his Gladiator (N2279). He at once radioed for assistance, a Vincent and a Blenheim quickly arriving, and all three aircraft then attacked the submarine. The Blenheim missed with its bombs, and the Vincent almost managed to blow itself up with the depth charges it was carrying. In the meantime the destroyer HMS *Kandahar* and the sloop HMS *Shoreham* had been sent out to intercept, but did not arrive until darkness had fallen. At 1830 the submarine surfaced and was foolish enough to break radio silence. *Kandahar* was able to get a good 'fix' on her and approached, but the submarine dived and a depth charge attack failed to inflict any damage before contact was lost.

Friday, 19 June 1940
An early search by Blenheims of 203 Squadron the next morning failed to see anything, the submarine again being submerged at this time. At 1137 however, she was discovered by the Asdic of the anti-submarine trawler *Moonstone*, which also delivered a depth charge attack, but again lost contact. Half an hour later contact was re-established and more depth charges dropped, causing *Galileo Galilei* to surface at 1230 and open fire on *Moonstone* with her two 100mm/47 guns from a mile astern. Turning swiftly to present the smallest possible target, *Moonstone* opened fire with her own World War I four-pounder, her Lewis gunners raking the decks of the Italian vessel which caused the gun crews to dive for cover and their shooting to be inaccurate as a consequence. When the range closed to 500 yards every spare hand on *Moonstone* opened fire with rifles, while two hits were obtained on the conning tower with the four-pounder. At 1225 the whole crew of the submarine rushed on deck waving white clothing, and the trawler ceased fire.

Capitano di Corvetta Nardi had been killed by one of the shells on the submarine's conning tower, and other officers and ratings had been wounded, but three officers and 37 ratings were taken off by *Moonstone*, which put aboard a prize crew. The submarine was then taken into Aden under her own power, arriving early on the 20th.

19 June also saw the first sortie by a Blenheim of 11 Squadron when one of these aircraft accompanied five from 39 Squadron to attack Diredawa where a hangar was damaged and a petrol dump set ablaze. The main event of the day in the air occurred in the south however — with most unsatisfactory results for the SAAF.

Three Ju 86s of 12 SAAF Squadron were escorted to attack Yavello by two Hurricanes of 1 SAAF Squadron on their first operational mission. A flight of CR 32s of the 411ª Squadriglia had recently moved to the airfield, and two of

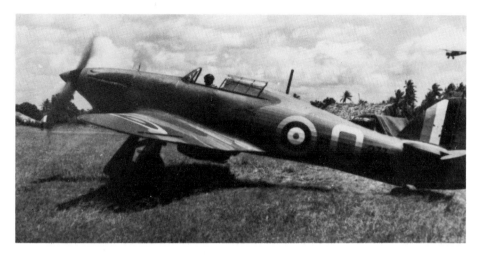

One of the original four Hawker Hurricane Is to be supplied to South Africa, 'O', No 277, is seen here after arrival at Port Reitz, Kenya, with 1 SAAF Squadron in June 1940. Hurricane 'D' can be seen in the left background, while to the right a light aircraft of the Kenya Auxiliary Air Unit (probably a DH Puss Moth) is approaching to land. *(via K. Smy)*

these scrambled on the approach of the South African formation; unaware of this, the South Africans made straight for the Ca 133s of the 66ᵃ Squadriglia, which were parked on the airfield, the Hurricanes diving down to strafe these.

At this point the Italian fighters, flown by Tenente Aldo Meoli and Maresciallo Bossi, dived out of the sun to attack, hitting one Ju 86 (they identified the bombers as Blenheims on this occasion, claiming one probably shot down) and damaged it badly, a fuel tank being holed and the gunner and observer both slightly wounded. The Hurricane flown by 2/Lt B.L. Griffiths was then attacked and shot down in flames, the pilot being killed. The second Hurricane, flown by Capt St. E. Truter became involved in a strenuous dogfight with one fighter, which Truter took to be a CR 42, and at last it reeled away, pouring smoke, landed and turned over on its back; the pilot, Ten Meoli, was slightly wounded and the CR 32 was a complete write-off.

Throughout the combat Air Sergeant Jeffries, the dorsal gunner in one of the Ju 86s, had been firing at the CR 32, and he claimed that his bullets were still hitting the aircraft as it went down; his squadron subsequently maintained that he was responsible for its destruction, but the victory was credited to Truter. The two undamaged Ju 86s and the remaining Hurricane returned to base, the damaged third bomber following somewhat later. Charles Jeffries, the gunner, was later to be awarded a DFM, and was commissioned; he would be killed in action over the Western Desert on 23 December 1941.

Saturday, 20 June 1940
As a result of the loss of one of the Hurricanes, the six Furies of 1 SAAF Squadron moved up to Port Reitz the next day. Three more 411ᵃ Squadriglia CR 32s flew down from Addis Ababa to reinforce the two still at Yavello in case a further, heavier attack should be forthcoming. In France on this date all fighting ceased and the Italians made a number of reconnaissances over French Somaliland to discover if the French there did indeed intend to fight on.

From Lugh Ferrandi the Ca 133s of the 9ᵃ Squadriglia now moved to a new base at Belet Uen, and the Squadriglia SMS Sud moved from Mogadishu to Villaggio Duca di Abruzzi. In the morning five Blenheims of 8 Squadron attacked Diredawa without causing any real damage. Three Italian fighters dived on the British bombers and attacked the outside aircraft, failing to inflict any damage, although they claimed to have hit one; with their superior speed, the Blenheims made good their escape.

Sunday, 21 June 1940

Apart from the usual Ca 133 sorties over the front, the main activity on 21 June was over French Somaliland, eleven Ca 133s of the 27° Gruppo from Dessie raiding Jibuti in three waves; bad weather prevented detailed analysis of the results of the attack, although fires and explosions were seen. Two aircraft returned early due to engine trouble, and three more returned safely to Dessie. However, substantial anti-aircraft fire had been encountered and two Capronis failed to come back, the other four landing individually at Assab, Sardo, Elidor and Gauani.

A pair of S 81s bombed Berbera, British Somaliland, individually, but one was forced to land south of the port due to fuel shortage, and the crew were then massacred by native tribesmen. Three Vincents of 'D' Flight, 47 Squadron, had flown forward to an advanced landing ground at Malakal, Sudan, on the 20th, and now these raided an Italian outpost at Asosa successfully. Plt Off J.E. Dennant in K4683 ran short of fuel during the return flight and had to force-land, but the other two aircraft, K4685 and K6362, returned safely to base. Italian anti-aircraft crews claimed to have shot down a bomber over Asosa, and it was later reported that the wreckage was found near Kurmuk on 2 July with the crew dead. This clearly must have been an aircraft shot down elsewhere on another date, for K4683 was undamaged. Indeed, on the 24th a runway was cleared and fuel flown in, Dennant taking off and flying back to Malakal.

Savoia S 81 at Diredawa. *(C. Ricci)*

During June 1940 11 SAAF Squadron aircrew returned to South Africa to collect Fairey Battles, handing over their Hawker Hartbeestes to a new army co-operation unit, 40 SAAF Squadron. Three of 40's aircraft are seen on their way to the front. *(SAAF)*

Monday, 22 June 1940

Further RAF raids on Assab and Diredawa on 22 June inflicted damage, and at the latter airfield one CR 42 was burnt out, while a CR 32 had its engine damaged. Italian efforts were again concentrated on the French at Jibuti; three S 81s had bombed the port during the night, and by day eight more set out in three waves, two of which returned early due to bad weather. Five Ro 37bis, four CR 42s and a CR 32 also strafed and bombed Jibuti airfield; the reason for these raids was to prevent any incursion from French Somaliland by British aircraft, using Jibuti as an advanced base. Another S 81 carried supplies to the crew of an Italian submarine which had been beached the previous day on the island of Bare Mussa Seghir, also guiding another submarine to its assistance.

From Kenya twenty-one members of 11 SAAF Squadron now returned to South Africa to collect their new Battles. Around this time another unit of the SAAF arrived at Nairobi: this was a photo/survey flight equipped with an Airspeed Envoy and a BA Double Eagle. This unit was later to be expanded and would initially be known as 62 Squadron, and later as 60 Squadron.

Wednesday, 24 June 1940

On 24 June came news that an armistice had been signed between Italy and France, and further action over Jibuti was suspended. Around midday four Blenheims of 39 Squadron and two of 11 Squadron in two flights of three approached Diredawa for the fifth raid on this airfield. A CR 32 of the 410[a] Squadriglia, piloted by Serg Magg Giardina, was up on standing patrol, and at the approach of the British bombers two CR 42s were scrambled.

Giardina dived out of the sun on the leading flight and attacked them very effectively, all three bombers being damaged. He was seen by his unit commander to pass over the area in pursuit of the bombers, one of which was trailing white smoke and another appeared to be losing oil. The Blenheim flown by Plt Off Hunter began to lag behind with one engine stopped, but Giardina's guns now jammed and he was forced to retire.

At this juncture the two CR 42s joined the fight. The Blenheims jettisoned their bombs and engaged these fighters as they began attacking Hunter's crippled aircraft, which was last seen losing height steadily. It was later found by British troops force-landed in British Somaliland, the pilot wounded and the gunner missing.

The Italians reported another raid, this time on Asmara, by ten Wellesleys. Fighters intercepted, but during the combat one CR 32 suffered an overheating engine and returned to land, turned over and caught fire; on the ground an Ala Littoria Ca 133 was slightly damaged by bomb splinters.

Thursday, 25 June 1940

Blenheims, Wellesleys, Ca 133s, S 81s and Ro 37bis were again active on the 25th, and the first part of one flight of 40 SAAF Squadron moved forward to Isiola to begin operations with its Hartbeestes. A single Wellesley of 47 Squadron piloted by Sgt F.A. Sanders flew a photo-reconnaissance sortie intended to cover Asmara, Gura and Massawa; but shortly after leaving the first of these objectives it landed in Italian territory, obviously due to technical trouble. Sanders and his crew burnt their aircraft (L2696) before being made prisoners.

Friday, 26 June 1940

Various minor bombing raids were made by each side on 26 June, but at dawn a somewhat larger formation comprising four Wellesleys of 14 Squadron followed by five from 47 Squadron set out to attack Gura where airfield buildings were dive-bombed. The 14 Squadron aircraft flew at lower level as they had been modified to incorporate a unit-designed lower gun position. About seven CR 42s attacked at 0730, and three of the 14 Squadron aircraft were hit; each squadron claimed one fighter shot down, one being seen pouring smoke and the other apparently out of control. Only one Fiat was in fact hit, and the pilot was badly wounded, diving away to land his damaged aircraft.

Saturday, 27 June 1940

The Italians reported a raid on Assab airfield on 27 June by a lone Blenheim which damaged two Ca 133s and eight lorries; the bomber was claimed to have been hit by anti-aircraft fire and to have crashed into the sea. The previous day four Blenheims of 8 Squadron had been detached from Aden to Berbera, and now on this date one of these force-landed near the new airfield in unknown circumstances; it is possible that this was the aircraft mentioned in the Italian report.

During the 27th three Ro 37bis of the 110ª Squadriglia were despatched from Diredawa to Assab, and next day they were joined by three more CR 42s of the 414ª Squadriglia, Capt Lucertini and two more sergenti moving to this base. Three further fighters which had been assembled for this latter unit at Massawa were handed instead to the 412ª Squadriglia, and a final three were taken by Sottotenente Sola and two sergenti to Tessenei. In the afternoon a Blenheim of

Italian unit commanders at Assab — Capitano Lucertini, CO of the ill-fated 414ª Squadriglia (left), and Tenente Romano Palmera, CO of the 110ª Squadriglia. *(Stato Maggiore via Corrado Ricci)*

39 Squadron flown by Sqn Ldr Bowman led three Gladiators of 94 Squadron to Perim Island from where they were to make a dawn attack on Assab's Macaaca airfield. In the south Ca 133s again raided Wajir, while S 81s made several sorties against British warships in the Red Sea, three of these bombers being damaged by anti-aircraft fire from the ships.

Sunday, 28 June 1940

At dawn on 28 June Bowman's Blenheim and two of the Gladiators took off from Perim Island to attack a fuel dump at Assab. The Blenheim bombed, but missed. The Gladiators, flown by Sqn Ldr Wightman and Plt Off Carter, then set fire to some 100 drums of alcohol and petrol; the three British aircraft made good their escape before any opposition was encountered.

A little later in the morning three more Blenheims from 39 Squadron attacked the same base, destroying a bomb dump. One of the newly arrived Ro 37bis flown by Serg Magg Mario Di Trani had just landed from a one-hour flight, and was taxiing, when the pilot saw the three Blenheims diving on him and at once took off again. As he did so one bomb exploded, shaking his aircraft, and the bombers then attacked him one at a time. One then began turning with him, the gunner gaining many hits on his aircraft, damaging the undercarriage, the cockpit and the instruments. Di Trani had so far been unable to get into a position to fire himself, and tried instead to ram one of the bombers, but it was faster and left him behind. He then hit the slipstream of the aircraft and the Ro 37bis was thrown out of control, almost hitting the ground. Recovering control, he again tried to ram a Blenheim, and this time managed to open fire on it; he then went in to land, but his engine failed due to lack of fuel and he came down on the edge of the airfield safely, but with both tyres flat, and his brakes out of action. To add insult to injury he suffered from sunstroke while waiting to be picked up, and had to spend several days in hospital!

During a raid on the AGIP fuel depot at Massawa by four Wellesleys, the anti-aircraft defences claimed one shot down, but no loss was recorded. S 79s of the 7ª Squadriglia moved to Gura from Addis Ababa. Also that day the Italian authorities communicated with Général Legentilhomme in French Somaliland, requesting his implementation of the clauses of the armistice in respect of that territory, particularly that allowing the Italians the use of the Jibuti–Addis Ababa railway. Legentilhomme replied that he was unaware of the existence of the clause and declined to agree to its implementation.

At night three S 81s of the 10ª Squadriglia raided Port Sudan but meeting bad weather were late over the target, and were caught by the dawn.

Monday, 29 June 1940
At 0500 on the 29th Plt Off Hamlyn of 112 Squadron's Detachment scrambled in Gladiator L7619 and saw one S 81 3,000 feet above him, approaching from the south. Climbing to its level, he made an attack as he turned on to its tail, closing to very short range. After he had fired about 1,000 rounds the bomber suddenly swung to starboard and exploded, falling into the sea; flying debris damaged the attacking fighter. Two members of the crew survived, and were later picked up from a coral reef just offshore, one proving to be the Italian unit commander, Capt Umberto Barone.

Later in the day three S 79s raided Port Sudan, but found the airfield deserted. Three more of these bombers attacked Aden, but neither of these formations met any defending fighters. From Aden a single Blenheim photographed the Assab area and dropped some bombs, doing a little damage to buildings, but it was attacked and chased away by two CR 42s and a Ro 37bis. Three more Blenheims bombed Harar, hitting the living quarters of some drivers, 13 of whom were killed and 39 wounded.

Tuesday, 30 June 1940
Early on the morning of 30 June five Wellesleys of 223 Squadron set off to raid the AGIP depot at Massawa again, followed a few minutes later by four from 14 Squadron to attack another fuel dump at Acico Bay. The first formation met heavy anti-aircraft fire and fighters, Sgt Poskitt's aircraft failing to return. One aircraft of the 14 Squadron contingent turned back early, but the others also met heavy AA, though no fighters. The leading Wellesley was hit, but all aircraft returned. Damage to the targets was insignificant, and Italian fighters of the 412ª Squadriglia claimed two of the bombers shot down (one of them by Serg Magg Luigi Baron), AA claiming a third.

Various other raids and reconnaissances of a minor nature were made by Blenheims, Ca 133s and S 81s, and there were several movements of units. 47 Squadron despatched seven Wellesleys to Khartoum to operate from there for a week, while on the other side of the lines three Ca 133s of the 49° Gruppo moved from Jimma to Neghelli, and two 411ª Squadriglia CR 32s from Yavello to the same base. They were joined there by two more next day.

Wednesday, 1 July 1940
The moves made by the Italians at the end of June 1940 were preparatory to a new attack and on 1 July the whole of the 29° Gruppo moved its Savoia S 81s

from Mille to Dessie, and thence forward to Shashamanna, a new airfield still under construction. A substantial force of 'banda' then attacked the frontier fortress of Moyale in northern Kenya, where the garrison, a single company of the King's African Rifles, were surrounded and isolated. 237 Squadron was nearest to hand and four of the unit's biplanes took off to attack the enemy force. Unfortunately they bombed buildings still in British hands in error.

Thursday, 2 July 1940

Further north, the British now knew that at least five Italian fighters were present at Assab, and consequently a series of special attacks was laid on on the morning of 2 July in an effort to destroy them. A single Blenheim of 39 Squadron was off first, attacking the airfield at 0645; a Fiat CR 42 was seen taxiing. A little later an 11 Squadron Blenheim (L4924) operating from Ras Arar dive-bombed the area, where the crew reported seeing one fighter standing on its nose; the Blenheim was hit in one engine by a bullet from the ground and crash-landed on its way back to base, when still 25 miles short of Ras Arar.

At 0750 three more 39 Squadron Blenheims attacked individually, one being chased out to sea by two CR 42s, and another was chased all round the hills of Eritrea by another of these fighters. The third Blenheim, which was the second of the three to arrive over the airfield, saw a CR 42 taking off and at once attacked it, reporting that the aircraft crashed on the edge of the airfield. (In the light of the actual losses, it is possible that the CR 42 merely landed again under attack, having suffered some damage.)

Meanwhile three Gladiators of 94 Squadron had taken off to follow the Blenheims, arriving at Assab at 0836. Sqn Ldr Wightman at once made two attacks on a CR 42 on the ground and it burst into flames. He then saw two more CR 42s at 1,500 feet and attacked one, shooting it down in flames; the other attacked him, but he evaded it and set course for home. Meantime Sgt Dunwoodie had been strafing vehicles when he suddenly found he had a CR 42 on his tail; turning into it, he fired and the engine stopped, the fighter gliding towards the ground. He fired again and it crashed, first on to one wing and then the other.

It seems that the aircraft claimed shot down by Dunwoodie and by the 39 Squadron Blenheim may both have been fairly easily repairable, as both were reported by the Italians to be only slightly damaged. The aircraft shot down by Wightman was totally destroyed however, and the pilot killed, while the aircraft which he set alight on the ground was also a total loss. The position is not entirely clear, however, for it seems that the British claims may have been more accurate than Italian records indicate.

The commander of the 414ª Squadriglia reported that over Assab two of his pilots were shot down in combat, Serg Barengo being killed and Serg Celleri baling out. Since no other CR 42s were claimed over Assab by the RAF except on this date, it seems probable that Celleri's aircraft was also brought down on this occasion. The pilot was three times strafed on the ground by a Gladiator after baling out, and had to run like mad for cover. As a result he collapsed with heat stroke and spent two months in hospital.

During the afternoon five Wellesleys from 47 Squadron's detachment at Khartoum carried out a low-level bombing and strafing attack on Italian troops at Metemma. The bomber flown by Plt Off Bush (K7777) was hit by rifle fire from the ground and crashed, the crew being killed; the Italian soldiers claimed to have shot down two aircraft. Activity in this area was increasing, and during a return attack on Gallabat airfield by Italian aircraft, one of these also failed to return — probably shot down by British ground fire.

Friday, 3 July 1940
Raids and reconnaissances by both sides continued, and during 3 July three 14 Squadron Wellesleys were briefed to make a reconnaissance over Zula, Decamere, Gura, Asmara and Massawa. On leaving Decamere, the leading aircraft (L2652), flown by Flg Off S.G. Soderholm, was seen by the other two crews to turn suddenly and sharply towards the coast, but they then lost sight of it in cloud. This Wellesley was subsequently attacked and shot down by a CR 42 of the 412ª Squadriglia flown by Ten Visintini.

Saturday, 4 July 1940
The next day 8,000 Italian troops, supported by tanks and artillery, and by units of the Regia Aeronautica, advanced from Eritrea into the Sudan to attack the important communications centre of Kassala, while other forces from Metemma attacked the British fort at Gallabat. Three bomber squadriglie operated over Kassala, keeping up a regular attack for 12 hours, and two more squadriglie raided Gallabat. The small detachments of the Sudan Defence Force garrisoning these two centres withdrew after putting up a brief resistance, as they were grossly outnumbered. Several Italian aircraft were hit by ground fire during these operations.

Monday, 6 July 1940
Meanwhile operations in northern Kenya in the Moyale–Wajir–El Wak–Bura area continued on a small scale, and on 6 July three Hartbeestes of 40 SAAF Squadron flew up to Isiola to take part in operations here — a welcome reinforcement for 237 Squadron, which had been carrying the burden of army co-operation duties during recent days. Italian Caproni Ca 133s were active over the area during this period, but no engagements between aircraft of the opposing sides took place. On 6 July the flight of three Ro 37bis at Assab returned to Diredawa, their place being taken by two 413ª Squadriglia CR 42s from this latter base.

Tuesday, 7 July 1940
On 7 July 40 SAAF Squadron went into action for the first time. Six Hartbeestes, each carrying four 120lb and eight 20lb bombs, were led to Wajir by Capt Scravesande of 11 SAAF Squadron, and after refuelling took off again in the afternoon to attack enemy ground forces. Aircraft No 802, which had been specially fitted with armour plating against ground fire, spotted for the other aircraft during the attack. After again refuelling at Bura, a second attack was made during which eleven or twelve field guns appeared to have been silenced. From Dessie two S 81s now flew down to join those at Shashamanna.

In the north two Ca 133s attacked the garrison at Kurmuk in the Sudan in support of troops who, as soon as this raid was completed, advanced on the 70 Sudanese policemen who were holding the post, capturing most of them. The Italian column then halted and dug in.

Wednesday, 8 July 1940

Around midday on the 8th four Wellesleys of 14 Squadron attacked the landing ground at Zula, on the Eritrean coast. They then saw a lone S 81 flying below them to the east of the Dahlak Archipelago. This was an aircraft from the 10ª Squadriglia, 28° Gruppo, which had taken off from Gura for a long reconnaissance over south Sudan and the Red Sea, flown by Sottoten Salvatore Suella, but with a naval Sottotenente, Goffredo Franchini, as observer and aircraft commander. Flg Off C.G.S.R. Robinson, who was flying one of the 'up-gunned' Wellesleys (armed with four Lewis guns as well as his forward-firing Vickers), approached from astern and dived to attack the Savoia. This initial attack appeared to have no result, so he climbed back up, and repeated the attack. His gun then jammed, and as the Savoia's crew were now returning fire, he pulled away momentarily. Next, he pulled the Wellesley close alongside to allow the gunners to get a good shot; Cooke, the upper gunner, and Fell with the starboard side gun, both opened fire.

During these attacks Franchini, who was manning the Savoia's port side gun, was wounded, the dorsal turret gunner (the engineer) 1ᵉ Aviere Motorista Fiorindo Reggioni, then also being hit, as was the co-pilot, Serg Magg Piero Violetti. At this point the Italian aircraft broke away and attempted to land on a small island but was seen by the crew of the Wellesley to hit the ground with one wheel, bounce back into the air, and fly on. This was undoubtedly because the pilot, Suella, was hit and killed as he attempted to make the landing. Violetti got control, and flew on low over the sea. Robinson held the Wellesley alongside and slightly above, the gunners continuing to pump bursts down into the top of the Savoia between jams in their temperamental Lewis guns. About ten minutes after the initial attack, the S 81 at last succumbed, suddenly crashing into the sea with a violent splash, both wings breaking off.

The survivors, all wounded or injured in the crash, struggled free of the wreck with difficulty, three of them managing to get aboard a life-raft. Franchini had climbed on to a floating piece of wing, but realised that his weight added to those already on the raft would cause it to founder. After ordering the crew to head for the island they had almost landed on, he selflessly elected to remain behind, and was not seen again. (He subsequently received a posthumous award of the Medaglia d'Oro, Italy's highest decoration for courage.)

Once ashore on the tiny uninhabited island, the remaining three men realised that they would have to try to reach Dahlak Island if they were to survive. Living on birds' eggs found among the rocks, they paddled their way to their destination, arriving there two weeks later in a state of total exhaustion. Cared for by the local population, they were later picked up by a destroyer, finally reaching Massawa three weeks after being shot down. Meanwhile the victorious Wellesley crew had been somewhat sobered on return to base to discover that during the attack on Zula, their bombs had hung up in the wing containers, and had been aboard throughout the combat!

Thursday, 9 July 1940

Following an attack by five Blenheims on Diredawa on 8 July, British bombers hit Sardo and Macaaca airfields on the 9th, damaging a hangar at the latter base. In the afternoon nine more British aircraft were reported by the Italians to have bombed Macaaca, one being claimed shot down by fighters and one by AA; apparently one of these aircraft fell near the base, the pilot being killed, but the other two members of the crew were taken prisoner. No details of such a raid or loss have been discovered on the British side, and the possibility must be considered that the date given was in error.

Two more S 81s from Dessie flew to Shashamanna for operations during the day, and three more of these aircraft from the 63ª Squadriglia left this former base for Diredawa.

Friday, 10 July 1940

Next day, these three latter aircraft attacked Berbera airfield, causing a number of casualties and some damage. Meanwhile from Aden another attack was launched on Assab airfield, a Blenheim of 39 Squadron making an early reconnaissance at 0700; over the airfield it made several dive attacks, but during the fourth of these a fighter attacked the aircraft, chasing it for 20 miles and hitting it three times.

At 0820 three 94 Squadron Gladiators and a Blenheim of 8 Squadron attacked the same base again, Flg Off Haywood shooting up two CR 42s on the ground and seeing them start to burn. All pilots then turned their attention to a crashed CR 42, but despite several attacks this aircraft refused to be set alight. A single CR 42 was seen in the air, but this flew away before it could be engaged. This raid put an end to the 414ª Squadriglia, which had now lost all its six aircraft at Assab, two in combat and four on the ground. In its short period at this base the unit had undertaken numerous scrambles, but failed to achieve any success.

Saturday, 11 July 1940

During the evening of 10 July, three Hartbeestes of 40 SAAF Squadron flew up to join 237 Squadron at Wajir in preparation for operations over the front on the 11th. Early that day three Ca 133s of the 9ª Squadriglia from Lugh Ferrandi approached Wajir. Two Hartbeestes were scrambled to intercept them and attacked one bomber, gaining hits. The Ca 133 retreated, trailing smoke from the starboard and centre engines, but managed to regain its base with one member of the crew dead and two wounded. The other bombers completed their attack, gunners firing on the two Hartbeestes (which they identified as 'probably Hawker Demons', and optimistically claimed to have shot both down). Lt N.K. Rankin's machine was hit and one tailplane strut was shot away so that he was unable to take part in the subsequent bombing attack on the Moyale area. This however was the full extent of any damage inflicted upon the South African aircraft.

The attack on Moyale was carried out in the face of heavy ground fire, but on return one Hartbeeste ran out of fuel and had to force-land in the bush, while a second landed at Buna to refuel. Here this aircraft was attacked by two Ca 133s, and the air gunner, Sgt Lewis, was machine gunned while trying to draw their fire away from the aircraft by driving a truck on to the airstrip; the Hartbeeste was not damaged and was later flown back to Wajir.

Three more Hartbeestes had now flown up to Wajir, and in the early afternoon these took off, accompanied by Lt Rankin, whose aircraft had by now been repaired, to make a repeat attack around Moyale. There they encountered three more Ca 133s, these being from the 66ª Squadriglia at Yavello, escorted by three CR 32s of the 411ª Squadriglia, all intent upon attacking British troops in the area. The fighters attacked the South African aircraft, and Lt Rankin was last seen in a tight spin with one Fiat on the tail of his aircraft; he and his gunner,

A pair of 40 SAAF Squadron Hartbeestes on their way to the front. *(SAAF Official)*

Air Sgt D.H. Hughes, were both killed. Lt L.H.G. Shuttleworth's aircraft was also hit and he jettisoned his bombs, making good his escape. Lt Jubber's aircraft was damaged to a lesser extent, and after evading his attacker, he carried out his attack, but then ran out of fuel and had to make a force-landing. Fuel was flown up to him next day.

The Italians reported meeting five aircraft and claimed to have probably shot down two of them, one of these being claimed by Serg Magg Enzo Omiciolli of the 410ᵃ Squadriglia, who was on a brief attachment to the 411ᵃ. It is noteworthy that the SAAF pilots reported their opponents as five Capronis and six Fiats. While this combat was taking place, a Savoia S 79 of the 6ᵃ Squadriglia, flown by Capt Serafini from Addis Ababa, also appeared over the area and made two attacks on a 237 Squadron Hart (SR106) while it was being refuelled at Bura; fourteen bombs were dropped, but no damage was done.

From Aden a Blenheim of 8 Squadron, L8505, flown by Flg Off P.A. Nicholas, made a reconnaissance over Jijiga. Here CR 32s of the 410ᵃ Squadriglia flown by Sottoten Veronese and Serg Magg Giardina, intercepted and attacked the bomber, claiming to have probably hit it. The aircraft was in fact badly damaged and force-landed at Jibuti where two of the crew were taken to hospital.

Sunday, 12 July 1940

Around midday on 12 July eleven Wellesleys from 14 and 47 Squadrons attacked Massawa airfield. Italian fighters intercepted the formation, shooting down Sgt F. Nelson in K8520, and also claiming a probable. On this date 47 Squadron's base, Erkowit, had its name changed to Carthago to avoid confusion with Erkowit village, a few miles distant. At the time the Squadron had a single Supermarine Walrus amphibian, L2214, and this was now handed over to 14 Squadron at Port Sudan for general reconnaissance duties over the Red Sea.

To the south activity continued around Moyale, and Wajir was again raided — this time reportedly by a pair of S 79s, although Italian records do not confirm

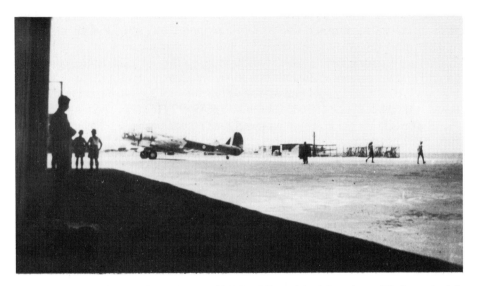

Martin 167F on arrival at Khormaksar on 13 July 1940, to join 8 Squadron. *(H. Lunt via A.S. Thomas)*

this. At Isiola Capt W.L. Kriel of 40 SAAF Squadron took off in Hartbeeste 859 with a load of ammunition, but this shifted as the aircraft got into the air, causing it to crash; Kriel was killed.

Monday, 13 July 1940

At Aden on 13 July 8 Squadron was reinforced by the arrival of two ex-French Armée de l'Air Martin 167F bombers and a Blenheim, all flown by French crews in RAF uniforms. The Martins had escaped from Syria at the time of the French armistice, having been serving in that country with GB I/39. Early on this day Plt Off Carter of 94 Squadron accompanied one of 39 Squadron's Blenheims from Aden to attack a fuel dump in the salt pans south of Assab. There his Gladiator, L9042, was intercepted by CR 42s of the 413ª Squadriglia and he was shot down.

Wednesday, 15 July 1940

The Squadron suffered further losses two days later when on the morning of 15 July Plt Off Sanderson's aircraft suffered a broken oil pipe and he force-landed at Little Aden. In the afternoon two Gladiators collided while on patrol south of Little Aden and N2279 crashed into the sea, Plt Off Bartlett baling out and being picked up safely; Plt Off Hogg made it back to base in the other aircraft.

Events in French Somaliland now took a turn detrimental to the British with the arrival of Général Germain. This officer had been despatched by the new Pétain government to replace the recalcitrant Legentilhomme and to implement the terms of the armistice; no more help would be forthcoming from that quarter. Within two days he was met by Generale Trezzani to discuss Italian use of the railway.

Thursday, 16 July 1940

Early on the morning of the 16th five 223 Squadron Wellesleys took off to bomb Agordat. Shortly after take-off the leading aircraft suffered a burst oil tank and landed, but the crew transferred to a standby aircraft and took off again. One more aircraft also returned due to fabric stripping off, but the four in the air reached the target, claiming twelve hits and four near misses with 250lb bombs. 254 Wing reconnaissance later reported three to five aircraft destroyed on the ground and the target totally obliterated; in fact damage had been insignificant!

More Wellesleys from 14 and 47 Squadrons then raided Asmara, but over the target two collided, one (L2641) piloted by Sgt W.C.H. Style, crashing. It seems that the reason for the collision was an attack by enemy fighters, as intercepting Italian pilots claimed one and one probable. The second aircraft, K7771, reached its home airfield, where it was written off. A reconnoitring Blenheim of 39 Squadron over Chinele was also attacked by a CR 42 and received a bullet in an aileron.

In the south further Italian raids were made on Wajir and the Moyale area, the former airfield being bombed just after a flight of SAAF Junkers Ju 86s had left for Nanyuki after refuelling here. Three S 81s operating from Neghelli claimed to have destroyed two aircraft on the ground during this attack.

Friday, 17 July 1940
Further attacks followed next day and over Buna a Ca 133 of the 65ᵃ Squadriglia reported being attacked by two Hawker biplanes, claiming one possibly shot down; the bomber was slightly damaged. 237 Squadron's main base at Wajir was now raided by three S 79s, three more of these bombers and two Ca 133s attacking Bura, to which 'B' Flight had just moved, damaging one Audax on the ground.

Saturday, 18 July 1940
Further raids were made by Italian bombers on this southern front on 18 July, three S 79s from Neghelli attacking Wajir and Buna, claiming one fighter shot down over the former base. One S 79 was hit by AA fire and a photographer on board was wounded. In return four SAAF Ju 86s — which the Italians identified as 'Handley Pages' — bombed and strafed Neghelli, destroying a barracks and setting fire to aviation fuel. During the return flight Maj du Toit landed 18 miles from Nanyuki due to oil pressure trouble, but was able to take off again and fly on to base next day. From Yavello the five CR 32s of the 411ᵃ Squadriglia returned to Addis Ababa, one crashing while landing and being destroyed.

Sunday, 19 July 1940
At Aden on the 19th intelligence reported that four CR 42s and two S 79s were due at Assab's Macaaca landing ground. A Blenheim of 39 Squadron and three 94 Squadron Gladiators flew over to attack, but found nothing there.

In the south two Ca 133s bombed Buna after dark, but one failed to return for unknown reasons; the crew came back safely on foot two days later.

Wednesday, 22 July 1940
Minor raids by Ca 133s continued during the next few days, but not until the 22nd did the RAF again operate in force. On that date, however, a major effort was launched by Aden-based Blenheims; at 0730 and 1200 flights of three 8 Squadron aircraft raided Diredawa, followed at 1315 and 1645 by similar flights from 39 Squadron. The 1315 raid was intercepted by a CR 42 and two CR 32s,

but without result. The results were not impressive for the British either; two CR 32s, a hangar and an officers' mess were slightly damaged!

Thursday, 23 July 1940

Formations of Wellesleys, four from 14 Squadron and three from 223 Squadron, raided Massawa around midday on the 23rd within half an hour of each other. Italian fighters were scrambled, two CR 32s chasing the 223 contingent for 25 minutes and repeatedly hitting Plt Off Ellis's aircraft, which gradually lagged behind. The Italian pilots thought it was about to force-land in Eritrean territory and claimed it probably shot down, but in fact it managed to get back and landed without the aid of flaps. A CR 42 attacked the 14 Squadron formation as the Wellesleys were on their way back to base, but the rear gunners reported a flash being seen on its engine following their fire, whereupon the CR 42 stalled and dived away; no damage was actually inflicted on the fighter.

Friday, 24 July 1940

It will be recalled that since before the outbreak of war a large part of 1 SAAF Squadron had been at Abu Sueir in Egypt, training on Gauntlets. They were then supplied with Gladiators, and with 18 of these aircraft on hand, 'C' Flight, led by Maj Niblock-Stuart, began the flight down to join the rest of the Squadron in Kenya, arriving four days later with nine of the new fighters. Other South African contingents were arriving there also, infantry of the 1st South African Brigade beginning disembarkation at Mombasa on the 24th.

The security of British Somaliland was now causing some concern, following the ending of French support, and six Gladiators from 94 Squadron in Aden were detached to Berbera to cover British troops there.

On 24 July 1940 'C' Flight of 1 SAAF Squadron, arrived in Kenya from Egypt with Gladiators, reinforcing the handful of Hurricanes and Furies. Within a few weeks the two Flights in Kenya became 2 SAAF Squadron. Note the African 'raid-spotter' in the tree. *(SAAF)*

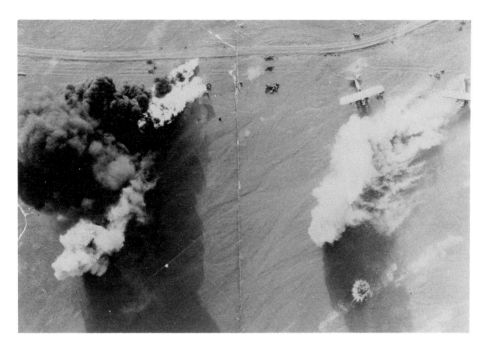

Bombs from a trio of 8 Squadron Blenheim Is exploding on Mille airfield on 27 July 1940. Note the two Caproni Ca 133s in the top right corner. *(8 Squadron via A.S. Thomas)*

Saturday, 25 July 1940
Next day three S 81s of the 4° Gruppo from Diredawa bombed military installations up the coast at Zeila. On the same day four Wellesleys of 14 Squadron raided a fuel dump at Massawa, suffering a determined attack by three CR 42s which seriously damaged one of the bombers.

Sunday, 26 July 1940
Two of the Blenheim IVFs of 203 Squadron from Aden made a strafing attack on Mille airfield on the 26th, where three Ca 133s were seen on the ground in a close 'V'. These were strafed and two were damaged. One of 203's Blenheim fighters returned early the next morning (27 July), leading three Blenheim Is of 8 Squadron to attack the same three Italian aircraft, and this time one was completely destroyed, the other two again being strafed. Three S 79s of the 44° Gruppo flew to K92 at Scenele, Diredawa, from Addis Ababa, and from there on the 28th they raided Aden port, claiming damage to one ship. The steamer *Mathura* was indeed damaged.

Wednesday, 29 July 1940
Early in the morning of 29 July five 223 Squadron Wellesleys set off to raid Sheik Island at Massawa; heavy and accurate AA was met and one aircraft was damaged. Then at 0805 two CR 32s attacked the last two Wellesleys and the air gunner in one was hit in the head. In the other, the ammunition pan on the gunner's Lewis gun was hit and blew up, knocking the unfortunate airman unconscious momentarily; he recovered, put a new pan on the gun and continued firing, claiming to have hit one fighter which dived away vertically. No loss or damage was reported by the Italians. On return to Summit these two Wellesleys, both badly damaged, landed first, and the air gunner with the head

Blenheim Is of 45 Squadron prepare to depart Helwan, Egypt, for Carthago in the Sudan on 29 July 1940. In the foreground is OB-W, L8612. *(45 Squadron via A.S. Thomas)*

wound was taken to hospital but died that night. One of the Wellesleys, K8524, was subsequently written off.

At 1115 Sgt J.J. Barry of 11 Squadron from Aden in Blenheim L4817 made a lone attack over Assab and Macaaca, but his aircraft was shot down by AA and all the crew killed. Reinforcements arrived in the Sudan at Carthago in the shape of a detachment of Blenheim Is from 45 Squadron in Egypt. 112 Squadron's Detachment moved three Gladiators forward to a landing ground close to the front at Gedaref. Over Aden five S 79s of the 44° Gruppo again attacked the port, claiming hits on two ships and a petrol dump.

Thursday, 30 July 1940

The three Gladiators of 112 Squadron at Gedaref were in the air early on the 30th, escorting five Wellesleys of 47 Squadron and three Blenheims of 45 Squadron to attack Kassala airfield, now in Italian hands. Further attacks were made during the day by 223 Squadron which sent six aircraft in two flights, 45 minutes apart. Soon after midday three Wellesleys from 14 Squadron attacked a railway station and positions west of the Gash river, all three aircraft being badly hit by ground fire, and one air gunner wounded.

Italian Ca 133s again bombed in the Wajir and Buna areas, but preparations were now being made for an advance into British Somaliland, and the nine CR 32s of the 411ª Squadriglia moved from Addis Ababa to Diredawa, where three of them joined the 410ª Squadriglia.

Friday, 31 July 1940

The 18ª Squadriglia from Dessie moved into Diredawa's Scenele landing ground with six Ca 133s, and the next day the Comando Tattico Aeronautico was set up there under Generale Collalti for operations over Somaliland. Early on the 31st the Gladiators at Gedaref attacked Tessenei landing ground looking for CR 42s, but none was there.

Saturday, 1 August 1940

The first day of August was to see considerably more action in the skies than was normal, starting at 0830 when a Gladiator of 112 Squadron's Detachment

Bristol Blenheim I 'OB:A' of 45 Squadron, RAF, over the Agordat area.

operating from Gedaref and flown by Plt Off P.O.V. Green (K7974), was scrambled after a single Ca 133 reported on reconnaissance over the area. He saw it at once, 500 feet above, and chased it for 50 miles, making twelve attacks; one member of the crew baled out and the starboard engine began to smoke, after which the Caproni force-landed in a clearing. Vincents of 47 Squadron's 'D' Flight searched for survivors for several days, finally bringing back the badly wounded wireless operator on 5 August. Three more Italian crew members, two officers and an airman, were brought to Khartoum by train next day; the pilot of the aircraft was reported to be the commanding officer of his unit. Meanwhile, during the afternoon of 1 August the three Gladiators at Gedaref returned to Khartoum.

Early that afternoon several flights each of three S 81s were despatched to attack shipping in the Somaliland port of Zeila, and while these attacks were taking place a British raid from Aden on the landing ground at Chinele, near Diredawa, got under way. Chinele had only that morning been discovered by the British and bombers were reported there. A dozen Blenheims, six each from

Vickers Vincent KU-B, K4683, of 'D' Flight, 47 Squadron, at the forward landing ground at Gedaref in July 1940. *(Grp Capt J. Pelly-Fry via A.S. Thomas)*

Capitano Ricci of the 410ª Squadriglia with his Fiat CR 32 at Diredawa in September 1940. Just visible beneath the port wing is one of the bomb shackles fitted to these aircraft. Pilot on the left is Sottotenente Folcherio. *(Corrado Ricci)*

8 and 39 Squadrons, escorted by two Blenheim IVFs of 203 Squadron, were sent off. The bombers approached at 16,000 feet and dived to 10,000 feet to bomb. AA fire was encountered and fighters from Diredawa, eight miles away, attacked the two Blenheim IVFs which were escorting the 39 Squadron formation, which had bombed first. One of the fighter Blenheims was hit by one bullet, and a possible hit on one CR 42 was claimed. Later than the rest of the fighters at Diredawa, Capt Corrado Ricci, commanding officer of the 410ª Squadriglia, had taken off in his CR 32 as the second wave of bombers approached, and he chased and attacked these, shooting down Blenheim L8406 of 8 Squadron, Sgt Franks and his crew becoming prisoners.

Leaving Chinele, the bombers passed over Zeila on their return flight, and there they saw below them one of the flights of S 81s attacking the port. Blenheims of 39 Squadron flown by Plt Off J.E.S. White and Sgt Crehan dived on these bombers and attacked the formation, which broke up. Two of the Savoias closed up their formation, but the third straggled and was hit, black smoke pouring from the starboard engine; it went down apparently in flames, and made a force-landing. Two of the crew had been killed, but the others set the aircraft fully ablaze before walking back to Italian territory.

Attacks by Wellesleys on Asmara and Massawa, and by Ju 86s on Yavello completed the day's actions; at Asmara the Ala Littoria hangar was hit, a Ca 133 and a fighter under repair there both being destroyed. Italian raids were again made in the south, and on Port Sudan.

Sunday, 2 August 1940

Early next morning Blenheims of 45 Squadron's Detachment attacked Asmara again, bombing five Savoia bombers on the ground, while 39 Squadron aircraft raided Chinele once more. The Blenheims were intercepted by CR 42s, one pilot claiming to have hit a bomber, but no damage was in fact suffered by any aircraft taking part. One CR 42 piloted by Capt Corrado Santoro, CO of the 413ª Squadriglia, was hit in the engine by return fire and had to force-land.

From Summit at 0820 two Gladiators of the 112 Squadron Detachment scrambled after three S 79s, but were unable to catch them, Flt Lt Savage's fighter being hit by several bullets during the chase.

Monday, 3 August 1940

Italian aircraft made several raids in the south on 3 August, S 81s and Ca 133s attacking targets around Wajir and Buna, while ground forces occupied Debel in Kenya; they left again, hastily, soon afterwards when reconnaissance reports came in of strong British columns much superior in strength approaching.

At Wajir now was a detachment of Furies of 1 SAAF Squadron and during the morning three of these were ordered off as a lone Ca 133 of the 8ᵃ Squadriglia approached on reconnaissance. One fighter could not be started but the other two, with Flt Lt Robert S. Blake and Lt Rushmere both almost naked as they had been sunbathing, scrambled and attacked the Italian aircraft. Almost at once Rushmere's guns failed, but Blake made a number of frontal attacks, firing a long burst into the cockpit, whereupon the Capitano piloting the aircraft attempted to land, but crashed in the bush about seven miles from Wajir, the aircraft bursting into flames. All the crew perished apart from the pilot, who was pulled out by rescuers. Badly burned and injured in the crash, he gallantly attempted to rescue his crew, but was forced back by the flames and died later. Blake, a native of South Africa, was a serving officer in the RAF, but had been attached to the SAAF for operations. It was considered that Rushmere's burst of fire had hit home before his guns ceased, and this victory was therefore credited to him and Blake jointly. Next day two Furies were lost when they collided over Nanyuki; both pilots baled out unhurt.

At around 1400 on the 3rd three S 81s attacked Berbera individually, but one of 94 Squadron's Gladiators there, N5778, was scrambled with Flt Lt Reid at the controls. He saw all three bombers, attacking one flown by Capt Parmeggiani, commander of the 15ᵃ Squadriglia, for several minutes, last seeing it losing height with black smoke pouring from it. It landed at Jijiga badly damaged and with one member of the crew dead; two others were slightly hurt.

At Khartoum 'D' Flight of 47 Squadron from Carthago was now formed into an independent unit as 430 (Army Co-operation) Flight, equipped with Vincents and Gauntlets. Five Gauntlets had arrived on 30 July, being flown down from Egypt by three RAF pilots who remained with the Flight, and two SAAF pilots

Gloster Gauntlet II of 430 Flight. (*S.M. Coates via A.S. Thomas*)

In August 1940 203 Group was set up to control all RAF units in the Sudan. Commander of the new Group was Air Commodore L.H. Slatter (right), seen with General Sir Archibald Wavell, GOC-in-C, Middle East, and a Wellesley. *(Imperial War Museum)*

who returned to Egypt. A sixth Gauntlet had force-landed en route with a burnt-out exhaust ring. These aircraft were some of those which the pilots of 1 SAAF Squadron had been training on at Abu Sueir, pending the issue of Gladiators.

Tuesday, 4 August 1940
At 0745 on 4 August a formation of bombers took off from the Sudan to attack Massawa; ten Wellesleys, five each from 14 and 47 Squadrons, were to attack Sheik Said Island and stores south of Otumlo, while three Blenheims of 45 Squadron came in low from the sea to attack three submarines moored at Abdul Kadar jetty. The attack went in in the face of very heavy AA. The Blenheims scored a direct hit on a submarine depot ship moored next to one of the submarines, and another between two of the subs; the ship was slightly damaged. The 14 Squadron Wellesleys were engaged by two CR 42s and one bomber was very badly shot up, the undercarriage collapsing when it landed.

Later that day French Martin 167F No 102, piloted by Warrant Officer Trecan, flew a long reconnaissance from Aden; over Dogahbur airfield the crew spotted two aircraft on the ground and strafed both. Italian records reported that the attacking aircraft was a Blenheim, and noted that one of three Ca 133s suffered damage to one engine.

During the day two of the 94 Squadron Gladiators at Berbera moved to a strip at Laferug, while at night a Bristol Bombay bomber/transport of 216 Squadron, which had flown down to Aden from its base at Heliopolis, was bombed up and took off to raid Diredawa. An electrical storm caused it to direct its attack on Zula instead. Two S 79s of the 44° Gruppo moved to Diredawa on that date.

On 13 July 1940 two ex-French AF Martin 167F reconnaissance-bombers and a Blenheim, with Free French crews, reached Aden to join 8 Squadron, RAF. The two Martins are seen here flanking the French personnel. Rear row (l. to r.): Sergent Chef Cunibil, Sgt Chef Poisson, Sgt Mery, Adjutant Roland, Commandant Ritoux-Lachaud, Cdt Dodelier, Lt de Maismont, Adj Chef Trecan, Sgt Portalis and Sgt Lebato de Faria. Front row (ground crew, l. to r.): Soldats Montillaud, Delautre, Pinson, Delpino and Casson. Roland, Ritoux-Lachaud and Lebato de Faria were all killed when Martin No 82 was shot down on 8 September 1940, while de Maismont was taken prisoner. Dodelier and Trecan were killed in Martin No 102 on 16 December 1940, and Cunibil became a real prisoner. *(E.C. Armées)*

Wednesday, 5 August 1940

Pressed by the authorities in Rome to operate with all possible speed, the Italians now moved into British Somaliland and occupied Hargeisa. On 5 August Ro 37bis aircraft of the 110[a] Squadriglia flew reconnaissance sorties and covered advancing columns, while Savoia S 79s raided Zeila, Berbera, Aden and Burao. Two more S 79s moved up to Diredawa from Addis Ababa for these operations, and three Caproni Ca 133s arrived there from Dogahbur. The Italian force employed for the Somaliland operations comprised some 34,800 men from the Eastern Sector, commanded by Generale Nasi, and included 26 battalions of infantry, 21 batteries of artillery, half a company of medium tanks, a squadron of light tanks and some armoured cars, together with 'banda' groups. Air support was to be given initially by 27 bombers, 23 fighters and seven reconnaissance aircraft. The force moved in three main columns, that in the centre, led by Generale De Simone, being the one that took Hargeisa, while the columns to the right and left were led by Colonelli Bertello and Bertoldi respectively.

The British forces available for the defence of Somaliland were very weak, and the colony was difficult to defend. The only viable place where a stand could be made was in the mountain passes around Tug Argan on the Hargeisa–Berbera road. It was realised that once the Italians, with their vastly superior strength and greater preponderance of artillery, were able to outflank these positions (which the defenders would be too few in numbers to prevent them doing), the road across the coastal plain to Berbera would be open, and evacuation would be inevitable. Two airstrips at Berbera and Laferug were available, but the only AA defences were concentrated for the defence of the port facilities at Berbera, and concerted air attack would swiftly render these strips untenable. It would then be impossible to give adequate fighter support to bombers operating from Aden, or to provide cover for the ground forces.

During the day trios of Blenheims from 8 Squadron attacked motor convoys west of Hargeisa on three occasions; during the third mission Plt Off Felstead and his crew in L8375 were shot down in flames by a patrolling CR 32 flown by Sottoten Folcherio of the 410[a] Squadriglia.

Thursday, 6 August 1940

The Italian advance continued on the 6th but strongpoints prevented the use of the Jijiga–Hargeisa track, necessitating detours for the time being over difficult country that slowed the pace considerably. Blenheims of 8 and 39 Squadrons flew reconnaissances and bombing missions against the columns. One aircraft from the former unit was damaged by CR 42s which made twelve attacks; the Italian pilots claimed one Blenheim shot down and one probably damaged.

Other British bombers from the Sudan attacked the Massawa submarine base again, hitting and badly damaging the torpedo-boat *Acerbi*, which reported 15 dead and 16 wounded. An AA gun exploded while firing, killing one more and injuring another seven men. Numerous Italian reconnaissances were flown, together with an attack on Gebeit in the Sudan. In the south two 9ª Squadriglia Ca 133s from Baidoa bombed Wajir and Harbow airfields, claiming to have destroyed three fighters on the ground and burnt a fuel dump. They reported being attacked by three aircraft and claimed to have shot down one of these. Their interceptors were in fact again two Furies, the pilots of which claimed that they had put the central engine of one of the Capronis out of action. The South Africans suffered no loss.

Friday, 7 August 1940

With Hargeisa firmly in their hands, the Italians flew in two CR 32s and two CR 42s from Diredawa on 7 August. Fighter patrols over Somaliland were at once instituted, while in the south Ca 133s were again in action over the front areas.

The 112 Squadron Detachment Gladiators had been trying to catch S 79s over the Sudan, and indeed only bombers of this type were now appearing there in daytime. Their speed, and the small number of defending fighters available, made interceptions very difficult. At this juncture the other nine Gladiators of 1 SAAF Squadron arrived at Khartoum from Egypt on 5 August, led by Capt S. van Schalkwyk, but here they were held by Air Commodore Slatter to assist in the defence of the Sudan.

Saturday, 8 August 1940

At Berbera meanwhile an Italian attack put an end to the local air defence. Two 94 Squadron Gladiators were on the ground at 0600 when two CR 32s and a CR 42 from Hargeisa attacked them. The standby pilot had got into the cockpit of N5778, but had not got the engine started when the attack began, and as Capt Ricci's CR 32 opened fire, he leapt out and ran to shelter. Failing to inflict telling damage in the first pass, Ricci returned for a second attack, and this time he set the Gladiator alight and it burnt fiercely, being totally destroyed. The second Gladiator was also set on fire by the attacks of Serg Magg Tellurio and Sottoten Komienz, the rear fuselage and tail being burnt off. When news of this attack reached Laferug, the other two Gladiators there were at once ordered to be flown back to Aden.

Blenheim IVFs of 203 Squadron were despatched to patrol over Berbera instead of the Gladiators, and during the middle part of the day Plt Off Corbould engaged three S 79s which were bombing the port and attacked one, damaging it and killing one of the crew. This aircraft was subsequently reported by the British to have crashed later, but in fact returned to its base. This was one of several raids over British Somaliland made by the Italians during the day; three

On the morning of 8 August 1940 the Italians put paid to the RAF's fighter defence of Berbera, British Somaliland, destroying two 94 Squadron Gladiators on the ground. N2284 was set on fire by Capt Ricci of the 410ᵃ Squadriglia (above), while N5890 was damaged by his fire (below). *(94 Squadron via A.S. Thomas)*

S 81s attacked positions on the Godojere Pass during the morning, while three Ca 133s attacked the Karim Pass, and two S 79s made an earlier attack on Berbera; Ro 37bis flew several reconnaissances, and fighters patrolled throughout the day, although one CR 32 and one CR 42 were damaged in landing accidents at Hargeisa. In the south four Ju 86s of 12 SAAF Squadron bombed and strafed Neghelli airfield, burning one Ca 133 and damaging two more.

Sunday, 9 August 1940

Early next morning, two CR 32s and a CR 42 again strafed Berbera airfield, but this time there was only a crash-landed Blenheim to shoot up; they were given a warm reception by the airfield defence party and by the quadruple 'pompoms' of the Australian cruiser HMAS *Hobart*, which was in harbour; one

Italian fighter was believed to have been hit. During the day the damaged Gladiator was dismantled and shipped back to Aden.

Five Wellesleys of 47 Squadron attacked Gura, hitting an ammunition dump which blew up. They were attacked by fighters, and several Wellesleys were badly damaged, one flown by Sgt Colvin crashing on landing when the damaged undercarriage of K7756 collapsed. The formation passed Italian bombers returning from an attack on 47's own base at Carthago, where fifteen aircraft on the ground had been bombed without effect.

A Hartbeeste of 40 SAAF Squadron on a reconnaissance over the southern front was attacked by two aircraft which the crew identified as Ro 37s, which came out of the sun; all the aircraft of this type were operating over Somaliland at this time, and the identity of the aircraft involved is uncertain, although they were probably CR 32s. After fighting with them for some time, fire from the ground hit the radiator of the Hartbeeste and Capt Lemmer had to land at the strip at British El Wak, which was in Italian hands. Here he was taken prisoner by 'banda', but his gunner, Air Sgt Lewis, tried to put up a fight and was killed.

Monday, 10 August 1940

By 10 August one column of the Italian advance had reached the coast, but progress along the road towards Zeila was interrupted by bombardment by Royal Navy cruisers, and by the attacks of Aden-based aircraft. The column was finally halted due to tyre damage caused by the rough ground over which it was passing. The main column had been in contact with the Tug Argan defences since the 8th, but only on this day did the real battle here begin. A further CR 42 and two CR 32s flew up to Hargeisa from Diredawa, joined by a single Ca 133 of the 52ª Squadriglia; five S 79s from Addis Ababa moved to Diredawa.

During the morning three Blenheims of 8 Squadron dive-bombed Italian troops in the Tug Argan area, a CR 42 making a frontal attack and damaging one Blenheim. Three more Blenheims returned in the afternoon to dive-bomb the village of Dubato, but during the return flight two collided in the air and both crashed in flames. These were L8503 and L8506 flown respectively by Flg Off A.G. Curtis and Plt Off A.J.G. Bisson.

Tuesday, 11 August 1940

During 11 August the main Italian thrust from the direction of Harar towards Berbera was heavily involved in the Tug Argan battle, but the Italians were finding the terrain difficult for their supply vehicles, and their advance generally was now proceeding very slowly. In support of the attack six Ca 133s and three S 81s bombed and strafed fortifications in the Godojere Pass at low level during the morning; one S 81 was shot down in flames by Bren gunners. While this attack was under way three CR 32s strafed lorries and a fuel dump in the Laferug area, and a little later an S 79 bombed the British headquarters there. Italian reports claimed a Blenheim shot down during an attack on their troops during the day, but no losses are recorded.

Wednesday, 12 August 1940

At dawn next morning a Blenheim of 11 Squadron, L8395, piloted by Flt Lt Smith, and one of 39 Squadron, L8387, flown by Plt Off Rowbotham, left Aden to attack guns in the Darboruk area. Considerable AA fire was met, and as

39 Squadron lost another Blenheim on 12 August, L8387 flown by Plt Off Rowbotham who was attacked by two Italian fighters over Darboruk and crash-landed at Berbera. His aircraft too was removed to Addis Ababa, where it is seen in a hangar. *(Corrado Ricci)*

Smith attempted to drop a message to British troops he was attacked by CR 42s, his aircraft being badly shot up, although he managed to reach Aden. Rowbotham's aircraft was attacked by two more fighters and was also badly damaged, causing the pilot to crash-land at Berbera.

A couple of hours later three more Blenheims from 39 Squadron arrived to attack similar targets; over the front a CR 32 of the 410ª Squadriglia flown by Sottoten Alberto Veronese attacked the leading bomber, but Flt Sgt Thomas in

On 12 August 1940 Flt Sgt Thomas of 39 Squadron flying this Blenheim I, L8402, was engaged in an air battle over British Somaliland with Sottotenente Veronese of the 410ª Squadriglia. Badly wounded and losing blood, Thomas flew the 40 miles to Berbera where he crash-landed; he was later awarded the DFM. Italian troops are seen examining the aircraft after the capture of the port.

Thomas's Blenheim after it had been dismantled and removed to Addis Ababa. 39 Squadron's code letters, 'XZ', have never previously been illustrated. *(Corrado Ricci)*

the third Blenheim, L8402, seeing this, jettisoned his bombs and attacked. The fighter made a head-on attack on this aircraft, the observer being killed and Thomas badly wounded in the right shoulder. Stemming the flow of blood with a handkerchief, he managed to reach Berbera, 40 miles away, and crash-land; he subsequently received a DFM for his courageous action. Veronese, the attacking pilot, was also slightly wounded in this encounter.

While the second Blenheim attack was under way a Blenheim IVF of 203 Squadron left to patrol over Berbera, encountering three S 79s bombing the airfield there. The pilot gave chase for 15 minutes, but a bullet then entered the cockpit, wounding both the pilot and the observer, and the pursuit was broken off.

Italian activity in support of their main attack, and of the other columns,

The evacuation of Berbera by British forces on 19 August 1940 was covered by fighter Blenheim IVFs of 203 Squadron from Aden. One of these, NT-J, is seen here on Khormaksar airfield during the month. *(via A.S. Thomas)*

Pilots of the 410ª Squadriglia in a sandbagged shelter at Jijiga. On the left is Sottotenente Alberto Veronese and on the right, enjoying a banana, Capitano Ricci. *(Corrado Ricci)*

continued all day, six Ca 133s raiding defences at Mandera and Laferug. During the afternoon a column reached Zeila from the direction of Bulhar, and in the Adadleh area British outposts were gradually overcome, although some were retaken — mainly with the help of artillery fire.

In the south a new Comando de Gruppo Tattico was set up at Yavello, and the 65ª Squadriglia moved there from Neghelli. In Kenya meanwhile the crews of 11 SAAF Squadron had returned with fifteen Fairey Battles, and moved to Archer's Post on 12 August.

Thursday, 13 August 1940

On the 13th four of these aircraft flew their first mission to Jimma, meeting AA and fighters; Capt J. de Wet's aircraft was hit by both a CR 32 and an AA shell, and he set course for home in the wrong direction. Finally realising his mistake, he eventually reached Lokitaung where he crashed, the aircraft being written off.

In British Somaliland Italian attacks continued, mainly in the area east of Adadleh. Ca 133s bombed Jerato Pass, and CR 32s twice strafed the crash-landed Blenheims at Berbera. On the second occasion one of these fighters, flown by Ten Pesce, was hit by rifle fire and force-landed in British territory. Three more S 81s moved to Diredawa from Shashamanna to take part in operations over the area. Outflanking of the Tug Argan positions was now making their continued defence precarious, and British units began withdrawing on Berbera.

To assist the Aden-based aircraft in operations over Somaliland, eleven Wellesleys of 223 Squadron now flew to Aden, landing at Perim Island during the afternoon. On the way Sqn Ldr Larking's aircraft suffered an engine fire and he had to make a forced landing on poor ground, his aircraft being badly damaged. Two 8 Squadron Vincents flew to Dar Majahar and found him, dropping messages advising him to make for Khar Umeir landing ground, 16 miles away. He and his crew hired camels from local inhabitants, and in a temperature of 120°F, reached the landing ground in five hours, being flown out successfully.

Friday, 14 August 1940

The Italians reported bombing attacks on both Zeila and on one of their columns moving between that port and Berbera, anti-aircraft gunners claiming to have shot down one bomber in flames; no losses are recorded. Regia Aeronautica aircraft were also busy, S 79s bombing shipping off Bulhar, while three S 81s and three Ca 133s raided a fort north of the Godojere Pass, and troops retreating down the road to Berbera from there. Three CR 32s strafed vehicles at Mandera and Laferug, and on the track to Berbera.

In the south three Ca 133s from Baidoa attacked Wajir, claiming to have destroyed two fighters on the ground here. Lt A. Colenbrander of 1 SAAF Squadron in one of the newly arrived Gladiators intercepted the bombers and damaged one, which returned with four of the crew slightly wounded. Colenbrander reported that his attack had caused the Capronis to jettison their bombs. During the day a Vickers Valentia transport of 50 SAAF Squadron flew up to Lokitaung from Nairobi. Here the pilot, Lt C. Kearey, joined by several officers of 11 SAAF Squadron, prepared a bomb from an oil drum and in the early hours of 15 August he unofficially unloaded this on an Italian fort nearby. Although the Valentia was hit by 93 bullets, it was not badly damaged, and Kearey was able to keep his attack secret until it was picked up by the intelligence services from a Rome broadcast. An inquiry was held, and a month later he was transferred to a bomber squadron.

Saturday, 15 August 1940

On 15 August — one of the major days of the Battle of Britain — Italian forces overcame an outpost of Rhodesian troops on the road to Laferug, taking some prisoners and counting a number of dead. Bombers continued to provide support, three Ca 133s bombing positions at Laferug, three S 81s hitting others in the Mandera area, and three S 79s attacking troops and vehicles near Berbera.

To reinforce the squadrons in Aden, a flight of six Blenheim Is from 84 Squadron in Iraq had flown to Port Sudan, arriving from Ismailia on the 14th; on the morning of 15 August these aircraft took off for Aden, but while passing to the north-west of Kamaran Island they spotted beneath them a single S 81. Flt Lt Cattell led all six Blenheims down to attack and three of them opened fire. The S 81 attempted to turn towards the coast, but suddenly its starboard wing caught fire, an explosion then causing this to fold back and break up, and part of the tailplane fell off. The bomber went down vertically into the sea in flames, two of the crew being seen to jump out and attempt to open their parachutes before they hit the water. The Blenheims landed at Sheik Othman and were handed over to the squadrons there, the 84 Squadron personnel leaving on the return journey to Shaibah, Iraq, in two Bombays next day.

Blenheims of 39 Squadron were twice attacked by fighters during operations on this date, but in neither case was any damage inflicted.

Sunday, 16 August 1940

By 16 August the small British forces in Somaliland had all withdrawn into

1430 Flight Vincents at Gordon's Tree. KU-4 is K6354, KU-6 is K4685, but KU-3's serial is not known. *(F. Paget via A.S. Thomas)*

Berbera and evacuation began. Italian raids now concentrated on the port, and at dawn two S 81s bombed vessels there, both bombers being damaged by AA. Around midday two S 79s attacked but one of these was also hit. When a third flight of three S 79s attacked in the afternoon, they were intercepted by the two Martin 167Fs of 8 Squadron's French contingent, which were sharing patrols over the port with 203 Squadron's Blenheim IVFs; Flt Lt Ritoux-Lachaud claimed to have shot down one of the bombers, although this was not officially confirmed to him. Despite this, the S 79 flown by Sottoten Luigi Conti, which he had attacked, did in fact fall in flames a few minutes after the attack, the Italians in the other aircraft identifying their attackers as Blenheims.

Had the S 79s been fitted with radio communication, Conti and his crew would almost certainly have survived; following Ritoux-Lachaud's attack, the other crews noted a thin stream of black smoke trailing beneath Conti's bomber, but this had obviously not been noticed by the occupants. The men aboard the other aircraft made vigorous and increasingly more desperate signs to Conti in an effort to warn him, but he and his crew merely waved back as the trail of smoke thickened; suddenly the stricken Savoia exploded into a ball of flame and fell to the ground near Sheik.

The component at Diredawa for the Somaliland operations was reinforced further during the day by the arrival of two S 79s of the 44° Gruppo and three CR 32s of the 411ª Squadriglia from Addis Ababa, and three S 81s from Shashamanna. In the Sudan the newly formed 430 Flight was now divided into two sub-flights, 'A' with Gauntlets and 'B' with Vincents. That night, however, high winds caused damage to two of the former and three of the latter.

Monday, 17 August 1940
Fighting over British Somaliland continued on the 17th, five Blenheims raiding Hargeisa airfield, while five Ca 133s escorted by two CR 32s attacked the residency of the British commander in the Sheik area. A Blenheim of 39 Squadron on reconnaissance over the Bulhar–Zeila area was hit in the bomb-bay by AA and had to ditch in the sea; the crew were picked up after 30 minutes by the cruiser HMS *Ceres*.

Three of the 4° Gruppo's S 81s now returned to Shashamanna from Diredawa as the fighting approached its close, two 44° Gruppo S 79s flying back to Addis Ababa, where they were joined by three more of these aircraft from Gura.

These latter bombers were from the 10ᵃ Squadriglia of the 28° Gruppo, which had just exchanged its S 81s for these more modern aircraft; this change was made possible as reinforcements of S 79s were now flying direct from Italy via Libya. In Aden 39 Squadron transferred two of its Blenheims to 11 Squadron, giving each unit five operational aircraft — a sign of the attrition of the constant operations over the last weeks.

Tuesday, 18 August 1940

Leaving Aden at 0535 on 18 August, three Blenheims of 11 Squadron made a high-level bombing attack on Italian vehicles near Laferug but were attacked by two CR 32s flown by Sottoten Veronese and Serg Magg Volpe of the 410ᵃ Squadriglia, Blenheim L1479 flown by Sgt Gay being shot down in flames by Veronese north-west of Laferug. All the crew managed to bale out, but only one survived, wounded and badly burned; one man died almost at once, and the other in hospital a little later.

Five minutes after the Blenheims had left the ground, five Wellesleys of 223 Squadron were up from Perim Island and attacked Addis Ababa in very poor weather; AA fire was encountered and a lone CR 42 made several determined attacks from all angles, four Wellesleys being hit, one badly. The Squadron claimed the destruction of two hangars with two more damaged, and of four S 79s with two more badly damaged; it was also reported that the Duke of Aosta's private aircraft was destroyed in one of the hangars. Actual losses were one S 79, one S 75 and three Ca 133s destroyed, with one S 79 and one S 81 badly damaged.

S 79s twice bombed Berbera on this date, three appearing over the port fairly early in the morning and three more, escorted by two CR 42s, attacking in the early afternoon, the escort driving off a patrolling fighter Blenheim.

During the 18th the Italians broke through the second line of defence in front of Berbera, but the defenders had done their job.

Wednesday, 19 August 1940

On this day the evacuation of 7,000 troops from British Somaliland was completed. A last raid was made by three S 79s, but before the morning was out British aircraft were arriving from Aden to attack Italian columns moving into the port and airfield. On arrival the Italians found much of the town burning, and on the airfield were the remains of four British aircraft, three showing evidence of having been strafed by Italian fighters. The campaign cost the British ground force 38 killed, 102 wounded and 120 missing; Italian casualties totalled 465 killed, 1,530 wounded and 34 missing.

Between 5 and 19 August Aden-based units of the RAF flew 184 sorties and dropped 60 tons of bombs, losing seven aircraft with ten more badly damaged; twelve aircrew were killed and three wounded. In the final four days, 16th to 19th, 12 reconnaissances and 19 bombing-reconnaissances had been made, together with 72 bombing sorties against enemy troops and transport, and 36 fighter patrols over Berbera.

Several important lessons had been learned, notably that the airfields did not have sufficient AA defences and consequently had quickly become unusable. As a result there had been no protection for the bombers from Aden, which had proved vulnerable to fighter attack. Despite the activities along the coast of British Somaliland, an important convoy had passed through the Red Sea

As the fighting in British Somaliland reached its peak, far away in Kenya 11 SAAF Squadron flew its first sorties with its new Fairey Battles on 13 August 1940.

early in the month, and another entered the area on the 19th. These were escorted by Wellesleys of 14 Squadron, as 203 Squadron's Blenheim IVFs were involved over Berbera.

With operations over British Somaliland ended, Italian aircraft at Diredawa began to disperse on the 22nd, three CR 32s of the 411ª Squadriglia going to Addis Ababa, three S 79s of the 10ª Squadriglia to Gura, and three Ca 133s of the 52ª Squadriglia to Miesso. From Aden the Wellesleys of 223 Squadron returned to the Sudan. The dispersal of the Italian units was completed on 26 August and the Comando Tattico dell Settore Aeronautica Ouest was disbanded. Three further 52ª Squadriglia Ca 133s flew to Dessie with one from the 18ª Squadriglia, while two more from the latter unit went to Jijiga.

To the south on this date the newly arrived Battles of 11 SAAF Squadron made the first of a series of raids on Mogadishu, refuelling at a strip at Habaswein in the Northern Frontier District. At this stage the Battles, like the Italian bombers, could not intercommunicate in flight, and only the leader navigated; this state of affairs continued until January 1941.

During the raid on the 19th the Battles split into sections, attacking the AGIP store at Mogadishu, Lugh Ferrandi airfield, Vittorio d'Africa, Neghelli and Bathie. On that day, however, a Hartbeeste of 40 SAAF Squadron flown by Lt G.J. de Greef failed to return from a sortie over the front; months later, in March 1941, the wreckage of this aircraft was to be discovered by advancing troops at Bardera.

Thursday, 20 August 1940

Dessie suffered its first air attack early on the 20th when five Wellesleys of 223 Squadron, which were still based at Perim Island, bombed the airfield, damaging several buildings. Forty minutes later four Blenheims of 39 Squadron and one of 11 Squadron, RAF, attacked the Ala Littoria hangar at Diredawa; this target was hit and damaged, an S 81 under repair being burnt and a CR 32 damaged by splinters. While on the run-up to the target the bombers were attacked by two CR 42s of the 413ª Squadriglia and Plt Off Jago's Blenheim (L8474) was

Capitano Corrado Santoro, CO of the 413ª Squadriglia, about to take off in his Fiat CR 42 from Addis Ababa. It was a surprise picture and he was telling the photographer, 'Please don't. To be photographed before a combat brings bad luck.' Later in the campaign while attacking a bomber, Santoro received a bullet in the leg, which permanently crippled him. *(via Corrado Ricci)*

shot down in flames by Capt Corrado Santoro, the crew being killed. Santoro also hit the 11 Squadron aircraft which was badly damaged and crash-landed on return to Aden.

In the Sudan the 112 Squadron Detachment was reorganised as an autonomous flight, known as 'K' Flight. It was administered by 14 Squadron and now comprised about a dozen pilots under Flt Lt K.H. Savage with seven Gladiators. During the night high winds in the Sudan again played havoc with 430 Flight's biplanes, one Gauntlet and three Vincents being damaged. To be nearer to the front, three Gauntlets and six Vincents were ordered to the landing ground at Gedaref.

Friday, 21 August 1940

In the south six Battles of 11 SAAF Squadron carried out their second raid on the Mogadishu area on 21 August, claiming to have destroyed five Ca 133s on the ground and damaging others. Two of the Italian aircraft awaiting overhaul were so badly damaged as to be beyond repair, only the engines being recoverable; one under repair was badly damaged, and three more were slightly damaged, one further aircraft without engines being set on fire. In addition, two lorries and fourteen parachutes were destroyed, two hangars badly damaged and various other damage was done. Over Cocaia, 'banda' claimed to have shot down one aircraft with rifle fire, but no losses are recorded. However, Lt C.A. van Vliet's Battle was hit five times during an attack on Habaswein, and the observer, Lt Chapman, was hit in one leg.

Monday, 24 to Thursday, 27 August 1940

During the next few days Regia Aeronautica Ca 133s were again active in small numbers over the southern front, and on 24 August four SAAF Battles returned to Mogadishu once more to bomb and take photographs. Three Ro 37bis which had just moved there to provide a modicum of defence were scrambled but were unable to catch the bombers. A repeat reconnaissance in similar strength was made next day, but again could not be intercepted.

In the north three Blenheims from 11 Squadron, RAF, refuelled at Perim Island and bombed Dessie's Combolcia airfield on the 24th. Also on that day 430 Flight flew its first sorties from Gedaref, two Vincents and two Gauntlets bombing Gallabat fort. On 26 August five Wellesleys of 223 Squadron attacked Asmara where heavy AA was encountered. Two fighters attacked with great determination as the bombers turned away after the attack, one closing to within 50 yards when it was hit by fire from all the air gunners; it broke away suddenly and was believed to have been shot down. The other fighter shot down Plt Off J.C. Smitheram's Wellesley (K7731), the last in the formation which fell in a flat spiral in flames and crashed; no parachutes were seen. From Khartoum two 1 SAAF Squadron Gladiators were sent to defend an important bridge at Atbara; they were to remain there until the end of September, but no Italian air attacks were to develop.

Friday, 28 August 1940
11 SAAF Squadron was busy again on 28 August, making no fewer than three raids on Mogadishu; the last two were intercepted by Ro 37bis, but the Battles were able to outrun these biplanes once again. A substantial vehicle park of some 1,000 trucks was dive-bombed and 800 were destroyed. This, however, was by no means the great victory it at first appeared, for when the town was subsequently captured and the wrecked lorries were examined, they were found to be ancient vehicles that had been dumped as worn out at the end of the conquest of Ethiopia several years before!

Saturday, 29 to Sunday, 30 August 1940
Further raids were made next day and three 223 Squadron Wellesleys attacked Agordat, strafing a Ca 133 on the ground after bombing. On 30 August a detachment of RAF personnel with Fairey Swordfish biplanes arrived in Aden and was posted to 8 Squadron.

Tuesday, 1 September 1940
The first day of September saw a temporary increase in activity over the East African theatre generally. From Aden Blenheims of 8, 11, and 39 Squadrons attacked Assab naval base, badly damaging a requisitioned tug, destroying naval barracks, a store of 1,500 shells, and a copra store; 12 men were killed and over 30 wounded. One bomber was claimed probably destroyed by the defences, but in fact all returned safely. A single Wellesley of 14 Squadron piloted by Sgt Norris (L2669) made a photographic reconnaissance over Harmil Island, but was attacked by fighters scrambled from Massawa and crash-landed on the island, the crew being taken prisoner.

Over the northern front three Gladiators of 1 SAAF Squadron were patrolling in the Kassala area when two CR 42s climbed up to challenge them. The South Africans got in first, Maj van Schalkwyk and Lt J.J. Coetzer claiming one shot down each; one CR 42 was seen to spin and crash while the other was chased to its airfield at Tessenei, where it was reported to have crash-landed. The identity of the Italian pilots remains unknown since no account of this combat can be found in their records. Indeed, a little confusion surrounds this engagement, as apparently Coetzer's claim was shared by Lt J.L. Hewitson, who recorded it in his logbook as occurring on 18 September!

Three S 81s from Diredawa now moved to Shashamanna, while the commanding officer of the 110ª Squadriglia, Ten Romano Palmera, also left this base to join the detachment of his unit at Mogadishu.

Wednesday, 2 September 1940

Next day S 79s attacked Aden, and it was later learned by the Italians from British radio reports that two motor torpedo-boats had been left in a sinking condition. With a Valentia carrying the necessary ground crews and supplies, three Vincents and four Gauntlets of 430 Flight moved from Gedaref to Azzoza for operations on this date.

Thursday, 3 to Friday, 4 September 1940

On the morning of 3 September three Ju 86s of 12 SAAF Squadron raided Yavello airfield, destroying three Ca 133s on the ground. Lt R.G. Donaldson's bomber was hit by ground fire and crashed, bursting into flames; the crew of seven all perished. Shortly after midday on the 4th three S 79s from Diredawa bombed Aden port again. This time two 94 Squadron Gladiators were scrambled, and one intercepted, firing on one Savoia which suffered slight damage. The bomber crews claimed to have shot down one Gladiator, but neither was in fact hit. Other Italian bombers raided the steamship *Velko* in the Red Sea, damaging her seriously. British bombers attacked the railway station at Aiscia, Kassala, and the airfield at Baidoa, where four Ca 133s were badly damaged.

Saturday, 5 September 1940

Further British raids on the 5th included an attack on Assab where a battery of 120mm naval guns was hit and put out of action, together with a munitions dump and other targets. Five S 79s raided a convoy known by the code 'BS 3½' in the Red Sea; an escorting Blenheim IVF attacked, but was hit and damaged by return fire.

Sunday, 6 September 1940

Next day a single S 79 attacked the convoy again, while three more Savoias from Addis Ababa bombed Aden. Six Gladiators were scrambled and two made contact, making astern attacks but failing to see the results of any damage inflicted. One S 79 was hit in the centre engine and oil tank, landing at Adigolla in a damaged condition; a second bomber hit a tree while landing at Diredawa and was also damaged. One Gladiator was claimed shot down in flames, but no loss was in fact suffered. S 79s were once more active on the 7th, this time raiding Port Sudan.

Monday, 7 September 1940

Over the northern front on 7 September two Gauntlets, each carrying eight 25lb incendiary bombs, took off at 1120, accompanied by two Vincents; their target was Metemma airfield. As they left the ground one Vincent hit some trees and was damaged, landing again. At 1305 the other Vincent had just begun dive-bombing the target when a Ca 133 was observed coming in low, apparently oblivious to the British aircraft, and dropping supplies by parachute. Flt Lt A.B. Mitchell in Gauntlet K5355 dived and made a head-on attack on the Caproni, which at once dived into the ground and stood on its nose; Mitchell reported that the centre engine was rammed right back into the cockpit. He then climbed to 4,000 feet and dived again to drop his incendiaries on the bomber; these had no apparent effect, so he carried out three strafing attacks. While this action was briefly recorded by the Italians, no mention was made of any damage to the Ca 133, although it seems likely from this detailed report of the combat that some was almost certainly suffered.

In the south 11 SAAF Squadron returned again to Mogadishu, intent upon finishing off the vehicle park attacked on 28 August. On arrival the South Africans noted twelve Ca 133s on the airfield and attacked these instead, claiming one destroyed. This was in fact an unserviceable machine which was badly damaged in the attack. Ro 37bis again attempted to intercept, but were left behind. Three Ca 133s raided the Bura area of northern Kenya, while two more attacked targets around Boma in the Lower Sudan.

Tuesday, 8 September 1940

During the morning of 8 September Martin 167F No 82 from 8 Squadron at Aden left on a long-range reconnaissance. The pilot, Adj M.R. Rolland, strafed the airfield at Moggio, causing a fire here, but the aircraft was attacked and shot down in flames by a CR 42 of the 413ª Squadriglia. Only Flg Off P.C. Rupert, the observer, managed to bale out and he was taken prisoner; the rest of the crew were killed. Port Sudan was again bombed by S 79s, which attacked the airfield on which were seen eighteen aircraft. Fighters attacked, and the bombers claimed one shot down; no British loss was recorded. In the afternoon three Ca 133s of the 25° Gruppo from Gobwen bombed the airfield at Garissa, causing fires.

Wednesday, 9 September 1940

Following an overnight stay at Ras Ara, three Blenheims of 39 Squadron and two of 11 Squadron attacked Dessie again on the 9th. They were attacked ineffectively by two CR 32s, which did however cause the bombers to jettison their bombs short of the target; the fighters claimed one bomber possibly shot down. Meanwhile 11 SAAF Squadron launched its longest-ranging raid to date, four Battles attacking Shashamanna airfield where fourteen Italian aircraft were counted on the ground. In the afternoon five Battles returned to the target, but this time one was shot down by AA fire, Capt R.A. Blackwell and Air Sgt F.A. van Zyl being taken prisoner. The Italians identified the attacking aircraft as Wellesleys, and reported total losses during the two raids as one S 81 burnt out, two S 81s and a Ca 133 slightly damaged; they claimed one of the South African bombers shot down, and four more badly damaged.

In the Sudan six more Blenheims of 45 Squadron arrived at Summit from Egypt, led by Flt Lt Troughton-Smith, while far away in South Africa a new fighter squadron, 3 SAAF, began forming at Waterkloof under Maj L.A. Wilmot for service in Kenya.

Thursday, 10 September 1940

During the night of 9/10 September British forces launched a limited attack on Italian positions at Kassala. In support of this attack three Wellesleys of 14

Squadron bombed these positions during the morning, but as they began their return flight, they were attacked by two CR 42s which shot down K7763, the No 3 aircraft, in flames; only the pilot, Plt Off J.A. Ferguson, managed to bale out. The fighters claimed a second bomber probably destroyed. Following this raid, the attack on the ground was brought to a halt and repulsed by Italian artillery fire.

During the three months since the outbreak of hostilities in East Africa the Italians had suffered a considerable number of aircraft destroyed or damaged in landing accidents, and by this date the total number of aircraft destroyed or written off from all causes had risen to 84; 143 air force personnel had been killed and 71 wounded or injured.

Saturday, 12 September 1940

Four Ju 86s of 12 SAAF Squadron raided Jimma airfield on the morning of 12 September, attacking eleven aircraft which were seen lined up on the ground. The South Africans claimed nine aircraft destroyed and two damaged; Italian records noted that five Ca 133s were damaged and a hangar hit, where several work benches were destroyed. An hour later three Battles of 11 SAAF Squadron raided Shashamanna again, dive-bombing the airfield, hitting the headquarters building and destroying an S 81; a second was damaged. Fighters were already in the air when the Battles approached, and four CR 32s attacked; the aircraft of Lt E.G. Armstrong was shot down in flames.

A fourth Battle, detailed to photograph the results of the bombing, then flew over the base at 2,000 feet, but as it turned for home Maresciallo Gobbo of the 411ᵃ Squadriglia in one of the CR 32s suddenly appeared from the clouds below and opened fire. Air Gunner V.P. McVicar and Air Sgt L.A. Feinberg, the photographer, were both wounded and the aircraft began to burn. Lt J.E. Lindsay managed to force-land in clear ground between some trees, but while doing so the aircraft hit and killed a local villager, then burst into flames.

The Battle's crew got out swiftly, but were at once attacked by armed natives; at that moment the ammunition in the burning aircraft began to explode and the natives fled. Italian troops then arrived and took the crew prisoner; the Italians did not at first realise that the Battle had been brought down by one of their fighters and thought that the crew had burned it themselves after force-landing.

Sunday, 13 September 1940

On 13 September a Regia Aeronautica Ro 37bis on reconnaissance from Mogadishu spotted a small warship off the coast. Two hours later two Ca 133s escorted by another Ro 37bis attacked the vessel, which turned out to be a motor torpedo-boat; it was bombed again late in the afternoon, the latter pair of bombers claiming to have hit the stern of the vessel. For the second time in 48 hours an S 79 on reconnaissance over the Gulf of Aden was attacked by a 94 Squadron Gladiator, but escaped; a further similar interception was to take place next day with similar negative results, and then again on the 15th.

Monday, 14 September 1940

On 14 September the new detachment of Blenheim Is from 45 Squadron began operations, and on the same date three Blenheim IVs with crews arrived for 14 Squadron, which was to begin conversion to these aircraft. During the night of

14/15 September a number of raids were made on Asmara and Gura by the RAF; a Ca 133 and two S 79s were damaged at the latter base. Italian bombers also remained active, three Ca 133s of the 49° Gruppo from Jimma attacking the Boma area, where a fort was hit; one bomber was slightly damaged by AA.

Wednesday, 16 September 1940
Allied bombers were over several targets on the 16th, and at sunset three 223 Squadron Wellesleys left to attack Gura; Plt Off Walker's aircraft failed to return. From Baidoa the Ca 133s of the 9ᵃ Squadriglia moved to Vittoria d'Africa for better dispersion.

Friday, 18 to Saturday, 19 September 1940
With the availability of 40 SAAF Squadron, now at full strength in Kenya, and with the shortage of army co-operation aircraft on the northern front, 237 Squadron began moving up from its Kenyan base to Khartoum on 18 September. The remaining Harts and Audaxes were left behind, and the first five Hardys left on this date, followed by six more on the 19th and the final six on the 20th. Minor raids by both sides continued, and on 19 September five S 79s attacked a convoy in the Red Sea; two 94 Squadron Gladiators were as usual unable to catch them.

Sunday, 20 September, 1940
Next morning the three new Blenheim IVs of 14 Squadron flew their first mission, attacking Massawa. AA fire hit the port engine of one, and set it on fire, the aircraft force-landing north of the port, where the crew were taken prisoner.

Two strafing attacks were made on Tessenei landing ground during the day, one by Flt Lt Mitchell of 430 Flight in a Gauntlet, and one by three pilots of 1 SAAF Squadron from Khartoum, these latter shooting up a Ca 133 on the ground. S 79s again attacked the Red Sea convoy, claiming hits on two ships. One bomber was slightly damaged by AA, but two escorting Blenheim fighters were unable to intercept them. Wellesleys were now frequently operating at night, but the first signs of opposition to such incursions were noted during the night of 20/21 September when two CR 42s twice attacked an aircraft of 223 Squadron over Massawa without inflicting any damage. Such aircraft may well have been responsible for shooting down Plt Off Walker's aircraft from this squadron four nights earlier.

Monday, 21 September 1940
Following the recent attacks on Mogadishu and Shashamanna by the South African Battles, the Italians now planned a raid on the base of 11 SAAF Squadron at Archer's Post, and three S 79s moved to Yavello on 21 September to undertake this. Allied monitors picked up details of this operation however, dummy aircraft being set up on a mock satellite airfield. When the bombers approached, they were met by four Gladiators of 1 SAAF Squadron and chased off. The Italians claimed to have hit one fighter during this engagement. One bullet passed through the exhaust manifold of Lt Colenbrander's aircraft.

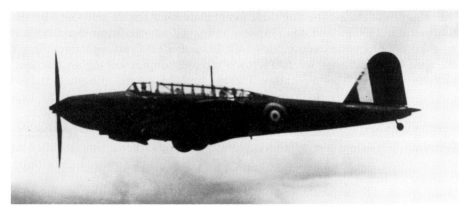

Fairey Battle of 11 SAAF Squadron operating from Nanyuki. *(SAAF)*

Tuesday, 22 to Thursday, 24 September 1940

The first substantial reinforcement of ground troops for the British in the Sudan arrived at Port Sudan on 22 September 1940, units of the 5th Indian Division beginning disembarkation that day. Italian air raids on the port were redoubled, and during the day an attack on the nearby airfield was made, ten British aircraft being seen and bombed. Four of 1 SAAF Squadron's Gladiators were sent down from Khartoum to reinforce 'K' Flight there, although in the event the attacks stopped before they could get into action.

Other raids were also carried out against Aden, Savoia S 79s attacking by day and S 81s by night. At night RAF Wellesleys of 14 Squadron attacked Mai Edaga airfield, claiming to have destroyed two fighters on the ground and to have strafed three bombers. Two days later on 24 September, S 79s again raided Aden, claiming to have shot down one British fighter, although none was in fact recorded as lost.

Friday, 25 September 1940

The whole of 45 Squadron now arrived in the Sudan from Egypt on 25

Vickers Wellesleys of 223 Squadron, RAF, at Summit landing ground, Sudan, being armed with 250lb bombs (note bomb doors open). Wellesley L2714 'AO:A' (foreground) was the aircraft of Flt Lt James Pelly-Fry, then commander of 'A' Flight.

September, and during the day three Blenheims from the detachment already there attacked Gura and Mai Edaga; a CR 42 attacked one bomber and damaged it. During the morning a 430 Flight Gauntlet, flown by the indefatigable Flt Lt Mitchell, was scrambled to intercept five approaching aircraft, but these turned out to be Wellesleys. Passing over Metemma airfield, Mitchell observed three Ca 133s on the ground and strafed one of them; this aircraft had just landed, and suffered some damage from his attack.

Just after midday two Vincents and two Gauntlets returned to this airfield to repeat the attack on these aircraft.

Sunday, 27 September 1940
The whole of 45 Squadron was ready for operations on 27 September, three of its aircraft attacking Assab airfield to add to the almost daily attacks small formations of Blenheims were now making throughout Eritrea. Some movement of Italian aircraft occurred at this stage, three CR 42s of the 413^a Squadriglia moving from Addis Ababa to Bahar Dar, two CR 32s of the 411^a Squadriglia going from Dessie to Shashamanna via Addis Ababa, while two more from the 410^a Squadriglia moved from Auax to Diredawa, and an S 81 of the 62^a Squadriglia also moved to Shashamanna from Diredawa.

Wednesday, 30 September 1940
Early in the morning of 30 September three 45 Squadron Blenheim Is raided Gura, but there all the bombers were attacked by CR 32s and CR 42s, Flt Lt G.J. Bush's Blenheim L6665 being shot down. An hour later six more of the Squadron's aircraft appeared over Gura and on this occasion suffered no loss, although fighters were seen again. It seems very possible that Bush had been shot down by Ten Visintini of the 412^a Squadriglia, for his commanding officer has recorded that he was credited with shooting down two Blenheims over Gura during this period.

From Khartoum 1 SAAF Squadron despatched a further detachment under Capt Boyle to the very primitive forward strip at Azzoza, where they joined the detachment of 430 Flight. From there they would on several occasions escort General Heath, commander of the 5th Indian Division, on personal reconnaissances over the front, the General being carried aloft in a 237 Squadron Hardy.

Aden again received an attack by a lone S 79 from Diredawa on 30 September. Two Gladiators of 94 Squadron intercepted, and the bomber dived away trailing black smoke from one engine; on return the S 79's crew claimed that they had probably hit one of the fighters. Due to the low-grade fuel used in East Africa by the Regia Aeronautica, when the throttles of aircraft were opened the engines frequently gave out smoke, sometimes even misfiring, and as no damage was suffered on this occasion, it seems likely that this is what had occurred.

With much of 1 SAAF Squadron still in the Sudan, and likely to remain there, the two flights of the unit in Kenya now became 2 SAAF Squadron, while the flight at Khartoum, plus its detachments at Port Sudan and Azzoza, took on the full mantle of 1 SAAF. The victories of 19 June and 3 August, claimed over the Southern Front, were now credited to the new unit, which had on hand at the time of renumbering, nine Hawker Furies, five Hurricanes and nine Gladiators. These were stationed in detachments at Mombasa, Nanyuki, Archer's Post,

Early warning equipment at Ndege's Nest airfield, northern Kenya. The platform was manned by an alert spotter during daylight hours. *(SAAF)*

Garissa and Ndege's Nest. The performance of the Fury in the tropical climate was leaving much to be desired, the engine coolant often boiling at 3,000 feet, while at Garissa 20 minutes were needed to reach an altitude of 20,000 feet. These aircraft were now being used mainly to supplement 40 SAAF Squadron's Hartbeestes on army co-operation and ground-attack duties.

Friday, 2 October 1940

At dawn on 2 October three Blenheims of 45 Squadron from the Sudan approached Gura, but were attacked short of the target by six 412ª Squadriglia CR 42s, which concentrated upon the leading aircraft, flown by the commanding officer, Sqn Ldr J.W. Dallamore. The Blenheim (L8452) at once began to burn

Gloster Gladiators N5851 and N5815 of 2 SAAF Squadron. These fighters were subsequently passed on to 1 SAAF Squadron, in the Sudan. *(O.G. Davies)*

Serg Magg Luigi Baron of the 412ª Squadriglia climbs into the cockpit of his CR 42. He ended the campaign as the second most successful of the Italian fighter pilots in East Africa. *(N. Malizia)*

and Dallamore was seen to jettison his bombs; the air gunner then baled out, but the pilot remained at his controls to allow the navigator to follow suit. Before Dallamore could himself get out, the aircraft hit the ground and exploded. The other two Blenheims now broke formation and fled, chased by the fighters for some distance; Serg Magg Baron claimed to have shot down two Blenheims during this combat, and to have shared in the destruction of a third.

In the course of the morning waves of Blenheims from Aden attacked Assab, hitting the AGIP fuel dump, army stores, the central telephone exchange and the area of the naval base. In a raid on Afmadu by Allied aircraft, Italian records claimed a further aircraft shot down, the machine reportedly being discovered semi-destroyed at Beles Gugani, but with no trace of the crew; the identity of the aircraft is unknown.

It was more than a month since the opposing fighters had met, but now they clashed once more. At the start of October as mentioned, Capt Boyle had led six 1 SAAF Squadron Gladiators to Azzoza, near Gedaref; only six mechanics accompanied the detachment to this rudimentary base, where the pilots even had to prepare their own belts of ammunition for their guns. Early warning was almost non-existent, consisting of a native in the bush with a field telephone, whose only words of English were 'Aircraft over Gallabat'!

Sunday, 4 to Monday, 12 October 1940

Following such a warning on 4 October, three Gladiators were scrambled, climbing over Metemma where they saw three CR 42s in line astern approaching them 500 feet higher. Climbing to meet them head-on, the Gladiators attacked and the six aircraft broke up into a dogfight. Lt S. de K. Viljoen shot down one Fiat in flames, the pilot baling out, but Capt Boyle's aircraft was hit and damaged; despite this, he continued to attack one of the Fiats, seeing it fall away apparently out of control, trailing smoke. Subsequently the ground forces sent

Aircrew of 11 SAAF Squadron, being briefed on the next raid by Major R.L. Preller, DFC. Emblem on the nose of the Fairey Battle is a hog named 'Musso'. The Squadron attacked targets as far apart as Mogadishu and Neghelli. *(SAAF)*

in a report that this second aircraft had crashed, but the Italians recorded the loss of only one aircraft (that destroyed by Viljoen), claiming in return one of the Gladiators shot down. It is possible that Boyle's victim force-landed in a repairable condition, or managed to struggle back to base. Almost certainly their opponents were from the 412^a Squadriglia.

During the day the Battles of 11 SAAF Squadron dropped propaganda leaflets for the first time, Yavello being the target; such missions were to become increasingly frequent. On 5 October Flt Lt Mitchell and Plt Off A.N. Johnstone of 430 Flight in two Gauntlets, each armed with eight 20lb fragmentation bombs, escorted three 47 Squadron Wellesleys to bomb Gallabat fort, but this was the last operation by Gauntlets for some weeks. In the south Lt D.C. Uys of 2 SAAF Squadron stalled his Fury whilst making a practice attack on a Hartbeeste and crashed near Wajir, suffering severe burns. He was pulled from the wreckage by a sergeant of the Gold Coast Regiment, recovering to lose his life over Italy in 1945, at the controls of a 34 SAAF Squadron Liberator.

A period of relative quiet in the air now settled over the whole area, small British and Italian raids continuing on the usual targets on a rather limited scale. From Yavello on 11 October three S 79s and two CR 32s moved back to Addis Ababa, and the next day a detachment of Wellesleys from 47 Squadron moved to the advanced landing ground at Gedaref to fly sorties in support of patriot guerrilla forces in the Lake Tana area.

Tuesday, 13 October 1940

After losing its commanding officer on 2 October, 45 Squadron did not again attempt to attack Gura until the 13th, but on this date three Blenheims once more set course for this objective; one was forced to return early with engine trouble. The other two aircraft continued, but again found 412ª Squadriglia CR 42s waiting for them. Both Blenheims (L8463 piloted by Flg Off G.C.B. Woodroffe and L8502 flown by Plt Off G.A. Cockayne) were shot down, the crew members all perishing. During the same morning a single S 79 raided Aden, three 94 Squadron Gladiators scrambling to intercept. Flg Off Haywood got close enough to open fire, the bomber being slightly damaged and two of the crew killed.

Wednesday, 14 October 1940
Next day Italian AA crews claimed to have shot down one British aircraft over Massawa, the bomber reportedly falling into the sea, but no loss was recorded. In the south three Battles attempted to attack Jimma airfield around midday on the 14th, one more following to photograph the results of the raid. Two CR 32s intercepted, the pilots reporting that they had caused the bombers to jettison their loads short of the target. However, Lt van Vliet reported that he had bombed the airfield, claiming one Caproni destroyed. The Italian pilots claimed damage to two of the intruders, and van Vliet's aircraft was indeed hit, causing him to force-land at Lokitaung. However, he was able to fly back to Lodwar next day after repairs had been carried out.

Thursday, 15 October 1940
British bombing raids were increasing again by mid-October, and during the night of the 14th/15th two attacks on Diredawa caused damage to two S 79s, two S 81s and a Ca 133. The next day, in the afternoon, three S 79s of the 6ª Squadriglia, 44° Gruppo, took off from Diredawa to attack a strongly escorted convoy ('BS 6¼') which was sailing up the Red Sea, covered by Aden-based aircraft. The bomber crews reported being attacked by two Gladiators and a Blenheim, claiming the latter shot down and one of the former damaged. They claimed that the Blenheim, while a considerable distance away, was seen to ditch by one of the ships, after making a prolonged attack on the Savoias. This Blenheim was not in fact shot down, and the aircraft, a fighter Mark IVF of 203 Squadron, did indeed make an attack lasting a considerable time on one of the bombers, Plt Off Barnitt then breaking away suddenly, giving the Italians the impression that his aircraft had been hit by their combined fire. The bomber he had fired on was that flown by Sottoten Gheradini, who had been the pilot of the aircraft damaged by Flg Off Haywood on the 15th, and had insisted on flying on this date against the advice of his unit commander, in order to avenge the members of his crew killed in the earlier fight. Now, with two engines out of action, Gheradini nursed his badly damaged aircraft towards the coast, trying to make a force-landing at Jibuti in French Somaliland. As he began his landing approach his aircraft became uncontrollable, turned on its back, and crashed into the sea. The crash was witnessed by the crew of HMAS *Parramatta*, some six miles to the east, and subsequently Barnitt received credit for the destruction of this aircraft.

Friday, 16 October 1940
In the early hours of 16 October Flt Lt Mitchell of 430 Flight, this time piloting a Vincent, attacked Tessenei airfield. He was followed back to Gedaref by a Ca 133, which bombed the landing ground without effect; but the Italians now knew where the aircraft which had been operating around the Lake Tana region

during recent weeks were based. A strike was laid on at once. At 0525 an S 79 flown by Generale Piacentini himself led in nine CR 42s of the 412ª Squadriglia (the British identified the attackers incorrectly as one S 79, four CR 42s and three CR 32s). The Savoia dropped its bombs without causing much damage, but the fighters then strafed and totally destroyed all eight Wellesleys of 47 Squadron's detachment (K7742, '7762, '7779, '7781, L2650, '2675, '2677 and '2688) and two of 430 Flight's Vincents (K4657 and '4731). An attempt to telephone the fighter detachment at Azzoza was foiled, as the line between Gedaref and Azzoza was found to have been cut — a final polish to a well planned and well executed attack. Italian claims were very accurate, eleven aircraft being claimed destroyed, together with a munitions dump and a lorry.

Sunday, 18 October 1940

In a reprisal raid two days later, three Gladiators of 1 SAAF Squadron, flown by Capt Boyle and Lts Pare and Duncan, approached Barentu airfield at 100 feet to see three CR 42s of the 412ª Squadriglia about to take off, and dispersed around the field an S 79 and five Ca 133s. Attacking in formation, the South Africans set all three fighters on fire and then broke up to strafe the bombers individually, claiming hits on all of them. A subsequent army report claimed that all six multi-engined aircraft were destroyed in addition to the fighters, but this is not confirmed from Italian records, although it is likely that some, or all, may have been slightly damaged. However, such damage could not have been important, for no mention of it was made in the wire reporting the destruction of the CR 42s. To congratulate the fighter detachment at Azzoza, General Heath sent a present of champagne.

Tuesday, 20 October 1940

While Allied raids on ports and airfields continued, a new British convoy now approached up the Red Sea. Italian bombers were again active against this in small numbers, and on 20 October a lone S 79 was engaged by an escorting fighter Blenheim of 203 Squadron; the Italian bomber was last seen in a steep dive south of Massawa. The attacking pilot was again Plt Off Barnitt, victor over an S 79 on the 15th, and he was again credited with the destruction of the bomber; on this occasion, however, it had in fact completely escaped damage, and returned safely to its base.

Later in the day three Ca 133s from Gobwen undertook a dusk raid on Garissa airfield, claiming the destruction of two aircraft on the ground, while they also claimed one of two intercepting fighters shot down. Only one had taken off — a Fury of 2 SAAF Squadron's 'H' Detachment at this airfield, flown by the detachment commander, Lt H.J. Burger. Burger attacked one bomber and shot it down, the Caproni force-landing and the crew of five being made prisoners (after they had set fire to their aircraft). The supply situation for the Italian forces was now becoming critical, and on 22 October the Regia Aeronautica became subjected to rigid petrol rationing, instructions being issued to obtain horse-drawn transport for all ground movements.

During 20 October five Blenheims from Aden refuelled at Perim Island, then bombed Alomata. Serg Magg Ugo Zoino of the 411ª Squadriglia attacked three of these in his CR 32, but as he opened fire one of his explosive shells detonated, puncturing the oil tank so that hot oil blew back all over his face. Disengaging, he tried to land, but found that bombs were exploding on the airfield; he then saw a lone Blenheim of 8 Squadron close by his aircraft, and tried to manoeuvre on to its tail, opening fire with his remaining gun, although his goggles were awash with oil. At this point his gun jammed and he attempted to hit the tail of the bomber with his propeller, but his goggles then blew off and his eyes filled with oil, blinding him. He at once pulled away violently and dived for the ground, convincing the gunner in the Blenheim that he had shot the fighter down.

As Zoino landed, his aircraft was strafed and he leapt out, hiding in a ditch. With the Blenheims gone, he attempted to pull his CR 32 off the field, but two more bombers then attacked, and he again had to dive for cover; in neither of these attacks was his aircraft further damaged, however. This date also saw the first bombing sortie over the Northern Front by the Hardys of 237 Squadron, but it was to be the only such mission of the month for the unit.

Saturday, 24 October 1940
In Kenya 24 October saw the arrival of the new 3 SAAF Squadron from South Africa, bringing with it an initial complement of nine Hurricane Is. Seven more were soon to follow, and the Squadron was despatched in sections to airstrips between Mombasa and the frontier. The arrival of these modern aircraft permitted the GOC, East Africa, to direct the despatch of some of 2 SAAF Squadron's Gladiators to reinforce 1 SAAF Squadron in the Sudan.

Sunday, 25 October 1940
During the evening of 24 October Flt Lt R.S. Blake and Lt D.H. Loftus of 2 SAAF Squadron borrowed two of 3 SAAF Squadron's newly arrived Hurricanes and flew them up to the forward strip at Lokitaung, near Lake Rudolph, where a raid was expected. Next morning sure enough three S 81s of the 29° Gruppo from Yavello approached, led by Capt Tito Zucconi, the others being flown by Sottoten Argento and Sottoten Titi. They had been ordered to take photographs and to bomb Lodwar, and also to see if the reported arrival of Hurricanes in the area was correct. Near Lokitaung Zucconi, busily searching the ground, led the formation into a 360° turn which gave the Hurricanes, which had by now scrambled, time to intercept the bombers right over the heads of the Imperial troops on the ground. Blake attacked and shot down Argento's aircraft, the

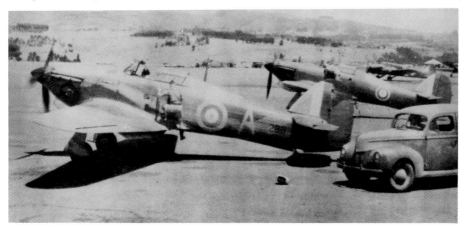

Hawker Hurricanes of 3 SAAF Squadron, in Kenya. Note 3's 'Fighting Wasp' emblem on the noses of both aircraft. '289' in foreground. Behind are an Anson and a Battle. *(SAAF)*

When three Savoia S 81s of the Italian AF's 29° Gruppo arrived over Lodwar on 25 October 1940, they were met by a pair of Hurricanes of 2 SAAF Squadron, which shot down two of the bombers. This S 81, flown by Sottotenente Titi, was hit by Lt D.H. Loftus, crash-landed and was then set on fire by its crew. South African personnel are seen inspecting the remains. *(SAAF)*

pilot being killed immediately; the co-pilot, a sergente, tried to land the blazing S 81, but touched down at too high a speed, crashing into some large trees. The wireless operator, Signorelli, leapt out through the fuselage door and survived unhurt, but the rest of the crew were killed in the crash.

Meanwhile Lt Loftus had at the same time attacked Titi's aircraft until his guns jammed; his third burst smashed the instrument panel in the cockpit, and

Pilots and Gloster Gladiators of 2 SAAF Squadron, in Kenya. After the Gallabat offensive in November 1940, these aircraft were passed on to 1 SAAF Squadron, in the Sudan to make good the latter's recent losses. *(SAAF)*

with two engines out of action and fuel pouring into the fuselage from the punctured tanks, Titi hastily jettisoned his bombs and force-landed on the bed of a dried-up river at Lokitaung; as they went down the Hurricane flew alongside, Loftus saluting them as he passed. The crew swiftly set fire to the petrol-soaked Savoia and set off for the frontier, but were taken prisoner by British police, who arrived on the scene in three cars.

While these two bombers were falling, Blake had also attacked Zucconi's aircraft, claiming to have badly damaged it, and it was later reported to have force-landed. This was not the case, however, for it managed to reach its base safely. When the Hurricanes were inspected after landing it was found that only one of their combined total of sixteen 0.303in machine guns had not jammed, and that as a result less than fifty per cent of their ammunition had been expended. Three S 79s from Gobwen then appeared over Kenya, bombing Port Reitz from 15,000 feet and claiming to have hit a camouflaged depot on an airfield. 2 SAAF Squadron's 'D' Detachment scrambled, but was unable to catch the fast bombers.

SAAF fighter strength had been weakened when 2/Lt A. McDonald of 2 SAAF Squadron crashed to his death at Nanyuki during a training flight in a Gladiator on 23 October, while Lt C.T. Gould of 3 SAAF Squadron was also killed four days later whilst landing a Hurricane at Nairobi.

Monday, 26 October 1940
In the Sudan 14 Squadron was now steadily re-equipping with Blenheim IVs, the Wellesleys being handed to 47 and 223 Squadrons as conversion took place. On 26 October one of the Blenheims was mistaken for an S 79 by defending Gladiators, and was attacked, the pilot being wounded in the arm and the aircraft badly damaged; T2057 was written off as a result. The unit's second full bombing mission with these aircraft was to be flown on the 30th when three aircraft led by Flt Lt J.K. Buchanan, DFC, attacked Massawa. The end of the month was also to see the award of a further decoration for the air forces in the area, Sqn Ldr A.McD. Bowman of 39 Squadron in Aden receiving a DFC.

Saturday, 31 October 1940
During late October an Italian officer, Colonello Rolle, had led a column of 1,500 men on a daring raid from Ethiopia into the Sudan, almost reaching Rosières. Halted by units of the Sudan Defence Force, and attacked from the air, he was forced to turn back and make for Beni Shangui to prevent his lines of communication being cut. On 31 October his column of 90 lorries was spotted in a narrow defile between Gondar and Metemma, and was at once attacked by Wellesleys and Vincents, escorted by 1 SAAF Squadron Gladiators. Twenty lorries were hit, ten of which were destroyed, and casualties were also inflicted. A Ca 133 bombing Rosières spotted the bombers taking off and attacked them, claiming one shot down. Another Caproni raided Metemma, reporting being attacked by British fighters, and was forced to land in friendly territory with one dead and two wounded aboard. No details of either of these combats have been found in British records; did one Italian aircraft perhaps attack another?

In Kenya General Cunningham now arrived to take over command of all forces in the area, and during the day the South African Prime Minister, General Jan Smuts, arrived on a visit of inspection. Accompanied by Air Commodore Sowrey, the General and his party were carried in two Ju 86s and a Rapide on

Gladiator pilots of 2 SAAF Squadron (l. to r.): 2nd Lt B. Fritz, Lt A.M. Colenbrander, and Lt B. Guest. *(SAAF)*

a flying visit to the frontier airfields, escorted by a pair of Hurricanes. While en route to Nanyuki to visit 11 SAAF Squadron, the formation passed over Archer's Post without the normal recognition signal, which consisted of lowering the undercarriage and waggling the wings. Under the impression that the formation was Italian, three Furies of 2 SAAF Squadron's detachment there, led by Capt J. Meaker, were scrambled and intercepted the formation. One pilot initially failed to recognise the aircraft as friendly and opened fire on the leading Ju 86; fortunately no damage was done.

Despite all problems, reinforcements were gradually trickling in for the Empire forces, and by the end of the month 94 Squadron had sufficient Gladiators on hand to become a two-flight unit at last; Flg Off G.S.K. Haywood received a well deserved promotion to lead the second flight. In Kenya the last Airspeed Envoy of the SAAF's Survey Flight was flown back to the Union, Ansons having arrived to carry out this duty instead.

Sunday, 1 November 1940

The first day of November 1940 saw a resumption of attacks on columns of Italian troops and transports in the northern areas of Eritrea and Ethiopia. On that day three Gladiators of 1 SAAF Squadron escorted bomb-carrying Gauntlets of 430 Flight to the target. Italian AF Caproni Ca 133s were out bombing British troops in the Gallabat area as they approached, and one of these was spotted passing overhead by the South African fighters. Lt R. Pare climbed unseen to make an astern attack, followed by a beam pass, and the bomber then dived steeply and crashed; two of the crew were seen to get out but both were wounded, as were all other members of the crew save one, who was killed. The biplanes continued to their target, all attacking at low level in the face of heavy return fire; all were hit, but returned safely to Azzoza. At this base the whole of 1 SAAF Squadron had now arrived from Khartoum and Port

Sudan, and on the 4th a detachment of three Gladiators of 'K' Flight also arrived at Azzoza fom Port Sudan, led by Flt Lt Savage.

Monday, 2 November 1940

During 2 November an S 79 of the 44° Gruppo which was on a reconnaissance over Noggara was reported to have been attacked by five Gladiators at 0930, the crew claiming to have shot one of these fighters down and to have seen the pilot on his parachute. No record of a combat of this nature has been found in British records although apparently the bomber did sustain slight damage.

Preparations were now being completed for the first British offensive — a limited attack on Gallabat fort. A total of 27 aircraft had been mustered to support this, and all were now moving up to advanced landing grounds. Italian air strength available for operations over the area was of the order of 17 fighters and 32 bombers. On the ground the 10th Indian Infantry Brigade Group, commanded by Brigadier W.J. Slim, later famous as commander of the 14th Army in Burma, and supported by six cruiser tanks and six light tanks, approached the area during the night, reaching positions for the start of the assault before dawn on 5 November.

Wednesday, 4 November 1940

While preparations for the attack were still under way, the South African Gladiators again clashed with the Fiat CR 42s of the 412ª Squadriglia. On an early patrol over Metemma on the 4th three Gladiators were attacked from above by four of the Fiat fighters, but swiftly turned the tables, Lt L.leC. Theron shooting down one from which the pilot baled out, while Capt Boyle and Lt A. Duncan claimed two more (one of which apparently was not confirmed). The Italian pilots claimed to have shot down one Gladiator and reported the loss only of the aircraft shot down by Theron.

Elsewhere that day a fighter Blenheim of 203 Squadron on an early convoy escort sortie engaged an S 79 over the Red Sea, Flt Lt Pike damaging the bomber and sending it racing for Zula with two dead and two wounded aboard. To the south two Battles of 11 SAAF Squadron raided Neghelli with bombs and leaflets, but one bomber was hit by anti-aircraft fire and crash-landed three miles from the airfield, where Lt B.L. Hutchinson and his crew got out and set fire to the aircraft. A crowd of locals quickly gathered to watch, but the heat detonated the bombs and killed about 20 people. The Italian authorities at first thought that the captured airmen had set off a time bomb in their aircraft! At Kismayu Italian AA artillery was less fortunate, one of the elderly naval 76/40 guns exploding while in use, killing one of the gun crew and wounding two more.

Thursday, 5 November 1940

Next day the detachment of 'K' Flight Gladiators joined 1 SAAF Squadron on a patrol, their first operation from Azzoza; in the evening Capt Boyle led one flight of the South African unit forward to a rough strip named 'Heston', 75 miles nearer to Gallabat, ready for operations.

Chapter Two

THE FIRST BRITISH OFFENSIVE OF THE WAR

Friday, 6 November 1940

At dawn on the 6th the first British offensive of World War II began with an artillery barrage on Gallabat, Wellesleys and Vincents bombing the radio station and fort, while Indian and English infantry, supported by tanks, moved forward through the wire. The Italians were initially taken by surprise but reacted swiftly, and called up air support. While the bombers were making their attack, the three Gladiators of 'K' Flight had also arrived overhead to patrol at low level over the advancing troops. No sooner had they begun patrolling to the east of Metemma, where they could head off any enemy bombers approaching the area, than a number of 412ª Squadriglia CR 42s led by the unit commander, Capt Raffi, and estimated to be six or seven strong, attacked the Gladiators from out of the sun. Flt Lt Savage in L7614 was shot down and killed and Plt Off Kirk baled out of K7969, neither having seen what had hit them; Plt Off Hamlyn's L7612 was badly hit and he force-landed, returning later on foot.

Meanwhile Maj van Schalkwyk of 1 SAAF Squadron had also taken off from Azzoza, but on arriving over the front was also attacked by the CR 42s. Observers on the ground at once rang the strip at 'Heston' to report the lone Gladiator in combat with eight opponents, and despite thick mud caused by an unexpected downpour during the night, Capt Boyle at once took off, arriving just in time to see the commanding officer's Gladiator going down in flames,

Gloster Gladiator N5821 of the SAAF in East Africa. *(D. Becker)*

74

the pilot taking to his parachute with his clothes on fire; he did not survive. Immediately Boyle was also attacked, bullets entering the cockpit and wounding him in hands and legs; desperately he fought on until the engine of N5852 stopped, and he had to crash-land between the lines. He was subsequently awarded a DFC for his gallant action in going single-handed to van Schalkwyk's assistance. Raffi reported that four victories were claimed as a result of these engagements, but Sottoten Rosmino's aircraft was hit and he returned with his parachute pack riddled with bullets.

The situation everywhere was bad for the British. Within the first hour of the battle five Gladiators had been shot down without a single loss being inflicted on the opposition. By 0800 Indian troops had taken Gallabat Ridge, but three tanks had been knocked out by mines and six had damaged their tracks on rocks, only one cruiser and two light tanks remaining serviceable. The Italians now threw 20 bombers into the fight, Ca 133s keeping up a steady attack in waves. On Gallabat hill the troops were almost without cover, and the rocky surface offered no chance of digging slit trenches. Bomb splinters and flying slivers of rock quickly caused considerable casualties, and a lorry bringing up spare parts to repair the damaged tanks was demolished by a direct hit.

During the morning another 'K' Flight Gladiator was flown up to the front, and shortly after midday Flg Off Haywood (not to be confused with G.S.K. Haywood of 94 Squadron) in his aircraft, K7977, joined four Gladiators of 1 SAAF Squadron from 'Heston' in another patrol over the front. There five Ca 133s were seen at 7,000 feet, 2,000 feet lower than the Gladiators, approaching the battle area. As the fighters prepared to attack, they were bounced from above by six CR 42s and Haywood's aircraft was seen to crash in flames. The South Africans at once split up into pairs, Lts Coetzer and Pare taking on the fighters while Lts Duncan and J.L. Hewitson went after the bombers. The Caproni attacked by Duncan crashed on the Metemma–Gondar road, while Hewitson's fell out of control and also crashed; he made an astern attack on a third bomber. The crew of one of the shot-down bombers survived, and was to return on foot several days later.

Pilots of the Italian AF's 412ª Squadriglia in front of one of their Fiat CR 42s at Gura (l. to r.: Tenente Cacciavillani, Ten Visintini, Sottoten D'Addetta, Ten De Pauli, Capitano Raffi, and Sottoten Levi. *(Nicola Malizia)*

While this was going on, the two pilots fighting the CR 42s had managed to drive them off, each claiming one of the fighters shot down; no losses of CR 42s were recorded however, although either or both of those attacked may have been damaged, and force-landed. Two more victories were claimed by the Italians to raise their total for the day to six, two or three of which were credited to Ten Visintini.

By the end of the day, despite the loss of air superiority by the British forces, Gallabat Fort had been captured and the garrison virtually annihilated. However, the Capronis returned that evening to attack again.

Saturday, 7 November 1940

Early next morning four South African Gladiators were once more in the air to escort five Wellesleys of 47 Squadron over the front. Four CR 42s were seen and chased, Lt R. Pare claiming one shot down; another four CR 42s then attacked him and he had to go into a long dive to evade them. Finally, after losing these fighters, he suffered engine trouble and had to force-land at Gherigana. Italian fighters patrolling over Metemma during the morning failed to report any engagement, however. While the Gladiators were so occupied, five S 81s and five Ca 133s which the CR 42s had been escorting got through without interference and made a damaging attack on the ground forces at Gallabat.

Despite the odd success gained by the South Africans, the Italians were now virtually masters of the air thanks to the considerable successes of the 412ª Squadriglia on the previous day, and in consequence it was decided that Gallabat Fort was untenable. While the artillery pounded Metemma, the defences at Gallabat were demolished and Slim's troops withdrew to the

Italian troops of the Savoy Grenadiers embark in a Caproni Ca 133 of the Squadriglia dello Stato Maggiore dell Settore Centrale at Addis Ababa for transportation to Gallabat. Behind is an IMAM Ro 37bis of the 110ª Squadriglia. *(via Corrado Ricci)*

surrounding hills from where the shelling of Metemma could be continued. British casualties in the two days had been 167, while the Italians suffered 428.

Thursday, 5 to Sunday, 8 November 1940

While this attack had been going on, further north the 12th Frontier Force Regiment had assaulted Tehamiyan Wells near Kassala on 5 November, taking the position by the afternoon. Next day they moved up to attack the main Italian positions in the area, but were attacked three times by Ca 133s and CR 42s, no air cover being available to them due to the Air Force's involvement in the Gallabat operations. On top of this, the Italians proved to be in strongly entrenched positions, and in these circumstances the force withdrew.

During 7 November Air Commodore Slatter flew down from Khartoum to take direct command of air operations, and the five remaining Gladiators of 'K' Flight arrived at the same time at Azzoza. Next day four of these joined three 1 SAAF Squadron aircraft on patrol, similar sorties of seven or eight Gladiators being continued during the next two days. Capt G.J. le Mesurier joined this latter unit during the day as temporary Commanding Officer following the loss of van Schalkwyk. Italian bombers and fighters continued to appear frequently, and attacked the British and Indian troops as they dug into their new defensive positions in the hills, but after 8 November their attacks began to die down.

Monday, 9 to Tuesday, 10 November 1940

On 9 November three Gladiators from 2 SAAF Squadron in Kenya arrived in the Sudan to be handed to 1 SAAF Squadron, having been led to this latter destination by a Lodestar transport, which was to carry the pilots back to their home base. As they came in to land Sudanese Home Guards opened fire, damaging the Lodestar and two of the Gladiators, one of which was crash-landed by Lt Dimmock on an island in the Nile and was wrecked. Next day 'K' Flight returned to Port Sudan from Azzoza.

While the British air forces rested and reorganised their sparse resources after the recent fierce fighting, Italian raids on the army positions around Gallabat continued. On the 9th British troops reoccupied the fort to deny it to the Italians, withdrawing at night, but returning again the next day.

Wednesday, 11 November 1940

The 412ª Squadriglia reported combat with Gladiators in the Metemma area on 11 November, claiming one shot down and possibly two more probables; 1 SAAF Squadron was involved, one Gladiator receiving a single bullet hole from a CR 42. The unit then returned to Khartoum on the 13th, having suffered no further losses since the 6th.

Thursday, 12 November 1940

A Blenheim IV of 14 Squadron reconnoitred the Dahlak Archipelago on 12 November, seeking an Italian flying boat reported the previous day at Sheik el Abu Island. The machine was reported seen at anchor at Zula, the Blenheim pilot attacking and claiming it destroyed. What had actually been seen and attacked is uncertain, since no flying boats or floatplanes were based in Italian East Africa at that time.

Saturday, 14 to Sunday, 15 November 1940

On 14 November three 8 Squadron Blenheim Is took off after dark to attack Diredawa; Plt Off Young's aircraft, L6648, was hit by AA fire, and after jettisoning his bombs, he force-landed at Ras Ara on the Arabian coast. Next morning two S 79s attacked Port Sudan, Plt Off Wolsey of 'K' Flight taking off to intercept. He managed to get close enough to open fire on the Italian bombers but was unable to press home his attack due to lack of speed, although he saw numerous hits on both aircraft.

Monday, 16 November 1940

At midday on 16 November Flt Lt Buchanan, DFC, of 14 Squadron attempted to attack Gura in a Blenheim IV in heavy cloud. After finding and bombing the landing ground he was attacked by three fighters, one of which closed to 50 yards, but he managed to lose his attackers in cloud, and returned to see what damage he had caused to the airfield before returning to base. The Italian pilots thought they had probably shot down the British aircraft.

Hawker Hardys of 237 Squadron were now in action in support of the forces at Gallabat, and while dive-bombing in the Metemma area K5915 flown by Plt Off Campbell, was hit in the water manifold, causing the pilot to attempt a force-landing; this failed and the aircraft crashed in wooded country. At Massawa AA gunners claimed one Aden-based bomber shot down during a raid, and it is believed that this was in fact Wellesley L2695 from 223 Squadron. Far to the south, SAAF aircraft raided Callam in the Lake Rudolph province; Italian anti-aircraft again claimed one aircraft shot down. Their victim was a Battle in which Lt van Vliet was undertaking a reconnaissance sortie. The aircraft was hit in the radiator, and he force-landed, the crew then setting fire to it. They evaded capture and were subsequently brought to safety by troops of the King's African Rifles.

Wednesday, 18 to Thursday, 19 November 1940

On 18 November a Royal Navy cruiser, HMS *Dorsetshire*, launched a Walrus flying boat from its catapult to attack targets in the Massawa area, a store of naphtha being bombed with little effect. Next day Italian bombers raided Imperial troops in the Gedaref area, but one Ca 133 failed to return; although a search was made, it could not be found. A Blenheim of 45 Squadron made a lone attack on the Keren area on this date, but two 412[a] Squadriglia CR 42s were scrambled and drove it off, damaging the aircraft and slightly wounding Sqn Ldr Ray, the pilot. Over the Red Sea a 203 Squadron Blenheim IVF crashed while on escort patrol, all the crew being lost.

Friday, 20 to Saturday, 21 November 1940

For the second night in succession S 81s raided Aden, one aircraft of the 15[a] Squadriglia leaving Jijiga in the early hours, flown by Colonello Francesco Via, the Diredawa base commander, with Sottoten Vincenzo Priore (now a monk) as co-pilot. From Aden Sqn Ldr Wightman of 94 Squadron scrambled in Gladiator II N5627 at 0430 and intercepted the bomber, shooting it down in flames into the sea three miles off the coast. Three members of the crew, including Via and Priore, baled out and were picked up by the Royal Navy, becoming prisoners.

In the early afternoon of 21 November two S 79s raided Port Sudan again.

Flg Off Scott Vos taxiing a Gladiator of 94 Squadron, RAF, at Sheik Othman in late 1940. *(Scott Vos via Ian Simpson)*

There the cruiser HMS *Carlisle* opened fire and two Gladiators of 'K' Flight scrambled to intercept. Flg Off Green and Plt Off Smither attacked the bombers at 16,000 feet, hitting both, but one fighter was hit and damaged by return fire; the gunners in the Savoias claimed to have shot down both Gladiators. One S 79 was badly hit and returned with three wounded aboard. British radio interceptions led to the belief that the S 79 had force-landed at Karet, near Elghena, and Blenheim IVs of 14 Squadron were despatched to destroy it, but failed to find it there; it had in fact reached its home base in a damaged condition.

Sunday, 22 November 1940

On 22 November Italian bombers attacked Rosières airfield in Central Sudan, claiming to have burned one of four Wellesleys on the ground. During the day 1 SAAF Squadron returned from Khartoum to Azzoza for resumed patrolling over the Gallabat front. It was in the south that action came on this date, however; Capt D.W. J. Allam of 11 SAAF Squadron made a photo-reconnaissance flight over Italian Somaliland in a Battle, but was intercepted by CR 42s from Kismayu. Because he was unable to see them approaching from behind due to the aircraft's large tail unit, his bomber was hit and began to burn. He spiralled down through cloud and crash-landed, setting fire to his aircraft fully before he was taken prisoner. On his subsequent release in April 1941 he reported that many of the aircraft that his squadron had been attacking at Shashamanna were in fact dummies built of plywood and fabric, indistinguishable from the real thing at 200 yards range. The genuine articles were brilliantly camouflaged and were very hard to spot from the air.

In Kenya the new fighter squadron, 3 SAAF, had its first combat, three Hurricanes scrambling to intercept three Ca 133s raiding Bura. Lt Allen shot down the leading aircraft, five of the crew being killed and the only survivor suffering severe burns; the other two bombers escaped in cloud. One had been badly hit by the fire of 2/Lts Glover and Kershaw however, and crash-landed in Italian Somaliland with the starboard engine out of action. The crew tried to walk back to their base, but were intercepted and captured by an African patrol.

More S 79s were now available to the Italians, having flown in by the long air route from Libya, and on 22 November the 14^a Squadriglia of the 4° Gruppo converted to these aircraft, handing its remaining S 81s to the 15^a Squadriglia. By this time other changes had also taken place. Late in October the 66^a Squadriglia was disbanded, and the 65^a Squadriglia, reinforced by the personnel of the former unit, came under the control of the S 81-equipped 29° Gruppo at Shashamanna, although the Ca 133-equipped 65^a Squadriglia remained at Yavello for the time being.

In Aden too there were some considerable changes, as due to the drop in activity in this area, and to the approaching British offensive in the Western Desert, 11 and 39 Squadrons were ordered to Egypt. At the same time a special General Purpose Flight was formed at Khormaksar for policing operations against dissident tribesmen in the Aden Protectorate, and 8 Squadron's sixteen Vincents were transferred to this, the Squadron retaining its Blenheim Is and a few Swordfish.

In the Sudan 47 Squadron moved to Sennar and 237 Squadron to Gordon's Tree, but while three 1 SAAF Squadron Gladiators were making practice attacks on one of this unit's Hardys, one fighter (N5850) hit the ground at high speed and burst into flames, Lt W.H. Morris being killed. The South Africans at this time received four more ex-2 SAAF Squadron Gladiators as reinforcements.

Thursday, 26 November 1940

Early on the 26th six of 14 Squadron's new Blenheim IVs set out to raid the station at Nefasit, but over Dessie Island three fighters attacked and the bombers turned out to sea. The second aircraft of the second flight, flown by Flg Off Mackenzie, was hit in the starboard engine and fell away, as did one of the fighters, but the rest of the bombers outdistanced their attackers and bombed instead the small island of Sheik el Abu, where a listening post was situated. After the attack Mackenzie's aircraft was seen force-landed, and the Commanding Officer, Sqn Ldr Selway, landed alongside; the downed crew got into Selway's aircraft which then took off and returned to base.

Friday, 27 November 1940

Next day over the Metemma area a 237 Squadron Hardy, K4311, was attacked by two 412^a Squadriglia CR 42s and badly damaged, Sgt A.P. Burl, the gunner, being shot through the head and killed. Flg Off P. Holdengarde managed to force-land in friendly territory at Guriangana. The Squadron now welcomed more modern equipment with the arrival from Egypt of five Westland Lysander I army co-operation aircraft.

Saturday, 28 to Sunday, 29 November 1940

45 Squadron, after several weeks in the Sudan, returned to Egypt on the 28th, on which date the SAAF Survey Flight in Kenya was redesignated 60 Photographic Squadron. On the 29th one of the Royal Navy's catapult Walruses was again launched from a cruiser in the Red Sea to attack a target thought to be of military importance. After it had finished bombing, the cruiser itself opened fire and pumped 40 shells into the building, totally destroying it; it was in fact a tunny-fish tinning plant! The Italians gained the impression that the British were trying to destroy their possible source of food, thinking this to be a wasted effort considering the numbers of cattle and other supplies available.

Monday, 30 November to Thursday, 3 December 1940

The month ended with an attack on Gedaref airfield by three CR 42s, where they claimed to have burnt a Wellesley; it was in fact a dummy Hardy. Next day (1 December) British bombers raided an Italian column in the Metemma area, causing severe casualties, while other aircraft raided Kassala; there one was claimed shot down by anti-aircraft fire, but no loss is recorded. 'K' Flight received two new Gladiator IIs on 2 December, and the next day Flg Off Chapman and Plt Off Wolsey moved to Khartoum to assist 1 SAAF Squadron's detachment with the defence of this town. At the front five South African Gladiators escorted three 237 Squadron Hardys to attack a bomb dump at the Gwanda River crossing where nine Italian personnel were killed and 22 wounded during the raid. From Diredawa two S 79s of the 14ª Squadriglia moved to Gura, coming under the command of Settore Nord for operations.

Friday, 4 December 1940

Two Blenheim IVs of 14 Squadron were off on 4 December, one making a diversionary attack on the station at Adarte, between Agordat and Keren, while the other, R2270, flown by Flg Off Rhodes, made a photo-reconnaissance run over the Mai Atal and Ghinda area. This latter aircraft was intercepted by 412ª Squadriglia CR 42s and shot down.

Saturday, 5 December 1940

In the south on 5 December a Junkers Ju 86 of 12 SAAF Squadron on reconnaissance over Mega and Moyale was hit in one engine by AA fire. Attempting to return to base, it struck some jagged mountain peaks 40 miles south of Mega and crashed. While three of the crew remained with the wreckage, the other three set off southwards; a search was instituted by three Battles of 11 SAAF Squadron, but one of these also crashed (on the 13th), Lt M. MacDonald and his crew being killed. The members of the Ju 86 crew who had remained by the aircraft were eventually found five days later, but the other three were not seen again. Many weeks later the body of the pilot, Lt Vermeulen, was discovered in the bush.

At Nanyuki three Martin Maryland Is had arrived from the Union, Nos 1601, 1602 and 1603, and these formed the basis of a new squadron, 14 SAAF, the initial nucleus being formed by crews provided from 12 SAAF Squadron; Maj C.E. Martin, DFC, became the Commanding Officer. An Operational Training Unit was set up under Maj Preller, until recently CO of 11 SAAF Squadron, to train crews on the new aircraft. On an early flight however, one Maryland was just taking off when a Hartbeeste landed on top of it, both aircraft being badly

Above: SAAF Hawker Hurricane in East Africa. *(D. Becker). Below:* By January 1941 the detachment of Martin Maryland I reconnaissance-bombers with 12 SAAF Squadron was extremely active over Italian Somaliland. *(SAAF)*

damaged. The other two aircraft were then attached to 12 SAAF Squadron for the time being as a reconnaissance flight. On 5 December Maj Martin flew the first sortie in one of the new aircraft, a reconnaissance over Kismayu, Harbow and Jelib. He was pursued by a fighter but eluded it with ease.

Sunday, 6 December 1940

Four Wellesleys of 47 Squadron took off during the morning of the 6th to attack the village and fort at Burie, one bomber returning early with engine trouble. The others were attacked by CR 42s which shot down Plt Off Witty's aircraft, K8521, from which the crew were seen to bale out. A second Wellesley was attacked without success but the Italians claimed to have shot down a total of three of these bombers on this occasion.

One CR 42 was now moved to Burie, and three more to Gura for operations in the north; two of the three at Mogadishu now returned to Addis Ababa, the third remaining behind due to technical trouble. Experiments were being carried out at this time to fit the CR 42s with radio receivers so that contact from the ground might be maintained. The Italians were also pressing ahead with a policy of dispersal of bases and stores, and the remaining 87-octane petrol was being distributed to secret stores and dumps.

Wednesday, 9 to Thursday, 10 December 1940
On 9 December 'K' Flight despatched six Gladiator IIs and a Mk I, accompanied by a Wellesley carrying a fitter and a rigger, to Heliopolis to reinforce 112 Squadron. Next day the two aircraft at Khartoum returned to Port Sudan, where about half the pilots of the flight remained with a handful of Gladiators. In the south however, the forces in Kenya were preparing for an assault on the Italian frontier fortress of El Wak, and Hartbeestes were busy photographing the locality.

Friday, 11 to Saturday, 12 December 1940
Six Battles of 11 SAAF Squadron raided Yavello on 11 December, burning three Ca 133s and badly damaging another, while four more were damaged to a lesser degree. Italian raids continued on a small scale, but on 12 December the 412ª Squadriglia launched another of its successful airfield strafes, this time on the advanced strip at Gaz Regeb, where 237 Squadron's 'B' Flight was now based. At 0610 an S 79 flown by Ten Col Liberati led five CR 42s over the airfield, three of the latter making an attack on the parked Hardys and destroying K4053, '4308, '4055 and '4307. Capt Raffi made several attacks on

Hit by ground fire during a raid on Gaz Regeb on 12 December 1940, Capitano Raffi, CO of the 412ª Squadriglia, was forced to land his CR 42 near Aroma. He was rescued by Tenente Mario Visintini in another CR 42 who took his CO aboard and, seated on Raffi's knees (as here), flew back to Asmara. *(via Corrado Ricci)*

one aircraft which consistently refused to burn, but his own aircraft was then hit in the oil sump by fire from the Sudan Defence Force detachment guarding the airfield. Trailing smoke, he headed away from his base, but the engine finally seized and stopped some 100 kilometres from the target and he force-landed east of Aroma, near the Atbara River. Ten Mario Visintini, the unit's most successful pilot, landed alongside; the parachute was dispensed with, and Raffi then sat in the cockpit with Visintini sitting on his knees to fly the aircraft, taking off again successfully after they had set fire to the crippled CR 42. The Italian pilots claimed to have destroyed five Vincents on the ground at Gaz Regeb, together with some armoured cars. Successive attacks were made on Raffi's CR 42 to ensure its total destruction.

Sunday, 13 to Wednesday, 16 December 1940

In Egypt and Libya the British offensive which had been launched on the 9th was going well and General Wavell, the Supreme Commander in the Middle East, had taken the courageous decision to pull the experienced 4th Indian Division out of the line and despatch it to the Sudan in order that a full offensive might be launched there also. The convoy carrying these troops was due to dock at Port Sudan on 16 December and, fearing heavy air attack, reinforcements were ordered from Kenya to join 1 SAAF Squadron in the Sudan. First to arrive were two Hurricanes — original 1939 ex-2 SAAF Squadron machines — flown by Maj L.A. Wilmot and Capt K.W. Driver from 3 SAAF Squadron. Although initially only attached to 1 SAAF, both pilots were to remain, Wilmot relinquishing command of 3 SAAF to take over the vacant command position in 1 SAAF.

Over Eritrea during the night of 12/13 December, Italian fighters operated in an attempt to intercept some of the growing number of British bombers now relying on the cloak of darkness for protection. One bomber was claimed shot down with a second probably destroyed, both being credited to the 412ª Squadriglia's Ten Visintini, but in fact no losses were reported by the British squadrons.

Hurricane No 285 which was despatched from Kenya by 3 SAAF Squadron on 16 December 1940, to join 1 SAAF Squadron in the Sudan. The aircraft still carried the former unit's 'Fighting Wasp' insignia on the nose. *(A.J. Thorne via A.S. Thomas)*

Close-up of the nose of Hurricane No 285, showing the 3 SAAF Squadron insignia. *(A.J. Thorne via A.S. Thomas)*

By mid-December 1940 all was ready for the Imperial forces' new offensive in Kenya. The attack was to be made by the 24th Gold Coast Brigade, 1st South African Brigade and 1st South African Light Tank Company, supported by nine Hartbeestes of 40 SAAF Squadron, three Ju 86s of 12 SAAF Squadron and 'B' Flight of 2 SAAF Squadron under Flt Lt Blake, with four Hurricanes; the Hurricanes and Hartbeestes were to operate from Ndege's Nest.

Unlike the Gallabat operation where numbers on each side had been roughly equal on the ground, this was a very large attacking force for a small objective, but the attack was organised as much as an exercise to give commanders experience of moving large bodies of troops over long stretches of open country, as it was for any strategic or tactical reasons. It would also give the troops valuable experience of active duty.

The offensive began on 15 December, on which date a Hartbeeste flown by Lt J. Human spotted an ammunition dump, leading troops to capture it. The attack went in on the 16th, Junkers Ju 86s dive-bombing the fort and village at El Wak, causing several fires, while the Hartbeestes flew 17 sorties in support of the troops on the ground. By evening the fort had been taken, with 13 guns and 44 prisoners, but at this stage it was learned by Intelligence sources that an Italian air attack was likely next morning at dawn. As it would be dark by the time the Hurricanes had returned from their patrols, Hartbeestes were used instead, one patrolling over the area at once, and three more arriving overhead just before dawn on the 17th.

Sure enough no sooner had they arrived than three Savoia S 81s appeared and bombed the village, but the troops were bivouacked some way off and no casualties were caused. The Savoias were followed by three Caproni Ca 133s of the 8ª Squadriglia from Berbera, led by Capt Raoul Gamba which had been ordered to bomb El Wak and then search for a column of enemy armoured cars and bomb them also. The formation attacked the fort, and as it did so the Hartbeestes were warned from the ground by Aldis lamp. As his two wingmen had expended all their bombs on El Wak, Gamba ordered them to return to base and continued on his own, but almost at once he was attacked by the three Hartbeestes, which the crew took to be Harts, and these began to pour bullets into the Caproni. Capt Gardner attacked first, vapour (probably leaking petrol) and smoke streaming from the bomber; Maj Durrant then jettisoned his bombs and took up the assault, but Lt Human's guns jammed when he opened fire. Under Durrant's fire the aircraft went down to crash-land.

Gamba's version of the event was somewhat different. He reported that immediately after the biplanes had attacked, a single Hurricane — the first he had seen — appeared and opened fire, putting his starboard and central engines out of action, after which he had to crash-land. He reported that the pilot of the Hurricane then threw him some cigarettes and a medical kit. SAAF records make no mention of a Hurricane taking part in this combat and state that it was Capt Gardner who dropped his medical kit and cigarettes to the Italian crew. He then fired warning shots in an effort to prevent them from setting fire to the downed aircraft, but without success, the shattered Caproni dissolving in flames and smoke. Gamba, although wounded in the leg, had first removed two badly wounded members of the crew from the aircraft. He then set off for friendly territory, which he reached safely, but was subsequently hospitalised for a considerable time.

During the rest of the day Hartbeestes dropped maps to forces on the march and patrolled over roads to the north of El Wak, keeping a lookout for Italian reinforcements approaching.

During this period there had also been sustained air activity over Port Sudan as a convoy of ships from Egypt arrived with the 4th Indian Division aboard. On 15 December ten S 79s of the 44° Gruppo moved up to Gura to operate over this area, and a photographic mission was flown over the port and surrounding areas. Next morning, 16 December, at 1145, three S 79s approached just as Capt Driver was making a demonstration flight in one of the newly arrived Hurricanes. Three 'K' Flight Gladiators and the other Hurricane scrambled, Flg Off Chapman, Plt Off A. Tofield and Plt Off. S.R.F. McPhee of the former unit all opening fire and seeing hits on some of the aircraft. Driver then joined the attack firing first at the No 2 aircraft, which escaped in cloud, and then at the No 3, which fell in flames. Two of the crew baled out, but the other three were killed, two of them leaping out of the blazing aircraft without parachutes.

Two more formations, each of three S 79s, appeared at 45-minute intervals, neither being intercepted as they bombed the harbour, although fighters scrambled on each occasion. The final intrusion came at 1335 when the tenth bomber of the 44° Gruppo arrived alone. Two Gladiators and a Hurricane again scrambled, and Maj Wilmot attacked the S 79, causing one engine to stop. Although this aircraft was not seen to fall, Wilmot was subsequently credited with its destruction. The 44° Gruppo reported that the day's attacks cost one S 79 lost, with two more damaged, these latter aircraft returning with a total of three dead and seven wounded — every member of both crews had been hit.

In the evening Capt Boyle and Lt Duncan of 1 SAAF Squadron arrived from Khartoum bringing in two more ex-Kenya Hurricanes, Nos 272 and 273. When three more of the 44° Gruppo's S 79s approached to attack the airfield next morning at 0915, three Hurricanes and two Gladiators were able to take off to intercept. The bombers escaped in cloud, but Capt Driver kept after them, finally seeing them again 36 miles down the coast near Suskin. After a long chase he opened fire on one and reported having seen the starboard engine cease to function before he was forced to break off and return; this aircraft was subsequently confirmed as destroyed by the authorities, but in fact all three S 79s returned safely to Gura, two slightly damaged.

An hour and a half later four S 79s from Asmara bombed the port area, two Hurricanes and two Gladiators getting off after them. Maj Wilmot attacked one, but it escaped in cloud and the formation returned unscathed. This virtually brought to an end the series of attacks on the port, although next morning five Asmara-based S 79s attacked the railways at Haja Junction.

Despite the operations in the north and south, Italian bombers continued to attack ground forces in the Gallabat area and in central Sudan generally; one Ca 133 from Vittorio d'Africa was badly hit during one such attack on 16 December.

Also on the 16th the remaining French Martin 167F in Aden, No 102, flew an early morning reconnaissance over Diredawa, where two 410ª Squadriglia CR 32s were on a standing patrol. As the fast reconnaissance aircraft approached from the direction of Dancalia, the AA opened up, and seeing this, the two fighters — which had climbed much higher — dived almost vertically to intercept. Pulling out of his dive, Sottoten Veronese arrived close behind the tail of the Martin and opened fire, but almost at once the greater speed of the monoplane began to tell, and he fell behind. He had hit the intruder however, and it began to trail a thin tail of black smoke, and the starboard engine stopped. Feeling ill — probably from anoxia due to operating at high altitude with no oxygen supply — Veronese then had to land and was taken to sick quarters.

The Martin was slowing down now, as it continued with only one engine, and Serg Magg Athos Tieghi took up the attack, setting the aircraft on fire, whereupon it crashed. The observer, named as Flt Lt J.M. Boulet (actually Capt J. Dodelier), was killed, the other two members of the crew baling out; the parachute of Adj Chef Y. Trecan opened too soon and caught on the tail of the aircraft, the unfortunate pilot being carried to his death. Only the engineer, Sgt Chef Cunibil, survived.

Several moves and changes were taking place for the Italians at this time. The 65ª Squadriglia transferred from the 29° Gruppo to the 49°, which controlled the 61ª and 64ª Squadriglie; the unit withdrew to Jimma, leaving two Ca 133s at Yavello. Four of the 29° Gruppo's S 81s moved to Shashamanna, and three CR 42s of the 413ª Squadriglia moved from Burie to Addis Ababa, three more of this unit's aircraft moving from this latter base to Lugh Ferrandi. On 19 December 29° Gruppo aircraft moved to join the force which had gathered at Bardera for operations over El Wak; but from Gura and Asmara in the north the 44° Gruppo's S 79s all returned to Addis Ababa.

Friday, 18 December 1940

A small Italian air component had marshalled at Bardera, and early on 18 December three Fiat CR 42s from Addis Ababa, three Ca 133s from Vittorio d'Africa and two IMAM Ro 37bis from Mogadishu flew in. In the afternoon an Ro 37bis piloted by Ten Romano Palmera made a reconnaissance over the El Wak area, seeing a column of vehicles and also a Hurricane just beginning its take-off run from Ndege's Nest landing ground. This was Flt Lt Blake's aircraft and Palmera swooped to attack, firing on the Hurricane which was hit by three bullets. The Italian then made off, using the speed he had gained in his dive to escape at low level before the fighter could get fully airborne and attack him.

By early 1941 Avro Anson Is had arrived in Kenya to equip two SAAF units, 34 (Coastal) Flight and 60 (Photographic Survey) Squadron. *(SAAF)*

Blake thought his attacker had been a CR 42 which had underestimated his take-off speed. By now Italian aircraft were raiding El Wak heavily at night, but already the Imperial force was withdrawing, its objective successfully concluded.

The end of operations over El Wak and Port Sudan heralded another lull. In Kenya the arrival from the Union of 34 Coastal Flight, SAAF equipped with six rather worn ex-RAF Anson Is, commanded by Maj A.J. Mossop, released one of the flights of 12 SAAF Squadron which had been held back from the active zone, using its Ju 86s for coastal reconnaissance duties. During mid-December the regular Italian raids on the Gallabat area were interspersed with several small missions to attack the forces still near El Wak, but little damage was done.

Monday, 21 December 1940

On 21 December 12 SAAF Squadron recorded the second sortie of the newly arrived Marylands, a reconnaissance over Kismayu and Bardera. In the north 47 Squadron, RAF, moved to the airfield at Gordon's Tree, Khartoum, but kept a detachment close to the front at a strip named 'Blackdown', which was shared with the Gauntlets and Vincents of 430 Flight, which were still co-operating with the ground forces in the Gallabat area.

Thursday, 24 December 1940

In this same area 237 Squadron's Hardys were still active and on 24 December Flg Off MacIntyre with Sgt Collins as his gunner in Hardy K5923 encountered a formation of three Ca 133s bombing British troops north of Kassala. Attacking these he managed to shoot one down in flames; the gunners in the other Capronis claimed to have shot down the attacking 'fighter' in return, but MacIntyre returned with his aircraft undamaged to his airfield. On this same date Lt J.D. Niblock-Stuart of 2 SAAF Squadron was killed when he accidentally crashed one of the unit's Furies at Archer's Post.

Sunday, 27 December 1940

Following a quiet Christmas, 1 SAAF Squadron's detachment at Azzoza was alerted early on the 27th with the news that six CR 42s of the 412ᵃ Squadriglia were again making one of their strafing attacks on Gedaref. This formation is believed to have comprised Capt Raffi, Sottotenenti Sola, Provinciale and Rosmina, and two other pilots; they saw two landing grounds, strafed a single aircraft on one and a detachment of Indian cavalry which was exercising on the other.

Five Gladiators were ordered to scramble, but only three got off, these being directed on to two more CR 42s which were covering the strafing aircraft. Attacking these, the Gladiators cut off the rearmost aircraft which attacked them head-on with great desperation. Capt le Mesurier's guns jammed as soon as he began firing and an explosive bullet from the Fiat struck the propeller of Lt T. Condon's aircraft. Despite this, he shot down the Italian fighter in flames five miles east of Gedaref, the pilot (believed to be Sottoten Sola) being killed.

Monday, 28 December 1940

On 28 December a Maryland was sent on a photo-reconnaissance mission over Kismayu, Gobwen, Afmadu, Jelib and Bardera. At the latter base three S 81s were noted before the Maryland was driven off by three CR 42s which scrambled but were unable to catch it. These fighters were a small detachment from the 413ᵃ Squadriglia.

Tuesday, 29 December 1940

Following the evidence of this reconnaissance, a raid was planned on Bardera for the 29th by 'B' Flight of 2 SAAF Squadron, and at 1525 four Hurricanes (Nos 7382, 3254, 4103 and 4104) led by Flt Lt Blake, took off, flying in pairs, one at 3,000 feet and the other at 6,000 feet. On reaching the Italian airfield the lower pair, flown by Capt A.Q. Masson and Lt A.M. Colenbrander, went down to strafe in the face of fire from an armoured car; the three S 81s were hit and one began to burn.

At this stage the three CR 42s, which were at a satellite strip, and were expecting the attack following the appearance of the Maryland on the previous day, were scrambled again. Ten De Micheli and Sottoten Bartolozzi got off first, but Serg Strano had to wait for the dust they had raised to subside before he could follow. This same dust brought the Hurricanes down on him as he began his run and one attacked him, firing two bursts; the first of these hit the left side of the aircraft and put 17 splinters into his body, also damaging the throttle control, while the second burst struck the right side, puncturing the compressed air cylinder. He continued his run, however, taking off under attack. Without compressed air he was unable to operate his guns and had to manoeuvre wildly to escape being shot down. He later landed with the tyres flat and the fabric stripped completely from the rear fuselage. The Hurricanes meanwhile continued their strafing, unaware that two CR 42s had already got into the air.

Flying cover, Flt Lt Blake saw the Italian fighters climbing up, but as the Hurricanes were not at this stage fitted with radio, was unable to warn either his wingman, Lt J.A. Kok, or the other Hurricane pilots who were now making their third strafe. Although Blake made a dummy pass on Kok's aircraft in an effort to attract his attention, the latter did not catch on in time, and Ten De Micheli was able to engage Kok in a dogfight, while Bartolozzi similarly engaged Blake. The fight continued, according to observers on the ground, for around seven to nine minutes, De Micheli then shooting down Kok's Hurricane in flames; the pilot baled out and became a prisoner, having been slightly wounded. Bartolozzi finally managed to get a good burst into Blake's Hurricane from below, wounding the pilot in the foot and setting fire to the fuel tank. Burned around the waist and legs, Blake was unable to climb out of his cockpit, so he turned his aircraft on its back and fell out at 700 feet. On landing by parachute he was almost immediately surrounded by 'banda', followed soon after by an Italian officer. Meanwhile Masson and Colenbrander returned to base, quite unaware of what had transpired above their heads.

Blake was removed to the airfield sick quarters, being now in bad shape from his wounds; here Serg Strano had just been brought in. Blake was later moved to the town hospital for more extensive treatment, as the wound to his foot was quite severe, and there he remained for some time, occupying a bed near Capt Gamba, the Ca 133 pilot shot down on 17 December, who came to know him quite well.

The above combat shows well that the CR 42 could be more than the Hurricane could handle if it tried to turn with the Italian fighter in a traditional dogfight. Blake, the most successful fighter pilot in East Africa with the Imperial forces up to this time, was not greatly enamoured to find that his victor, a pilot of the 410ª Squadriglia on loan to the 413ª, had only been flying the CR 42 for about a week! This disastrous combat, and a few further Italian incursions over the El Wak area, brought 1940 to an eventful close.

Summary for 1940

Up to this point the Regia Aeronautica had performed most creditably and had certainly given as good as it got. Now, however, the precarious supply position began to have an increasingly deleterious effect, and when the position on the ground began to deteriorate the Regia Aeronautica was to disintegrate as a decisive force with considerable rapidity. Although reinforcements had been arriving from Italy, these had not even managed to keep the strength of the first-line units at their previous levels, much less replenish reserves, although they did raise slightly the percentages of more modern aircraft available for operations.

By the end of 1940 seventy-four new aircraft had arrived, many of them S 79s, and three S 81 squadriglie had re-equipped with these aircraft. Two S 82s had also been sent, one fitted with a bomb bay for bomber operations, and one with extra long-range tanks; this latter aircraft had crashed during December. CR 42s were now also arriving, these fighters being dismantled in Italy and stowed within the capacious fuselages of S 82s for carriage to East Africa by air; thirty-six fighters had been delivered in this manner by 31 December and fifteen more were to come during 1941, plus seven more S 79s. These, however, were to be the only reinforcements received during the new year, and after 24 March 1941 nothing further would be sent due to the loss of Cyrenaica to the British.

Italian losses during 1940 had totalled 137 aircraft, 83 shot down or destroyed on the ground by enemy action, the rest destroyed or damaged beyond repair in flying accidents or other non-operational mishaps, or written off due to old age or general wear and tear. Of reserves there were now none; indeed as early as 10 October (the last date for which records are available) only eight aircraft had remained in store, and these were quickly distributed to units as the month progressed.

Deliveries of Fiat CR 42s, which were carried dismantled in Savoia S 82 transports to East Africa, caused these fighters to be slightly more numerous in early 1941.

By 1 January 1941 the number of serviceable aircraft on hand with the squadriglie and gruppi stood at 132 — a reduction of 45 (all bombers), the percentage of which to the total had dropped from 75.82% to 70.45%, although the percentage of modern aircraft (S 79s) had risen from 8.89% to 29.03%. The number of fighters remained the same — 35 — though the percentage of CR 42s had risen slightly from 50% to 62.85%.

The only reserves available to the Italians were those aircraft undergoing repair or overhaul; 85 of these were at the main air force workshops (SRAM) or with civilian contractors for major works, while 40 more were still with the units undergoing lesser works — see table.

ITALIAN AIRCRAFT STRENGTH, 1 JANUARY 1941

(i) Serviceable aircraft on hand with units:

Settore	S 79	S 81	Ca 133	CR 32	CR 42	Ro 37bis	Ro 1	Total
Est	2	1	6	3	–	–	–	12
Ouest	11	4	15	6	3	1	1	41
Sud	–	3	13	–	3	2	–	21
Nord	14	6	18	4	16	–	–	58
Total	**27**	**14**	**52**	**13**	**22**	**3**	**1**	**132**

(ii) Aircraft under repair at workshop level*:	**85**
(iii) Aircraft under repair at unit level*:	**40**
(iv) Transport force:	**19**
Grand total	**276**

* A breakdown of the types making up these sub-totals of 125 aircraft is not available

The British and South African air strength had now achieved at least parity in numbers with the opponents, and was in the process of overtaking them; the quality of equipment was also rising, and the Imperial forces were increasingly able to concentrate locally superior forces at situations of their choice. The major campaign in Libya, which was now approaching a successful conclusion, had led to some denuding of the units in the north, Aden suffering particularly here when, as has already been related, 11 and 39 Squadrons were lost to Egypt. During December 94 Squadron had been ordered to pack and despatch to

Egypt five of its recently acquired Gladiator IIs. In the Sudan 45 Squadron had returned to Egypt, but re-equipment of 14 Squadron with Blenheim IVs had now been completed, and indeed 'B' Flight was converting its aircraft to Mk IVF fighter configuration with an eye to ground-strafing operations.

The Wellesleys remained the mainstay of the long-range bomber force, although 223 Squadron was now operating almost entirely at night. During December 47 Squadron had undertaken a number of 500-mile flights to the Ethiopian province of Gojjam to attack Italian brigade centres at Bahrdar, Giyorgis, Burye, Dangila and Debra Markos in an effort to support and hearten the Ethiopian patriot partisan forces, now being readied to rise in support of their exiled ruler, Haile Selassie. This monarch was now in the Sudan awaiting the propitious moment to re-enter his country.

1 SAAF Squadron was now virtually the only fighter unit in the north, as the greater part of 'K' Flight was still in Egypt with 112 Squadron. The South African unit, so swiftly and unexpectedly elevated to full squadron status, had suffered greatly from its almost total lack of a proper ground echelon, but now substantial numbers of RAF personnel were posted in to undertake these duties.

In the south another army co-operation squadron, 41 SAAF, was ready for action. Equipped with Hartbeestes, it had been formed in the Union in mid-October under Maj E.A. Pope, and had moved to Kenya at the beginning of December. After a month spent training its inexperienced crews, it now moved its three flights to Garissa, Ndege's Nest and Bura to support the 11th and 12th African Divisions. 40 SAAF Squadron had assembled at Marsabit, with a detachment at the very rough strip at Lokitaung, to support the 1st South African Division, which was soon to begin offensive operations against forces in the far north of Kenya, and the Galla Sidamo province of southern Ethiopia.

Operational strength of the SAAF in Kenya was now 94 aircraft, the units being as follows:

2 SAAF Squadron (Hurricanes and Furies), HQ Nanyuki, detachments at Archer's Post, Lokitaung, Marsabit and Ndege's Nest
3 SAAF Squadron (Hurricanes) HQ Nairobi, detachments at Mombasa, Lamu, Bura and Garissa
11 SAAF Squadron (Battles), Archer's Post
12 SAAF Squadron (Ju 86s), Nairobi
14 SAAF Squadron (Marylands), two aircraft only, attached to 12 SAAF Squadron at Nairobi
40 SAAF Squadron (Hartbeestes), Marsabit and Lokitaung
41 SAAF Squadron (Hartbeestes), Garissa, Ndege's Nest and Bura
50 SAAF Squadron (Valentias, Lodestars, Junkers Ju 52/3ms and a Rapide), operating between the Union and Kenya with Lodestars and Ju 52/3ms, and within Kenya with Valentias and the Rapide
60 SAAF Squadron (Ansons), Nairobi
34 Coastal Flight, SAAF (Ansons), Mombasa and Dar-es-Salaam

In the Sudan with 203 Group, RAF, were:

1 SAAF Squadron (Hurricanes and Gladiators), Port Sudan and Azzoza
14 Squadron, RAF (Blenheim IVs), Port Sudan

The frontier fort of Wajir on the Kenyan/Ethiopian border. Overhead is a Gloster Gladiator of 2 SAAF Squadron. *(SAAF)*

47 Squadron, RAF (Wellesleys), Gordon's Tree, with a detachment at 'Blackdown'
223 Squadron, RAF (Wellesleys), Summit
237 Squadron, Southern Rhodesian AF (Hardys and Lysanders), 'Blackdown'
430 Flight, RAF (Vincents and Gauntlets), Azzoza
'K' Flight, RAF (Gladiators), Port Sudan, but greatly under strength, with most of the flight's aircraft and personnel detached to Egypt

In Aden was now a much-reduced force:

8 Squadron, RAF (Blenheim Is), Khormaksar
94 Squadron, RAF (Gladiators), Sheik Othman, under strength
203 Squadron, RAF (Blenheim IVFs), Khormaksar
GP Flight, RAF (Vincents and Swordfish), Khormaksar, for internal security duties in the Protectorate

2 SAAF Squadron in Kenya was just about to have its teeth drawn, for on 3 January 1941 its remaining Hurricanes, together with two of 3 SAAF Squadron's aircraft, were sent to 1 SAAF Squadron in the Sudan. 2 SAAF Squadron was then left with a strength of twelve Furies (a number of ex-RAF machines having been supplied to supplement the original South African machines) and three Gauntlets, one of which was in such bad shape that it was cannibalised for spares. It is believed that these aircraft had previously served with 430 Flight, since the records of this latter unit ceased after the autumn of 1940, and it appears to have operated only Vincents during 1941.

Chapter Three

A NEW YEAR DAWNS; THE ADVANCES BEGIN

Saturday, 4 January 1941

The new year of 1941 began quietly enough, belying the violent actions which were soon to come. On 4 January while dive-bombing Italian forces in the Metemma area, two Hardys of 237 Squadron were hit by anti-aircraft fire. Flg Off Christie's aircraft, K4314, began to burn, but the gunner, Sgt K. Murrell, managed to fight the flames and keep them down while the pilot jettisoned the bombs and force-landed at 'Heston', a landing strip close to the front; Murrell was subsequently awarded a DFM for this action. The second Hardy took a bullet in the radiator, following which the engine seized, and with no power it was force-landed on the Gedaref–Gallabat road, receiving severe damage.

Wednesday, 8 January 1941

A few days later on 8 January Italian AA claimed one British bomber shot down in the sea during a raid on Massawa. Next day six South African Battles attacked a satellite landing ground at Yavello in two waves, destroying two Caproni Ca 133s on the ground. Also that day British patrols in the Sudan moved forward to occupy frontier posts which it was discovered had just been evacuated by the Italians, who were drawing back to consolidate their defences in the face of an expected British offensive.

Saturday, 11 January 1941

On 11 January the Viceroy, the Duke of Aosta, telegraphed Rome for agreement to a withdrawal. He reported that he was now faced on the Northern Front by about 60,000 enemy troops, 20,000 around Gallabat, with the rest to the north, facing Agordat. At Gallabat malaria had decimated his troops, forcing a slow withdrawal to Ammanit between Celga and Metemma. It was his opinion that the main forces would attempt to outflank him and push on the Tessenei–Azaki area and Mount Maman, then making for Keru and Agordat. The ground here facilitated such a move, as the bush was not thick enough to hinder the movement of all types of mechanised vehicles.

Until now the greater part of the Duke's strength had been sub-divided into nucleii of a few battalions posted on all the principal routes along which the British might advance, but these were threatened by the possibility of a surprise flanking move. A direct attack on any of these small forces would bring defeat for the defenders. Already as a result, he had pulled back the greater part of his force to a line from the crossroads east of Tessenei to Sabderat and Keru.

He now wished to give up Kassala and Tessenei, as a stand on this line held little chance of victory, and would lead to a retreat to Keren and the loss of the whole western part of Eritrea.

From a purely military point of view he wished to consider the line at present held, as an intermediate one pending a withdrawal to the Agordat–Barentu area where the terrain would limit the use of motor vehicles and give a major possibility of victory. However, he appreciated that such a withdrawal would mean the abandonment of a substantial part of Eritrea which would have grave internal repercussions in the capital of Asmara, and on the international scene. He therefore needed Rome's consent to his proposed course of action. The abandonment of Tessenei was to be a particular blow as its airfield was used by aircraft flying in from Libya, and its loss would reduce the possibility of reinforcement, as well as bringing British aircraft to a base within a short distance of the Italian lines.

Sunday, 12 January 1941

Despite these ominous preparations 12 January proved to be another good day for the Italian fighters. Three Fiat CR 42s escorted a Savoia S 79 on a reconnaissance over Aroma, where two Gladiators of 1 SAAF Squadron intercepted, opening fire and damaging two of the Italian aircraft. The Fiats turned on the attackers and shot down one in flames, Lt J.S.R. Warren being killed. Over Tessenei another CR 42 intercepted a 237 Squadron Hardy — K5922, crewed by Plt Off Simmonds and Sgt Gray — and claimed to have shot it down; the Hardy was extensively damaged, but managed to remain in the air for 25 minutes before force-landing a mile south of Tessenei, the crew returning to base on foot.

Meanwhile, as the Italians were awaiting the expected British offensive on the Eritrean frontier with Sudan in the north, General Cunningham's troops struck first from Kenya on 14 January. Supported by Hartbeestes of 41 SAAF Squadron, the 11th and 12th African Divisions began the long trek across the desert of the Northern Frontier District to attack the port of Kismayu in the south of Italian Somaliland. The 12th Division moved off first, one brigade making for Buro Erillo to threaten the road junction at Jelib, while the 1st South African Brigade travelled south from the Wajir area to capture Gobwen and cut the retreat of the Kismayu garrison. When these moves had been completed, it was planned that the 11th Division would assault the town itself, supported by bombardment from ships of the Royal Navy lying offshore. The routes to be covered were long and arduous, the tracks poor, and the water supplies sparse. Consequently some days would be needed before the 12th Division's units could be in position to make their first attack, with their supplies adequately built up.

Thursday, 16 January 1941

As the main forces moved up to the Kismayu area, the 1st South African Division (not to be confused with the 1st South African Brigade, which was at this time serving as a part of the 12th African Division) was preparing to enter action far to the west, and just before dawn on the 16th, its columns began the long journey northwards towards El Yibo, a Kenyan frontier post in Italian hands. Roads, tracks and conditions generally were even worse than those across which Cunningham's other forces were marching. The Division was supported from the air by the Hartbeestes of 40 SAAF Squadron which next day bombed El Yibo prior to the assault; when the first troops arrived on the scene on the 18th, they were to find the post already abandoned.

From Aden on 16 January Blenheim L8456 of 8 Squadron made a lone high-altitude bombing raid on targets in Eritrea, but failed to return. It seems that it may have flown on to attack Jijiga, where a lone Blenheim made a surprise attack, strafing and slightly damaging one CR 32. The pilot of this fighter took off nonetheless, and fired at the Blenheim without obvious results; he reported that it appeared to have a white band painted round the fuselage, similar to those carried by Italian aircraft. In the circumstances it may be that some of his bullets struck home, for the bomber was found by British reconnaissance aircraft two days later, having force-landed in French Somaliland. It had been wrecked and partially burned, the crew having been interned by the French. At this time 8 Squadron received two Blenheim IVs, handed to the unit by 203 Squadron after re-conversion to the bomber configuration.

Friday, 17 January 1941

All was now ready for the big assault in the north and on 17 January the supporting air units began moving nearer to the front. All the various detachments of 1 SAAF Squadron rejoined the parent unit, which moved to a new strip, 'Oxo', situated 35 miles west of Kassala. Six 47 Squadron Wellesleys moved to 'Blackdown' and 'Sarum'. Before the offensive began, however, the Duke of Aosta's preparations started to take effect, and during the night of 18/19 January Italian forces evacuated Kassala and moved back into Eritrea. Next day the British force moved forward, entering Kassala and crossing the border, while Wellesleys of 47 and 223 Squadrons hammered Barentu and Agordat airfields and the Caproni workshops at Mai Edaga.

In the south the Marylands attached to 12 SAAF Squadron were extremely active, flying far and wide to photograph key areas; the survey Ansons of 60 SAAF Squadron were also busy, often operating well over Italian territory. On 17 January two Marylands reconnoitred the whole of the coast of Italian Somaliland as far as Mogadishu, discovering the previously unknown airfield at Vittorio d'Africa, where seven bombers were spotted hidden among some trees; both aircraft strafed, but without apparent results.

Saturday, 18 to Sunday, 19 January 1941

Next day three Marylands were again over the coastal airfields, seeking any signs

Martin Maryland of 12 SAAF Squadron, over the Southern Front. *(SAAF via R.C. Jones)*

of impending air attacks on the troops approaching Kismayu. On the 19th six Junkers Ju 86s of 12 SAAF Squadron bombed a vehicle park at Neghelli; it was believed that most of the 150 vehicles there had been destroyed or damaged, preventing their use for carrying reinforcements down to the area where the 1st South African Division's activities were just beginning.

Monday, 20 to Tuesday, 21 January 1941

On 20 January the Regia Aeronautica reacted fully to the new threat in the north, and attacks were thrown in throughout the day on the British motorised columns moving on Agordat, which were now beginning to establish contact with the Italian rearguards. It proved to be a disastrous day in the air for the Italians, not due to opposing fighters, but to ground fire. CR 42s strafed the columns, burning two lorries and immobilising five others, but two of the fighters were badly hit and had to force-land within their own lines. The attack was then taken up by S 79s and Ca 133s, but four of the latter were hit hard, and three force-landed, being damaged beyond repair; one crew member was killed and four wounded. One of the S 79s was also hit and crashed in the Adi Ugri area with the loss of the whole crew.

An attack west of Mount Tebu by S 81s was undertaken next, but while taking off one of the bombers crashed for no apparent reason, all the crew being killed. The CR 42s then strafed again, but one suffered engine trouble on the way to the target and attempted a force-landing; the aircraft failed to make it and crashed, a total write-off although the pilot was unhurt. Without meeting any opposition in the air, the Italians had lost six aircraft, with three more badly damaged: eleven crew members were dead and four more wounded.

The time was now ripe for Emperor Haile Selassie to return to Ethiopia and rally his supporters. During the day he was flown from Khartoum to Umm Idla on the border in a 47 Squadron Wellesley, escorted by Hurricanes of 1 SAAF Squadron. Next day 1 SAAF Squadron moved to Kassala to be nearer the front, and there it was divided into three flights. 237 Squadron also began operating on a three-flight basis, 'C' Flight having just arrived from Egypt equipped with five brand-new Lysander IIs. Over the front Italian bombers attacked vehicles in the Aicota and Auascia areas, while fighters made strafing attacks and escorted other bombers to attack British forces moving forward in the Gallabat/Metemma area also. Their efforts were to no avail, and before the day was out the 5th Indian Division had occupied Aicota.

In the south 11 SAAF Squadron's Battles were engaged in bombing airfields from where raids might be launched on the 1st South African Division's advancing columns, and having hit Yavello with little success on the 20th, six Battles now raided Shashamanna where six Italian aircraft had been reported; 216 fragmentation bombs and 480 incendiaries were dropped on half-a-dozen S 81s, and it was claimed that four of these were burned and a fifth lost a wing and its tail. In fact only one bomber was burned, others being slightly damaged, and it therefore seems likely that some of the aircraft seen burning were actually the dummies referred to earlier.

Wednesday, 22 January 1941

On the northern front further raids were made by the Regia Aeronautica on 22 January, one attack on Tessenei airfield claiming to have damaged a single British aircraft. Two Ca 133s with fighter escort then bombed a large concentration of transport and armoured cars near Keru, but on this occasion were intercepted. Operating from Kassala, two Hurricanes and two Gladiators of 1 SAAF Squadron had been ordered to patrol to Keren, and these saw the Italian formation which they incorrectly reported as comprising three Capronis (the Italians reported being attacked by two Hurricanes and four Gladiators). Lt O.B. Coetzee in one of the Hurricanes, attacked one Ca 133, seeing it jettison its bombs and some small flames appear. He was then driven off by CR 42s, but reported seeing the bomber falling in flames and the crew baling out. Lt H.J.P. Burger in the other Hurricane had also attacked a Caproni, which fell in flames, four of the crew baling out. The two men were credited with a shared victory, but Coetzee may in fact have attacked another aircraft, then seeing Burger's victim falling in flames, for a second bomber was hit and damaged, returning to Agordat with three of the crew wounded. Three members of the crew from the missing aircraft subsequently returned to base on foot.

A first-hand account of this action from the Italian side has been provided by one of the survivors:

'On the morning of 22 January 1941 a formation of three Caproni Ca 133s of the 18ª Squadriglia, 27° Gruppo, took off from Asmara to bomb the enemy advancing from the north. Tenente Passetto was in command and I, a Sergente, was the second pilot. The aircraft on the right was flown by Sottotenente Nicoletti and Serg Belcaro, while that on the left was flown by an officer whose name I do not remember, and Serg Dichino. After take-off I took over control from Ten Passetto who gave me the course and altitude. Over Agordat we received an escort of two Fiat CR 42s which stayed 200 metres above us. Not long after, the Observer Commander of the aircraft came into the cockpit and, staying between the two pilots, indicated to the Tenente to look down to the left. After a moment I saw a shower of flak coming from below and I then saw two Hurricanes. The Tenente ordered us to jettison the bombs, took over control and started to bank in the direction of home. A Hurricane attacked from behind and the aircraft on the left crashed in flames, while that on the right was hit, dived away and disappeared from our view.

'We were alone in the sky, the Tenente banked again, increasing speed. I saw the needle of the tachometer move forward and stop at 175 km/hr. The Hurricane turned back, attacking us again. We were hit by one bullet after another and the Observer Commander was wounded in the thigh. Our radio operator was very good; he was firing with a Lewis gun to the rear and was managing to reload very swiftly. In the meantime the engineer was manning another Lewis but was only getting off single shots.

'The next thing that happened was that the petrol tank was hit by a burst of fire. I saw a torrent of fuel pouring over the engineer, the floor, and eventually disappearing through the doors, leaving a grey trail behind us . . . I was looking at all that fuel and worrying about the engine exhaust. We were then attacked again from the right — the Hurricane was determined to finish this old Caproni that was still flying! The right engine was hit. I heard the sound of bullets hitting metal parts all round the aircraft, but fortunately none of us was shot. Our escort did intervene, but from my seat I couldn't see a thing. Those who could see said that there were four Gladiators present also.

'The Tenente landed at Agordat, the tyres burst and the Caproni ran on the wheel rims with a terrible noise; after that it drew to a halt. A moment later Sottoten Nicoletti's Caproni also landed, damaged and with one wounded. When banking I had thought I saw for a moment a very, very small Caproni far below. It was Sottoten Nicoletti; up higher something bright was coming down very slowly. These images disappeared very quickly from my vision. When we landed a mechanic explained the mystery. It was the radio operator of the plane that had been shot down in flames; he had been soaked in fuel and caught fire as he baled out, falling like a burning torch on his parachute — ironically his surname was Fuoco (fire).

'The ambulance arrived and picked up the wounded. The engineer complained that he was very sore because of being showered with fuel and was longing for a proper shower! After this action the 18ª Squadriglia had no more aircraft. The Officer, Sergente and engineer (wounded in the shoulder) from the aircraft shot down, had been able to bale out and arrived in our lines on foot. Out of the three crews there was one person dead and three wounded. The mechanics were able to repair the damage to Sottoten Nicoletti's Caproni just sufficiently to allow the aircraft to fly back to Asmara. However, I confirm that in the afternoon the Hurricanes returned and blew up my Caproni; it carried the number 18-4.'

In the afternoon Lts Burger and Hewitson attacked Agordat airfield in Hurricanes, destroying the damaged Caproni and claiming damage to another.

In the south a Ro 37bis of the 110ª Squadriglia on reconnaissance over Gerille was reported to have been attacked by a fighter, engaging it in combat and returning with slight damage. In the same area a 41 SAAF Squadron Hartbeeste was shot down reportedly by two CR 42s, but in the absence of fighter claims by either side it is assumed that these biplanes had in fact been fighting each other.

Thursday, 23 January 1941

On 23 January units of the 1st South African Brigade moving southwards from Wajir came under air attack in the Digh Merer–Diff area; only the Hartbeestes of 40 SAAF Squadron could reach this area to operate at this time, so no adequate air cover was forthcoming.

In Eritrea 1 SAAF Squadron moved again, this time to Tessenei, the first airfield captured in this country. From there the unit continued to patrol over the advancing columns. Italian fighters reported intercepting a formation of escorted bombers attacking a bridge on the Agordat–Keren road, and claimed to have shot down one Hurricane. During another raid on Biscia a Blenheim was seen to swerve away trailing smoke after attack by fighters and this was presumed shot down by the Italian pilots. Italian bombers made attacks on armoured cars and tanks on the Aicota–Mela road, escorting fighters claiming one more British aircraft probably shot down.

Friday, 24 January 1941

Further Italian raids were made on troops in northern Eritrea next day, and also on concentrations near Metemma and Gallabat. Fighters patrolled over the front, fighting aircraft of 1 SAAF Squadron and claiming two shot down; none was in fact lost, although Lt E.A. Jarvis's Gladiator did suffer some damage;

Capt le Mesurier of this unit claimed to have badly damaged a CR 42, while Lt Hewitson strafed a Ca 133 in a clearing 40 miles west of Agordat. In the south troops of the Transvaal Scottish in the Digh Merer area had now been under attack for several days, Ca 133s and a few Savoias, usually escorted by Fiats, coming over daily and attacking unopposed.

Sunday, 26 January 1941

On 26 January three Ro 37bis aircraft shot up the Gerille area. A patrol of Hurricanes of 3 SAAF Squadron sent over the area at maximum range failed to see any of the attackers.

One rather unusual combat did, however, take place as an Italian formation of Ca 133s was returning to base after one such attack. Over the Afmadu area escorting fighters reported seeing two aircraft, and shot one down, claiming it as a Battle; the crew were killed. One aircraft was indeed over the Liboi–Afmadu area, but it was an Anson (No 1827) of 60 SAAF Squadron on a survey mission, flown by Lt E.A. Gebhart, a peacetime survey pilot of the Aircraft Operating Company. This aircraft's crew saw below them three Ca 133s flying east at 1,200 feet and dived on them, going through the formation firing. It was reported that one Caproni gunner fired a single burst that killed Gebhart, who fell forward over his controls; the second pilot tried to take over, but before the crew could bale out, the aircraft hit the ground and burst into flames, everybody aboard being killed. From the Italian account, however, it seems clear that the Anson was claimed by the escorting fighters, which were returning from strafing British troops, and not by any of the gunners.

By early 1941 Avro Anson Is had arrived in Kenya to equip two SAAF units, 34 (Coastal) Flight and 60 (Photographic Survey) Squadron. Picture shows aircraft of 34 Flight; the dorsal turret gunner is taking aboard ammunition pans for his Vickers 'K' machine gun. *(SAAF)*

Over Eritrea during the morning a Hardy of 237 Squadron on reconnaissance over Agordat spotted two CR 42s and signalled to a pair of escorting Gladiators which engaged these; Italian fighters during the day claimed one fighter shot down and two others probably destroyed over Eritrea.

Monday, 27 January 1941

The advance continued to make new airfields available, and on the 27th 237 Squadron moved to Umtali. Six Hurricanes and six Gladiators of 1 SAAF Squadron, using Sabderat as an advance landing ground for refuelling, attacked Gura airfield during the day, many aircraft being seen there. While three fighters remained above as top cover, the other nine strafed, claiming hits on nine S 79s, seven S 81s and three Ca 133s; two pilots then strafed four more S 81s at Adi Ugri. The Italians reported that three S 79s and four S 81s were substantially damaged.

Damaged Hawker Hartbeeste of 40 SAAF Squadron, hit by AA fire on 29 January 1941, being retrieved by South African troops. *(D. Becker)*

Tuesday, 28 January 1941

Next morning in the south Gauntlets of 2 SAAF Squadron escorted Hartbeestes of 41 SAAF Squadron covering the move of South African troops of the 1st Division from Buna towards Moyale; there Maj Pope spotted the wreckage of a Hartbeeste which had been shot down on 11 July 1940 when the pilot, Lt Rankin, was in combat with CR 32s and Ca 133s. The Hartbeestes then spotted for artillery fire, but Lt C.H. Beech's aircraft was hit by AA and he had to force-land on the strip at British Moyale, where he found himself under fire and made a dash for cover. This attack on Moyale was, however, only a feint to cover preparations for a major move against El Gumu and Gorai, which was now ready to begin. Next day another Hartbeeste, flown by Lt A.D. Maxwell, was also hit by AA fire from a hidden pom-pom, and he too had to force-land and run for cover. At night gunners of the 4th Field Brigade went out to collect the aircraft cutting off the wings and towing the rest to safety.

Meanwhile over Eritrea on 28 January six Wellesleys of 223 Squadron attacked the road bridge at Shaikatu, near Asmara, while three Blenheims of 14 Squadron bombed railway sidings at Keren. Two Hurricanes, flown by Capt Driver and Lt Hewitson, set off to attack Asmara airfield, but became separated. Driver strafed the target, firing on three aircraft which he identified as S 79s; they were in fact very similar S 73 transports, and two were damaged. Hewitson meanwhile apparently attacked Gura, claiming to have hit an S 79, an S 81 and two Ca 133s, although no record of such an attack was noted by the Italians. Two more South African fighters scrambled from Sabderat to meet CR 42s over Agordat, Lt Burger's aircraft being damaged in combat with two of these.

Wednesday, 29 January 1941

Early in the morning of 29 January, eight Blenheims of 14 Squadron attacked the airfields at Gura and Mai Edaga; a pair of CR 42s attacked three of the bombers, damaging two of them although both managed to return safely. At

Bristol Blenheim IVs of 14 Squadron, RAF, made several attacks on Italian airfields on the Southern Front. Note the rare LY code. *(R. Whittard)*

1400 1 SAAF Squadron took off to attack in the same area, eight Hurricanes and five Gladiators approaching Gura where it was intended that the latter should strafe. As they approached however, several S 79s and a large number of CR 42s were seen over the airfield, the bombers having just returned from a raid over the front, and the fighters having scrambled at the approach of the South African aircraft. Capt Driver at once attacked an S 79 as it was going in to land, and shot it down in flames, two members of the crew baling out.

Capt Raffi, commander of the 412ª Squadriglia, was above with two of his pilots, Cacciavillani and Soffritti, and he saw the Hurricane shoot down the S 79 before he could intervene. He then spotted the Gladiators, which he believed to be six strong, and at once a great dogfight began, during which the South Africans saw many Fiats falling away. Driver meanwhile had seen Adi Ugri landing ground on which four S 81s were dispersed, and attacking these, he left one in flames.

On return to base the combat with the Fiats was fully discussed, and it was decided that five had been shot down, one each by Lt H.P. Smith and Lt E.A. Jarvis, the other three being impossible to allocate to individual pilots. This proves how easy it was to overestimate the damage caused, and indeed the numbers involved, in a whirling dogfight. Although several CR 42s were hit and damaged, none was in fact shot down. Raffi's own aircraft was hit five times, while Cacciavillani's was badly damaged by 50 hits, and Soffritti's was also damaged. All the SAAF aircraft returned safely, although one Gladiator had been hit by a single bullet. Other Italian fighters claimed one aircraft shot down over Barentu when they were escorting bombers on a raid; this claim possibly refers to one of the 14 Squadron Blenheims.

To the south Capronis again attacked Dif, while Savoias hit Colbio, but little damage was done. Apart from the shooting down of Lt Maxwell's Hartbeeste by AA, which has already been mentioned, this was the only activity on this front.

Thursday, 30 January 1941

Early on the morning of 30 January Capt Driver of 1 SAAF Squadron led four Hurricanes back to Adi Ugri to attack again the remaining three S 81s which he had failed to destroy on the previous day. Diving down, he set one of the bombers on fire, and Lt Duncan burned a second. Actually all three were

Wreckage of a 237 Squadron Westland Lysander II; this is believed either to have been L4676, lost over the Barentu area on 30 January 1941, or N1206, shot down on 2 February. *(F. Paget via A.S. Thomas)*

already beyond repair, and were being employed as dummies to attract just such an attack. Lt Hewitson strafed a pair of S 79s at Terammi.

During the day one of 237 Squadron's new Lysanders, L4676, flown by Flg Off Miller, somehow strayed over the Barentu area while on a non-operational flight, and was forced to land in this area, the crew being taken prisoner. The burnt-out aircraft was later discovered by advancing troops, but the reason for the force-landing is unknown.

From Kenya a Maryland of 12 SAAF Squadron flown by Lt Tennant made a photo-reconnaissance sortie over Kismayu, being attacked by a CR 42. The rear gunner fired at the attacking fighter which appeared to be disabled, and broke off the attack. Tennant then dived to ground level to strafe some Ca 133s on the airfield at Gobwen. The existence of this airfield had not previously been suspected by Headquarters in Kenya.

In an effort to facilitate the despatch of further reinforcements of fighters, the Duke of Aosta now reported to Rome that the British were on the way to gaining numerical and qualitative superiority over the Regia Aeronautica, and that the ground troops were becoming worn out in the face of fresh enemy troops brought in from Egypt via Port Sudan. Despite the growing Imperial strength in the air, and the attrition being suffered, the Regia Aeronautica continued to operate in strength however, particularly over the Northern Front, where the 5th Indian Division had now begun the assault on Agordat.

Friday, 31 January 1941
On 31 January bombing and strafing attacks were made by the Italians in the Gallabat, Metemma, Zeriba, Laquatat, Ooche, Chibabo and Sanero areas.

Two Hurricanes of 1 SAAF Squadron were patrolling over Agordat at 1000 when their pilots saw two S 79s engaged in one such raid and gave chase. Capt Driver attacked one S 79 and set the fuselage on fire; four of the crew baled out, but the pilot remained in the aircraft, diving down to zero feet. Driver kept after him and fired another burst, whereupon the pilot jumped clear and the bomber crashed. During the day Italian fighters were engaged in combat over the front, claiming one aircraft shot down, but one CR 42 was damaged and force-landed with the pilot slightly wounded; it was a write-off.

On the north Kenya border the feint attack on Moyale had been suspended, and the advance on El Gumu had been held up by a roadblock near Gorai fort. In the early afternoon armoured cars, supported by mortars and air bombardment carried out by 40 SAAF Squadron Hartbeestes, broke through this obstacle. The aircraft then harassed the retreating enemy troops. The advance continued next day, and the defenders of El Gumu were swiftly withdrawn; nine Hartbeestes then attacked Hobok, a small town due east of El Gumu. Some hundreds of miles to the south-east the first forward landing strips were now ready at Aligabe, near Liboi, and at Galma Galla, from where proper support could be given to the troops moving on Kismayu and the Juba River defences. Three Hurricanes of 3 SAAF Squadron at once flew up to Aligabe.

Saturday, 1 February 1941
In Eritrea the northern offensive by the British Imperial forces was going well by early February 1941, and on the first day of that month fighters of 1 SAAF Squadron were successful in breaking up one attempted raid by five escorted Savoia S 79s as Indian troops on the ground stormed into Agordat, from where the Italians were evacuating their forces.

The Italian Viceroy now advised Rome of the plight of the Regia Aeronautica. Since 17 January seventeen aircraft had been destroyed by the enemy in combat or on the ground, and three more had been lost in accidents. On top of these losses, twenty-four more had been badly damaged and would not be serviceable until March at the earliest. Aircraft available for operations totalled 82: 37 Ca 133s, 15 CR 42s, 14 CR 32s, 7 S 79s, 6 S 81s, 2 Ro 37bis and 1 S 82. These figures gave a false impression of the capabilities of the air force, however, as due to the substantial number of Hurricanes and Gladiators now appearing on all fronts, it was virtually impossible to employ the Ca 133s without strong fighter escort. If activity in the air continued at the present level for another fifteen days, the ability of the Regia Aeronautica to continue effective operations would cease, unless adequate numbers of reinforcement machines were sent at once to save the situation. Meanwhile, to bring the greatly weakened 110ª Squadriglia up to strength, it had received four CR 42s, the first sorties with these being flown on this date.

Sunday, 2 February 1941
Early on 2 February two of the 3 SAAF Squadron Hurricanes which had moved up to Aligabe took off on patrol flown by Capt J.E. Frost and Lt J. Howitson, but saw nothing. On a second sortie they flew to Afmadu airfield where Frost strafed a Ca 133, seeing it begin to burn. Frost, who was very shortly to make a big name for himself in action, had been recipient of the Sword of Honour at the South African Military College in 1938.

On the north Kenya front Hobok was assaulted by armoured cars and infantry, following an air attack by Hartbeestes of 40 SAAF Squadron and an artillery barrage. During the attack Lt J.D.W. Human of this squadron silenced a machine gun post and also attacked an Italian armoured car. His Hartbeeste was hit by ground fire, but he remained over the target losing height to allow Air Sgt J. Jackson, the gunner, another shot at the vehicle. At this stage the engine seized, and Human had to crash-land in front of the advancing infantry.

He subsequently received a DFC for this action, Jackson being awarded a DFM.

Elsewhere in the south there was considerable action during the day. The aircraft carrier HMS *Formidable* was sailing up the coast of East Africa on her way to the Mediterranean, carrying 21 Fairey Albacores of 826 and 829 Squadrons, and a dozen Fairey Fulmar fighters of 803 Squadron. During the early hours of 2 February nine Albacores had bombed Mogadishu, killing a large number of natives, but doing little other damage, while other Albacores laid magnetic mines in the harbour. These were later to give considerable problems to the British and South Africans, who had difficulty in clearing them after the fall of the port.

On the far left of the Kenyan front, the 25th East African Brigade began an advance up the western shore of Lake Rudolph, entering Ethiopia between the Sudanese border and the western part of the Galla Sidamo province. The troops, supported by 'A' Flight of 40 SAAF Squadron, reached Kalam, but there they were opposed by the Merille, a warlike tribe that supported the Italians — mainly because the British supported their neighbours and local rivals, the Turkanas. At this stage 'C' Flight of 40 SAAF Squadron at Lokitaung lent a hand, attacking a Merille fort at Todenyang at the northern end of the lake at dawn. Another Hartbeeste, flown by Lt Roberts, bombed the camp of the chief of the tribe, but was hit by small arms fire on the return flight and had to force-land near Todenyang.

One more Hartbeeste was hit when dropping a message, but returned to base, loaded up with 20lb bombs, and went out again to attack the tribesmen. The aircraft was again hit, this time in the radiator, and Lt Smith had to force-land. Two more aircraft were badly shot up during the morning, and later in the day Capt Stableford's Hartbeeste was hit while covering troops who were now withdrawing; he force-landed near Smith's aircraft. The Commanding Officer, Maj Durrant, flew up with four new aircraft, a couple of mechanics and a load of spare parts. These were landed by the two stranded aircraft, which were repaired and flown out.

Three Battles of 11 SAAF Squadron were thereupon called in to bomb the tribesmen from 4,000 feet, but even one of these was hit by one of the sharp-eyed natives. General Cunningham then ordered the advance to be called off and the 25th Brigade to go over to the defensive. Subsequently the Merille were persuaded to turn on the Italians, following an assurance that the British would not occupy their territory.

Further back, 1 Bomber Brigade SAAF was now re-titled 2 Wing. At the same time the OTU at Nakuru was temporarily closed and the Audaxes and Wapitis held ready as a reserve should the two army co-operation squadrons run short of aircraft. All other aircraft — Valentias, Rapides and light types — were pressed into service for ambulance and communication duties. Air Commodore Sowrey then ordered several units to move closer to the fronts, and during the next few days the squadrons took up the following locations:

2 SAAF Squadron, Garissa East, with detachments at Garissa West and Husseini
3 SAAF Squadron, Garissa West, with detachments at Aligabe and Galma Galla
11 SAAF Squadron, Husseini
12 SAAF Squadron, Garissa West

Communications, transport and ambulance aircraft were to go to Garissa East, where the Rapide and two Gauntlets for escort purposes were set aside for General Cunningham's personal use.

On the Northern Front during the morning of 2 February a Lysander of 237 Squadron, N1206 flown by Flg Off M.A. Johnson, was on a tactical reconnaissance over the Scipitole–Tole road when it encountered three Ca 133s dropping supplies to troops at the front. Johnson at once attacked one of the bombers, forcing it to land and crash; unknown to him however, the Capronis were escorted by three 412ª Squadriglia CR 42s, and these now attacked the Lysander. Sgt J.G.P. Burl fired three pans of ammunition at them with the rear gun, seeing smoke from the engine of one fighter, but he was wounded in the wrist. The Lysander's controls were shot through however, and it crash-landed violently to the east of Tole, the pilot being rendered unconscious; the aircraft was claimed shot down by Maresciallo Arnaldo Soffritti, one of the more recently arrived fighter pilots with the unit. Under fire from the fighters which were strafing the wreckage, Burl managed to pull Johnson clear, both members of the crew subsequently being decorated.

Monday, 3 February 1941

On 3 February 3 SAAF Squadron Hurricanes at Aligabe made two early scrambles over the Dif area, but saw nothing. Lt Marsh then escorted 41 SAAF Squadron Hartbeestes to attack Afmadu, meeting five CR 42s over the town and engaging one of these which evaded him in cloud. At Aligabe meanwhile Capt Frost made his third scramble of the day, this time spotting three Ca 133s which were bombing the camp of the Transvaal Scottish at Dif again. Diving out of the sun to position himself between the bombers and their base, he made a frontal attack on the third aircraft as they turned for home, but before he could achieve anything, he was attacked by two CR 42s, one from in front and one from behind.

Eluding these, Frost flew several miles ahead of the eastbound formation, and swinging in, turned to fire at two Capronis, but again the CR 42s attacked him, both coming in head on. He fired a long burst into one of these, which pulled up in a steep climb and was seen to crash into the bush and burst into flames. He then returned to the bombers which were beginning to break formation, and attacked one from which the pilot at once baled out; the co-pilot, a sergente, took over the controls and crash-landed the aircraft. The second bomber at once succumbed to a burst of fire, and crashed; the third, after two passes by the Hurricane, also crash-landed. The whole combat had taken place above the heads of the exultant troops, who took eleven prisoners from the crashed aircraft. The sergente who had taken over the first Caproni was later introduced to Frost, and insisted on shaking his hand and congratulating him. Although all four aircraft were reported to have been seen to crash from the ground, only the three bombers were reported lost by the Italians, one CR 42 being reported badly damaged in the combat. However, a photograph was taken of the wreckage of a CR 42, reputed to be the one shot down in this fight, so the records may in this case not be fully correct.

At 1130 three more of 3 SAAF Squadron's Hurricanes at the strip at Galma Galla took off to escort three Ju 86s to attack Gobwen. The formation flew over the sea to gain surprise skirting the heavily defended area of Kismayu. The fighters then went in first, five minutes ahead of the bombers. Capt S. van Breda

Wreckage of a Fiat CR 42 near Gobwen. It is believed to be the aircraft shot down by Capt J.E. Frost of 3 SAAF Squadron, during the battle over Dif on 3 February 1941. *(SAAF)*

Theron strafed a CR 42 on the ground at a satellite landing ground, and claimed to have shot down another as it took off. While Lt Upton stayed above as cover, Lt Dudley then attacked the main Gobwen airfield where he set a Ca 133 on fire. The three fighters then climbed up as the bombers approached, and Dudley dived back at the airfield to indicate the target to the Junkers' crews, strafing another Caproni which began to burn. Lt Upton followed him down to set light to a third Caproni, although a fourth refused to burn.

In Eritrea on the 3rd six Gladiators of 1 SAAF Squadron flew forward to a new strip named 'Pretoria', where they refuelled, taking off again at 1145 to strafe airfields in the Gondar area. South of Azozo a landing ground was seen on which five Ca 133s were being bombed up, and these were strafed, all being claimed in flames and blowing up; only one was reported as actually destroyed in this attack by the Italians. The Gladiator pilots then spotted another airfield nearby from which CR 42s were taking off, and after one strafing pass on some S 81s on the ground here, the Gladiators were attacked by the Fiats and a big dogfight began, during which Captains Boyle and le Mesurier each claimed one CR 42 shot down. On return Lt Smith's Gladiator was badly damaged during a force-landing at Azozo. The Italians reported the loss of two CR 42s, although only one over Gondar, the other being reported lost in a battle over Gura with eleven bombers and five escorting fighters.

One of the Italian fighter pilots lost on this date was Serg Magg Enzo Omiccioli who, during the attack on Gondar, took off but after a brief dogfight with the Gladiators was shot down. One of the best pilots of the 410ª Squadriglia, he had been loaned to the 412ª Squadriglia early in the campaign, and was still with this unit at the time of his death. A calm, brave man, he was greatly liked and respected by all, and his CO had been about to recommend him for a commission when he was killed. He was posthumously awarded Italy's highest decoration for valour, the Medaglio d'Oro (Gold Medal), having claimed a Hawker fighter over Moyale while flying a CR 32 during a brief attachment to the 411ª Squadriglia right at the start of the campaign (probably

---

Lt Rankin's 40 SAAF Squadron Hartbeeste). Omiccioli had gone on to take part in the destruction of two Blenheims while with the 410ᵃ Squadriglia, and had then claimed four more aircraft over the Northern Front with the 412ᵃ Squadriglia, as well as taking part in many ground strafing missions.

Sergente Maggiore Enzo Omiccioli of the 410ᵃ Squadriglia, seen in a Fiat CR 32, who was killed in action on 3 February 1941 and was posthumously awarded the Medaglio d'Oro; he was credited with seven victories. *(Corrado Ricci).*

Tuesday, 4 February 1941

On 4 February three Hurricanes and three Gladiators from 1 SAAF Squadron flew to Metemma to refuel and then attacked Bahar Dar airfield where three Ca 133s were seen on the ground. Lts Coetzer and White set two of these on fire, and Capt Driver the third — all confirmed by Italian records. Driver's Hurricane received one bullet in the mainplane from the ground, and one Gladiator was damaged. Four more of the unit's Hurricanes escorted Wellesleys to bomb the Gura area, when they met a formation of three Blenheim IVs from 14 Squadron, RAF. Not expecting these aircraft, the South Africans took them to be hostile and attacked, damaging one bomber (T2115) which had to crash-land at Port Sudan on return. These Hurricanes then engaged four CR 42s, and Maj Wilmot closed on one at low level over Asmara, seeing it fall away towards the town, following which a large cloud of dust was observed rising among some buildings. He did not make a claim, but it is possible that this was the aircraft reported shot down over Gura on the previous day in Italian records. It is noted that a total of at least three CR 42s were later reported lost during these two days, and Sottoten Dadetta of the 412ᵃ Squadriglia is known to have been shot down and killed by Hurricanes over Gura around this time.

From Aden two Blenheim IVFs of 203 Squadron, flown by Sqn Ldr J.M.N. Pike and Flt Lt Gethin, made a low-level strafing attack on Makale airfield where three S 79s were left in flames, hits being claimed on three more also; of the three bombers destroyed one had already been damaged, and another was undergoing repairs. The Blenheims were then attacked by two fighters identified as CR 42s; they were in fact CR 32s from the 410ᵃ Squadriglia on detachment to Makale, and flown by Tenenti Veronese and Folcherio. Both Blenheims were hit and one had to crash-land at base.

Wednesday, 5 February 1941

The RAF bombers in the Sudan were now involved in intensive operations over the Eritrean battlefront, the Wellesleys of 223 Squadron frequently using Agordat as an advanced base. The army co-operation aircraft were also active, and during 5 February Hardys of 237 Squadron attacked troops, columns of vehicles and a rail bridge east of Keren. The fighters were again over the front, four Hurricanes and two Gladiators of 1 SAAF Squadron carrying out a patrol during which six CR 42s were met and engaged. Capt Driver attacked the leading Fiat head on, and hit the engine, the pilot breaking away and making

Safe conduct document issued to all British Commonwealth airmen operating over Ethiopia. It was known to the aircrews as a 'Goolie Chit'! *(G.R. Whittard)*

for Asmara. Driver fired again and the Italian fighter crash-landed just short of the airfield. Lt Coetzer, flying one of the Gladiators, claimed a second CR 42 which crashed, and a third was claimed by Capt le Mesurier. Italian records show that one CR 42 crash-landed, badly damaged and with the pilot slightly wounded, while a second was shot down, the pilot baling out; he was badly wounded and died later that day. One Gladiator was damaged during this engagement.

Thursday, 6 February 1941
On 6 February the 5th Indian Brigade was attacked by Italian aircraft in a valley near the Keren area, after which 1 SAAF Squadron began a six-day period of intensive defensive patrolling. British bombers were again active, bombing Keren and Assab, the shipyard at the latter port being badly damaged. Early next day a Hardy of 237 Squadron on a tactical reconnaissance over the Keren area was engaged by a 412ª Squadriglia CR 42 and shot down in flames; the crew of the Hardy, K4313, Flg Off Taylor and Sgt Stowe, were both killed. Two Wellesleys from 47 Squadron flown by Flg Off Helsby and Sgt E.E. Blofield made a road reconnaissance from Barentu to Adi Ugri; over the latter location they were also intercepted by the 412ª Squadriglia and were both shot down, one being claimed by Mar Soffritti; one was K8525. On a later mission Soffritti was to claim a Hurricane, and the unit also claimed one further aircraft probably shot down, but no losses are known. In the afternoon two Aden-based Blenheim IVFs of 203 Squadron, again flown by Sqn Ldr Pike and Flt Lt Gethin, attacked Alomata where nine Ca 133s were seen. These were machine gunned most effectively and eight were left in flames, all being destroyed.

Tuesday, 4 to Friday, 7 February 1941
To the south bombers from Kenya raided Lugh Ferrandi and Yavello airfields, and 41 SAAF Squadron moved forward 'B' Flight going to Colbio and 'A' Flight to Aligabe. On 4 February the 12th African Division had captured Beles Gugani and begun construction of a landing ground deep in the bush there. On the 7th the troops in the area were bombed by Italian aircraft, but by the 9th the strip was completed. 'C' Flight of 41 SAAF Squadron then flew in from Ndege's Nest and was joined later by three Hurricanes of 3 SAAF Squadron.

Saturday, 8 February 1941
Four Blenheim IVs of 14 Squadron took off at 0905 on 8 February to raid the aircraft workshops at Asmara, but while over the target T1818 was hit by anti-aircraft fire and spun into the ground, the crew and Plt Off T.H. Scorrer of 'K' Flight who had gone along as a passenger, all being killed. Four Hurricanes of

1 SAAF Squadron flew an offensive patrol over Asmara during the day, but these were bounced by five CR 42s, and another dogfight began. Capt Driver got a good burst into one Fiat which crashed 25 miles west of the airfield, and Lt van der Merwe claimed to have damaged another. In Aden Sqn Ldr Wightman of 94 Squadron was informed that he had been awarded a DFC for his splendid work during 1940.

Sunday, 9 February 1941

On 9 February the 412ᵃ Squadriglia achieved a resounding success with a surprise dawn strafing attack, this time Agordat and its satellite airfields being the targets. Five CR 42s made the attack, the pilots claiming to have destroyed five Hurricanes, five Hawker biplanes, two Gladiators, two Wellesleys, a Valentia and a 'Martin' Lysander; actual losses were two Wellesleys of 47 Squadron (K7713 and L2665), two Hardys and two Lysanders of 237 Squadron, while four other aircraft were damaged.

Monday, 10 February 1941

Six 1 SAAF Squadron Hurricanes were again on offensive patrol in the Asmara area next day, flying in two sections each of three aircraft. It was a cloudy day, and when five CR 42s were seen, a dogfight in and out of the clouds began. Capt Boyle leading one section, attacked one fighter, claimed as a CR 42, and shot it down in flames, the pilot baling out. Capt Driver, who was leading the other section, having fired at two Fiats and lost them in cloud, shot at a third and saw it in flames, but his own aircraft was then hit and he had to break off. He was chased for some way by two fighters which shot up his aircraft badly, and indeed claimed to have shot it down, but he eventually escaped them and landed at Agordat. During this combat only one Italian fighter was shot down, and this was a CR 32; Boyle and Driver may have double-claimed. The pilot is believed to have been Serg Marlotti of the 412ᵃ Squadriglia, who was attacked by Hurricanes from above in cloud and shot down. He baled out at low altitude as his fighter fell below the clouds, but was found dead near the wreckage of his fighter with his parachute unopened.

Monday, 10 to Tuesday, 11 February 1941

The attack on Afmadu, in Italian Somaliland, was now soon to be made, and while the artillery barrage began, air attacks were also laid on. Alternate waves of Ju 86s and Battles went in in threes, each wave being escorted by a pair of 3 SAAF Squadron Hurricanes; in all nine Ju 86s and six Battles took part in this attack during which thirty-six 250lb bombs and 384 fragmentation bombs were dropped, all aircraft also making strafing attacks. The weight of the explosives, splinters and bullets proved too much for the defenders, and that night the 9th Italian Colonial Infantry Brigade abandoned the village, attempting to reach the Juba River. Next morning the 22nd East African Brigade was able to enter Afmadu unopposed at 0820, and the first Hartbeeste landed there shortly afterwards. The rest of 41 SAAF Squadron quickly followed, and by dusk on 11 February the 1st South African Brigade also began arriving from the north-west.

In the north on 11 February 1 SAAF Squadron put eleven fighters up on patrols over Keren and on one of these two Hurricanes encountered three CR 42s which dived away in thick cloud. Lt S. de K. Viljoen followed and failed

Sole operational users of the Fairey Battle in East Africa — or on the African continent for that matter — were the South Africans and the aircraft of 11 SAAF Squadron, continued their bombing missions until the end of the campaign. Here a SAAF Battle is prepared for action. Note 0.303in machine gun in the starboard wing leading edge. *(SAAF)*

to return; running low on fuel, he had to land near a village, fortunately within territory in British hands. He obtained petrol, and attempted to take off next morning, but crashed; he then returned to Agordat on foot. His aircraft was later recovered and repaired.

It seems that the CR 42s which he had chased were aircraft of the 412ª Squadriglia, engaged in a strafing attack on British troops in front of Keren. Two of these fighters, flown by young sergenti, force-landed at a forward landing strip due to the bad weather. On learning of this on his safe return to base, the formation leader Capt Mario Visintini decided that he should at once fly back to guide his inexperienced pilots home through the clouds. During the flight it seems that Visintini was blown off course by high winds and while descending through cloud, he crashed into the side of Mount Nefasit and was killed.

Visintini was without doubt the most successful fighter pilot of the campaign. He had taken part in the successful strafing attacks at Gedaref and Gaz Regeb in October and November 1940 and at Agordat two days previously; he had also flown in Spain, but it is the number of victories in combat claimed by him over Eritrea that remains uncertain, due to the lack of records for the 412ª Squadriglia. Apart from his early successes against the Wellesleys over Massawa and Gura, where he had also claimed two of the first Blenheims to appear, his CO, Capt Raffi, records that he had more recently shot down three more Blenheims in three separate combats. On one occasion he set an engine of one of these bombers on fire, then flew alongside signalling the pilot to land. Only when the pilot ignored these signals and continued to fly out to sea, did Visintini administer the coup de grâce. His score has been quoted by those who flew with him as about 17 — certainly not less than 15. Since in the same period the 412ᵃ Squadriglia seems to have claimed at least 50 victories (of which 29 can be confirmed from British records) and 16 probables in the air, plus many on the ground, this total seems in no way unlikely. He received the Medaglio d'Oro posthumously for his outstanding combat record, and for noteworthy work as deputy commander of the Squadriglia. His brother Licio would also receive a posthumous Medaglio d'Oro following his death in a daring underwater 'human torpedo' attack on Gibraltar harbour on 7 December 1942.

Wednesday, 12 February 1941

On 12 February an Italian cargo ship, *Leonardo da Vinci*, escaping from Mogadishu for Diego Suarez in Madagascar, was intercepted and attacked by a British cruiser. Another ship, *Ascari*, was bombed in harbour at Brava and set on fire. On the north Kenya front 40 SAAF Squadron moved to Dubana, with one flight at Kunchurro, and from there the Hartbeestes were to assist the 2nd and 5th South African Brigades in an attack on Mega. The Suez Canal had been rendered temporarily impassable by air-laid mines and HMS *Formidable* was still waiting for these to be cleared to pass through to the Mediterranean. During the night of the 12th/13th therefore, an attack was made on Massawa by fourteen Albacores, seven of which carried bombs and seven torpedoes. Low cloud turned the attack into a shambles, and although one ship was hit (the steamer *Moncalieri* of 5,723 tons was destroyed), this was the only real damage; two of the bombers were shot down, two crew members being killed and six taken prisoner.

Thursday, 13 February 1941

With morning, five Hurricanes of 1 SAAF Squadron patrolled over Asmara, intercepting five fighters which they identified as CR 42s. Maj Wilmot saw one evade a Hurricane and stall and he fired on this, causing the engine to stop and black smoke to issue forth; Capt Boyle then attacked this aircraft and set it on fire, the pilot baling out and the fighter crashing east of Asmara. Lt Duncan saw another Fiat in cloud and dived vertically on it; from this too the pilot baled out, the aircraft crashing in flames 12 miles south-east of the town. Capt Driver attacked another, but lost it in cloud, while a fourth was also attacked by other pilots but escaped. One of the fighters shot down was indeed a CR 42 of the 412ᵃ Squadriglia, the pilot being badly wounded; he is believed to have been Ten Luigi De Pol, who later died in hospital. The second aircraft lost was a CR 32 — the last available in Eritrea — from which the pilot also baled out. However, it was reported that he was machine gunned on his parachute by a Hurricane, and on landing was rushed to hospital where an arm and a leg were amputated, but he died shortly afterwards; this was Ten Bossi. Three more CR 42s were damaged in this combat, and one had to force-land, the pilot having been slightly wounded.

It seems against the ethos of the South African pilots that they would have attacked a pilot on his parachute. Certainly, it was recorded that one of the SAAF pilots did fly past the unfortunate Bossi as he fell, but it is much more likely that he had already been seriously wounded by his attacker's fire before evacuating his cockpit.

A raid on Zula by Aden-based aircraft caught a Savoia S 82 transport on the ground which had just arrived from Italy, and this was badly damaged. 'K'

Flight's Gladiators had at last returned from Egypt, together with a new commander, Flt Lt J.E. Scoular, DFC, a veteran of the Battle of France with some 12 and two shared victories to his credit. Two Gladiators and three pilots, Scoular included, now moved forward to Mersa Taclai to begin general reconnaissance over the area Kelanet, Kub-Kub, etc.

In the south Capt O.G. Davies of the Maryland detachment with 12 SAAF Squadron made an early morning reconnaissance over the Mogadishu area. He strafed a staff car on the Jelib–Mogadishu road, causing it to crash into some trees, and then fired on some lorries and two tankers near Brava. Seeing Vittorio d'Africa airfield he dived to attack five Ca 133s, damaging two, but was then intercepted by a CR 42 flown by Capt Palmera, which shot up the rear of his aircraft, causing considerable damage; 732 holes were subsequently counted in the tail of the Maryland. Six 11 SAAF Squadron Battles bombed the Berbera

On 13 February 1941 the Gladiators of 'K' Flight moved up to the front to support the advance in Eritrea; previously they had mostly been attached to 112 Squadron in Egypt, whose code letters 'RT' appear on the Gladiator in the background. The identity of the pilot is not known. *(Imperial War Museum)*

area, but two were hit by AA, one landing at Afmadu and the other force-landing at Beles Gugani. During the morning elements of the 1st and 2nd Gold Coast Regiments advanced on Bulo Erillo across open ground, suffering heavy losses, but the Italians were now showing all the signs of confusion, and to add to this, during the day a pontoon bridge across the Juba at Jelib was bombed and destroyed by Ju 86s.

Italian bombers were still doing what they could, and during the night a raid had been made on Afmadu during which one attacking S 81 was hit and damaged by AA. While the attack on Afmadu by the Imperial force had been going on, a second column of African infantry had closed on Kismayu, the port coming under attack by Fairey Swordfish from the carrier HMS *Hermes*, and by gunfire from the cruiser HMS *Shropshire*. In an effort to forestall capture, the steamship *Pensilvania* left Kismayu harbour, but was attacked by the cruiser and damaged, beaching herself to allow at least a proportion of her cargo of fuel, which it had been intended she would carry to the Red Sea ports, to be salved. A Walrus was catapulted from *Shropshire* and this attacked Brava with little effect, but Italian bombers launched a return attack, claiming a near miss on one ship.

Friday, 14 February 1941
Following the initial Imperial successes on the Kenya/Somaliland frontier,

Vincent I KU-4, K6354, of 430 Flight en route to Kassala. *(F. Paget via A.S. Thomas)*

elements of the 22nd East African Brigade moved into the port of Kismayu on 14 February 1941; they found the town undefended due to the large number of civilians present. At the same time the 1st South African Brigade advanced on Gobwen. As this move started, six Junkers Ju 86s of 12 SAAF Squadron bombed the defences and partially sunk another pontoon bridge over the Juba, while Battles pounded motor transport on the Jelib–Bardera road; one Battle was badly hit by AA and force-landed at Beles Gugani. Eight Hartbeestes of 41 SAAF Squadron patrolled overhead, providing such assistance as the South African infantry required.

Over Eritrea operations continued, Italian ground forces claiming to have shot down an RAF Vincent of 430 Flight. As night fell three Wellesleys of 223 Squadron left to attack the Caproni workshops at Mai Edaga, Flg Off Willing's aircraft (K7788) being shot down by AA.

Saturday, 15 February 1941

The next morning a Wellesley of 47 Squadron reconnoitred Mai Edaga to observe the result of the previous night's attack, but three Fiat CR 42s were seen climbing up, one of which attacked the bomber. Three 1 SAAF Squadron Hurricanes were patrolling over the Gura area in support of the Wellesley, and spotted the CR 42s flying towards Massawa, attacking and driving them away from the bomber. One was claimed shot down by Capt Boyle, who saw this crash and the pilot crawl out and limp away. Capt Driver then led a sweep over Asmara by four Hurricanes and two Gladiators to prepare the way for a big Wellesley attack the next day. Six CR 42s were seen in pairs and Driver forced down the leading aircraft, seeing it crash-land at high speed on the airfield.

General Cunningham's successful troops in the south were preparing to continue their advance now that the port of Kismayu was available.

During the preceding night Italian bombers had raided forces approaching Jelib, but one Caproni Ca 133 was badly damaged by AA fire. With daylight

Wellesley L2673 of 47 Squadron, RAF, at Belaiya, Ethiopia, 11 February 1941. In the centre group are (l. to r.) Capt Dodds-Parker who was flown in (by Plt Off Collis) and Col Sandford and Major Orde Wingate who were lifted out. *(via C.C.H. Cole)*

another of these bombers was hit by the guns and had to force-land in Italian territory. Nine Ju 86s bombed and strafed Italian troops at Jelib, while the cruiser HMS *Shropshire* was escorted by Hurricanes to the area of Brava, shelling Modun where the headquarters of the Army of the Juba were situated. The gunfire was directed by a Maryland flown by Capt Davies, who was subsequently to receive a DFC for these operations; he also indulged in another of his general strafing attacks. Savoia S 79s raided South African troops near Jelib, but were intercepted by a Hurricane of 3 SAAF Squadron flown by Lt Glover, who attacked and badly damaged two of the three bombers involved. The Savoias returned with one dead and two wounded aboard.

Sunday, 16 to Tuesday, 18 February 1941

With all the bridges across the Juba damaged or destroyed, General Cunningham was now seeking a suitable crossing place for his forces, and on 16 February he was flown in a 41 SAAF Squadron Hartbeeste from Gobwen on a reconnaissance up the river. Meanwhile, however, Brigadier Dan Pienaar of the 1st South African Brigade discovered a good point for such an operation at Yonte, and three 12 SAAF Squadron Ju 86s were at once despatched to blast the opposite bank, while six Battles dive-bombed Jelib as a diversion. At dusk the crossing was made, and next morning the South Africans were ensconced on the eastern bank, beating off an Italian counter-attack which developed at dawn, inflicting heavy casualties. The South Africans then moved south to take Jumbo from the rear. Battles meanwhile raided the airfield at Iscia Baidoa, between Mogadishu and Lugh Ferrandi.

To the north-west of these operations, an Italian force had left Yavello on the 16th to reinforce Mega, but a South African force from El Gumu intercepted the column north of the fortress, and after a brief but sharp engagement it withdrew. On 17 February the attack on Mega began, Hartbeestes of 40 SAAF Squadron providing support as best they could in conditions of heavy cloud, but by the early afternoon of the 18th the garrison had surrendered. In support of the attack six Battles had flown north to bomb Yavello during the day.

Over Eritrea on 16 February Hurricanes of 1 SAAF Squadron escorted fifteen Wellesleys of 47 and 223 Squadrons to attack Gura airfield, the fighters also strafing, and claiming to have set two S 79s on fire. Next day in the Mescenti area an S 81 engaged a 430 Flight Vincent and claimed to have shot it down; absence of records for this unit prevent definite confirmation. Early in the morning of the 18th two 203 Squadron Blenheim IVFs from Aden strafed Makale airfield, one S 79 being claimed set on fire and two others hit. Sottoten Veronese of the 410ᵃ Squadriglia in a CR 32 attacked and shot down Blenheim T2053, flown by Sqn Ldr A.L.H. Solano, the aircraft force-landing in the Piana del Sale with two of the crew dead. Veronese chased the other Blenheim, T9173, flown by Sqn Ldr Scott, out to sea and fired at it without apparent effect. It was badly damaged, however, and crash-landed on its return to Aden.

On 17 February the Duke of Aosta again reported to Rome on the condition of the Regia Aeronautica. From 17 January to 16 February, he stated, 22 enemy aircraft had been claimed definitely shot down, with eight more probables and 18 destroyed on the ground — a total of 48. In the same period 53 Italian aircraft had been destroyed and 23 damaged, equivalent to three-quarters of the first-line strength. Among the personnel, 33 had been killed in this period, including ten officers, 46 had been wounded, again including ten officers, and 16 were missing, bringing the total casualties since the outbreak of war to 110 dead, 182 wounded and 161 missing — a total of 453 out of a strength of 1,926 aircrew, almost equivalent to 25% of the force.

Wednesday, 19 February 1941

Italian bombers made a number of raids on the Northern Front on the 19th, attacking Tessenei and Agordat airfields, and troops at the front. Generale Pinna had now advised the withdrawal of all aircraft from Eritrean airfields to Ethiopia, where they would be beyond the range of fighter strafing. 1 SAAF Squadron now escorted ten Wellesleys to Asmara, where a considerable number of Italian aircraft were seen on the ground about to depart for the south, and these were attacked. Hurricane pilots strafed and claimed to have burned two CR 42s, three S 79s and two Ca 133s; aircraft actually destroyed were one CR 42, one S 79 and two Ca 133s. On a later operation of a similar nature, a further claim for a CR 42 was submitted.

On the Juba meanwhile, the 11th African Division was now also getting across the river at Makungo, covered by Hurricanes of 3 SAAF Squadron, while Hartbeestes of 41 SAAF Squadron flew reconnaissances over the Jelib–Bardera road in support of this move.

Thursday, 20 February 1941

Next day Jumbo was taken, and Ju 86s of 12 SAAF Squadron for the first time used Gobwen as an advanced base. The intrepid Capt Davies of this squadron's Maryland detachment again flew over Mogadishu and Brava, this time on a photographic sortie. He once more went down to strafe on completion of his primary mission, but was attacked by a CR 42, again flown by the recently promoted Capitano Romano Palmera, CO of the 110ᵃ Squadriglia, who had intercepted the Maryland on a previous occasion. This time Davies escaped with five explosive bullets in the starboard wing of his aircraft.

Three Hurricanes of 1 SAAF Squadron, over northern Eritrea. *(SAAF)*

At midday in the north, four Hurricanes of 1 SAAF Squadron attacked airfields at Massawa, Decamere and Adi Ugri, claiming four CR 42s and a Ca 133 hit. This time the pilots had underestimated, four CR 42s, two Ca 133s and two S 81s being damaged, and ten tons of fuel burnt.

Friday, 21 February 1941

Air reconnaissance had reported new CR 42s being assembled at Massawa after delivery by transport aircraft, and at 0800 on 21 February Maj Wilmot and six other 1 SAAF Squadron pilots left Agordat in Hurricanes, refuelling en route at a forward landing strip, and attacking the airfield at midday. A small number of aircraft was seen outside the hangars, but the number inside was not known, so all six hangars were attacked, the pilots approaching at zero feet and firing directly into them; all were left in flames, the roof of one being blown right off. Six Ca 133s and a CR 42 were strafed in the open, and claimed in flames, while Lt Pare wiped out an anti-aircraft gun position and crew. In fact, three Ca 133s and two S 81s, all of which had been damaged the previous day, were destroyed, and one more of each was damaged. Lt J.J. Coetzer was shot down by AA fire, his Hurricane crashing in flames. Seven Albacores from HMS *Formidable* also attacked Massawa, bombing the harbour in shallow dives; four were hit by AA but all returned safely.

While the Hurricane attack was under way, six Blenheim Is from 8 Squadron and six Blenheim IVFs from 203 Squadron flew from Aden to bomb Diredawa's Chinele airfield in Ethiopia. The 8 Squadron aircraft found it difficult to keep formation with the Mark IVFs due to the latter's poor climb rate. Over the target the attack became broken up in cloud, and the bombs hit the town instead, destroying the post office and the office of public information. Italian bombers raided British positions near Keren, two S 79s being hit by AA and both force-landing, one being destroyed.

Saturday, 22 February 1941

On the Juba Front the 1st South African Brigade was now engaged in fighting at Margherita, while over Jelib Italian fighters claimed to have shot down a Hurricane from which the pilot baled out. On 22 February Jelib was taken by troops supported by 41 SAAF Squadron Hartbeestes, and the airfield there was quickly put into use. The Hartbeestes then began a series of attacks on enemy forces retreating from the area. They were joined in this task during the afternoon by three Battles of 11 SAAF Squadron, which bombed vehicles on the Lamma Garas–Duduma road, destroying eight. As the bombers turned for home one was attacked and shot down by Capt Palmera of the 110ª Squadriglia; the pilot, Lt B.S.M. Hamilton, was killed, but the gunner, Flt Sgt J.W. Dixon, managed to bale out. He was taken prisoner and an Italian officer ordered a native NCO to escort him to headquarters. On the way Dixon apparently boasted of having taken part in recent raids on Mogadishu, where a lot of locals had been killed. His guard of locally recruited colonial troops at once sentenced him to death and shot him. Ironically, the raid which had caused the casualties had been carried out by Royal Navy Albacores, and not by the South African Battles. Subsequently the Italian officer mentioned above was captured by Imperial forces, and was put on trial, accused of responsibility for Dixon's death.

'K' Flight saw its first action since its return to operations on this date. Flt Lt Scoular on an early patrol over Mersa Taclai in Gladiator N5828 saw some Blenheims passing and escorted these to Massawa. There he spotted a lone S 79 in flight, and shot it down; there is no Italian record of this loss and it may in fact have been one of the transport Savoias.

Sunday, 23 February 1941

On 23 February seven Hurricanes of 1 SAAF Squadron flew forward to Tole where they refuelled. In the afternoon three took off to strafe Makale landing ground, while the other four, which were to provide top cover, also escorted a Wellesley which was to attack the same target. The bomber became lost, but Maj Wilmot, leading the lower section of three Hurricanes, saw dust rising over to his left, and heading for this, arrived over Makale where the fighters at once began shooting up the airfield. They set fire to a CR 32 which was on the ground with its pilot Sottoten Folcherio of the 410ª Squadriglia in the cockpit, about to take off. He leapt out under fire and managed to reach a trench. Without their top cover the Hurricanes were vulnerable to surprise attack, and at that moment another CR 32, with Sottoten Veronese at the controls, appeared overhead and dived on Wilmot's aircraft, shooting it down. Lt Duncan was on the Fiat like a flash and shot it down in flames, the pilot baling out slightly wounded; Wilmot had in the meantime carried out a crash-landing, and became a prisoner. Capt Driver, leading the four top-cover Hurricanes, now saw smoke rising, and dived down to join in the strafing, five S 79s being set on fire.

Alberto Veronese's wounds prevented him taking any further part in the fighting; up to this time he had been the most successful pilot in the 410ª Squadriglia, and of the CR 32 in East Africa, with his four individual and two shared victories. He was evacuated home to Italy by air, via Arabia, and later served with the Italian Co-Belligerent Air Force, on the Allied side. He was to be killed on 4 November 1944 when his Spitfire V was shot down by ground fire during a strafing attack on a column of German artillery in Greece.

In the south the few CR 42s of the 110ª Squadriglia again put in an appearance, Capt Palmera and Sottoten Malavolti attacking a Hartbeeste of 41 SAAF Squadron between Jelib and Merca, and engaging it in a seven-minute battle. Sgt McWilliam, the gunner, stood in his cockpit returning fire and claimed to have hit the first attacker with a long burst, seeing a trail of grey smoke from the cockpit area as it left the combat. The second pressed home its attack, but overshot on its second pass, Lt Shuttleworth, the pilot, pulling up the nose and firing a long burst at it with the front guns. Both fighters then broke off, returning to base; neither had in fact been damaged, and Palmera claimed the Hartbeeste as a probable. In fact the damaged biplane managed to return to Jelib.

Another Hartbeeste, this time from 40 SAAF Squadron, and flown by Capt C.P. Kotze on the north Kenyan front, made a reconnaissance over Moyale on this date as the 1st South African Division was now moving south from Mega to attack this post. It was seen by Kotze to have been evacuated however, and this brought an end to operations in this zone. The successes at Kismayu and on the Juba River made further operations in the area unnecessary now that the Italians had been driven well back into southern Ethiopia, thus securing Cunningham's left flank against sudden attack. The 1st South African Division would now go into reserve.

Monday, 24 to Friday, 28 February 1941
In Italian Somaliland the advance was gaining momentum now that the Juba, the only real defensible position in the area, had been crossed. Against only slight resistance, the 22nd East African Brigade entered Modun on 24 February, finding it deserted; Brava was also taken on this date. The Italians now declared Mogadishu, the capital, an open town, and the Imperial forces pressed on, taking Merca on the 25th and entering the city that same evening, the garrison surrendering next day.

The capture of this major port opened up new possibilities and the SAAF began moving up. On 24 February 12 SAAF Squadron had moved to Gobwen, but next day it flew on to Margherita. Now the Advanced Air Headquarters, which had only recently moved up to Kismayu, arrived at Mogadishu, and on the same day (27 February) 41 SAAF Squadron landed at the airfield there, where eleven Ca 133s and ten other types were found destroyed. A demonstration of strength was then made with a flight over the city by SAAF Ju 86s, Battles, Hurricanes, Hartbeestes and Furies. By this time the Army of the Juba had been overrun; the 102nd Colonial Infantry Division had been totally destroyed, and the 101st largely so. While the victorious 11th African Division consolidated around the city and prepared to swing its advance northwards towards Harar, the 12th African Division pressed north-west up the Juba, swiftly capturing Bardera, Iscia Baidoa, Lugh Ferrandi and Dolo. It was only necessary for a token force to remain in Italian Somaliland to press on to clear up the small garrisons in the eastern half of that country.

In the north raids had continued over the Keren front, and on 24 February three Blenheims of 203 Squadron attacked Addis Ababa airfield. On the 26th Plt Off Wells, a Gladiator pilot of the 'K' Flight detachment at Mersa Taclai, had been patrolling over Kub-Kub in N5815, when army personnel on the ground drew his attention to two CR 32s above him, and apparently oblivious of his presence. Climbing beneath them, he attacked one and shot it down over Keren in full view of the troops. Also that day Capt A. Duncan of 1 SAAF Squadron (newly promoted) made an offensive reconnaissance on his own over Zula airfield. There he saw a Savoia S 82 which had just arrived from Italy, and attacked this, setting it ablaze. He also fired on a hangar close by, and this blew up violently. On the last day of the month two Wellesleys of 47 Squadron, using Sennar as an advanced landing ground, raided Burye: there Flt Sgt Wimsett's bomber (K7765) was shot down by AA, the crew surviving and being taken prisoner. Other bombers attacked Ellaberet railway station near Asmara, damaging it and causing considerable casualties amongst the native population.

Saturday, 1 March 1941
From Mogadishu a mobile column of Nigerian troops from the 11th African Division left on 1 March to press on north-eastwards up the Strada Imperiale towards the Ethiopian border, and Harar. In six days they would cover a fantastic 354 miles, one of the longest, fastest advances in history, and a true indication of the completeness of the victory on the Juba. 2 Bomber Wing moved to Mogadishu, together with 12 SAAF Squadron and part of 3 SAAF Squadron; 11 SAAF Squadron moved to Vittorio d'Africa.

Massawa, on the Red Sea coast, was again attacked by five Albacores from *Formidable*, this time operating from the landing ground at Mersa Taclai in Eritrea; no results of the bombing were recorded. A lone Blenheim IVF of 203 Squadron from Aden flew a reconnaissance along the Alomata–Dessie road, and over landing grounds at Mille and Sarda. On a strip near Alomata two Ca 133s were seen, and these were both strafed and destroyed in flames. On this date 430 Flight was renumbered 1430 Flight; this was occasioned by the decision in England to number all Commonwealth squadrons serving with the RAF in the '400' series. 1 SAAF Squadron had by now become fully equipped with Hurricanes, and the unit's remaining Gladiators were handed to 'B' Flight of 237 Squadron for army co-operation duties.

Attrition during February had virtually halved the Regia Aeronautica's operational strength in East Africa, which was now down to 42 aircraft, despite deliveries of CR 42s from Italy and repaired machines from the workshops.

By the start of March 1941, 1 SAAF Squadron was fully equipped with Hurricane Is, and had moved flights up to forward landing grounds close behind the front. One of these aircraft is seen on such an airfield, with its pilot preparing for a sortie. *(IWM)*

Tuesday, 4 March 1941

In central Ethiopia, Maj Orde Wingate's 'Gideon' Force, which was accompanying Haile Selassie and his patriots, captured the fort at Burye on 4 March, the garrison withdrawing. In Somaliland that day Hurricanes and Ju 86s landed to refuel on the newly captured airfield at Belet Uen, then flew on to raid Gabredarre airfield. This was found to be deserted, with white flags much in evidence.

Wednesday, 5 to Saturday, 8 March 1941

On 5 March Lt J. van der Merwe of 1 SAAF Squadron made an early reconnaissance over the Massawa–Demke area, where he strafed a train. Returning to the area later in the morning while escorting a Wellesley on a photographic sortie over Keren, he spotted the train still stationary at the same spot, and attacked it again. Returning a third time in the afternoon, he escorted three Wellesleys to Asmara, and watched two of these bomb this same train, following them down for a third and final strafe himself.

Next day a 12 SAAF Squadron Maryland flew from Mogadishu to reconnoitre as far north as Harar, finding the Italian forces evacuating as far back as the Harar–Jijiga line; heavy AA was encountered over Harar. Activity by the RAF and SAAF in the Keren area was intense during this period in support of the ground forces. On 7 March fighters strafed the Italian airfields at Zula and Makale, defending AA claiming to have hit one over the latter base. On this date Italian bombers attacked 'Gideon' Force at Dembeccia and Burye, but one S 79 was hit by ground fire and had to force-land.

The three Marylands of the detachment with 12 SAAF Squadron, which were now at Mogadishu, were undertaking reconnaissance missions up to 700 miles from this base, and on 8 March Capt Davies flew as far north as Awash, where he photographed a bridge over a gorge. Measurements of the bridge from the photo allowed a Bailey bridge to be built in advance, which would later be laid across the gorge after the Italians had blown down the permanent structure. Six Battles of 11 SAAF Squadron refuelled at Belet Uen on this date and flew to attack concentrations of troops at Harar; due to heavy cloud only four aircraft found the target, which they dive-bombed. From Moyale 40 SAAF Squadron now began moving back to Wajir, ready for service elsewhere.

Sunday, 9 March 1941

Six Blenheims of 8 Squadron from Aden bombed Diredawa early on 9 March, six CR 42s and a single monoplane being reported seen on the ground, although in fact only two or three fighters were actually present; the monoplane was an S 81, already damaged beyond repair, but retained as a decoy. Three CR 32s of the 410ª Squadriglia approached the bombers head on, and the leader, Capt Ricci, turned sharply to attack the right-hand Blenheim. This manoeuvred to evade him and Ricci found himself formating closely with the leading aircraft, L8504 piloted by Sqn Ldr Hanlon. The turret gunner opened fire on him and incendiary bullets struck the wings of his Fiat. Bouncing around in the bomber's slipstream, Ricci opened fire as it began to pull away from him, and saw his bullets exploding on the rear of the right-hand engine nacelle. Thinking he had damaged it badly, he then attacked another Blenheim and fought with it for minutes before his guns jammed and he had to land. He was credited with the bomber as probably destroyed, and two more were claimed damaged during the fight. Sqn Ldr Hanlon had to force-land on Perim Island during the homeward flight as a result of the damage sustained.

Little damage had been done to the airfield, but the native quarter was hit and 20 of the inhabitants killed. For Ricci it was a particularly memorable combat as his aircraft had at last been fitted with a radio receiver that he had been requesting for months, and as a result of guidance given from the ground, he was able to intercept the bombers and attack them before they had dropped their bombs. Another raid by Sudan-based aircraft on Gondar was more successful, nine drums of petroleum being burned.

Tuesday, 11 to Wednesday, 12 March 1941

The Italians despatched aircraft on reconnaissance to discover the latest position of the 11th African Division's columns, an S 79 bombing one of these at Gabredarre. The bomber was hit by AA, and an army observer who was aboard was badly wounded in the stomach, dying later. To provide cover against any more attacks of this nature 'B' Flight of 3 SAAF Squadron was moved up to Gorrahai, a few miles south of Gabredarre. Next day, however, Dogabur was taken, and 41 SAAF Squadron Hartbeestes at once flew up to this new location, reporting the airfield there to be suitable for use by Hurricanes. On receiving this news, 'B' Flight, 3 SAAF Squadron followed the Hartbeestes to this base on the 12th; they were now very close to the major Italian airfields at Jijiga and Diredawa.

Meanwhile in Eritrea 237 Squadron had moved up to Barentu, and 203 Group was about to receive some small reinforcements. Far away at Fort Lamy the Free French bomber flight, GRB 1, was ordered to send all its serviceable Blenheim IVs and their crews to the Sudan, and three were at once prepared for despatch. On 11 March three Hurricanes of 1 SAAF Squadron attacked Keren airfield, Capt Driver and Lt Hewitson burning a lone S 79 on the ground and then strafing an unidentified small biplane, before Capt Boyle joined them for a general strafe. On the 12th Asmara and Gura were attacked, one S 81 being slightly damaged and an AA position at Massawa also being strafed. On each of these attacks one Hurricane suffered slight damage to AA fire.

Thursday, 13 March 1941

During the morning of 13 March two S 79s which had been sent to attack vehicles in the Dogabur area, passed over the airfield there at 6,000 feet. Before these bombers reached the area, Lt Venter of 3 SAAF Squadron had taken off to escort a Hartbeeste of 41 SAAF Squadron on the first incursion over Jijiga from the new airfield. Over the target he lost his charge in heavy cloud, became lost himself, and ran out of fuel, force-landing 50 miles east of Dogabur. He paid two Somalis who came on the scene to carry a message to the base, and these met a South African armoured car almost at once, and passed the information to the crew, who radioed Dogabur. Here Lt L.R. Dudley had already been despatched to search for Venter, but at once encountered the S 79s, engaging them for nearly 15 minutes before he was joined by Capt S. van Breda Theron, who had scrambled when the Italian aircraft appeared overhead. Dudley found that the Savoias used cloud cover to evade his attacks, and he had swiftly used up all his ammunition, managing only to claim damage to one.

Theron, meanwhile, pursued the bombers for over 100 miles, but also lost his target in cloud. However, he saw a fire on the ground and was subsequently

Capitano Romano Palmera, CO of the 110ª Squadriglia, began flying Fiat CR 42 fighters, with which his unit was partially re-equipped (primarily an observation squadron with Ro 37s), in February 1941. He achieved several successes but on 13 March was shot down and became a PoW. *(Generale Palmera via Corrado Ricci)*

credited with having shot one bomber down. In fact, the badly damaged S 79, flown by Ten Lattarulo, managed to reach Diredawa and land with one of the crew dead and three wounded. Although in a bad state, the aircraft was repairable.

That afternoon, with news in of Venter's whereabouts, Theron took off again to look for him. Spotting Venter's aircraft, he landed alongside, and siphoned off some of the fuel in his own tanks into the stranded Hurricane.

Taking off together, they flew back to the airfield, but as they approached they saw Lt Dudley taking off and being attacked by two CR 42s, his Hurricane crashing and bursting into flames. He had been shot down by Capt Palmera of the 110ª Squadriglia who with his wingman, Serg Magg Tominello of the 413ª Squadriglia, now went on to try to shoot up six Hartbeestes on the airfield. At the approach of the other two Hurricanes, both Fiats tried to climb away, but Theron pulled up behind one which had entered a loop, and shot down Tominello's CR 42, which crashed straight into the ground in flames from 1,000 feet. Venter then shot down Palmera's aircraft, also in flames, the pilot baling out. He was picked up by troops of the 11th African Division and handed over to the pilots of the two squadrons at Dogabur, who entertained him in their mess for the rest of the day before he was evacuated to Mogadishu. Recently promoted Capitano, and despite his late start on CR 42s, Palmera was already on his way to being one of the more successful Italian fighter pilots in East Africa when this combat cut short his operational career.

The detachments at Dogabur were now to be reinforced, for 'C' Flight of 3 SAAF Squadron which was still back at Mombasa, was now ordered forward to undertake offensive operations over Diredawa.

An Italian AF Caproni Ca 133 which force-landed in British-held territory in Eritrea. After repairs it was flown to the Sudan by an RAF pilot. *(Imperial War Museum)*

Chapter Four

THE BATTLE FOR KEREN; ERITREA SECURED
AND ADDIS ABABA TAKEN

Saturday, 15 March 1941

In Eritrea unsuccessful attempts had been made in early February 1941 to breach the extraordinarily strong defences of the natural fortress which the Italians had established at Keren. British and Indian forces had subsequently been built up for a new attack, while in the interim the pressure was maintained on the defenders both in the air and on the ground. Now on 15 March the attackers, numerically inferior to the defenders, but well-equipped, well-trained, with high morale and air superiority, launched the final all-out attack on one of the toughest natural fortresses to be assaulted in any country throughout the course of World War II. The attack began at 0700, bombers of 14, 47 and 223 Squadrons, RAF, keeping up a shuttle service to drop 38,800lb of bombs on the defences during the day.

Side gun position in a Wellesley. This rather cramped position did not offer a particularly wide field of fire. *(IWM)*

Sgt Turner, DFM, of 47 Squadron in the upper gun position of a Wellesley, displays his wounds, received whilst fighting off Italian fighters during a raid on the Keren area, in which the aircraft was badly damaged. *(IWM)*

In the south the newly arrived Hurricanes of 3 SAAF Squadron launched their own assault on Diredawa. During the night Blenheims of 8 Squadron from Aden bombed the airfields there, and in the morning six fighters from Dogabur approached the main airfield at the same time as Junkers Ju 86s of 12 SAAF Squadron arrived to bomb. There the Hurricane pilots found three Fiat CR 32s of the 410ᵃ Squadriglia in the air, the South Africans identifying these as two CR 32s and a CR 42. One of the CR 32 pilots, Serg Magg Giardina, had just begun an attack on a Ju 86 when he suddenly spotted a Hurricane approaching to attack him, and a dogfight began. Sottoten Bartolozzi rushed to Giardina's aid without checking his own tail, next moment hearing an explosion and being hit in the face and neck by splinters. He immediately broke away and began turning with his attacker, avoiding two more bursts of fire; he landed with 188 holes in his aircraft, but no serious damage. Bartolozzi, normally a CR 42 pilot, had just landed at Diredawa before the raid because his aircraft was in need of repair. At the outset of the attack he had taken off again in one of the 410ᵃ Squadriglia's CR 32s. Giardina meanwhile fought on for several minutes, returning fire, and at last the Hurricane left; he was then able to land, his aircraft also exhibiting a few holes in the fabric. The third CR 32 escaped undamaged. In this combat the South Africans considerably overestimated the results of their fire against the nimble Fiats, Capts Theron and Frost each claiming a CR 32 shot down, while Lts Morley and Venter claimed a shared CR 42.

With the opposition in the air disposed of, the Hurricanes strafed, and the following claims against aircraft on the ground were made: Capt Frost — one S79 in flames and one damaged, one CR 32 or Romeo damaged; Capt Theron — one S 79 in flames, one CR 32 or Romeo in flames; Capt Harvey — one CR 32 or Romeo in flames; all pilots together — three CR 32s or Romeos damaged. One fighter and two Ro 37bis aircraft were actually damaged.

Returning to Dogabur to refuel, the Hurricanes attacked again in the afternoon, but this time a single machine gun post manned by an engineer of the 410ᵃ Squadriglia named Coppoli, opened up with accurate fire, and Capt Nöel

Harvey's aircraft was hit when in a low dive, bursting into flames and crashing into a building. Capt Theron and Lt Morley claimed to have set two more S 79s on fire and damaged a third. Capt Frost claimed to have damaged a CR 32, but his Hurricane was hit and he force-landed on the satellite strip K92; Lt R. Kershaw covered him as he went down and then landed alongside. Frost attempted to set fire to his aircraft by firing his Very pistol at it and then climbed in behind Kershaw, who taxied to the end of the runway. There Frost sat on Kershaw's knees, took over the controls and flew back to base. Capt Theron's

Above: Frost's Hurricane, 'W' of 3 SAAF Squadron, after it had force-landed on the satellite airfield at Diredawa. Note Squadron badge on nose. *(Corrado Ricci). Below:* Lt R.H. Kershaw (left) wearing the medal ribbon of the DSO which was awarded for his exploits of 15 March 1941, when he rescued Capt J.E. Frost (right) from an Italian satellite airstrip. *(SAAF)*

Flight reported strafing Frost's Hurricane and claimed to have destroyed it, but in fact it survived this attack as it had Frost's hasty attempt to burn it, and was later inspected by the Italians. The aircraft seemed to possess a charmed life, for when Diredawa was being evacuated Capt Ricci was ordered to strafe and destroy it. He made three firing passes in his CR 32, but finally gave up in disgust and landed; he then ordered a native NCO to dowse it with petrol and set fire to it.

Kershaw was recommended for the VC for his action, but in the event the award of a DSO was made, the first to a pilot in East Africa. During the two attacks the South Africans had claimed a total of nine aircraft destroyed on the ground; actual losses were one S 79 and four Ca 133s destroyed, with two more S 79s, three Ca 133s, two Ro 37bis and a CR 42 damaged. That night 8 Squadron returned to attack again, an S 81 under repair being damaged.

Sunday, 16 March 1941

With the advance into southern Ethiopia now going well, a force had been organised in Aden under the command of Air Vice-Marshal Reid, and this now sailed into Berbera harbour on 16 March in the face of only light opposition, going ashore in British Somaliland. Colonial troops of the garrison were already withdrawing from the country to avoid being cut off by the 11th African Division's swift advance from Mogadishu, but in the event the Imperial forces were to reach Jijiga first, and many of the Italian units were cut off and captured.

At Keren action in the air erupted again on the 16th, and during the day 40 Wellesley, 15 Blenheim, 9 Gladiator, 11 Hardy and 12 Lysander sorties were flown. All available Italian aircraft (three S 79s, two Ca 133s and twelve CR 42s) were brought forward to Dessie to take part in the critical battle, the rest — a handful of bombers and CR 32s — being retained in Ethiopia to face Cunningham's forces.

During one of the raids over Keren, Wellesleys of 47 Squadron were attacked by five CR 42s, which shot down K8527 flown by Plt Off Leuchars, only one of the crew being seen to bale out. At the time Plt Off P.H.S. Simmonds of 237 Squadron was dive-bombing the north-east slopes of Mount Sanchil in Gladiator N5789, and he was also attacked by a CR 42, which damaged his aircraft. He turned on the Fiat and shot it down, the aircraft crashing and bursting into flames.

Monday, 17 March 1941

The continual attacks by 203 Group on the Keren defences were causing grave losses to the Italian colonial units, and were having a bad effect on their morale, many desertions occurring. On 17 March four Hurricanes of 1 SAAF Squadron were led on an offensive reconnaissance by their new CO, Maj Ross Theron, during which Capt Driver shot up some lorries and Lt Pare destroyed an S 82 on the ground at Danuba, also destroying some 30 drums of petroleum.

During the day the Italians lost one of their precious remaining S 79s in a take-off accident, while in the Sudan the first Free French Blenheim arrived at Gordon's Tree where it was attached to 47 Squadron. In Ethiopia Nigerian troops reached the plain of Jijiga 774 miles from Mogadishu, finding the hamlet empty. In the south elements of the 12th African Division moving up the Juba River had crossed the border into this sector of southern Ethiopia and were now moving on Neghelli. 12 SAAF Squadron moved forward to Gorrahai for

Free French Blenheim IV Z9583 of GRB 1, which was attached to 47 Squadron in the Sudan. *(E.C. des Armées)*

operations over the Marda Pass, three Ju 86s attacking a road block on the road from Jijiga. 11 SAAF Squadron also moved forward, going to Belet Uen, although two Battles were left at Mogadishu for the defence of the port; Advanced Air Headquarters joined the Ju 86s at Gorrahai.

Tuesday, 18 March 1941
Next day 12 SAAF Squadron sent out the Ju 86s to attack the Marda Pass road block again and also to strafe vehicles on the Harar road. 40 SAAF Squadron left Wajir for Ndege's Nest, where it awaited a new assignment.

In Eritrea that day five CR 42s of the 412ª Squadriglia appeared over Agordat at dawn to strafe the aircraft on the ground. They reported seven Hurricanes and a Wellesley present, and saw five fires after their attack. Wellesley K7786 of 47 Squadron was destroyed and two Hurricanes of 1 SAAF Squadron were hit — one badly. Twenty minutes later two S 79s came over and bombed, one Hurricane being burned. One of the CR 42s had been hit by ground fire, but was repaired the next day.

During the day four CR 42s 'bounced' the Gladiators of 'K' Flight over Keren, claiming four badly damaged, two of them probably shot down. All the Gladiators returned to base. In the afternoon two of 237 Squadron's Hardys were out over Keren, Plt Off Storey observing the other aircraft flown by Flt Lt N.S.F. Tyas with Sgt Horobin as gunner, involved in a battle between Wellesleys and CR 42s; the latter shot down Tyas's Hardy, both members of the crew being killed.

Wednesday, 19 to Thursday, 20 March 1941
On 19 or 20 March more strafing in the Keren area followed heavy fighting on Dologorodoc mountain, where an Italian counter-attack was launched. While two 1 SAAF Squadron Hurricanes were patrolling over the area they were

attacked by three 412ᵃ Squadriglia CR 42s, Mar Soffritti claiming to have shot down one of the South African fighters; Capt Boyle's aircraft was damaged but he returned safely to base.

In Ethiopia the SAAF now took a calculated risk, moving its bomber squadrons forward to the newly captured Jijiga airfields, which were in a rather rough state. AAHQ stipulated that only communications aircraft be left on the main airfield, all Battles and Ju 86s being dispersed well away from the runways, as the area was within range of all Italian aircraft at Diredawa, Addis Ababa, and other smaller fields.

Next morning three Ju 86s escorted by a single Hurricane dive-bombed enemy troops concentrated on the Harar–Diredawa road, and also bombed two trains. Over Diredawa itself violent AA was met and two CR 32s attacked one of the bombers at 2,000 feet as it came out of its dive. Capt Theron in the Hurricane at 10,000 feet spotted them and dived to attack, catching one Fiat at the top of a stall turn, but it suffered nothing worse than a few holes in the fabric.

Other bombers of the SAAF meanwhile began a series of attacks on the railway system.

The forces which had landed at Berbera from Aden had at first been covered by Blenheim IVFs of 203 Squadron, but now one of these led four Gladiators of 94 Squadron over to Berbera, from where they were to begin operations. Sqn Ldr Wightman, 94's CO, was promoted Wg Cdr but at his own request he remained with the unit.

Friday, 21 March 1941
At 0515 on 21 March three 1 SAAF Squadron Hurricanes took off on an offensive reconnaissance, and 15 minutes later four more followed to patrol over Keren, while a Lysander of 237 Squadron set out on an artillery observation mission. The Lysander, R1988, flown by Flt Lt G.A. Smith, was attacked by

Keren, scene of the major battle of the East African Campaign, which began on 15 March 1941 and ended in victory for the British Empire forces on 27 March. *(Imperial War Museum)*

129

five CR 42s and damaged, the pilot being slightly wounded; the gunner, Sgt A.K. Murrell, DFM, claimed to have damaged one of the attackers in return. The four Hurricanes on patrol spotted four CR 42s in line astern and attacked. Capt Driver hit the third aircraft in line and saw it crash. Lt Pare meanwhile had chased the last fighter in the line, but it escaped. He then attacked the second, which crashed in flames, the pilot baling out. The leading Fiat then attacked him head on, and they became involved in a dogfight which ended with the CR 42 crashing four miles north of Keren and bursting into flames.

The Italians reported that two CR 42s were shot down, while a third fighter was damaged. This returned to Asmara, but while landing was strafed by Capt Duncan in one of the three Hurricanes that had taken off first. The Italian pilots claimed both Smith's Lysander and Driver's Hurricane shot down, also claiming a Wellesley during the day; two other Hurricanes were claimed hit and probably shot down. That evening Capt Duncan's DFC award was announced.

During the day all available bombers were put into the air by the Italians to attack the British at Dologorodoc, but ground-fire was heavy, two S 79s and two Ca 133s being hit and damaged. Other bombers were escorted by CR 32s to attack units of infantry and cavalry from 'Gideon' Force at Dembeccia, but here one S 81 was hit by ground-fire also. South African bombers attacked the railway at Diredawa, while six Blenheims from Aden bombed the airfield.

From Jijiga Hartbeestes of 41 SAAF Squadron operated over the Marda Pass, where Nigerian troops were engaged in fairly heavy fighting during the afternoon, but the defenders were seen to be withdrawing. Further to the west the 12th African Division now occupied Neghelli.

Saturday, 22 March 1941

Next day the Marda Pass was taken, and anti-aircraft guns were at once moved forward. Thirty minutes later two S 79s made a half-hearted attack, while in the afternoon three Italian fighters led by Sottoten Folcherio of the 410ᵃ Squadriglia strafed. 3 SAAF Squadron was then ordered to send Hurricanes to join the bombers at Jijiga, to cover convoys which were now moving through the pass towards Harar.

Early in the morning a Blenheim of 14 Squadron from the Sudan on reconnaissance saw a 'K' Flight Gladiator that had force-landed 30 miles south of Mersa Taclai, and landing alongside, picked up the pilot. A little later two Hurricanes of 1 SAAF Squadron escorted six Wellesleys and six Blenheims to Asmara, but south of the town three 412ᵃ Squadriglia CR 42s were seen, one of which at once disappeared. Lt L. le C. Theron attacked the leading fighter and his fire killed the pilot, the aircraft crashing in flames 20 miles south-east of the town. A second CR 42 was claimed by Lt J.B. White, also reportedly seen to crash. During the day 237 Squadron moved to Umritsar, and two CR 42s were despatched from Addis Ababa to Diredawa, to meet the growing threat from the SAAF units at Jijiga.

Sunday, 23 March 1941

At 0500 on 23 March Lts Pare and W.J.A. White of 1 SAAF Squadron began a patrol over Keren but became separated at 19,000 feet. Pare then saw six CR 42s at 22,000 feet and climbed after them. Overtaking, he made a frontal attack on one, which he believed was damaged, but was attacked by all the others which hit his aircraft; however, he managed to return to base.

In Ethiopia Italian bombers attacked vehicles in the bush near Jijiga, while Ju 86s bombed two ammunition trains which blew up. Two of the CR 42s which had just moved to Diredawa, joined by two CR 32s, flew to Jijiga to strafe aircraft on the ground; failing to see any, they returned to Addis Ababa. It was noted that the Italians were beginning to withdraw from Diredawa to Sire, Guma and Meta Mara.

Monday, 24 March 1941

3 SAAF Squadron was now at full strength at Jijiga, where at 1100 on 24 March two unidentified aircraft passed overhead, making for Diredawa. Capt Frost and Lt Venter were at once ordered off to follow, and at Diredawa they reported eight to ten aircraft on the ground. Both pilots made several strafing runs and claimed to have left two Savoias in flames. In fact, the only aircraft present were an S 81, already partially burnt out after many attacks, two S 79s in a hangar, which were not damaged, a CR 32 and a CR 42 hidden beneath acacia trees, and a burnt-out Ca 133.

It was on this date that the Aden force at Berbera suggested that the railway between the frontier of French Somaliland and Diredawa be attacked, to prevent the Italian 70th Colonial Division from Berbera escaping. At once Battles from Dogabur dive-bombed and destroyed several bridges on the Jibuti section of the line; ground fire was encountered, and Capt Britz's aircraft was hit 22 times. It was thought possible that the fire may have come from French troops across the frontier.

In the north the only Free French Blenheim of GRB 1 which had so far arrived in the Sudan made its first sortie to attack Debra Marcos. Over Asmara Italian fighters claimed one British fighter as a 'probable'.

Tuesday, 25 March 1941

The detachment of 47 Squadron Wellesleys at Agordat made sixteen sorties over the front on 25 March as the battle for Keren drew to a climax. One bomber, K7715, was attacked by two CR 42s and the air gunner, Sgt German, was mortally wounded; with the aircraft on fire, Plt Off Kennedy dived vertically, the slipstream blowing out the flames. He returned to base where he crashed on landing. Agordat had now become known as the 'Wellesley Burial Ground' as six bombers had already crashed here, and more would.

14 Squadron also attacked in the Keren area, three CR 42s intercepting two Blenheims and damaging both, though both got back with their crews unhurt. The Italians claimed one shot down by Mar Soffritti of the 412ª Squadriglia, and the other badly damaged. Gladiator N5853 of 237 Squadron was operating over Keren and the pilot saw two CR 42s, but was himself attacked by a Hurricane at that point, the biplane being damaged. 1 SAAF Squadron engaged CR 42s twice during the day, once in the morning when one was hit by Lt Irvine, but no result seen (possibly the 237 Squadron Gladiator). In the afternoon engagement Lts Pare and White met two Fiats at 15,000 feet, one of which Pare shot down in flames, but the other escaped from White. Pare went after this one also and caught it near Asmara where he reported that it blew up. The Italians recorded one CR 42 shot down and a second so damaged as to be a write-off. Two more CR 42s were damaged in combat during the day, and both pilots were wounded; two Hurricanes were claimed shot down. Three S 79s and three CR 42s bombed and strafed a strong column of vehicles near Babile on this date,

On 25 March Wellesley K7715 of 47 Squadron was hit by Italian fighters near Keren and set on fire. Plt Off Kennedy dived the aircraft to blow out the flames and crash-landed at Agordat, where he is seen inspecting the damage. *(Imperial War Museum)*

but intense AA was encountered and all aircraft were slightly damaged, one CR 42 force-landing.

In the south Capt Glynn Davies of the Maryland detachment with 12 SAAF Squadron set off from Jijiga to reconnoitre the roads and railways in the Harar, Barada and Diredawa areas, seeing two S 79s on the ground at the latter location, and meeting a third in the air. He gave chase, closing to 250 yards, but could not bring his guns to bear; the Italian pilot dived to increase speed, but crashed in a valley; the Italians did not record this loss.

Wednesday, 26 March 1941

The Nigerians were now approaching Harar, but the Italians were already preparing to withdraw, and the town was taken the next day. Italian fighters and bombers from Addis Ababa bombed vehicles approaching Harar during 26 March.

On that day six Ju 86s dive-bombed trains at Miesso, causing a series of violent explosions, but one bomber was hit in the tail by AA fire. As they returned to Jijiga, they were followed at a distance by three CR 42s led by Ten Meoli, intent upon strafing their base. As the Italians approached the area they saw communications aircraft on the main airfield, where three Ju 52/3ms were just coming in to land, carrying AAHQ personnel. Making an engineless glide out of the sun, the Fiats strafed the transports as they rolled to a halt. All three Ju 52s were badly damaged, as were a Rapide and a Vega Gull. Fighters from 3 SAAF Squadron were rapidly scrambled and chased off the attackers.

At Keren British troops cleared the final roadblock, and that night the bulk of the Italian troops and guns began withdrawing. During the attack the 4th and 5th Indian Divisions had suffered nearly 4,000 casualties; 3,000 men of the 4th

Junkers Ju 52/3m of 50 SAAF Squadron. On 26 March three of these transports were badly damaged by Italian fighters just after landing at Jijiga. *(SAAF)*

Division had scaled the near-vertical rock face of Mount Sanchil, but had failed to capture the ridge and peaks, which were defended with spirit by the Savoy Grenadiers. During this attack all but one officer in the 3/18 Gharwal Rifles had been killed or wounded, but Italian morale had finally been broken.

The last straw had been the arrival of British forces in a position overlooking one of the key defences, after they had found and made their way through a railway tunnel which the Italians had failed to demolish or guard. This incursion spelt the fall of the front, whatever the defenders then did. 1 SAAF Squadron flew several sorties over the area, during one of which Maj T.R. Theron claimed to have shot down a CR 42. Italian fighters claimed one Hurricane damaged, but two CR 42s were hit, both however returning to base.

From Neghelli in Galla Sidamo province, the 12th King's African Rifles had moved on to capture Yavello, and now 'B' and 'C' Flights of 40 SAAF Squadron flew up from Ndege's Nest to support these troops. On the main and satellite airfields the wreckage of sixteen Ca 133s and a CR 32 was discovered. The Hartbeestes went straight into action, attacking Soroppa where the Italian Carabinieri were resisting stubbornly. Two 250lb and eight 20lb bombs were dropped, and the defences were also strafed.

Thursday, 27 March 1941

Keren fell at last on 27 March 1941 with an estimated loss to the Italians of 40,000 prisoners and 300 guns. During an early patrol Hurricanes of 1 SAAF Squadron saw signs of withdrawal and a series of strafes were laid on, Vincents, Gladiators, Lysanders and Hardys from 237 Squadron, 'K' and 1430 Flights, joined by Hurricanes, attacking the retreating columns on the Keren–Asmara road again and again. One Vincent (Plt Off M.R.C. Dyer) was shot down and three Lysanders were attacked by three CR 42s, Flg Off Walmisley's aircraft being badly damaged and the gunner, Sgt Marshall, wounded. Lt W.J.A. White of 1 SAAF Squadron on one patrol saw three CR 42s chasing two Vincents and drove them off.

A Lockheed Lodestar transport of 267 Squadron lands at 'Fowl' airstrip, Keren, after the fall of the fortress, bringing General Wavell and Anthony Eden, the Foreign Secretary, for a victory inspection. *(F. Paget via A.S. Thomas)*

From Harar in Ethiopia the 11th African Division pressed on towards Diredawa during late March 1941. Their objective was now only 50 miles ahead, although Addis Ababa was still some 320 miles distant, however, the country through which the columns were now passing was very wild and mountainous. In many places the Italians had demolished bridges over gorges, or blown down sections of cliff face to block the road, and the speed of the advance slowed considerably. With so few aircraft remaining serviceable, the Italians now had a substantial surplus of Regia Aeronautica personnel, both air and ground crews, and these had been formed into infantry units to join the Army in the ground fighting. On 27 March the first Battaglione Azzurro (Blue Battalion) entered the line at Diredawa.

Friday, 28 March 1941

Two long-range reconnaissances were flown over the area of central Ethiopia on the 28th. An RAF Blenheim IVF of 203 Squadron from Aden, T2255 flown by Flg Off P. Moller, was sent off to the Awash–Adowa area, but failed to return. A 12 SAAF Squadron Maryland flew over the airfields at Adama, Addis Ababa, Jimma, Soddu and Shashamanna. One aircraft was reported shot down by the Italians as it was strafing columns near Awash, this hitting the ground and burning; it was almost certainly the Blenheim. The Maryland crew discovered a satellite airfield near Moggio, where they saw three large aircraft and three fighters, and these were strafed, hits being claimed on two of the former. Two CR 42s and a CR 32 then took off and attacked, the gunner in the Maryland's dorsal turret claiming to have damaged the CR 32, the other Fiats being easily outdistanced. The Maryland flew on to Jimma, where seven aircraft, including three or four bombers, were seen, and to Addis Ababa, where something over twenty bombers were counted. Despite another attack by fighters, the Maryland returned safely to Jijiga.

From this same base Lt N.J. Pretorius of 41 SAAF Squadron on a tactical reconnaissance discovered large columns evacuating Diredawa, and at once strafed. On return to base, Advanced Air Headquarters refused to permit a further strike for fear that the columns might be the advancing elements of the

11th African Division — they were not — and Pretorius was subsequently allowed to repeat his attack next day.

On the Northern Front British bombers and their fighter escorts attacked Italian troops in the Ad Teclesan area all day. Italian aircraft managed a single raid and a few reconnaissances, and Mar Soffritti of the 412ª Squadriglia claimed to have shot down a Hurricane. Two Gladiators of 237 Squadron on an early reconnaissance saw a number of CR 42s, and chased an S 79 which returned with slight damage.

During the evening of the 28th five CR 42s under the command of Ten De Micheli had moved from Addis Ababa to Gauani, and now at dawn these, joined by two CR 32s, made another surprise attack on Jijiga. At 0700 four of the fighters suddenly strafed the main landing ground while the other three circled overhead as top cover. In the first pass a Ju 52/3m (No 660), Valentia (No 264) and a Hartbeeste were set on fire, two of the Ju 52/3ms damaged during the attack on the 26th also being shot up again, as was a Leopard Moth of the Comm. Squadron. The fighter satellite strip had again not been spotted, and two stand-by Hurricanes of 3 SAAF Squadron flown by Capt Theron and Lt Venter at once took off.

Theron was no sooner in the air than his aircraft received a bullet in the cooling system (from an airfield defence Lewis gun, it was suspected); he went in to land again, but as he did so he was attacked by Serg Magg Giardina in a CR 32, the Hurricane being set on fire, while Theron was wounded in the leg. As soon as Giardina saw Theron leap out on to the wing, which he did the moment his Hurricane touched the ground, the Fiat pilot ceased firing. A CR 42 then arrived on the scene and opened fire on the Hurricane, although to the personnel on the ground it appeared that it was the fleeing pilot who was the target. Venter meanwhile was attacked by three Fiats and his aircraft was riddled with bullets, but he managed to shoot down one Fiat which fell in flames and crashed, the pilot, Sottoten Silvano, baling out badly wounded. (This aircraft was claimed as a CR 42, but it was in fact one of the CR 32s.) AA gunners of the 5th Battery, SAA, claimed to have shot down a CR 42 also, but only the one aircraft was lost during the attack. The Italians claimed to have burned four aircraft on the ground and damaged three more, and to have shot down two Hurricanes. During the attack on the main airfield a 41 SAAF Squadron gunner had climbed into the rear cockpit of a Hartbeeste to return fire, while more Hurricanes were now scrambling, giving chase as the enemy fighters sped away towards the hills around Diredawa. Capt Frost chased two CR 42s flown by De Micheli (who was now commander of the 413ª Squadriglia) and Serg Magg Danesin, following them through valleys and over peaks, finally getting close enough to them without being seen, to shoot down Danesin's aircraft, the pilot being killed.

Immediately after this attack, 3 SAAF Squadron was ordered to move to another landing strip, ten miles away from Jijiga in case of a repeat performance. The Squadron was now running very short of Hurricanes, no replacements for the original complement being forthcoming. During the day a Blenheim of 203 Squadron led five more 94 Squadron Gladiators from Aden to Berbera, then leading six of these fighters to Jijiga where they were handed over to the South Africans; the British pilots returned in the Blenheim and a Rapide. Next day 94's last three Gladiators in Aden were brought over, going to Jijiga also. Three SAAF pilots were then flown up to Berbera in the Rapide to collect the final three aircraft still at that base, and the British unit's supply of spares was despatched by road. 94 Squadron then ceased operations pending re-equipment.

Saturday, 29 March 1941

During 29 March Diredawa was entered by Imperial troops, and at once the SAAF took over the airfield where the wreckage of eighteen aircraft was found. There was again considerable British activity over Ad Teclesan and Asmara in the north, the railway from the latter town being attacked by a substantial formation of bombers. A Hurricane was claimed shot down during an offensive fighter reconnaissance by CR 42s, but it seems that this was the aircraft claimed by Soffritti on the 28th, reported a day late; no loss was reported on this date by 1 SAAF Squadron. This unit now bade farewell to Capt B.J.L. 'Piggy' Boyle, DFC, Lt Hewitson, and two other pilots, who returned to the Union in a Ju 52/3m for a well-earned rest. Boyle had been credited with the destruction in combat of five Italian fighters and a share in a sixth, together with others on the ground. He was at this time one of the outstanding fighter pilots on the Northern Front.

Sunday, 30 March 1941

During the morning of 30 March Jijiga was again attacked, this time by two 44° Gruppo S 79s; this was the only Italian bomber unit still operating, all remaining bombers having been concentrated under its command. The bomber crews had been briefed to attack the same spot as that strafed by the Fiats the previous day, and a stick of bombs fell exactly where the Valentia and the other aircraft had been parked; unfortunately for the Italians all had been removed, except for a single Gauntlet, which escaped destruction. Only after dropping their bombs did the crews see the dispersed Hartbeestes of 41 SAAF Squadron, but by this time two Hurricanes and two Gladiators had been scrambled.

The fighters gave chase, but the Gladiators were soon found unable to catch the Savoias as usual; the Hurricanes could, however, and both bombers were well riddled by Capt Frost and Lt Howitson. The SAAF Squadron had no incendiary ammunition at the time and the bombers would not burn. Neverthe-less, one S 79 was so badly hit that it force-landed and crashed with two dead and three wounded on board; the other, flown by Capt Serafini, returned to Addis Ababa with one of the crew dead and another mortally wounded, and with more than 800 holes in the aircraft. Serafini had no back armour to his seat, and his parachute pack was hit by several bullets, the noses of these actually penetrating through to irritate his back without causing him any injury!

Later in the day 3 SAAF Squadron despatched several Hurricanes to Diredawa, followed by headquarters and 'B' Flight of 41 SAAF Squadron. At Diredawa a number of prisoners of war were released by the arrival of the 11th African Division, including several members of the SAAF. A Maryland of 12 SAAF Squadron again reconnoitred Awash and Addis Ababa, diving to attack three fighters seen over the capital; it was chased off by a CR 42. In the north Asmara was heavily bombed, and Dessie, between Asmara and Addis Ababa, was also attacked.

Monday, 31 March 1941

The final Italian defence at Ad Teclesan, which was still preventing the Indian

Divisions from breaking through to Asmara, was now almost in a state of collapse. At 0445 on 31 March two 1 SAAF Squadron Hurricanes left to patrol over the forward troops there. At 0620 they spotted the only three serviceable S 79s of the 44° Gruppo in a tight vic, led by Magg Nino Pasti, after these bombers had dropped their containers of fragmentation bombs on the troops on the ground. The Hurricanes gave chase and caught the bombers north-east of Asmara, but Lt J. van der Merwe misjudged his attack, passed too close to the Savoias, and was hit by the gunners, thick smoke pouring from his Hurricane. Capt Driver made three more attacks, the No 2 aircraft smoking from two engines, while the leader dropped its undercarriage, but all three then disappeared into cloud. Driver then saw van der Merwe circling and trailing smoke, but he finally crashed into the side of a mountain at Zogher, 20 miles north of Asmara, and was killed. It was later reported that one S 79 had crashed due to Driver's attack, and he was credited with a victory. In fact, all the bombers returned to base, although all were damaged.

Later in the morning three Blenheims of 8 Squadron from Aden bombed a dump north of Dessie, but two CR 42s intercepted and claimed two of the bombers shot down; it is believed that both were credited to Serg Magg Giuseppe Baron of the 412ᵃ Squadriglia, who claimed to have hit an engine of each aircraft with the same burst of fire. Only one in fact fell, this being Plt Off Barke's L8433, he and one other member of the crew managing to bale out, both wounded and both becoming prisoners. Barke was struck by the tailplane immediately after extricating himself from the aircraft, one of his ankles being broken by the impact.

Over Ad Teclesan three Gladiators of 237 Squadron strafed Italian ground forces in the face of heavy and accurate AA, Plt Off Simmonds in N5853 being hit and force-landing. Simmonds managed to reach friendly territory on foot, and subsequently reached Kassala on 8 April. During the day no fewer than forty-four bombing sorties were launched on the Ad Teclesan positions to aid the final breakthrough. In Galla Sidamo meanwhile, the Soroppo defences were finally subdued by 12th African Division troops, aided by 40 SAAF Squadron Hartbeestes. The final breakthrough was now close.

Tuesday, 1 April 1941

The next day saw the fall of the last defences at Ad Teclesan, and at 0630 that morning Asmara — capital of Eritrea — was in British hands. A little later in the day units of the 5th Indian Division reached the Red Sea coast; the Battle of Keren was at last completely over. British Empire casualties for the battle up to the fall of Asmara stood at 536 dead and 3,229 wounded; the Italians lost approximately 3,000 dead and 4,500 wounded, with further substantial losses to the colonial troops, who were now deserting in droves. At Asmara many aircrew prisoners were released and returned to their squadrons. During the day the Hurricanes of 1 SAAF Squadron again strafed retreating Italian columns, but while landing at an airfield at Tole after one such sortie 2/Lt J. Marais crashed into a telegraph pole and was killed. In the hope that the fall of Asmara would now lead to an early capitulation, a Maryland of 12 SAAF Squadron dropped messages on Adama, Awash and Addis Ababa, suggesting that an envoy be sent to Diredawa to discuss terms.

Realising that the main battlefield would be in northern Eritrea, and judging that the major Imperial force had been assembled there, the Duke of Aosta had concentrated nearly all his forces in this area, leaving the defence of the south in the hands of a meagre force of colonial troops which had been spread very thinly, relying on the Juba River as their main line of defence. The Duke also relied greatly on the difficulty of crossing the arid and inhospitable wastes of the Northern Frontier Territory of Kenya, but here he sadly underestimated the great technical expertise of the substantial South African engineering units, which built roads and landing grounds, bridged gullies, rivers and gorges, and sank wells vastly to increase the supplies of water naturally available. Production of modern motor vehicles in South Africa reached a truly prodigious rate, allowing General Cunningham's forces to become fully mobile in modern, reliable trucks and lorries, while the efficient home-produced Marmon–Herrington armoured cars were used to force a way through wherever the infantry was held up.

Once the Juba was crossed, and port facilities at Kismayu and Mogadishu eased the tenuous lines of communications, the Empire forces were able to advance in the face of only light resistance at a tremendous rate. Supplies had generally to travel on bad roads over distances greater than from London to Edinburgh, and sorties flown by the SAAF were often made at extreme range.

Throughout the whole of this period the fighting in the north continued, the main Italian armies steadily being broken upon the anvil of Keren, preventing any possibility of reinforcing the south. Indeed, the withdrawal of troops from the Galla Sidamo region, which had been dropped as the main route to Addis Ababa by Cunningham once the Juba was crossed, allowed columns from Kismayu to move up and occupy Neghelli and Yavello, and to threaten the capital from the south-west. The increasing strength of the patriot forces with Haile Selassie and 'Gideon' Force in the west posed a further, although relatively minor, threat to the Italians.

Now, as the forces at Asmara and Diredawa waited for either Italian surrender or the final advance, various small changes took place. Following intensive operations from rough forward airfields, the South African bombers were becoming badly worn, and several Ju 86s and Battles were despatched to Nairobi for overhaul; others were already flying north to attack the road from Addis Ababa to Dessie. At Diredawa a special Close Support Group was formed under Maj M.C.P. Mostert to operate under the direction of a liaison officer at the front against any obstacles hindering the forward troops. Four Gladiators of 3 SAAF Squadron and four Hartbeestes of 41 SAAF Squadron were allocated to this Group.

During the advance from Kenya, 2 SAAF Squadron with its collection of elderly biplanes had taken little part in the operations. In March nine Curtiss Mohawk IV fighters arrived at Mombasa to re-equip the unit, but the Wright Cyclone engines for these proved faulty and had to be shipped to England for major works. In the Sudan the three Free French Blenheims of GRB 1 had taken part in seven missions, but only one aircraft was now serviceable. Six British Blenheims were supplied to the flight, which now became integrated with 47 Squadron.

Wednesday, 2 April 1941

The fall of Asmara had left Massawa in danger of imminent attack, and Admirale Bonetti, the Italian Naval Commander, now ordered his destroyer force out on a final desperate mission to attack Port Said and Suez. They sailed late on 1 April, but one ship ran aground on a sandbank as it left harbour. At 1430 on 2 April the destroyer force was spotted steering north by a Blenheim of 203 Squadron, and by sheer coincidence a strike force ideally situated and trained to attack them was available.

The aircraft carrier HMS *Eagle* was awaiting passage through the Suez Canal from the Mediterranean, en route around the Cape to the Atlantic. The ship's two squadrons, 813 and 824, equipped with a total of seventeen Fairey Swordfish torpedo-bombers, had just flown from Alexandria to Port Sudan, led by Cdr C.L. Keighly-Peach, and during the 2nd two of these aircraft bombed and hit an Italian merchant vessel at Makra.

Thursday, 3 to Friday, 4 April 1941

Warned by Aden of the approach of the destroyers, six Swordfish were off at 0430 on 3 April and began a diverging step-aside search. Meanwhile as dawn broke Cdr Keighly-Peach took off on a lone reconnaissance of the approaches to Port Sudan, and at 0511 he spotted the Italian ships 28 miles to the east. Calling up three of the patrolling aircraft, he led an attack with 250lb bombs during which several near misses were claimed. While one of the Swordfish shadowed the flotilla, the rest returned to refuel and rearm, and at 0813 Lt A.G. Leatham led the second strike of seven Swordfish to the scene. These attacked the ships, one aircraft approaching from each beam and one from astern. Midshipman E. Sargent, RNVR, scored six hits with six bombs on *Nazario Sauro* and she sank in less than a minute; the rest of the aircraft achieved near misses which caused many casualties on the other vessels.

Five Blenheim IVs of 14 Squadron had taken off, and saw Sargent's attack, noting that a second destroyer was stationary in the water, but as they approached the crew took to the boats. The bombers attacked this ship, reporting that it caught fire, exploded and sank. It is possible that this was *Cesare Battisti*, later found beached and abandoned on the Arabian coast.

At 1010 another Swordfish strike, led by Lt (E) J.L. Sedgwick found the destroyers 100 miles away, leaving the area fast. This time Sub Lt S.H. Suthers hit *Daniele Manin* between the funnels with two bombs, the ship coming to a halt and the crew abandoning her; three other aircraft near-missed. Sedgwick continued to shadow the two remaining destroyers until 1100, by which time they were 130 miles away, going east fast. They were now getting out of range of the Swordfish, and further attacks were left to the RAF.

These two destroyers, *Pantera* and *Tigre*, in fact went ashore 12 miles south of Jedda, and there in the afternoon they were caught by Blenheims of 14 Squadron, Wellesleys of 223 Squadron, and the British destroyer HMS *Kingston*. The bombers claimed hits on both vessels, one of which caught fire, and they were then finished off by *Kingston*. One Wellesley had to force-land on the Arabian coast nearby, and a second landed alongside, but was unable to take off again. The remainder of the formation then all landed and taking aboard the crews of the two unserviceable aircraft, took off again for base. (K7720 and K8530 were burnt by their crews before they left.) Survivors from the two destroyers who had come ashore made no effort to interfere. This was the last operational mission to be flown in East Africa by the Blenheims of 14 Squadron.

One surviving Italian destroyer, *Vincenzo Orsini*, which had gone aground on the sandbank at Massawa, managed to get back to port, where it was scuttled by the crew on 8 April after being bombed by 813 Squadron Swordfish. The 670 ton torpedo boat *Giovanni Acerbi* was also sunk by air attack at Massawa. Three days later an MTB (MAS 213 — Sottoten Valenza) torpedoed the light cruiser HMS *Capetown* outside Massawa harbour, but on the 8th five MTBs, a torpedo boat and many merchant vessels, totalling 89,870 tons, were scuttled at Massawa. This included 11 Italian and six German ships, one of the former being the 11,760 ton liner *Colombo*. Eight more Italian steamers totalling 61,890 tons would be scuttled elsewhere on 10 April.

Meanwhile on 2 April an S 79 had dropped a message on Diredawa, stating that an envoy would land next day. Ready to enter Addis Ababa, the 1st South African Brigade moved to Miesso, joined by the new Close Support Group. The Hartbeestes from this unit patrolled over the Awash River to prevent the Italians blowing up a bridge; there was one five-minute gap between patrols, and in that short period the bridge was successfully blown. The 22nd East African Brigade had meanwhile arrived at Awash Gorge.

Next day the S 79, flown by Capt Serafini, landed at Diredawa, the envoy meeting senior Army and Air Force officers in conference at Harar. In the afternoon the bomber returned to Addis Ababa with terms which guaranteed the safety of the women and children in the capital in all eventualities, but demanded a full surrender; Aosta decided to continue the fight, as these terms were unacceptable to him. In the west, Wingate's 'Gideon' Force and the Emperor's entourage entered Debra Marcos, evacuated by the defenders under Colonello Maraventano, on their approach. From Addis Ababa three transport S 73s left for Jedda loaded with personnel who had been wounded in action. It was hoped that they would be able to fly back to Italy from there.

While it was decided that no bombing of Addis Ababa town would be carried

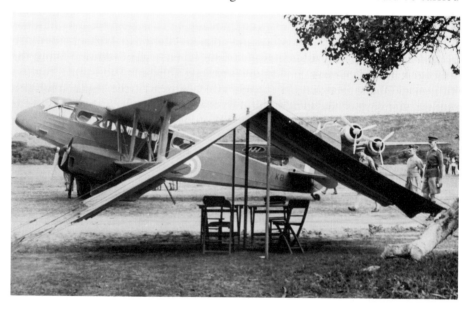

On 3 April a Savoia S 79 of the 44° Gruppo flown by Capitano Serafini landed at Diredawa's Scenele airfield carrying envoys from the Duke of Aosta to discuss armistice terms with the British High Command. The tent is where General Alan Cunningham met the Italian delegates. Behind is the DH Dragon Rapide, K8 (ex-VP-KCR) of the Kenya Auxiliary Air Unit, in which Cunningham flew to Scenele, with Serafini's S 79 in the background. The talks proved abortive. *(SAAF via Ken F. Smy)*

out following the surrender discussions on 3 April, the airfield was still a legitimate target, and one where much of the remaining Italian air strength was believed to lie. Consequently three Hurricanes were ordered to strafe, but this order was then rescinded, and a set-piece attack was laid on for 4 April by six separate waves of aircraft as a show of strength designed to hasten the Italians' willingness to cease resistance. First over the target were two Marylands of 12 SAAF Squadron intended to act as a decoy for any Italian fighters on patrol, while two Hurricanes of 3 SAAF Squadron from Miesso waited overhead to pounce. The Marylands passed over the target at 1200 and two CR 42s of the 413ª Squadriglia were scrambled, flown by Ten De Micheli and Serg Veronese; these attacked at once, each getting on the tail of one of the bombers. The rear gunners each fired at the aircraft on the other's tail, and the Hurricanes, flown by Capt Frost and Lt Marsh, dived to attack; Frost fired at the CR 42 on the tail of Capt Davies' Maryland and it

Six waves of SAAF and RAF aircraft raided Addis Ababa airfield on 4 April and another mass raid was made on Dessie airfield two days later. Here Junkers Ju 86s of 12 SAAF Squadron, are escorted by Gladiators of 3 SAAF Squadron, on one such mission. *(via Ken F. Smy)*

fell away in a spin, Frost believing that he had possibly shot it down, but neither side suffered much damage.

The Duke of Aosta decided to withdraw his forces from Addis Ababa to prevent air reprisals on the city, and the orders not to resist had arrived at the airfield only after the CR 42s had taken off. A smoke signal was at once set off ordering them to land immediately, which they did. There seems to have been some misunderstanding about the exact terms of the surrender of the town, for the authorities thought the airfield would not be attacked so long as no hostile action emanated from it. Indeed, several officers were under the impression that the massive bombing attacks that followed were as a direct result of the action of the two CR 42s — a completely false impression as it happens.

The Hurricanes now withdrew to refuel, but the Marylands remained. The first wave of bombers comprised four Battles of 11 SAAF Squadron, which dropped 208 fragmentation bombs without interference, one stick falling across eight aircraft parked in front of the main hangar, starting fires. As the Battles arrived, the Marylands left, flying at low level and strafing a convoy near Awash on their way back. Four Ju 86s of 12 SAAF Squadron escorted by two Gladiators then attacked, followed by three Blenheim Is of 8 Squadron which had flown to Jijiga from Aden to take part in the attack; they were escorted by two Hurricanes, again flown by Capt Frost and Lt Marsh. After the bombing, the Hurricanes patrolled overhead for 15 minutes, then returning via Moggio where three Ca 133s in pens were strafed. As at Diredawa, all the satellite strips here were seen to be ploughed up, as well as all but one runway on the main airfield.

The final wave of four Ju 86s went in at 1335, escorted by two more Hurricanes flown by Capt van Breda Theron and Lt Upton. The bombers gained direct hits on airfield buildings, and the Hurricanes strafed, setting fire to an S 79 and a Ca 133, and hitting four other aircraft. When the formation left, 15,670lb of bombs had been dropped on the target in under three hours.

Over Eritrea on 4 April Mar Soffritti of the 412ª Squadriglia claimed to have shot down a British bomber; no losses appear to have been recorded.

Saturday, 5 April 1941
At about 1345 Capt Frost led three other Hurricanes back to Addis Ababa for another strafe, claiming personally to have set fire to four bombers, while Lt Kershaw claimed two and Lt Glover reported hits on several others. Frost was back again before dusk with Lt Marsh, claiming two more bombers destroyed. It seems that many of the aircraft hit on this date were already abandoned, as although 30 burnt out and damaged aircraft were subsequently counted on the airfield, only an S 79 and two CR 42s were reported to have been destroyed on the 4th, one S 73 being damaged but repairable, and the other aircraft slightly damaged. Indeed, on the 5th most of the remaining aircraft had already evacuated to Jimma and Shashamanna in the south-west, and on this date the last aircraft left Addis Ababa, four CR 42s and three S 79s going to Dessie, and one CR 32 to Jimma. This latter aircraft had to make the flight unarmed, as it was a CR 32bis, and only ammunition boxes for CR 32quater aircraft were available; it had proved impossible to adapt these to fit.

In the afternoon Frost again returned and set fire to one more. In the city looting had already begun and the advancing Imperial troops found the Chief of Police waiting for them on the outskirts to organise an early occupation before the Ethiopians got out of control and many Italian civilians got killed.

Six Battles of 11 SAAF Squadron attacked a convoy of vehicles on the Sire–Aselle road, claiming at least twenty destroyed, while a Maryland spotted the main Italian retreat from Addis Ababa making for Jimma, where Generale Gazzera was setting up a stronghold. To the south of this town Hartbeestes of 40 SAAF Squadron from Neghelli spotted strong defences at Wadara, the unit coming under the command of Major-General Godwin-Austen to support the 12th African Division in an attack on this locality.

To the north 1 SAAF Squadron flew its last mission in Eritrea, five Hurricanes strafing Gondar, where all suffered damage from small arms fire. Capt Duncan strafed an S 81 on the ground at Azozo, claiming to have destroyed it. The unit had received the good news that Maj Wilmot and other prisoners of war at Adi Ugri had been liberated. 47 Squadron also welcomed back all its missing personnel who had been captured, with the exception of Plt Off Witty who had died in captivity. On that date 94 Squadron became the first unit to leave for Egypt since the fall of Asmara — it was soon to be followed by several more. The capture of Addis Ababa now allowed all remaining targets to be reached by SAAF units here, and much of 203 Group was therefore withdrawn to Egypt where the situation was critical.

Chapter Five

MOPPING UP

While success was everywhere in East Africa, this was far from the case elsewhere. In Libya the arrival of Erwin Rommel and the Afrika Korps, together with reinforcements from Italy, had sent the greatly weakened British Army scuttling back to the Egyptian frontier; while in Greece the Germans were about to launch a powerful Blitzkrieg which would throw the small Expeditionary Force out of the Balkans and on to the island of Crete in a matter of days. Everything possible would be needed in the Mediterranean area, and while the 4th Indian Division was due to embark for this area as soon as Massawa was taken, the 1st South African Division in Kenya drew in its scattered 2nd and 5th Brigades and also began leaving from Mombasa and Berbera for the same destination.

Fiat CR 32 of the 410ᵃ Squadriglia abandoned at Addis Ababa. *(via Ken F. Smy)*

Sunday, 6 to Thursday, 10 April 1941

From the Sudan 1 SAAF Squadron, having claimed 48 victories in the air and 53 aircraft destroyed on the ground for the loss of six pilots killed to all causes, took its Hurricanes to Egypt on 6 April. Among its pilots, Capt B.J.L. Boyle (who had returned to the Union) and Capt 'Andy' Duncan had already received

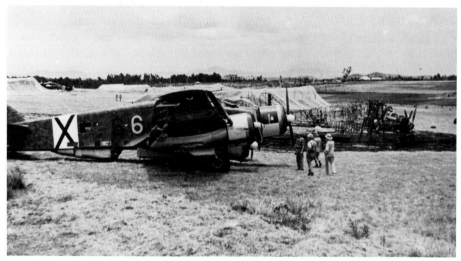

Above: Captured Fiat CR 42, probably of the 413ª Squadriglia, in Ethiopia. *(R.C. Jones).*
Below: By 5 April 1941 Addis Ababa was in the hands of British Empire forces. Many Italian aircraft were found on the airfield including this Savoia S 79 of the 6ª Squadriglia, 44° Gruppo, with its undercarriage collapsed; behind, the burnt-out skeleton of an S 81 and on the left another S 79. *(Imperial War Museum)*

DFCs, Boyle having been credited with five and one shared air victories and Duncan with four. Further awards were now to be forthcoming for Capt K.W. Driver, the most successful fighter pilot of the campaign on the British Empire side, credited with ten air and five ground victories, and for Lt R. Pare, credited with five in the air.

Three days later the South Africans were followed by the Blenheims of 14 Squadron, and on the 10th by 203 Squadron, which flew to Kabrit. 223 Squadron handed its last ten Wellesleys to 47 Squadron and also left, followed by 'K' Flight and 1430 Flight, both without aircraft. 'B' and 'C' Flights of 237 Squadron meanwhile moved to Asmara, while 'A' Flight flew to Khartoum to collect more Gladiators — presumably those left behind by 'K' Flight.

1 SAAF Squadron's leading pilots pose for an unusual group photograph at the conclusion of the unit's operations over East Africa. *(L. to r.*: Capt A. Duncan, DFC (four victories in East Africa); Capt K.W. Driver (Commonwealth top-scorer in East Africa with ten victories); Lt R. Pare (five victories); Maj L.A. Wilmot, commanding officer (one ond one shared victories in East Africa); and Capt B.J.L. Boyle, DFC (five and one shared victories). Driver and Pare both received DFCs after the squadron left Eritrea for Egypt early in April. *(IWM)*

With Addis Ababa in Imperial hands at last, the SAAF launched another big air attack on 6 April 1941, this time on Dessie airfield. The first wave, composed of six Battles, took off at 0640 carrying 20lb fragmentation bombs, but as they were approaching the main airfield, the leading formation passed over Combolcia landing ground where a fighter was seen landing. As the South Africans approached, Italian fighters had been ordered to scramble, but even as they rolled on to the runway, two Fiat CR 42s which had been patrolling over the front came in to land, preventing the take-off. Capt E.J. Kelly dived his Battle towards this airfield, and launched his bombs, claiming to have destroyed one fighter as it landed and damaged two others. The Battles then bombed buildings, while two escorting Hurricanes strafed about twenty fighters and bombers on the ground. Both Hurricanes, flown by Capt Frost and Lt Glover, were repeatedly hit by ground fire, and were damaged, Frost's being unserviceable on return to base. Frost claimed two CR 42s and two Ca 133s in flames, and Glover a Caproni in flames and an S 79 damaged.

At this point eight SAAF Junkers Ju 86s approached, escorted by Capt Theron, Lt Venter and Lt Van Ginkel in Hurricanes. By now three more CR 42s had returned from the front where they had been strafing, and although short of ammunition they attacked the bombers, damaging three of them. The Hurricanes were on to the Fiats like a flash, Capt Theron and Lt Van Ginkel each shooting down one. Ten Caldonazzo, a 412ª Squadriglia pilot, baled out over the airfield, but was hit — it was believed by fire from a Ju 86 — and was killed. A second fighter fell some way from the airfield, and while both South African pilots reported that the pilots of the aircraft shot down by them had baled out, the pilot of this one did not return. The third Fiat was hit and damaged, force-landing away from the field, but both pilot and aircraft survived. After seeing the Ju 86s on their way back to base, the Hurricanes returned to strafe, a S 79 and a CR 42 being claimed burnt, with two more Fiats and a

Romeo damaged. This brought SAAF strafing claims for the day to three CR 42s, three S 79s and one Caproni.

Actual losses on the ground in the attacks on this date amounted to two S 79s, one S 81, two Ca 133s and four CR 42s, with one S 79, one S 81, one S 75 and one Ca 133 badly damaged and others slightly damaged, but readily repairable. A final raid by three Blenheims of 8 Squadron, RAF, from Jijiga caused no further damage.

Next day the surviving aircraft at Dessie — four Ca 133s and three CR 42s — withdrew to Alomata. Three Battles of 11 SAAF Squadron patrolled over the front, but cloud was encountered over some mountains and Lt M.E. James' aircraft (No 906) hit a peak, the bomb load exploding. From Alomata, where the Italians were building up a small striking force, their fighters strafed British vehicles and flew reconnaissances.

On 8 April Scots infantry and Free French troops, both part of the 4th Indian Division, supported by Matilda 'I' tanks, captured the port of Massawa; virtually all Eritrea with the exception of Assab was now in British hands. Sudden heavy rains bogged in the Hurricanes of 3 SAAF Squadron on the 9th and an attack on Shashamanna airfield had to be called off, although five Blenheims of 8 Squadron managed to get off to bomb the Addis Ababa–Medani road. The attack on Shashamanna was made next day, Hurricanes and Battles finding the airfield deserted, and bombing some buildings. Two hidden bombers were then seen and strafed by the Battles without apparent result. Meanwhile the three Hurricanes had found two satellite fields on one of which Lt Howitson strafed two Savoias. Capt Frost then claimed two Capronis destroyed on the main airfield, Lt Torr meanwhile strafing another Caproni. Frost and Howitson then joined him in making repeated attacks on this aircraft, which refused to burn. In fact, two S 81s and three Ca 133s were destroyed during the raid. On the return flight the weather closed in again and one Battle, flown by Lt M.G.T. Ferreira, crashed, the wreckage not being found for a month.

Later the Hurricanes took off again, five of them in two flights flying to Jimma. Lt Glover's section went in to strafe some bombers, while Capt Frost's section engaged two fighters which were identified as CR 42s but were in fact CR 32s. Frost and Howitson attacked the CR 32 flown by Mar Mottet, engaging it in a hard dogfight during which a burst of fire cut the Fiat's controls, Mottet then attempting to land. In doing so he collided with an obstruction and crashed, the aircraft being written off though the pilot was unhurt. Lts Glover, Upton and Marsh meanwhile attacked four Ca 133s and a CR 32 on the ground, each burning one of the bombers; Frost's section then came down, Frost flaming the remaining bomber and the fighter, while Howitson set two alight in a hangar. Glover's section then came upon the second CR 32, among some clouds at 9,000 feet. Upton attacked and the Fiat turned and dived vertically; Glover then got in some good bursts and it flicked on to its back, the pilot baling out. His parachute caught the tail of the aircraft however, ripped in half, and he fell to his death.

Total losses actually suffered on the ground in this attack were six Ca 133s and two CR 32s, plus the two CR 32s shot down. The Regia Aeronautica now had left serviceable two S 79s, four Ca 133s, five CR 42s and two CR 32s, with hopes of getting three more Ca 133s, one S 79, one CR 42 and one Ca 148 airworthy.

Two Hartbeestes of 41 SAAF Squadron now found the column of 2,000

Italian troops with 12,000 armed natives and their families, led by Colonello Maraventano, which had retreated from Debra Marcos as 'Gideon' Force approached, and had been making for Addis Ababa when it fell. The column had at least 50 vehicles, and was at Tulla Milchi, near the Blue Nile, when seen. Five Hartbeestes and two Gladiators led by Capt T. van der Kaay were sent to strafe this target, doing so with such thoroughness that the troops had to abandon their vehicles and take to the bush, making for Dessie. Return fire was fierce, and one Hartbeeste was hit 33 times. Next day the column was attacked again, and this time Lt C. Collins had to force-land his badly damaged Hartbeeste. He and his gunner burnt the aircraft and were then taken prisoner, spending the next six weeks with the column.

Thursday, 10 to Friday, 11 April 1941

The Italians continued to hold out, and were now in four main areas. In the north they held Dessie, blocking the way to Amba Alagi, a fortress where the Duke of Aosta and Generale Frusci were facing the troops advancing southwards from Asmara. To the west of Amba Alagi was Gondar, another natural fortress of great strength, where the Italians were also well entrenched. West of Addis Ababa they were also at Jimma and Gambela, and to the south there were isolated but strong forces among the lakes around Soddu; these latter forces were being contained by patriot bands which roamed the countryside in considerable strength.

With the small Imperial forces available after Egypt had creamed off substantial reinforcements, and with the rainy season due in late May/early June, there was now little prospect of an early end to the campaign if the Italians were determined to hang on. This they were, having been ordered to fight for as long as possible to tie down the largest possible force which might otherwise swing the balance in the Mediterranean. Consequently a long period of 'mopping-up' operations now began.

The 12th and a part of the 11th African Divisions, supported by 3, 11, 40 and 41 SAAF Squadrons, would now operate in the Galla Sidamo and Gojjam provinces, while the 1st South African Brigade advanced northwards to Dessie, supported by the Close Support Group Hartbeestes and Gladiators. The Ju 86s and Hurricanes remained for the moment at Addis Ababa to attack the more distant targets and drop leaflets. In the north 47 and 237 Squadrons, RAF, and the Free French Flight, supported by three Ju 52/3ms of 51 SAAF Flight, remained to operate over Amba Alagi and Gondar in support of the forces still facing these objectives. The task was still formidable, for west of the capital alone Generale Gazzera had 40,000 men, 200 elderly guns and some armoured cars (trucks fitted locally with steel plate protection) — a far greater numerical strength than was now available to General Cunningham. One of the objectives of the campaign had been realised however, for on 11 April President Roosevelt declared that the Red Sea was no longer a combat area, and that United States shipping bringing war materials to the British in the Middle East might now sail through it.

Saturday, 12 to Sunday, 13 April 1941

Six Ju 86s of 12 SAAF Squadron tried to bomb Dessie on 12 April, but found the target obscured by cloud. Lt N.S. de Villiers ran short of fuel and had to force-land in French Somaliland, where he and his crew were interned. He

Captured Italian AF Caproni Ca 133 repainted with RAF roundels but still retaining its Italian rudder markings and fuselage code, 'SM-8', showing it to have been an aircraft of one of the Stato Maggiore squadriglie. *(SAAF)*

subsequently escaped, returning to his unit on 29 April.

Three Gladiators of 237 Squadron attacked Alomata airfield, claiming three Ca 133s and an S 79 destroyed; two Ca 133s and an S 81, all of them already unserviceable, were hit, and a Ca 148 was slightly damaged. At Jimma on the 13th, Capt Frost, flying alone, attacked, destroying a Ro 37bis and a Ca 148, both already unserviceable.

Tuesday, 15 April 1941
On 15 April two 237 Squadron Gladiators escorted a reconnaissance Lysander to Debarech, seeing an S 79 in the air. The fighters got to within 500 yards unseen and Plt Off Simmonds then opened fire and hit it from astern, but the pilot opened up his engines and escaped. It was now reported that between 1 November 1940 and 15 April 1941 the RAF and SAAF on the Northern Front had lost 26 medium bombers, 22 miscellaneous bomber and army co-operation aircraft and 19 fighters — a total of 67 aircraft, 49 of them to enemy action.

Wednesday, 16 April 1941
Next day three Ju 86s of 12 SAAF Squadron with Hurricane escort bombed workshops and buildings at Dessie, the fighters then going down to strafe. They claimed two S 79s on fire and damage to five fighters and a Ca 133; one Hurricane was hit and damaged by AA. It was believed subsequently that eight aircraft had been burned on the ground. Four of these were credited to Lt Howitson and three to Capt Frost, the last apparently being allotted to Lt Glover, who claimed only a damaged. In fact two S 79s already badly damaged on the 6th were burned, and a CR 42, also destroyed on the 6th, was hit again, as were several damaged fuselages. The Italians were able to launch a raid by one S 79 and two CR 42s during the day, vehicles in the Termaber area being attacked, while a Ca 133 bombed patriot forces near Deca.

Thursday, 17 April 1941
On 17 April 2 SAAF Squadron recalled its flights at Mega, Jijiga and Mogadishu, the CO and sixteen pilots leaving for Egypt where the Squadron was to be re-equipped and join the fighting over the desert; several pilots of 3

SAAF Squadron were also despatched to Egypt at this time to reinforce 1 SAAF Squadron. On the same date Brigadier H.C. Daniel left for the Union, Advanced Air Headquarters being taken over by Colonel H.G. Willmott just as the battle for Combolcia Pass, south of Dessie, began.

Saturday, 19 to Wednesday, 23 April 1941

Heavy air attacks on Dessie were ordered on 19 April and three Battles, escorted by three Hurricanes, raided, catching a convoy of 40 vehicles north of the town, leaving four oil tankers ablaze. Capt J.F. Britz's Battle was hit and force-landed at Combolcia with the undercarriage half retracted; Lt S.W. Murray landed to try to pick the crew up, but he put down too far away. Before he could taxi over, Italian artillery opened up, and Britz waved him off under fire; he and his crew were taken prisoner, although they were to be released only six days later. During the next few days both the SAAF and the Blenheims of 8 Squadron from Aden were very active over the area.

Ca 133s were now operating whenever possible to drop supplies to Colonello Maraventano's column, but raids on airfields used by these aircraft continued. Wellesleys attacked Belese on 19 April, while on the 21st two Gladiators of 237 Squadron again strafed Alomata, claiming two Ca 133s and an S 79; in fact, they destroyed one Ca 133 and damaged a Ca 148. Two CR 42s on reconnaissance over Bottego encountered three Gladiators, but without result. One Gladiator, an aircraft of 3 SAAF Squadron, flown by Lt Geraty, caught one of the Ca 133s over Debra Marcos and shot it down. On 22 April Combolcia was taken, and the remaining two S 79s and two CR 42s there were flown to Jimma.

The attack on Maraventano's column was repeated on the 23rd and on this date also 40 SAAF Squadron's Hartbeestes supported Gold Coast troops attacking Wadara; the attack was beaten off by the defenders on this occasion.

Thursday, 24 April 1941

It was believed that an aircraft might be trying to evacuate Generale Gazzera from Jimma, so on the 24th two Hurricanes of 3 SAAF Squadron, flown by the new commanding officer, Maj J.D. Pretorius, and Lt Howitson took off to attack. They circled over the airfield, Howitson giving cover, but his aircraft was suddenly hit by an AA shell and he was killed; he was buried by the Italians with full military honours.

14 SAAF Squadron, receiving no further Marylands after the initial few, had become a shadow squadron, and now — renumbered 24 to avoid confusion with 14 Squadron, RAF — it left for Egypt where it re-formed with a full complement of Marylands; the aircraft on detachment with 12 SAAF Squadron now became a part of that unit's establishment. At the same time 60 SAAF (Photographic) Squadron also left for Egypt.

Friday, 25 to Wednesday, 30 April 1941

The Italians reported two strafes on Bonava's Lekemti airfield on 25 April during which two Ca 133s were destroyed and two damaged; one of these was claimed by 3 SAAF Squadron's Lt Glover. One Ca 148 trying to supply the Maraventano column returned without accomplishing its mission when the pilot spotted two Gladiators in the area. Dessie was finally taken on 26 April, 10,000 men, including 6,000 Italians, 52 guns, 236 machine guns and 240 lorries being captured. Among the prisoners was Maresciallo Arnaldo Soffritti of the 412ª

Squadriglia, who had been credited with eight victories in air combat, together with a share in 15 destroyed on the ground.

To support the final assault on Amba Alagi from north and south, two flights of 41 SAAF Squadron now moved to Combolcia, while 237 Squadron moved to Makale. At Combolcia S 79s and S 81s, CR 32s and CR 42s, and Ca 133s were found burnt out or wrecked around the perimeter in considerable numbers. Not realising that the airfield was in British hands, two CR 42 pilots attempted to land, but were driven off by fire from captured Breda AA guns. On the arrival of the Close Support Group however, three Hartbeestes and two Gladiators crashed while landing, suffering various degrees of damage.

On the morning of 29 April three Gladiators of 237 Squadron took off to attack Alomata and Cer-Cer; at the former a Ca 133 was claimed in flames and at the latter Flg Offs Spencer, Simmonds and Robinson claimed a Ca 133, an S 79 and a CR 32. In the afternoon Flg Offs Spencer and Kleynhans returned to Cer-Cer, strafing the same aircraft, but this time the fighter was identified as a CR 42; the Italians admitted the destruction here of an S 79, a Ca 133 and CR 42. After the attack one S 79, the last serviceable, left for Shashamanna, two CR 42s flying to Gondar. Ju 86s from Addis Ababa bombed a brigade head-quarters at Wadara, and dropped leaflets.

Flt Lt E.T. Smith and Flg Off Simmonds of 237 Squadron returned to Cer-Cer again on 30 April, shooting up the same aircraft once more; these were also strafed by two of the unit's Lysanders. Capt Frost of 3 SAAF Squadron patrolled over Jimma and Agara, seeing the S 79 which had escaped from Cer-Cer the previous day, flying low along a valley just after it had taken off. He made two attacks on it and it climbed to 700 feet over some hills, allowing the crew to bale out; the pilot, Ten Curcio, also escaped before the bomber crashed. Frost then saw a CR 32 on the ground at Jimma and strafed it, causing it to burst into flames.

While celebrating having claimed the destruction of 101 aircraft as a result of these two victories, the Squadron was much sobered by Sir Pierre van Ryneveld's ruling that for totals, only those shot down in combat would count, not those destroyed on the ground. This reduced the unit's credited tally to 24, 77 having been claimed during strafing attacks.

Thursday, 1 to Tuesday, 6 May 1941

Reconnaissance at the start of May showed a substantial build-up of Italian forces in the west of Ethiopia. Generale Bertello's column had reached the Shashamanna–Soddu–Lake Margherita area of Ethiopia, while Generale Liberati's forces from Harar were now reaching the same area. Available to the SAAF now were two flights of Hurricanes and Gladiators of 3 SAAF Squadron at Addis Ababa, at which base 16 SAAF Squadron was just forming under Maj A.J. Mossop, taking over 12 SAAF Squadron's remaining eight Ju 86s as the latter unit withdrew to Kenya to re-equip. At Jijiga was 11 SAAF Squadron with Battles, while also at Addis Ababa were two flights of Hartbeestes of 41 SAAF Squadron. The Close Support Group was at Combolcia, supporting the attack at Amba Alagi, while at Neghelli were the seventeen Hartbeestes of 40 SAAF Squadron, assisting in the final attack on Wadara, which began on 3 May.

On 2 May thirteen sorties over Shashamanna by all types prevented any counter-attacks developing in either direction by breaking up Italian troop concentrations. On 6 May two Battles were despatched to join 16 SAAF

By the end of April 1941, 3 SAAF Squadron, had claimed over 100 victories, the majority of them on the ground. The Squadron's pilots are seen chalking their score on the fuselage of a captured Fiat CR 42. *(via Ken F. Smy)*

Squadron in these activities. Next day Capt Frost led the Hurricanes to Jimma to attack a fuel convoy, four oil tankers blowing up and five petrol tankers burning, preventing Generale Liberati withdrawing his 4,800 men and ten small tanks to the west due to lack of fuel. During the day Ju 86 No 652 had to force-land at Dalle, the crew becoming prisoners.

Thursday, 8 to Monday, 12 May 1941

On 8 May the 1st South African Brigade came under the command of the 15th Indian Division for the attack on Amba Alagi. The fortress and the airfield at Azozo, near Gondar, from where any air support would now be flown, were attacked throughout the day by Wellesleys and aircraft of 237 Squadron. 12 SAAF Squadron in Kenya had now re-equipped with Marylands, and this unit too left for Egypt.

Wadara fell on 10 May and the Italians fell back to Dalle into what was now becoming a vast trap. A new all-weather airfield had been prepared for the SAAF in the lakes district at Algato, Hurricanes, Gladiators and Battles now flying in here. Apart from a few CR 42s, the Italians had just two Ca 133s serviceable now, and one of these, flown by Ten Case, was carrying supplies to isolated garrisons during this period, repeatedly escaping discovery; the aircraft was hit by AA and damaged on 12 May while supplying the garrison at Jechi. On that day the 21st East African Brigade, supported by 40 SAAF Squadron, captured Giabassire. Two days later, on 14 April, Shashamanna fell to units of the 11th African Division, and as the Italians retreated towards Dalle, they met those retreating from Wadara, both columns then heading north-westwards through Soddu towards Jimma.

Tuesday, 13 to Thursday, 15 May 1941

Meanwhile the air attack on Amba Alagi and Azozo progressed. On 13 May a Free French Blenheim of GRB 1 was attacked by a CR 42 while raiding Azozo airfield, the gunner claiming to have shot this fighter down. Two days later four Gladiators of 237 Squadron attacked the same target, dropping bombs on a Ca 133 and an S 79, neither of which was serviceable. Plt Off W.M. Cooper of the same unit was shot down over Amba Alagi in Lysander P9189, crash-landing, but dying from his injuries. These were to be the last sorties in the area for this unit, for on 18 May, attacked from north and south, with the water supply precarious and without hospitals or proper medical care for a large number of wounded, the Duke of Aosta and his forces in Amba Alagi, totalling some 5,000 men with 54 guns and 250 machine guns, surrendered, the continued defence of the fortress being now almost impossible. The troops were allowed to march out with their arms in honourable surrender, past a Guard of Honour drawn from all the Imperial units involved, before being disarmed and removed to prisoner of war camps.

Monday, 19 to Monday, 26 May 1941

237 Squadron began moving on 23 May and by the 26th had left Kassala for Wadi Halfa. 47 Squadron with GRB 1 was now entirely at Asmara, the only RAF unit remaining in Eritrea. In Aden 8 Squadron, no longer able to reach the areas where fighting still continued, was re-formed with one flight of Blenheims and one of Vincents for general reconnaissance and policing duties.

In the west the SAAF continued its activities, while the fortress of Gondar was bombed from time to time by 47 Squadron. Ju 86s and Hurricanes were operating regularly over Jimma as the Italians prepared to defend the west bank of the Omo River, Gladiators and Battles attacking those forces still retreating through Dalle and Wondo, joined by Hartbeestes of 41 SAAF Squadron. One of the remaining Ca 133s, a Red Cross machine, had been used a couple of times to bomb patriot forces threatening the Italians, but after a note had been dropped warning that such use should cease forthwith, it was finally strafed and destroyed by a Hurricane on 19 May. The Caproni had by this time ceased its activities and was standing uncamouflaged in the open, but the British authorities had been incorrectly informed by local patriot forces that it was still being used for offensive purposes.

A new Close Support Group was now set up to assist the 11th African Division, as the 1st South African Brigade had been shipped to Egypt from Massawa after the fall of Amba Alagi. This new group comprised two flights of Battles, two of Hartbeestes and one of Gladiators. On 21 May 40 SAAF Squadron also flew its last operational sorties over Dilla but this unit, like so many others, then left, this time for the Union to re-equip. The sixteen service-able Hartbeestes were all handed over to 41 SAAF Squadron; these were Nos 805, 815, 817, 819, 824, 826, 835, 838, 839, 844, 845, 849, 852, 854, 857 and 863.

3 SAAF Squadron also suffered a great loss on 20 May when Capt 'Jack' Frost, top-scoring pilot of the unit with credit for eight and one shared victories in the air and a very substantial number on the ground, suffered an attack of acute appendicitis and was rushed to Nairobi for an emergency operation. He was later to lead a squadron in the Western Desert, becoming the SAAF's top-scoring fighter pilot of the war before his death in action. The Squadron's other outstanding pilot up to this time had been Capt Servaas van Breda Theron, with

five air and six ground victories; both Frost and Theron received DFCs.

Mopping-up operations continued throughout the middle of 1941. Soddu fell on 22 May, Generali Liberati and Baccari both being captured, and from there South African light tanks and armoured cars pressed on to the Omo River. It was crossings over this river that provided the main targets for the SAAF Junkers Ju 86s and Battles during the next few days. Lt Venter of 3 SAAF Squadron strafed a stationary truck on the 24th, but this proved to be a decoy, and his Hurricane was hit and damaged when it exploded violently; he crashed while landing as a result. Hurricane pilots were ordered in future to avoid strafing vehicles that were not on the move.

Monday, 26 May to Monday, 2 June 1941
Two Ju 86s of 16 SAAF Squadron were attacked by two Fiat CR 42s on 26 May while on an offensive reconnaissance along the Omo, each returning with one bullet hole. Two days later one of these fighters escorted a Caproni Ca 148, that had been repaired, to drop supplies over the front. On the 28th one of the Fiats, flown by Serg Magg Antonio Giardina, caught Capt D.R. Clyde-Morley, who had taken over 'A' Flight of 3 SAAF Squadron from Frost, and shot down his Hurricane over Jimma. Clyde-Morley, thinking he had been hit by ground fire, force-landed and hurt his head, wandering for hours until picked up by patriots and returned safely. Lt Venter of 3 SAAF Squadron was involved in an escort on 2 June, seeing a CR 42 over Soddu, but losing it in cloud. Next day he set off from Addis Ababa for Algato, but did not arrive, having crashed into the mountains 15 miles south of Soddu, losing his life; the rainy season with its resultant bad weather had arrived.

Thursday, 5 to Wednesday, 11 June 1941
The Omo crossings began on 5 June at two points 60 miles apart. All aircraft with the exception of the Ju 86s were now at Algato, where 11 SAAF Squadron had been renumbered 15 SAAF. During the crossings 7,000lb of bombs were dropped, bringing the total for the first five days of June to 18,000lb. At the southern crossing the 22nd East African Brigade got over at Abalti and pressed on towards Jimma, but one of the Hartbeestes giving support was shot down by AA on 3 June, Capt G.A. Giles, at 43 the oldest combat pilot with the SAAF, being killed; he had commenced flying with the RFC in 1916. On the northern crossing the 23rd Nigerian Brigade advanced on Lekemti.

Every flyable aircraft remaining to the Italians now left Jimma, one Ca 148 and two CR 42s flying from there to Gondar. En route they saw in the Lake Tana area a lone S 79 which appeared to have been painted with British markings, and attacked it. Lacking fuel, they were unable to continue the attack after the initial pass. At Gondar there was no 12.7mm ammunition for the fighters, which were grounded until 10 June when a fresh supply was flown in from Italy in a Savoia S 75. As the last defences on the river crumbled, the 24th Colonial Division, the last Italian force east of the Omo, surrendered as it was by then completely cut off in the mountains. Retreating Italian troops by passing Jimma were discovered at Cossa on the Little Didessa River on 9 June and were bombed several times by the Ju 86s and Hartbeestes, one of the latter being hit and force-landing. Only four of the twelve weary Battles were now serviceable, and these bombed Cossa again on the No 11th; 902 crashed into the mountains in cloud, the crew being killed. The wreckage was found by the Italians and

Generale Sabatini sent a message to the SAAF reporting the deaths of Lt E.J. Steyn and Sgt F.W. Kelly.

Monday, 16 June to Tuesday, 8 July 1941

Five Hartbeestes found five machine guns and four AA posts in action on 16 June, Lt D. Cobbledick silencing three of them, although he and his gunner were both hit and wounded; he landed at Wolchette with an oil lead cut by a bullet. Four days later Jimma fell, and there eleven bombers and four fighters were found burnt-out on the airfield. Generale Pietro Gazzera, now Supreme Commander in East Africa, still had 5,000 men left including 300 officers and nine generali, and he decided to stand at Dembidollo in the Gore region. From the Italians' rear a force of Free Belgians who had been assembled in the Belgian Congo and had moved across the Sudan, crossed the frontier near Gambela and moved eastwards to prevent any further retreat.

To support the final push, 'B' Flight of 41 SAAF Squadron moved to Jimma, while 'A' Flight went to a landing ground on the east bank of the Didessa. From there raids by these aircraft and the Ju 86s continued; 3 SAAF Squadron also completed the move to Jimma on 1 July, 'B' flight having arrived there on 24 June. During the first three days of that month 16 SAAF Squadron continually dive-bombed Gazzera's headquarters at Dembidollo, while Gore, Dembi and Gimbi all fell. The Italian position was now quite hopeless, and as the Free Belgians began their attack, Gazzera radioed Addis Ababa to open surrender negotiations, surrendering all remaining troops in Galla Sidamo to the Belgian commander, Major-General Gilliaert, on 6 July. The 4th Blue Battalion of the Regia Aeronautica was the last to surrender next day.

Around Gondar meanwhile the newly arrived CR 42s strafed British troops in the Debra Tabor area on 11 June and on the 19th Ten Case strafed and bombed them in his Ca 133, which was again hit and damaged by AA. On 20 June the Free French Blenheim crews of GRB 1 saw an S 82, which had just arrived from Italy, on the ground at Azozo and one of the aircraft dive-bombed this, the pilot claiming to have destroyed it; Italian sources reported that no damage was caused. Five Wellesleys of 47 Squadron, RAF, were attacked over Azozo by two CR 42s on 27 June without result, but on 2 July Sgt A.G. Brown of this unit was shot down over Gondar in L2713 by a CR 42, the aircraft falling in flames and all the crew being killed. During the day Ten Case's Ca 133 was once more repaired and ready to resume operations.

During the month a force of Indian troops, supported by the RAF in Aden, and by the Royal Navy and Royal Indian Navy, made a surprise landing at Assab, capturing the garrison including two generali; one of these was Generale di Brigata Aerea Pietro Piacentini, commander of Settore Nord, who had several times flown an S 79 to lead CR 42s of the 412ª Squadriglia to British airfields where their successful strafing attacks had been undertaken. By early July 1941 only Gondar remained in Italian hands, Generale Nasi being holed up there with 25,000 troops. The two African Divisions were too busy guarding the many thousands of prisoners recently taken, and although columns from the Sudan, Eritrea and Dessie, had closed on the fortress, there was insufficient strength available to reduce it. Added to this the heavy rains of the July/September period made movement on the ground difficult; so for the time being the RAF and SAAF were given the job of keeping the forces there on the defensive.

For this reason, following the end of the Galla Sidamo fighting, all SAAF units in the area were put at the disposal of 203 Group, RAF, and on 6 July 47 Squadron and GRB 1 made the first of a new series of systematic raids. At Gondar Colonello Dario Busoni commanded the air component, keeping his two CR 42s serviceable by cannibalising other unserviceable aircraft. The Ca 133 was used to carry supplies to the garrison to the north of Wolchefit Pass, and was kept hidden in a niche at the end of the airfield. The two CR 42s were camouflaged with netting in the open and were never to be discovered while on the ground. The equipment of the South African units was practically worn out by this stage, but some new aircraft were at last on the way.

Wednesday, 9 to Tuesday, 29 July 1941

Five Wellesleys raided Gondar on 9 July, a single CR 42 attacking and slightly damaging one of the bombers. Two days later the SAAF began moving in, three Ju 86s flying to Alomata, 120 miles from Gondar, while the Gladiators of 'B' Flight, 3 SAAF Squadron, arrived at Combolcia. They were followed on the 19th by 'A' Flight, comprising two Hurricanes and three more Gladiators.

The first SAAF raid was launched on 14 July by the three Ju 86s led by Capt C.M. Smuts, the Gladiators at Combolcia being at readiness in case Italian fighters should try to follow the bombers back. Lt G.E. Abbott found difficulty in keeping formation and over the target his bomber was hit by AA, falling behind. He dived to 30 feet over Azozo to attack a Ca 133, but then saw that it had no propellers and was a decoy. He attacked a hangar instead, but heavy machine gun fire hit his Junkers, No 643, and the speed fell to 70 mph as oil began to leak out; Abbott was forced to land in a ploughed field near Bandia, he and the rest of the crew escaping over the mountains to join the patriot forces.

Two Ju 86s repeated the attack on 17 July but were attacked for 15 minutes by the two CR 42s as they approached. Over the target their bomb releases failed to operate and both had to return still laden with bombs, one bomber having been damaged during the attacks.

During the day 'A' Flight of 3 SAAF Squadron began moving to Addis Ababa, but whilst landing on the rain-sodden airfield there, one Hurricane's wheels sank into the soft ground and the aircraft overturned, 2/Lt Lilienfeld, the pilot, being slightly injured. With 3 SAAF Squadron's flight now available in the area, the next bombing raid was to have an escort of two Hurricanes; another Ju 86 had flown up to bring the strength of the Alomata detachment to three again. Unfortunately the fighters were 15 minutes late taking off due to trouble with a trolley starter, and only met the bombers as they returned after being attacked by the two CR 42s again; this time all the bombers were damaged, two of them quite badly. The Hurricanes went on to strafe Azozo, where they claimed to have shot up a CR 42 on the ground; the telephone and electricity lines were damaged during the attacks on this date. Next day a Ju 52/3m arrived at Alomata carrying some reconditioned Pratt & Whitney Hornet engines to be fitted to one of the bombers.

Wednesday, 30 July to Saturday, 2 August 1941

41 SAAF Squadron was now also ordered up to Alomata, arriving during the next few days. At Gondar on 30 July one CR 42 patrolled while an S 75 landed uninterrupted after the flight from Italy, and on 1 August both Italian fighters

Captured Italian fighters, a Fiat CR 32 (left) and a CR 42, still in their national markings. In May 1941 the two aircraft were flown to South Africa where they were put on public display and subsequently preserved in a museum. *(SAAF)*

attacked a Blenheim of GRB 1, making several passes, but finally giving up. On 2 August Majors Biden and Klotze of 41 SAAF Squadron left for Nairobi, flying a captured CR 32 and a CR 42 respectively; these aircraft were to be used for training by home defence squadrons, neither surviving the war.

Saturday, 2 to Tuesday, 26 August 1941

By early August Colonel Preller had assembled his depleted force at Alomata, where 41 SAAF Squadron had all three flights together for the first time, 18 Hartbeestes being on strength. The other units were in much worse shape, 3 SAAF Squadron having three Gladiators and two Hurricanes serviceable, 15 SAAF Squadron two Battles, and 16 SAAF Squadron three Ju 86s. These aircraft were now to begin a maximum effort against Gondar itself, while 47 Squadron, which had been much involved recently in dropping supplies to troops at the front, and GRB 1, were to concentrate on Wolchefit and Debarech.

The new attack was begun by Hartbeestes and fighters, one Hurricane flown by Capt P. Hayden-Thomas being hit by AA and crash-landing at high speed near the Italian fortress. The pilot was helped to escape by friendly natives, and arrived later on muleback at Debra Tabor, finally being flown back to Alomata by Capt du Toit on the 22nd. A Gladiator was also hit and badly damaged, and one Hartbeeste ran out of fuel and force-landed on a road where it was wrecked.

Next day the attack was repeated by nine Hartbeestes, three Ju 86s, two Battles and a Hurricane. One Hartbeeste was hit by AA and Lt Anderson had to force-land it; he was picked up safely the next day. On 8 August three Hartbeestes and two Gladiators attacked the fortress, while two Battles strafed Azozo, rendering the Ca 133 unserviceable yet again; one Battle crash-landed on return to Alomata. A Ju 86 was written off on 9 August when its under-carriage collapsed on take-off, and on the 12th Lt Cobbledick wrecked a Hurricane in a taxiing accident. GRB 1 was ordered back to Fort Lamy on the 13th, leaving the Wellesleys and Hartbeestes as virtually the only effective attack force for the time being.

Three Hartbeestes raided Debarech on 14 August, but two were hit, Lt G.R. Andrews crash-landing, while Capt Chapman force-landed 50 miles from the target, his aircraft flipping over on to its back. He burned the aircraft, and he and his gunner were then captured by a band of brigands who luckily decided to hand them over to the patriot forces. Andrews and his gunner were found unhurt the next day.

'A' Flight of 41 SAAF Squadron moved up to Aksum on 17 August to increase the attacks on Wolchefit and Debarech pending an assault on the ground, but on the 18th another Hartbeeste was lost due to engine trouble. A new Coastal Flight, 35 SAAF, was formed on the 18th, and the remaining Ju 86s of 16 SAAF Squadron were transferred to this, the rest of the Squadron's personnel withdrawing to Nairobi; it was intended that the Flight should operate from Mombasa, but for the time being it remained in Ethiopia. Next day the last Battle flew its last sortie, and 15 SAAF Squadron withdrew to Kenya to re-equip. 16 SAAF's Commanding Officer, Maj Mostert, was promoted Lt Col and took over what remained of 2 Wing from Lt Col Preller, who also returned to Kenya.

The attack on Wolchefit by patriot forces led by Maj B.J. Ringrose began on 25 August and the SAAF was over the area in support, Hartbeestes of all flights claiming 32 direct hits on trenches, which they also strafed, while RAF Wellesleys bombed the same area. The patriots took 105 prisoners, but were then forced to withdraw by a counter-attack. Capt du Toit's Hartbeeste, No 865, was hit by Breda fire and set alight, but he managed to clear the area before force-landing on a road 15 miles south-east of Gondar; he returned later on foot with the assistance of patriots. Lt W. Arbuthnot in Gladiator No 1342 did not return from an offensive reconnaissance over Azozo; his aircraft had been hit in the oil cooler, and he was picked up safely by Allied ground forces some time later.

The fighters were alerted for aircraft trying to fly in to Azozo at this time, and on another mission over this airfield next day Lt Mitchell in Gladiator No 1344 was also shot down, crash-landing. He was pulled unconscious from the aircraft by patriots and returned safely to Alomata.

Wednesday, 27 August to Saturday, 27 September 1941

Twenty Curtiss Mohawk IVs with modified engines had reached Mombasa from England on 13 July, and were now ready for issue to units. Consequently on 27 August 'B' Flight of 3 SAAF Squadron withdrew to re-equip with these. The Squadron was now in such a depleted state that the small detachment remaining at Alomata was administered by 41 SAAF Squadron — it now included one Hurricane again, as one machine had been rendered serviceable — while 'B' Flight became known as 41 SAAF Detached Fighter Flight. This flight, under the command of Maj H. Borckenhagen and Capt J. Parsonson, took over its first Mohawks from 70 OTU at Nakuru, which had taken these aircraft on charge on 1 September.

Meanwhile, Air Commodore Sowrey ordered units to cease pressing home attacks at low level as the risks did not justify the losses. Seven of nine aircraft lost in the preceding three weeks had been to AA. However, on 4 September one of three Hartbeestes was hit while attacking Debarech and Wolchefit, Lt Harcourt-Baldwin crashing while attempting to force-land west of Alomata; he too returned safely. At Gondar by 8 September the Ca 133 was once more serviceable, and again began flying supplies up to Wolchefit, while the CR 42s patrolled, pending the arrival of an S 75 from Italy. The Hurricane intercepted

On 13 July 1941 twenty Curtiss Mohawk IVs arrived at Mombasa and after one or two mishaps (2506 illus.) began to re-equip 3 SAAF Squadron. *(SAAF)*

one of the CR 42s over Wolchefit on 11 September as it was being used to fly up supplies, but lost it again. Also that day two Ju 86s attacked motor boats operating on Lake Tana.

East Africa Command was formed on 15 September under Lt General Sir William Platt, commander of the forces in the north. The 25th East African Brigade had meantime been moved from the Lake Rudolph area of northern Kenya to the coast, and had then been taken by sea to Massawa; it now moved up to face the Wolchefit defences. On the 16th one of the remaining Ju 86s was hit by AA and force-landed 18 miles north-east of Debra Tabor.

It was now becoming clear that the Italian S 75 transports flying regularly in to Gondar were using the airfield at Jibuti in French Somaliland as a staging post. The Mohawk Fighter Flight was therefore ordered to move to Aiscia, close to the frontier, in an effort to intercept this traffic. Consequently on 16 September Captains Parsonson and Snyman, with Lt Strong, took off for Yavello, on the first part of their journey; Strong crashed at Mega, breaking an arm and a leg. By the 18th the rest of the Flight was ready at Aiscia and early the next morning Lt Turner was scrambled after two unidentified aircraft, which managed to escape before he could attack. Permission was given on 23 September to attack the S 75s on neutral Vichy French territory if necessary.

Meanwhile at Gondar on 21 September the Ca 133 was destroyed by fire at night, sabotage being suspected. With the last possibility of air reinforcement gone, and with the road to Gondar cut, the Wolchefit garrison surrendered on 27 September, 950 men having been killed or wounded there by air attack and artillery fire; no ground assault was necessary. During the day one of the CR 42s strafed.

Thursday, 2 to Wednesday, 15 October 1941

At Aiscia the Mohawks were found to be too few in number adequately to patrol the French Somaliland border, so on 2 October the three Ju 86s of 35 SAAF Flight were moved there also, joined by four Vincents from 8 Squadron, RAF, in Aden. Two days later it was reported that an S 75 was at Jibuti, and Capt Parsonson flew over, but was unable to see it. He returned at 0700 on 5 October making two more sorties later in the day. On the last of these he saw the aircraft on the airfield and dived on it twice, setting it on fire and totally destroying it. The French complained strongly, maintaining that it was a Red Cross aircraft, but despite this action the flights from Italy continued. Two more Mohawks arrived at Aiscia a few days later, and on the 14th the Flight reverted to its identity as 'B' Flight, 3 SAAF Squadron.

Both CR 42s flew reconnaissance sorties over Debra Tabor and Tacazze on 8 October, also strafing vehicles, but all was now being readied for the final assault on the fortress as the rainy season drew to a close. Since 4 August Gondar had received 96,290 lb of bombs and 74,500 rounds of ammunition from the squadrons of 205 Group. On 10 October the three Gladiators of 'A' Flight, 3 SAAF Squadron Detachment with 'C' Flight, 41 SAAF Squadron, moved to Dabat, near Wolchefit, and very close to the front; on arrival a CR 42 strafed the landing ground but caused no damage. It was clear to the Italians that the end would not now be long delayed, and Colonello Busoni informed Rome that if Gondar fell, Sottoten Ildebrando Malavolti and Mar Giuseppe Mottet, both volunteers, would take off in the last two CR 42s, one to attack Asmara and Gura airfields and then bale out, the other to attack Alomata and then fly to Jibuti.

Thursday, 16 to Friday, 31 October 1941

On 16 October the three Gladiators and remaining Hurricane tried to trap the two surviving CR 42s into coming out over Azozo, but when the one Italian fighter that did appear spotted the South African fighters, it fled. Success was not far off, however, for on the 24th Generale Nasi's headquarters wished to find out whether a small bridge at Kulkaber was still out of use, or if it had been repaired, and ordered an air reconnaissance to be made. Col Busoni did not like the order, as he had only one aircraft serviceable and considered it too risky to send one fighter alone over the area on a mission he considered to be of little importance. He therefore requested that the mission be postponed until the following day, when both CR 42s would be available. Army headquarters disagreed and Busoni received a direct order to despatch one aircraft immediately. When Sottoten Malavolti received the order to undertake the

Some of the last Italian AF personnel at Gondar, 23 October 1941. On the far left is Tenente Case who flew the last Ca 133 on many supply missions. Third left is Sottotenente Malavolti who was killed the next day when his CR 42 was shot down by a SAAF Gladiator in the last aerial combat of the campaign. *(Corrado Ricci)*

flight from Busoni, he too requested that it should wait until the other Fiat was ready. Reluctantly, Busoni had to order him off, Malavolti pleading that it was certain death to fly alone over the area due to the presence of the Gladiators. He took off convinced that he was unlikely to return.

At 1735 the South Africans at Dabat heard an aircraft overhead in heavy cloud and then sighted the CR 42. Lt L.C.H. Hope at once flew in the direction of Gondar, seeing it again 1,000 feet below; diving on it, he opened fire at 300 yards. Malavolti took violent evasive action, but Hope continued to follow, closing to only 20 yards and firing as the Fiat tried to dive away. There was a brief flicker of flame and the last Italian aircraft to be shot down over East Africa spun into the ground and burst into flames near Ambazzo. Next day the wreckage was found, the dead pilot still in the cockpit. Hope dropped a message on the Italian positions at Ambazzo:

> 'Tribute to the pilot of the Fiat. He was a brave man. South African Air Force.'

Two Hartbeestes with Gladiator escort bombed and strafed Guranba on this date.

Lt Hope was not to remain long in action himself, for late on 31 October he undertook an unauthorised evening strafe of motor boats on Lake Tana, also attacking a convoy on the way to the lake. He was hit by AA and crash-landed on fire at 200 mph hitting a tree and crashing in flames. He got out, burned, but was shot in the head by colonial troops who then beat him with their rifle butts. He was rescued by Italian officers, but was blind for two days. After the fall of Gondar and Hope's release, a Court of Inquiry was held on 30 November to consider the loss of his aircraft. The finding was that his unofficial act was prompted by excessive zeal and overkeenness.

Saturday, 1 to Wednesday, 12 November 1941

With the start of November came the final preparations for the assault on Gondar, for which the SAAF would have 45 aircraft, joined by the Wellesleys of 47 Squadron. On 1 November a Gladiator and a Hartbeeste attacked a large barge and other vessels at Gorgora on Lake Tana. The next day a Hartbeeste was damaged by AA. On the 6th another was hit and Capt du Toit had to dive it to blow out a fire in the cockpit. By 9 November, however, the Mohawks had arrived at Alomata ready for action and equipped to carry light bombs. 3 SAAF Squadron now had ten of these new aircraft with 'B' Flight, five more plus four Gladiators and one Hurricane serving with 'A' Flight; 41 SAAF Squadron still had 25 Hartbeestes. Only these two squadrons and the faithful old Wellesleys of 47 Squadron would take part in the assault.

The Mohawk's first action over the front was not a good start as one attacked an unmarked friendly position and was damaged by return fire. However on 11 November assistance was given to the 2nd Ethiopian Battalion attacking Gianda, and Lt Col Ormsby, the Artillery CRA, was flown over Gondar in a Hartbeeste. Within the fortress the Italians were now suffering mutinies from their colonial troops. Aircraft made heavy attacks south of Fercaber on the 12th, bombing and strafing ahead of advancing infantry. Two Hartbeestes were seen to go down: 2/Lt G.G.J. Van Dyk force-landing near Dabat, having shot off part of the cooling system of his engine with his own front guns; while Lt A.W.

Penver's aircraft was hit by AA and force-landed 70 miles east of Gondar. He was stranded there for thirteen days until flown out on the 25th. An S 75 from Rome had landed at Jibuti the previous day, as bad weather prevented its landing direct at Gondar. On that date it took off at dusk, approaching Gondar in darkness. There it struck a mountain peak near Debra Marcos and blew up.

Thursday, 13 to Thursday, 20 November 1941

The British force south of Gondar attacked Kulkaber on 13 November, took it, but was driven out again. More forces were brought up to attack from the rear when a new assault was ready to be launched. A rumour had grown that 15 German aircraft had arrived, and on the 14th four Wellesleys of 47 Squadron led by Sqn Ldr D.M. Illsley DFC, who had just become commanding officer, searched for these. Nothing was found of course, but for unknown reasons Illsley's aircraft, K7759, crashed and the crew was killed. On this date Celga was taken by the ground forces.

Nine Wellesleys, 24 Hartbeestes and 12 Mohawks raided Ambazzo, Defeccia, Gondar and Azozo on 17 November, dropping 10,880lb of bombs. Capt du Toit's Hartbeeste was again hit in the engine by AA, and he just made it to Dabat. Three days later fourteen waves each of three aircraft were sent out to assist in the attack on Fercaber and the Kulkaber Pass. One Mohawk stalled and crashed on take-off, Lt G.R. Jacobs being killed. Further attacks assisted the 25th East African Brigade in its assault on Kulkaber next day. The Italians there surrendered after 107 patriots had died attacking from the south and west, and 99 Imperial casualties had been suffered. Many Italians had been killed in the air attacks.

Saturday, 22 to Thursday, 27 November 1941

The last CR 42, flown by Mar Mottet, was sent out on 22 November; it attacked British artillery at Kulkaber and killed Lt Col Ormsby, the CRA, with the one burst it fired. This was to be the last Regia Aeronautica sortie to be flown. On the 23rd the Hartbeestes attacked the road at Gorgora, followed 15 minutes later by the Mohawks. The end was very near, and on the 26th the CR 42 was burnt to prevent its falling into British hands. At dawn the next day a great artillery barrage opened on the main fortress at Gondar, and aircraft were overhead all day, eight Mohawks, six Wellesleys and sixteen Hartbeestes dropping 12,544lb of bombs. Armoured cars had just reached Azozo when 2/Lt Robinson came in to land with the engine of his Hartbeeste badly hit by AA. By the end of the day Generale Nasi had surrendered, and the next day leaflets drafted by him were dropped to outlying outposts which were still resisting, informing them that the battle was over. 11,500 Italians, 12,000 Africans, 400 machine guns, 48 field guns and 24 mortars were captured.

So ended a long, hard campaign, fought by both sides with courage, determination, endurance and a high degree of chivalry. It had been fought in the face of supply problems that often seemed insoluble — indeed, for the Italians they were — and fought over very great distances with relatively small forces. Let there be no doubt that the Italian forces both on the ground and in the air performed most creditably, and that the Regia Aeronautica had given the RAF and the SAAF a very tough fight.

There only remained French Somaliland. Consideration was given to its invasion, but in the event it was simply blockaded in an effort to force the French into allowing the British to use the railway from Jibuti. 'B' Flight of 3 SAAF Squadron returned to Aiscia after the fall of Gondar to keep an eye on them, and while there saw one small piece of action. On 11 December 1941 Lt Gazzard had just taken off on patrol in a Mohawk when he saw a Vichy French Potez 631 from Jibuti dive over the airfield. He gave chase and the rear gunner opened fire on his aircraft; replying, he saw smoke pour from the port engine, but the aircraft escaped in cloud.

At this stage the final dispositions were:

> Nairobi: 3 SAAF Squadron HQ, 35 SAAF Flight HQ
> Aiscia: 3 SAAF Squadron 'B' Flight
> Addis Ababa: 41 SAAF Squadron HQ, 'A' and 'B' Flights
> Azozo: 41 SAAF Squadron 'C' Flight
> Mombasa: 34 SAAF Flight
> Dar-es-Salaam: 34 SAAF Flight Detachment

47 Squadron, RAF, had already left for Egypt to become a general reconnaissance unit, and 3 SAAF Squadron would soon return to the Union where its Mohawks were required for training fighter pilots for the Western Desert. The Coastal Flights were forced to carry on with their elderly and worn Ju 86s and Ansons for only a short while longer. The outbreak of war with Japan on 8 December 1941, and the imminent danger in the Indian Ocean in early 1942 was to lead to their re-equipment with Marylands and Bristol Beauforts.

VICTORY CLAIM TOTALS OF MOST SUCCESSFUL REGIA AERONAUTICA FIGHTER PILOTS

Cap Mario Visinitini	16*	412ª Squadrilgia
Serg Magg Luigi Baron	12 (+2 shared)	412ª Squadrilgia
Mar Aroldo Soffritti	8	412ª Squadrilgia
Ten Carlo Canella	7	412ª Squadrilgia
Ten Alberto Veronese	6 (+2 shared)	410ª Squadrilgia
Serg Magg Antonio Giardina	5 (+3 shared)	412ª Squadrilgia
Serg Magg Enzo Omiccioli	5	412ª Squadrilgia
Ten Osvaldo Bartolozzi	3 (+1 shared)	413ª Squadrilgia
Mar Giuseppe Mottet	2***	413ª Squadrilgia
Magg Corrado Ricci	2****	410ª Squadrilgia
Ten Franco De Micheli	2 (+1 shared)	413ª Squadrilgia

* Visinitini had previously claimed 1 in Spain
** Bartolozzi was to claim 3 more during 1943
*** Mottet had previously claimed 4 in Spain
**** Ricci had previously claimed 2 in Spain

(Listing via Giovanni Massimello)

SECTION II · IRAQ

Chapter Six

THE FIGHT FOR IRAQ — MAY 1941

The defeat of Turkey during World War I brought to an end the long-standing Turkish Empire. One of its former colonies, Iraq, an Arab state in the eastern Mediterranean area, was placed under British mandate immediately after the conflict and this mandate lasted until December 1927. At that time, a treaty had been signed between Britain and Iraq, recognising the latter as an independent state, and in October 1932 Iraq had been admitted to the League of Nations. The treaty guaranteed Iraqi assistance to Britain in the event of war and allowed passage of British troops through the country; a British Military Mission remained with the Iraqi army and two bases for the Royal Air Force were retained and were considerably developed. One of these was at Shaibah, near the port of Basra on the Persian Gulf, in southern Iraq; the other was at Habbaniya, situated on the River Euphrates and on the main Baghdad–Haifa highway, 55 miles (88 km) west of Baghdad. This large base contained, in 1941, an engineering depot, a communications flight, 4 Service Flying Training School and ancillary services.

Both bases were important staging posts on the route between Egypt and India, and both were protected by locally enlisted levies, recruited mainly from wandering Bedouin tribes. The loyalty of these levies was untested and uncertain at the outbreak of war in the Middle East in June 1940, but, in the event, they were to prove loyal, tough and efficient troops when the hour of trial came. Iraqi troops were responsible for the internal security of the country and for the protection of oil pipelines from northern Iraq to Haifa in Palestine and Tripoli in Syria. Of the two bases, Habbaniya was of the greater importance, but it was very vulnerable to attack. Situated on low ground by the Euphrates, it was overlooked by a high plateau some 1,000 yards (915 m) to the south, which rose to 150 feet (45 m). Beyond this plateau was Lake Habbaniya, used by the Short Empire flying boats of BOAC on the routes to the Far East.

Britain's main alternative route to the Middle East, should the Mediterranean become closed to her, was around the Cape of Good Hope, up the east coast of Africa and through the Red Sea to Suez. However, in case this route should also be closed by, for instance, the Italians in East Africa, a good alternative route had been planned. This involved the use of the Persian Gulf as far as Basra in southern Iraq; from Basra a railway ran to Baghdad, and from Baghdad a very good desert motor road to Haifa had been improved at great cost to the

British early in the war. As a result of this, any threat to the British presence in Iraq was obviously to be strongly resisted. From the start of World War II, however, the Iraqis had shown a marked reluctance to honour their part of the treaty, and had only broken off relations with Germany following British pressure. They did not follow this with a declaration of war as called for by the treaty, nor did they break off relations with Italy in 1940. The result was that, by early 1941, the Italian Legation in Baghdad was a veritable hive of Axis spies and other agents. Anti-British feeling ran high in certain quarters, and the Grand Mufti of Jerusalem with other Anglophobe Arabs from Palestine had found sanctuary within this city.

When war had broken out between Italy, the United Kingdom and France on 10 June 1940, all initial action had been well to the west of the Suez Canal, centring around Malta and the Libyan–Egyptian frontier. The early removal of France from the fighting left Italy with a somewhat freer hand in the Mediterranean, and in October 1940, an invasion of north-western Greece was launched from Albania, a country which Mussolini had annexed a couple of years earlier. At first it looked as if nothing could prevent Mussolini's forces sweeping all before them, and turning the Mediterranean into the Italian lake of which the dictator boasted. At the same time, as has already been recounted, other Italian forces from the East African colonies of Eritrea and Ethiopia occupied British frontier territory in Sudan and northern Kenya, and bombed Aden, threatening the all-important Red Sea route to Suez. As a result the importance of Iraq to the British increased greatly virtually overnight.

It was at the moment that German involvement in the Balkans seemed imminent, and as all earlier British successes in Libya crumbled into dust, that a *coup d'état* brought to power in Baghdad one Rashid Ali el Ghailani, a previous Prime Minister noted for his pro-Axis sympathies, who now proclaimed himself to be Chief of the National Defence Government. He was backed by four generals, known as the 'Golden Square' and also highly pro-Axis. The uncle of the young King of Iraq, Emir Abdul Illah, who was acting as Regent, and who was a friend of Britain, now learning of a plot for his arrest, fled to Basra where he and his chief followers were taken aboard a British warship, HMS *Cockchafer*, and conveyed to Transjordan.

In the face of these events, the British government decided to take action. General Wavell, Commander in Chief, Middle East, did not wish to become involved in any sort of military operations in Iraq due to the pressures on his command elsewhere. At this stage, the Government of India was responsible for Iraq and was asked if troops could be made available for despatch to Basra. A brigade group was about to leave Karachi for Malaya, but this was at once diverted to Iraq; it was not due to arrive until 18 April, so to expedite matters it was decided that 400 men of the 1st Battalion of the King's Own Royal Regiment should be transported by air. Rashid Ali was informed on 16 April that the British intended to invoke the treaty rights and to land troops for onward transmission to Palestine. At Karachi was 31 Squadron equipped with Vickers Valentia biplane transports; 'B' Flight of this unit was just in the process of receiving four Douglas DC-2s, taken over from civil airlines, and, on the 16th, both 'A' and 'B' Flights, aided by three civil Armstrong Whitworth Atalanta airliners, took aboard the battalion and began the first leg of the long flight to Basra.

Vickers Valentia SH-Y of 216 Squadron taking on passengers in Iraq, whilst an arab levy stands guard. *(via A.S. Thomas)*

Tuesday, 15 to Friday, 18 April 1941

At this time, apart from training aircraft at Habbaniya, the only British military aircraft in Iraq were the Vickers Vincent general-purpose biplanes of 244 Squadron based at Shaibah under Sqn Ldr H.V. Alloway. On 15 April, Flg Off Cleaver and two airmen pilots had arrived from Habbaniya with three Fairey Gordon biplanes, and next day another four of these arrived, all seven being attached to 244 in case of any trouble during the arrival of the main part of the brigade group from India. On the 17th, seven Valentias, four DC-2s and three Atalantas landed at Shaibah, and the 1st King's Own deplaned without trouble.

Vickers Vincent I, K6363, of 244 Squadron at Shaibah, South Iraq. *(via A.S. Thomas)*

165

On the next day, the 20th Indian Infantry Brigade, 3rd Field Regiment, RA, and the Headquarters of the 10th Indian Division began disembarking at Basra, the divisional commander, Maj Gen W.A.K. Fraser, taking over command of all land forces in Iraq. 31 Squadron was ordered to remain at Shaibah on detachment for the time being, first duty being to fly the 1st King's Own into Habbaniya to reinforce the garrison.

Friday, 18 to Saturday, 19 April 1941

Rashid Ali's immediate reaction was to request that no more troops be landed until those already in the country had passed through, but the British government refused to give any such undertaking. On the very day of the main disembarkation (18th), the Iraqis showed their hostility actively. This occurred when two of 31 Squadron's Valentias took off from Shaibah to begin flying the reinforcements into Habbaniya; en route one Valentia had occasion to put down on a landing ground at pumping station K-4 on the Tripoli oil pipeline where it was at once attacked by Iraqi troops. After a short skirmish, the crew and the 15 troops on board were taken prisoner and the aircraft was set on fire. The second aircraft also landed, but was unable to help and took off again under fire which wounded two of the crew. It flew on to Habbaniya where it landed safely. The next day, the rest of 31's aircraft moved down to Basra airport and began flying more men and stores to Habbaniya forthwith.

Saturday, 19 to Tuesday, 29 April 1941

By this date, the Wehrmacht had invaded Greece and sent the Greek and Empire forces reeling southwards in retreat, and the evacuation to Crete had already begun. Not surprisingly, Rashid Ali decided that he could count on Axis help should hostilities with the British commence. Indeed an indication had already been given to the Mufti of Jerusalem that the Germans would do anything they could to assist and this assurance had been passed to the Iraqi leader. With the position in Greece so grave and with the forces in the Desert building up for a new offensive, air reinforcements from the already overstretched strength available to the Empire forces was a difficult problem. However, on 19 April, six Gladiator fighters were despatched to Habbaniya from stocks in Egypt to add to three already at the base, and, on the 27th, 84 Squadron's Blenheim IV bombers were sent to Aqir in Palestine. Here 250 Squadron was in process of forming, using as a nucleus 'K' Flight — a fighter flight which had until recently been operating over Eritrea. Two days later, the pilots collected nine Curtiss Tomahawks, the first to be issued to a squadron in the Middle East; but the unit was by no means ready for operations, no matter how great the emergency.

Tuesday, 29 April to Thursday, 1 May 1941

This day, 29 April, was to be the decisive one. In complete opposition to Rashid Ali's request that no further forces be landed, a number of ancillary troops were put ashore at Basra. Again, this elicited no immediate reaction from the Iraqis, but in Baghdad, Rashid Ali and his supporters decided to surround the RAF base at Habbaniya with strong forces including artillery, as a show of strength. British strength was further augmented on this date when a force of four small warships, which had gathered at Basra under Commodore C.M. Graham, was joined by the aircraft carrier HMS *Hermes* and two cruisers. The *Hermes* was put on notice to operate her aircraft next day if necessary.

At Habbaniya the threat was clear: not enough troops were available to occupy the high ground overlooking the camp, but all British women and children in Baghdad were moving for their own safety to the base at the advice of the British Ambassador. Next day, the 30th, two BOAC flying boats took off from Lake Habbaniya, having evacuated the rest house, only six European male members of the Corporation staff being left behind. Later that same day, an Iraqi force, two brigades in strength, was seen by air reconnaissance from Habbaniya to be approaching from the east, and this occupied the plateau with guns, tanks and armoured cars, capturing the remaining BOAC staff and then beginning to dig in.

By the next morning, 1 May, the force investing the base had increased in size to about 9,000 men supported by 50 guns. A demand for their withdrawal was refused and all flying training ceased forthwith. Habbaniya was certainly as ready as it could be for such an emergency and everything possible had been done with what was available. Nearly 60 Hawker Audaxes and Airspeed Oxfords had been converted for bomb-carrying, the Audaxes to take a pair of 250lb (113kg) bombs each, while the Oxfords were to each carry eight 20lb (9kg) missiles fitted to improvised shackles. Intensive courses in bombing and air gunnery had been given to the instructors, some of whom were members of the Hellenic Air Force and spoke little or no English, and most of whom had seen no operational flying whatsoever. As there were only 35 instructors, the more promising pupil pilots were to be allowed to fly operations, while others, plus willing ground staff, were to act as observers, bomb aimers and gunners. Reconnaissance flights had already begun, and as previously mentioned, the approach of the Iraqi forces had been fully observed and reported.

Within the camp, the golf course and polo ground had been cleared to provide a landing ground inside the boundary fence in case the main airfield outside the camp should become untenable. For ground defence there were the 350 infantrymen of the 1st King's Own, about 1,000 airmen of all ranks, six companies of levies (about 1,200 men) and 1 Company, RAF Armoured Cars,

Oxford L4565 of 4 SFTS releasing 20lb bombs over Iraqi positions near Habbaniya. (*V. Cashmore via D. Vincent*)

4 SFTS Airspeed Oxford at Habbaniya, with bomb racks fitted beneath the fuselage for eight 20lb bombs. *(V. Cashmore via D. Vincent)*

with 18 rather elderly Rolls-Royce cars. There were rations for 12 days, but no artillery; fortunately two old World War I pieces were set on the lawns within the camp for display purposes and a Royal Artillery officer was flown in from Basra, reconditioning these and getting them into use for the later stages of the siege. This small force, then, had to defend a perimeter, including a river frontage, of some seven miles (11 km). Against a determined enemy the camp was virtually indefensible.

The aircraft of 4 SFTS were now formed into the Habbaniya Air Striking Force under the base commander, Grp Capt W.A.B. Savile; 'A' Squadron under Wg Cdr G. Silyn-Roberts would operate ten Audaxes from the main airfield; 'B' Squadron under Sqn Ldr A.G. Dudgeon would also fly from the main airfield with one Blenheim I, 26 Oxfords and eight Gordons (returned from their detachment to 244 Squadron at Shaibah); 'C' Squadron under Wg Cdr C.W.M. Wing was to fly its ten Audaxes from the polo ground and 'D' Squadron under Wg Cdr J.G. Hawtrey would operate its ten Audaxes with 'A' and 'B' Squadrons from the main field. The force was completed by the Fighter Flight, formed with the nine Gladiator Is under Flt Lt R.S. May which was to use the polo ground.

At Basra, in retaliation for the Iraqi action, British forces took over the airport, docks and power station, and Iraqi forces were given until the 2nd to withdraw from the town. Frantic efforts were now made to send more reinforcements. On 30 April, nine Vickers Wellington bombers of 70 Squadron under Wg Cdr Golding flew from the Canal Zone to Shaibah, but en route Flt Lt Blackburn suffered an engine failure and had to make a force-landing 30 miles (48 km) west of Habbaniya. One of 31 Squadron's DC-2s took off from this base and landed alongside to pick up the crew of the Wellington and three passengers that it had been carrying, and fly them on to Shaibah. On 1 May, eight more Wellingtons, this time from 37 Squadron, arrived at Aqir, and four

Royal Iraqi Air Force Hawker Nisr at Hinaidi. These aircraft served with 1 (Army Co-operation) Squadron at Mosul in May 1941. *(Sqn Ldr S. Sills via A.S. Thomas)*

Blenheim IVF long-range fighters of 203 Squadron, just returned from Crete, were led by Sqn Ldr Gethin to Lydda. Here they were shortly joined by three more under Sqn Ldr J.M.N. Pike, while the rest of the Squadron was sent to Kabrit, too far away to take part in activities. In Egypt, Wg Cdr Wightman of 94 Squadron, which was just about to re-equip with Hawker Hurricanes after service in Aden, was ordered to collect two Gladiator Is and three Mk IIs from a Maintenance Unit, and together with Flt Lt Sir R.A. MacRobert, Flg Off G.D.F. Herrtage and Sgts E.L. Smith and W.H. Dunwoodie, made ready to fly into Habbaniya.

To face this small and motley RAF contingent in the air was the Royal Iraqi Air Force, which, on paper at any rate, appeared to be a much more potent and formidable organisation. Disposition was as follows:

> 1 (Army Co-operation) Squadron at Mosul. This unit was equipped with Hawker Nisrs (Pegasus-engined Audaxes). Originally 35 of these aircraft had been purchased in 1934 for two squadrons, but one squadron had meanwhile re-equipped. About 25 Nisrs were still airworthy.
>
> 4 (Fighter) Squadron at Kirkuk. This unit was equipped with Gloster Gladiators, 15 of which had been purchased from Britain ex-RAF in 1939. About nine were airworthy.
>
> 5 (Fighter) Squadron at Rashid, Baghdad. Equipped with Breda Ba 65 attack aircraft, 15 of which had been purchased from Italy in 1937, 13 of these differing from those in service with the Regia Aeronautica in having a Breda L dorsal turret for rear defence.
>
> 7 (Fighter-Bomber) Squadron, also at Rashid. Equipped with Douglas-Northrop 8A-4 attack bombers, 15 of which had been purchased from the United States in 1939.
>
> Additionally, four Savoia SM 79B twin-engined bombers had been obtained from Italy in 1937, and these were also at Rashid and available for action. A number of other aircraft including de Havilland Dragons fitted to carry 20lb (9kg) bombs and with dorsal machine gun positions, Dragon Rapides, Dragonflies, Avro Ansons and Tiger Moths, were also available.

Douglas–Northrop 8A-4 attack-bomber of the Royal Iraqi Air Force 7 (Fighter-Bomber) Squadron, based at Rashid.

The British Command was thus faced with several objectives of varying degrees of urgency:

> (i) to defend the base at Habbaniya against the investing force;
> (ii) to relieve the garrison at Habbaniya at the earliest possible moment, and in the meantime to reinforce and support it in any way possible;
> (iii) to secure the removal from power of Rashid Ali el Ghailani and his government in order to neutralise the possibility of Axis intervention and eliminate the threat posed thereby to the rear of the important base and training areas of Palestine and the Nile Delta;
> (iv) to permit the prosecution of the war in the Western Desert with the maximum resources available in the Middle East from a secure base.

Following the refusal of the Iraqis to withdraw from around Habbaniya on 1 May, AVM H.G. Smart, Air Officer Commanding in Iraq, on receiving confirmation that the Foreign Office in London considered the Iraqi action as an act of war, now decided that he would attack the Iraqi forces at dawn on 2 May without prior warning.

Wellington IC of 70 Squadron over Iraq, May 1941. *(S.M. Coates via A.S. Thomas)*

170

Friday, 2 May 1941

In the early hours of 2 May 1941, eight Wellingtons of 70 Squadron and others from 37 Squadron took off to attack Iraqi positions on the plateau south of the camp, arriving at about 0500 and bombing gun positions, lorries and other vehicles. Wg Cdr Golding's bomber was hit by anti-aircraft fire and damaged, while Flg Off Anstey's aircraft suffered such damage that he had to force-land at Habbaniya. A mechanic at once set off on a tractor, escorted by armoured cars, and took the Wellington in tow, but the aircraft was then struck by artillery fire and set ablaze, the tractor also being hit. Immediately after the Wellingtons' attack, 35 Audaxes, Gordons and Oxfords took off and attacked the opposing positions. Although hits were scored on guns, armoured cars and machine gun posts, the Iraqis were well dug-in on broken ground which provided good cover and concealment, and they did not withdraw.

The Iraqis at once opened fire on the camp, and the aircraft using the main airfield had to take off in full view of the gunners. They taxied out of the gates at speed, straight on to the runway, and then took off in steep climbing turns away from the plateau. The aircraft using the polo ground were screened by trees, and were able to get off relatively unhindered. Fire from the ground was heavy, and several aircraft were hit. One Oxford flown by Flg Off D.H. Walsh was shot down in flames and one of the biplanes flown by Plt Off P.R. Gillespy also failed to return. By 1000, Iraqi aircraft were appearing overhead in some strength, but by this time the RAF attacks had already cut down the volume of fire from the Iraqi guns. Several strafing attacks were made by the Iraqi air arm and, before the day was out, had succeeded in destroying three aircraft on the ground. The Fighter Flight was active, Flg Off R.B. Cleaver intercepting one of the SM 79Bs over the camp, but his guns failed just as he began his attack. Flg Off J.M. Craigie was just about to land when he saw a Ba 65, and attacked this, causing it to break off its attack.

Six Blenheims of 84 Squadron took off from Aqir to take part in the attack on the troops on the plateau, escorted by three of 203 Squadron's Blenheim fighters, but the mission proved abortive, the formation being forced to turn back. At 1800, five Wellingtons from 70 Squadron returned for a second attack and were intercepted by two Northrop 8As and two Gladiators which attacked half-heartedly for 20 minutes, doing no damage whatsoever. One Wellington was hit by AA, however, and landed at Habbaniya. By the end of the first day, the aircraft of 4 SFTS had made 193 sorties bombing and strafing. Apart from the five aircraft already mentioned which had been destroyed, about 20 more had been damaged by one cause or another and were unserviceable.

Meanwhile, in southern Iraq, following an extension of the deadline, Iraqi troops had still not withdrawn from the Basra area in the afternoon, and they were then bombed and shelled, withdrawing northwards at once. Vincents of 244 Squadron attacked the railway between Shaibah Junction and Ur, encountering much rifle fire, as a result of which one Vincent crashed and Flt Lt G.B. Haywood, the pilot, was seriously injured. Plt Off F.G. Woolley landed alongside and picked up the crew, taking off again as Iraqi troops tried to reach the aircraft, and later being awarded a DFC for the rescue. During the course of the day, the Squadron made two raids on enemy trenches. On the first, two Vincents were damaged by ground fire and on the second, the aircraft flown by Plt Off S.C. Braybrook was shot down and its crew killed. 244 Squadron was shortly to be joined on operations in the south by the Fairey Swordfish torpedo-bombers of 814 Squadron from HMS *Hermes*, which were to use Shaibah as a land base. In the evening the Wellingtons of 37 Squadron moved from Aqir to join 70 Squadron's detachment at Shaibah.

Following the opening of hostilities, transport aircraft flying supplies and reinforcements into Habbaniya began taking out women and children to Basra. The Committee of Imperial Defence now decided that command of the land forces in Iraq should revert to Middle East Command, and General Wavell was pressed to organise a relief force to go to the aid of the Habbaniya garrison. Desperately short of troops of any sort, he was only able to start putting together a scratch formation comprising initially one mechanised brigade of the 1st Cavalry Regiment short of all equipment, one field regiment RA, a lorry-borne infantry battalion and three mechanised squadrons of the Transjordan Frontier Force. To be known as Habforce, it was short of all heavy weapons, and had no armour of any kind. It would have to cover over 250 miles (400 km) from Haifa to pumping station H-4 near the frontier to assemble, and then move another 285 miles (460 km) to Habbaniya. It could not be ready until about 10 May.

The Iraqi leaders now appealed to the Germans and Italians for aid, but the Germans were involved with the forthcoming invasion of Crete and were deploying also for the attack on the Soviet Union, while the Italians were slow to act, and it was some time before anything happened. The only support came from Général Henri Dentz, High Commissioner in the adjoining French-mandated territory of Syria, which was firmly in the hands of the Vichy government. Dentz, following German pressure, agreed that Axis aircraft en route to Iraq from Greece and Rhodes could use Syrian airfields for refuelling. The Vichy Foreign Minister, Amiral Darlan, a noted Anglophobe, subsequently agreed to supply Iraq with arms and ammunition from Syrian stores, and to pass on to the Germans military intelligence regarding the British forces in the area. These acts were to have very serious consequences for the French.

Saturday, 3 May 1941

During the first day's fighting at Habbaniya, the fire of the Iraqi artillery had not proved nearly so damaging as had been feared, and so well was the attack on the positions on the plateau being carried out by the Habbaniya Air Striking Force that AVM Smart decided that some of the effort on 3 May might be more profitably expended in attacking the Royal Iraqi Air Force at its bases in order to cut down the number of sorties its units were able to make against the RAF base. Consequently, at dawn, three Wellingtons of 37 Squadron took off to bomb the airfield at Rashid, while a fourth bomber attacked the lines near Habbaniya. At Rashid, several Iraqi aircraft tried to intercept, but the Wellington gunners claimed one Hawker Nisr shot down and damaged a second; one Wellington returned with six bullet holes in it. The damaged Wellington of 70 Squadron which had landed at Habbaniya the previous evening had now been repaired, and during the morning, this took off under fire, escorted by two Gladiators of the Fighter Flight, safely returning to Shaibah.

Throughout the day the Wellingtons of both squadrons and the aircraft of the Air Striking Force kept up steady patrols, bombing and strafing whatever movement was seen. The latter put up a further 119 sorties of this type. Iraqi aircraft again attacked, but accomplished very little; Flg Off Cleaver in one of the Gladiators again intercepted an SM 79B and made three attacks, firing 1,200

Unserviceable Hawker Audaxes, with their top wings removed. They were placed on the airfield as dummies, to persuade the Iraqis and their German allies that Hurricanes were present in numbers. The third aircraft in the far background is a Fairey Gordon. *(V. Cashmore via D. Vincent)*

rounds — the bomber was last seen diving steeply with smoke pouring from the port engine. Flt Lt May attacked a formation of Northrops, firing on one but without apparent result. During the day, Sqn Ldr Pike of 203 Squadron led four fighter Blenheims to Habbaniya. They were fired on by Iraqi machine guns while landing. Other Blenheims of this unit made a strafing attack on troops near the pipeline — fortunately without causing any serious damage as the recipients of their attention were members of the Royal Engineers and the Arab

Vickers Wellington ICs of 37 Squadron operating from Egypt over Habbaniya in May 1941. *(37 Squadron via A.S. Thomas)*

173

Legion! In the south, six Swordfish of 814 Squadron flew their first mission, a demonstration of strength over Basra.

To add to the problems of the British command, Iraqi police occupying a fort at Rutbah on the Haifa oil pipeline, some miles to the west of pumping station H-3, fired on British personnel working on the road nearby during the day. To prevent the possible use of the landing ground at Rutbah and that at H-3 by German aircraft, should these fly into Iraq as was feared, a small force was at once assembled at H-4 in Transjordan under the command of Grp Capt L.O. Brown. This force comprised a mechanised squadron of the Transjordan Frontier Force, a Desert Patrol of the Arab Legion and a company of the Essex Regiment flown to Lydda from Egypt in Bombay bomber-transports of 216 Squadron.

Sunday, 4 May 1941

37 Squadron was in the air again at dawn on 4 May, eight Wellingtons once more attacking Rashid airfield, while two others made for the lines at Habbaniya. At Rashid, buildings were bombed and aircraft strafed, a direct hit being scored on one small biplane. Fighters again took off and much rifle and machine gun fire was encountered. Sqn Ldr Rivett-Carnac's aircraft was attacked by a Northrop, but the rear gunner got in some good bursts and the Iraqi aircraft was last seen smoking and with flames coming from its engine. Sgt Noden was also attacked by either a Northrop or a Breda Ba 65 when ten miles (16 km) south of the target, this aircraft finally breaking away in a spiral dive with smoke streaming from its engine. Plt Off Castello had an indecisive engagement with a single-engined biplane over Baghdad, but Plt Off Rash flew low over a 20mm AA battery while being attacked from astern by a Gladiator. Both fighter and guns hit the Wellington and shortly afterwards it force-landed in

Two Douglas DC-2s of 'B' Flight, 31 Squadron at Habbaniya. DG478 (ex VT-APA) is nearest to the airfield fence. *(V. Cashmore via D. Vincent)*

hostile territory, the crew being taken prisoner. (They were to be held until the end of May, when all prisoners of war were handed back.)

At Habbaniya the guns had again opened a bombardment at dawn, but died away as soon as aircraft appeared overhead. At 0710, two of the 203 Squadron fighter Blenheims took off, Sqn Ldr Pike (T2189) and Flg Off Gordon-Hall (T2072) strafing Rashid and Baghdad airport. At the latter, a Gladiator and three Nisrs were strafed, while at the former an SM 79B, a Breda or Northrop and a Nisr were attacked, the Nisr being left in flames. A third Blenheim, flown by Sgt Hemsted, left at 1430 on a photographic reconnaissance mission to Mosul, Kirkuk, Baghdad and Solman Doh, strafing two Nisrs at Mosul and being hit in the tail seven times by return fire. Throughout the day, aircraft of 31 Squadron, which was now operating six Valentias and six DC-2s, kept up a shuttle service, flying more of the 1st King's Own in and refugees out. The number of sorties mounted by the Air Striking Force was down to 53, but that night it was decided that nocturnal sorties should be flown to deny the Iraqis their sleep, Audaxes operating if there was a moon and Oxfords if not.

At H-4, air support arrived in the shape of four Blenheims from 84 Squadron led by Flt Lt Plinston and two from 203 Squadron under Sqn Ldr Gethin, who was made commanding officer of RAF Detachment H-4. Ground crews from 84, 113 and 211 Squadrons, the latter fresh from Greece and Crete, arrived to service the aircraft. Initially duties involved mainly reconnaissance flights along the pipelines and the provision of cover to troops advancing on H-3 and Rutbah. The Transjordan Frontier Force occupied H-3 without opposition before the day was out, but refused to attack the Iraqi-held fort at Rutbah, being unwilling to fight fellow Arabs. In the south, operations against the Iraqis continued, four Swordfish from *Hermes* landing at Shaibah to refuel before making their first bombing raid on a rail bridge over the Euphrates. After dark, a Wellington of 37 Squadron took off from Shaibah but struck the boundary fence and crashed, catching fire at once.

Monday, 5 to Tuesday, 6 May 1941
Attacks were again made on the positions around Habbaniya on the 5th by

Blenheim IV of 84 Squadron under guard by Arab Legion troop at H-4 landing ground. *(IWM)*

Bristol Bombay SH-Y, L5857, of 216 Squadron on a transport sortie to Habbaniya in May 1941. *(216 Squadron via A.S. Thomas)*

Wellingtons and aircraft of the Air Striking Force which flew 80 sorties. At 1725, Flg Off Lane-Sansom of 203 Squadron took off in a fighter Blenheim (L9335) to strafe Baghdad and Rashid, firing at two SM 79Bs and a Gladiator at the latter. That night, demoralised by the continual air attacks, the Iraqis began leaving their positions. To the south, a Vincent of 244 Squadron was forced to land in the sea in the darkness. The pilot was later picked up, but both the air gunner and a passenger were lost. A dawn reconnaissance from Habbaniya on 6 May found the Iraqis leaving, and Col O.L. Roberts, commander of the ground forces at Habbaniya since the arrival of the 1st King's Own Royals, on receipt of this information, led the garrison in a sortie which, supported by Audaxes, drove the enemy from the high ground. Their morale broken by the constant air attacks, the Iraqis now began a disorderly withdrawal to Fallujah on the Baghdad road, the Air Striking Force keeping up a heavy assault and inflicting many casualties. The Wellingtons were again active, and at 0930 six from 37 Squadron raided Rashid once more, setting fire to a hangar and gaining a direct hit on a twin-engined aircraft, while others were claimed damaged. During the afternoon, a column of motorised infantry and artillery was seen approaching from the direction of Fallujah — the Iraqi High Command was sending in reinforcements. Forty aircraft were sent to attack these reinforcements and left them 'a solid mass of flames 250 yards long'.

The Air Striking Force made a total of 139 sorties on this date, one aircraft being damaged. One Gladiator intercepted a Northrop during an attack on the polo ground landing strip at Habbaniya, and got in two bursts before the Iraqi aircraft fled, but two of the Gladiator pilots on the ground were wounded by bomb splinters during the attack. The transport Valentias had rather a bad day, one crashing at pumping station K-3, while three more had to force-land in the open due to various causes. The transport force had, however, been considerably strengthened during the day by the arrival at Lydda of five Bristol Bombays and two Valentias of 216 Squadron on detachment. These flew troops and ammunition to both H-4 and Habbaniya throughout the rest of the month.

Wednesday, 7 to Thursday, 8 May 1941
At 1045 on 7 May, a lone Iraqi Nisr suddenly raided Habbaniya. Sgt Hemsted

of 203 Squadron scrambled his fighter Blenheim and gave chase, closing and shooting down the Nisr in flames. Two more of the unit's Blenheims, flown by Sqn Ldr Pike and Flg Off Gordon-Hall, flew a reconnaissance over Baquba at 1440, seeing 21 aircraft — Northrops, Bredas and Nisrs — on the ground and strafing these. At 1635, both pilots took off again, this time with a formation of Audaxes and Oxfords of the Air Striking Force, for a repeat attack. At Baquba, all the British aircraft bombed and strafed, the trainers destroying three aircraft and damaging others, while the Blenheims set another three on fire. Plt Off J. Watson in one of the Gladiators, who had accompanied the formation, engaged an Iraqi Gladiator from astern at point blank range, the enemy aircraft being last seen diving steeply.

In Egypt Wg Cdr Wightman's 94 Squadron detachment was now ready, and left Ismailia on the first leg of the journey to Habbaniya. With the arrival of these reinforcements, 'A' Squadron was re-formed next day as a fighter unit, 1 Flight, comprising the new 94 Squadron aircraft using the main airfield, while 2 Flight, with the old Fighter Flight Gladiators, remained at the polo field. The Air Striking Force completed 47 sorties over the Fallujah Plain against the retreating Iraqis, but on one of these Sgt H. Brattan was hit by small arms fire and killed while piloting an Oxford over the area. Aircraftsman K.E.W. Clifton, the air gunner, took over the controls, flew the aircraft back to base and managed to land it safely. During the day the first German aircraft to arrive in the area landed at Aleppo in Syria and then flew on to Mosul. However by this time the Royal Iraqi Air Force had almost ceased to exist as a result of the RAF's attentions.

The use of the training aircraft in the offensive role at Habbaniya and the aggressive defence put up by the small garrison had succeeded beyond all expectations by the evening of 8 May. Already the demoralised Iraqi forces were driven from around the base and had been forced on to the defensive at Fallujah. The attacks pressed home on the bases of the Royal Iraqi Air Force had also proved highly successful, and some 30 aircraft had been totally destroyed, most of them on the ground. Many others had been damaged and rendered temporarily unserviceable. To all intents and purposes Iraqi aircraft had disappeared from the skies and were no longer a serious factor for consideration. The makeshift Air Striking Force had added greatly to its laurels by taking part in the total destruction of the Iraqi reinforcement column approaching Fallujah. This entire episode had so far cost the RAF little more than a dozen aircraft, only three of these modern operational types. For the Iraqis the main hope now rested on speedy and adequate Axis aid. Aid was indeed on the way, but it was taking an unconscionable time in coming and, in the event, was to prove far from adequate.

As the second week of action started, the Order of Battle of the Royal Iraqi Air Force barely existed; it was no more than a handful of surviving aircraft, hidden as best as possible from further attention by the RAF. This latter force meanwhile had grown somewhat in strength, and was now disposed as follows:

Habbaniya

'A' Squadron	14 Gladiator Is and IIs
'B' Squadron	All remaining serviceable Oxfords, Audaxes, Gordons
'C' Squadron	and one Blenheim I
'D' Squadron	
203 Squadron (Det)	Four Blenheim IVFs

Transjordan

84 Squadron (Det)	Five Blenheim IVs at H-4
203 Squadron (Det)	Two Blenheim IVFs at H-4

Palestine

84 Squadron	Blenheim IVs at Aqir
203 Squadron	Blenheim IVFs at Lydda
216 Squadron (Det)	Five Bombays and two Valentias at Lydda
250 Squadron	Tomahawk IIBs at Aqir (non-operational)

Southern Iraq

37 Squadron (Det)	13 Wellington IAs at Shaibah
70 Squadron	
244 Squadron	Vincents at Shaibah
31 Squadron (Det)	Six Valentias, four Douglas DC-2s and three chartered A-W Atalantas at Shaibah
814 Squadron	Swordfish at Shaibah

Friday, 9 to Saturday, 10 May 1941

At 0520 on 9 May, Sqn Ldr Pike and Flg Off Gordon-Hall of 203 Squadron left Habbaniya to attack Mosul. As they approached the target, Gordon-Hall's aircraft suddenly climbed away and headed for home, but Pike continued his attack, destroying four aircraft on the ground. He then turned for base, but 30 miles (48 km) from Mosul he saw Gordon-Hall's Blenheim on the ground, having obviously crashed. Radio Baghdad subsequently announced that the pilot and observer had been captured, the gunner having died in the crash. While this attack was under way, in the south two Vincents of 244 Squadron carried out a dive-bombing attack on barracks at Amara. From Habbaniya the Air Striking Force made 53 sorties. A reconnaissance pilot over Rashid airfield saw an SM 79B, three Breda Ba 65s, a Nisr and a Moth, all of which he strafed; claiming to have destroyed the Savoia.

Early in the day the forces from H-4 were ready to attack the fort at Rutbah, and a Blenheim from the detachment dropped messages ordering the Iraqis to surrender. No reply was received, so four Blenheims from 84 Squadron attacked singly, each making two passes; all four were hit by small arms fire, Flg Off Goudge having to make a crash-landing near H-3, while the other aircraft were all rendered unserviceable and were forced to fly back to Aqir later in the day for repair and overhaul. The army reported that the attacks seemed to have improved the enemy's morale, rather than induced them to surrender! Following the departure of the 84 Squadron Blenheims, only Sqn Ldr Gethin's fighter

Mark IVF, L9174, remained at H-4. Consequently next morning Flg Off A. Watson was sent up from Lydda by 203 Squadron in another Blenheim (L9042), and at 1335 Gethin took off to attack the fort, followed ten minutes later by Watson. Each aircraft made several attacks on the fort, strafing and bombing, and while doing so the pilots noted two columns of armoured cars clearly engaged in a fight. Uncertain which were British, they refrained from attacking either. Heavy rifle and machine gun fire then hit both aircraft, and Gethin made off in the direction of the columns, but the aircraft suddenly pulled up and then crashed. Watson at once landed alongside, and he and Gethin, who had staggered from the crashed aircraft, tried to get out the other members of the crew, but heat and exploding ammunition drove them back. They then came under fire from hostile armoured cars and were forced to climb aboard the surviving Blenheim with all speed and take off for base. Tragically, Gethin was to die from the injuries he had sustained a few hours after landing back at H-4. One of the columns of armoured cars that they had seen was 2 Company, RAF Armoured Cars, which had just arrived after a 1,000-mile (1,610-km) drive and had gone straight into action.

Wellingtons of 37 Squadron again attacked Iraqi airfields during the day, bombing barracks at Mosul and Kirkuk. From Shaibah 814 Squadron's Swordfish made the first of a series of attacks on Iraqi army barracks, carrying old RAF 112lb (50.8kg) bombs of World War I vintage. On this occasion the barracks at Nazari were the target. At Aqir, 211 Squadron, recently back from Greece, arrived from Lydda equipped only with a few Blenheim Is. That night one member of the Squadron went as an observer aboard a Valentia of 216 Squadron making a bombing attack on Rutbah fort. The fort was to fall to the RAF armoured cars during the morning of 11 May, the whole area then passing into British hands. A little later reinforcements arrived and command passed from Grp Capt Brown to Maj Gen J.G.M. Clark, as the units from the attack on Rutbah became a part of 'Habforce'. It was intended that the main body of this force would hold the lines of communication, while a mobile flying column forming its spearhead, and to be known as 'Kingcol', would press on to Habbaniya as fast as possible. Under the leadership of Brigadier J.J. Kingstone, commander of 4th Cavalry Brigade, 'Kingcol' was about 2,000 strong and had some 500 vehicles; it comprised The Household Cavalry Regiment, a battery of the Royal Artillery, an anti-tank troop, various headquarters and service detachments and 2 Company, RAF Armoured Cars. It would cross the Iraqi frontier on the 13th, and advance via Rutbah to Habbaniya. To support this move the detachment at H-4 was reinforced with another of 203's fighter Blenheims from Lydda.

Sunday, 11 May 1941

Meanwhile, from Habbaniya at 0510 on the 11th, Sqn Ldr Pike and Sgt Hemsted of the same unit joined with Gladiators of 'A' Squadron in escorting Audaxes and Oxfords to attack Rashid again. Both Blenheims dive-bombed buildings while the Gladiators strafed dumps and the trainers bombed and strafed various targets. Pike and Flg Off Lane-Sansom escorted a similar mission at 0845, and others were flown during the day, being repeated daily for the next three days. In the south, raids were made by trios of Swordfish on barracks at Samawa and Nazaria, these sorties also being repeated next day. Luftwaffe aircraft were now flying towards Iraq at last, and for fighter operations the Messerschmitt Bf

110Cs of Olt Hobein's 4 Staffel of Zerstörergeschwader 76 had been transferred from Belgrade to Athens–Tatoi, from where, after being overpainted with Iraqi insignia, the fighters had been ordered to Mosul. During the day, three of these were overflying Syria when they were intercepted and forced to land by Morane-Saulnier 406 fighters of Groupe de Chasse 1/7 of the Armée de l'Air. At Aqir, 250 Squadron at last became operational on its Tomahawks, but ten pilots and aircraft were at once ordered on detachment to Amriya for the air defence of Alexandria.

Monday, 12 May 1941

The demands of the Western Desert were being felt elsewhere at this time, for next day the detachments of Wellingtons from 37 and 70 Squadrons flew back to Egypt. Since the end of the immediate threat to Habbaniya, both detachments had concentrated their efforts on attacking the Royal Iraqi Air Force's bases, a task which they had carried out with notable success. On this same date Flt Lt Plinston of 84 Squadron led a flight of six Blenheims into Habbaniya via H-4. A few Lysanders of 208 Squadron, another unit just back from Greece, were ordered from Gaza to H-4.

It was on 12 May that RAF reconnaissance aircraft first noted the presence in Iraq of Luftwaffe aircraft. Fliegerkorps VIII in Greece had now despatched a small contingent under the command of Oberst Werner Junck, who had been appointed Fliegerführer Irak. This force comprised:

4/ZG 76: 12 Messerschmitt Bf 110C twin-engined fighters led by Olt Hobein. The other pilots were Olt Herget, Lt Drewes, Lt Eisenach, Lt Froehling, Ofw Brandsetter, Ofw Neureiter, Ofw Piwarz, Uffz Hennies, Uffz Wenke, Uffz Ziegler and Ofhr Bob.

One Kette of ZG 26 comprising two Bf 110Cs led by Lt Woerner.

4/KG 4: seven He 111H-6 bombers led by Hpt Schwanhäuser.

Five He 111s left Italy on 12 May, arriving later that day in Syria. These were:

5J+AM	5J+AC
5J+LM	5J+BC
5J+GM	

Identified aircrew included Olt Schmidt, Olt Graubner, Lt Lothar Wolf, Ofw Thomas, Fw Prinz, Uffz Guretzki, Uffz Weber and Obgfr Oertel. These bombers flew in fully loaded, and carrying a skeleton technical staff. For the duration of the operation, Schwanhäuser was temporarily appointed an acting Major in the Royal Iraqi Air Force, his crews also receiving similar temporary promotions of one rank. Additionally there was a transport force of 20 Junkers Ju 52/3m tri-motors led by Hpt Harry Rother, and a 20mm Flak 38 battery, together with a few Junkers Ju 90 four-engined transports. All aircraft involved had been overpainted with Iraqi insignia before setting out from the Greek airfields.

For the Germans it was not to be the happiest of ventures; the first three aircraft to arrive had flown in on the 11th, on a preliminary reconnaissance, one He 111 carrying Major Axel von Blomberg, who was to act as liaison officer to

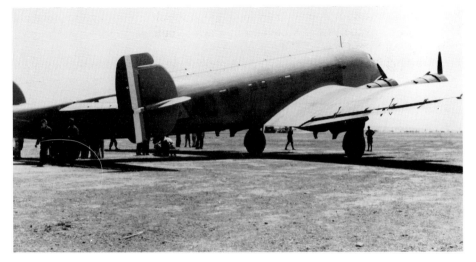

Above: The Luftwaffe begins arriving in Iraq. A Junkers Ju 90, repainted in Iraqi markings, is seen on its way to the Middle East, with a Junkers Ju 52/3m in the left background. *(Bundesarchiv).*
Below: The Junkers Ju 90, showing more clearly its Iraqi markings. *(Bundesarchiv)*

Rashid Ali. As the aircraft came in to land it was fired on by tribesmen, and when it came to a halt at Baghdad airport, von Blomberg was found to be dead with a bullet through his head. To add to this inauspicious beginning, the two main airfields, Rashid and Mosul, were found swiftly to be without camouflage or adequate dispersals, and to have very little in the way of anti-aircraft defences.

Tuesday, 13 May 1941
The first interception took place on the 13th, when a Bf 110 of 4/ZG 76 attacked a Blenheim fighter of 203 Squadron which was on reconnaissance over Mosul. No damage was caused, and the British pilot, Flg Off Lane-Sansom, was able to report that the fighter had attacked him four times without effect. Later in the day Flt Lt Plinston of 84 Squadron bombed the Mosul–Tel Awainot railway, also reporting seeing a Bf 110 in the air over the Mosul area. Plt Off Tulley of this unit had to make a force-landing on the Fallujah Plain during the day, but

Messerschmitt Bf 110C of 4/ZG 76 in flight, resplendent in Iraqi markings, but still with its ZG 76 'Shark's Teeth' on the nose. *(via K. Ries, Jr)*

was able later to take off again and return to base. The Air Striking Force, however, lost one aircraft during operations on this date. At H-4 the detachment was slightly reinforced by the arrival of a single Blenheim I from an Operational Training Unit, complete with an OTU crew.

Blenheim IVF 'B' of 203 Squadron in flight over Syria during one of the incursions in May 1941. *(203 Squadron via A.S. Thomas)*

Wednesday, 14 May 1941

From H-4 at 0615 next morning, Plt Off Watson of 203 Squadron flew an early reconnaissance over Syria to see if he could find out whether the Luftwaffe aircraft were landing there to refuel. Sure enough, at Palmyra in central Syria he spotted an aircraft, believed to be a Ju 90, just taking off. After returning to base, he flew a second sortie around midday in the OTU Blenheim I, this time noting four very large and three or four smaller aircraft refuelling. On his return this time, he asked Grp Capt Brown if he could take the fighter Blenheim and attack; Brown referred him to Maj Gen Clark. 'Do you want to declare war on Syria?' barked the soldier; 'That would be a bloody good idea!' came the response, to the delight of Clark's staff. Permission was in fact given forthwith to lay on such an attack, and arrangements were put in hand without delay. A few of 250 Squadron's Tomahawks were still at Aqir, and two of them — flown by Flg Offs G.A. Wolsey and F.J.S. Aldridge — left at 1440 to fly to H-4. From here at 1650 they took off again to undertake the first operational sorties of the war by Tomahawks, escorting two 84 Squadron Blenheims (which had also flown up to H-4 from Aqir) and Watson in fighter Blenheim IVF, T1820, to attack any German aircraft found at Palmyra.

Some confusion now exists regarding just what was at Palmyra when the formation arrived at 1740; Watson reported three very large transports, believed to have been Ju 90s, a Fiat CR 42 Italian biplane fighter, and two civil biplanes.

One of the first Curtiss Tomahawk IIB fighters to reach 250 Squadron, LD-Q is seen here at Aqir, Palestine, in early 1941. *(A.J. Thomas via A.S. Thomas)*

The Tomahawk pilots on the other hand reported the presence of four He 111s and a Ju 52/3m. The two bomber Blenheims attacked first, their bombs causing little apparent damage; Watson then dived and dropped some fragmentation bombs, then made a strafing attack. Following this, the Tomahawks, which had been circling overhead, also came down and strafed, but although several aircraft were seen to be hit repeatedly, none showed any signs of burning. KG 4 reported that the raid took place shortly after three Heinkels had taken off to fly to Mosul. The two remaining aircraft still on the ground were both destroyed, reportedly by a lone British fighter.

Meanwhile from Habbaniya Sgt Hemsted of 203 Squadron made a reconnaissance of several Iraqi bases during the early afternoon; at Erbil he spotted six monoplanes covered with native tents, and dived down to strafe two of these. During the attack he was hit in the shoulder by a rifle bullet, and was slightly wounded. At Aqir 11 Squadron now arrived, equipped with Blenheim IVs.

Thursday, 15 May 1941

Newly promoted Flg Off Watson, who was subsequently to receive a DFC for his recent activities over Iraq and Syria, was off again at dawn on the 15th to undertake a reconnaissance, which confirmed that all the German aircraft seen the day before were apparently still on the ground. At 1030 he again returned and made another strafing attack, but without visible effect. 250 Squadron reported that subsequent reconnaissance showed one He 111 to be burnt out, the other three and the Ju 52/3m all being damaged. At 1530 two of this unit's Tomahawks were off again, this time flown by Flg Off Aldridge and a young Australian, Plt Off C.R. Caldwell, soon to make his name as a fighter pilot over the Western Desert; they escorted eight Blenheims of 84 Squadron to Damascus to seek out more German aircraft. An He 111, two Ju 52/3ms and two Ju 90s were actually on this airfield at the time. Approaching the target, they saw below them a Morane 406, but lost this in heavy sea mist; they also lost the bombers in this same mist, so returned to base. Four of the Blenheims then bombed

Rayak airfield where they failed to do any serious damage, though one French officer was killed and several troops were wounded.

During the day Commandant Goumin, a Free French pilot, undertook a further reconnaissance over Damascus, and over Homs, Aleppo and Beirut, flying from Aqir in a Martin Maryland (No 1617), borrowed from 24 SAAF Squadron.

At Habbaniya three more pilots from 94 Squadron arrived from Egypt to join 'A' Squadron of the Air Striking Force; a number of pilots from 208 Squadron who were still without aircraft had also arrived. They were loaned Audaxes, and on this date began operations with the Air Striking Force; the main body of their unit continued re-forming at Gaza meanwhile.

At Aqir 211 Squadron took over four of 11 Squadron's Blenheim IVs for operations over Syria, and at once despatched two on a high-altitude reconnaissance mission over Rayak, Palmyra and Damascus. 'Kingcol', now well on its way to Habbaniya, was strafed during the day by a Bf 110, which inflicted a few casualties. Next day the column would strike soft sand to the south of Lake Habbaniya, which would cause delay, a detour to the south having to be made to avoid this hazard.

In the south 814 Squadron remained very active, and during the eighth of a series of attacks on barracks in the Basra area, three Swordfish attacked those at Samawa. Here one of the bombers was hit and made a very heavy force-landing. The aircraft was surrounded by Arabs, but these fell back when the pilot offered them a one dinar note. Another Swordfish, piloted by Lt J.H. Dundas, landed alongside and picked up the downed crew just as Iraqi troops advanced on them and opened fire, holing the fuel tank. Despite this, Dundas got the aircraft off again, Leading Air Mechanic Latham engaging the Iraqis with his Lewis gun; Dundas was later awarded the DSC.

This second week of operations in Iraq had been marked by several events, not the least of which was the ominous appearance of German aircraft. The Germans however had found conditions at their base at Mosul far from ideal, and frequent British air attacks had prevented them from taking any decisive part in the proceedings thus far. The week had also marked the discovery by the British of the Axis use of Vichy airfields in Syria as staging bases. This had led to the first attacks being made by RAF aircraft, although at this stage no state of hostilities between the British and the Vichy French in Syria existed. These attacks had also seen the operational debut (albeit on a limited scale) of the Curtiss Tomahawk fighter.

Perhaps, however, the most unsatisfactory feature had been the fiasco at Rutbah fort. During a period in which only five British aircraft were lost, two of these, both Blenheims that could ill be spared, fell at Rutbah, with others damaged sufficiently seriously to cause their withdrawal from operations for repairs. Such disproportionate losses for the negative results achieved were quite unacceptable, particularly when compared with the performance of the trainers at Habbaniya. Only Flg Off Watson's gallant attempt to rescue Sqn Ldr Gethin and his crew had redeemed this melancholy action.

While RAF losses had been much lighter during this second week, the number of Iraqi aircraft destroyed had also fallen to about half a dozen, mainly because there were few left undamaged. Initial attacks on Mosul airfield had already accounted for at least one of the newly arrived Luftwaffe aircraft, whilst German transports and two more bombers had been lost during the attacks on Syrian bases.

Friday, 16 May 1941

With the arrival of the Luftwaffe, activity for the Habbaniya-based units became more intense once more; at 0315 on the 16th Flg Off Lane-Sansom of 203 Squadron set off for Mosul and its two satellite fields, dropping two 20lb bombs on two German aircraft. He reported the presence of six Bf 110s, four Bf 109s, an He 111 and five unidentified types; what the aircraft purported to be Bf 109s were is uncertain, since it is definite that no aircraft of this type were despatched to Iraq. Lane-Sansom was coming down to strafe when a Bf 110 tried to attack him, but he managed to lose this, claiming that he had then caused an He 111 to burn.

Soon after Lane-Sansom's attack, Hpt Schwanhäuser led three He 111s off to raid Habbaniya. After a 90-minute flight they approached the base at 0935, Schwanhäuser leading in two of the bombers to attack at once, while Olt Graubner swung away to the left in order to bomb some parked aircraft. As his bombs were falling away, he saw below a plume of dust — a fighter taking off. This was a Gladiator which was being scrambled by Flg Off G.D.F. Herrtage of 94 Squadron. The three Heinkels made a second pass over the hangars, the two leading aircraft not having dropped their bombs, even though the attack had already caused more damage than had all previous Iraqi raids together! With the fighter in the air, however, the bombers turned for home, but Herrtage

Luftwaffe personnel in Iraqi uniforms prepare to bomb-up a 4/KG 4 Heinkel He 111H-6 at Mosul. *(via W. Bock)*

was able to cut across the turn, and thereby come within range, even though still climbing. Graubner reported:

> 'The fighter slowly climbed towards us. Soon it hung behind us, and we heard the clattering of machine gun fire — one could not tell whether it was our own, or the enemy fire hitting us. Fw Prinz and I suddenly saw many hits appearing in both wings, accompanied by a murderous roaring noise. I heard from behind, "Shot down!", and could not believe it when the voice of Ofw Thomas, the flight engineer, reported: "Now it is breaking up — now it has crashed!" The well-aimed return fire from Ofw Thomas and the radio operator, Uffz Guretzki, had succeeded! The first incontestable victory of our Gruppe!'

Observers on the ground reported that Herrtage's Gladiator had in fact been caught in the crossfire from all three bombers, and had crashed to the ground, the pilot probably already dead at the controls. He had however hit one of the bombers, and it was believed that this had crash-landed half a mile or so further from the camp. This was not so in fact, as Graubner's continued narrative explains:

> 'Our right engine began to shake and lose oil, and the temperature rose. The Kette still had to make a reconnaissance, so I broke off and set course for Mosul. We were at 2,000 metres and after ten minutes the damaged engine stopped. We could not now maintain height and began to sink at two metres a second, so we threw everything possible overboard, except for the guns and a little ammunition in case of a force-landing. We continued eastwards, at least to reach the Tigris valley. Slowly we dropped further, only desert beneath us. We tried to restart the "sick" engine, but it was no use and we had to turn the fuel off again. Still no sight of the Tigris; there must have been a strong headwind. "Everyone strap in!" — still ten metres above the ground. I lifted it over a ditch, there was a huge bump, and then we saw nothing but dust.'

Herrtage's victim had at last come down. This was to be the last attack flown by the KG 4 He 111Hs.

In the evening Sqn Ldr Pike and Flg Off Lane-Sansom of 203 Squadron made a dusk ground attack on Mosul; Pike made two strafing runs, reporting that one enemy aircraft caught fire and four others were damaged. Lane-Sansom also strafed two aircraft, one of these also being reported to have burned. On the return flight Pike reported being chased for 10 to 15 minutes by an aircraft identified as a Bf 109. This was the first of several such reports. Clearly the presence of German aircraft led pilots to identify every single-engined monoplane as one of the feared Messerschmitts. However, it is more likely that they were surviving Northrop or Breda types of the Iraqi Air Force.

Three more Blenheims from 84 Squadron arrived at Habbaniya during the day, joined by T1820, the last of 203 Squadron's Blenheim IVFs still at H-4. At this latter base Flg Off Watson remained, flying a reconnaissance in the OTU Mark I. Eight other Blenheims of 84 Squadron from Aqir raided Rayak, Damascus and Palmyra in Syria. The lack of French fighter reaction to these raids now released 250 Squadron's detachment, and a Blenheim of 211 Squadron

Heinkel He 111H-6 5J+LM demonstrates the Iraqi markings applied over its normal paintwork. *(via W. Bock)*

escorted Flg Off Wolsey and Plt Off Caldwell to Cyprus, where they were to be ready to defend the island against air attack.

However, during the day another reconnaissance was made by Free French personnel in a borrowed 24 SAAF Squadron Maryland, this time No 1063. Over Aleppo the aircraft was hit by anti-aircraft fire and Plt Off E.B. Smith, the only Briton in the crew, was badly wounded. Two MS 406s then pursued the aircraft without success, but a further AA hit wounded Adj Chef Contes, whose left leg had to be amputated after the aircraft had landed at Haifa.

814 Squadron completed its period of service at Shaibah with an attack on petrol tanks at Amawa by four Swordfish; the unit then flew back aboard HMS *Hermes*.

Saturday, 17 May 1941

On 17 May at 0710 two Gladiators flown by 94 Squadron Sgts Smith (in K7899) and Dunwoodie (in N5857) flew a reconnaissance over Rashid, where they saw two Bf 110s taking off. Diving on these, each pilot made a quarter attack on one, both German fighters being claimed shot down in flames. It is known that Leutnant Woerner, leader of the ZG 26 Kette, was killed in action in Iraq, together with his gunner, Uffz Fischer; it is assumed that theirs was one of the aircraft claimed shot down on this occasion. Subsequently six Gladiators escorted six Blenheims of 84 Squadron, led by Flt Lt Plinston, to bomb Rashid. Later in the day four Hurricanes arrived from Egypt at Habbaniya, and were handed to No 1 Flight of 'A' Squadron. They at once began operations, two escorting an Audax on a reconnaissance, while the other two made an offensive reconnaissance and strafed some motor transport.

From Aqir three Blenheims of 84 Squadron reconnoitred Aleppo, Palmyra, Rayak and Damascus during the morning, claiming to have destroyed two aircraft on the ground at Palmyra. The French reported that two German transports were badly damaged in this attack. A lone Blenheim from 211

Sgt W.H. Dunwoodie of 94 Squadron in front of one of the Messerschmitt Bf 110C fighters which he and Sgt E.L. Smith claimed to have shot down as they were taking off from Rashid airfield on 17 May 1941. Both were claimed in flames, but this aircraft, still bearing the 'Shark's Teeth' marking of II/ZG 76, appears to have crash-landed without suffering total destruction. Since the crew probably survived, this may well explain why this loss was not fully documented by the Luftwaffe. *(via A.S. Thomas)*

Squadron also raided Rayak, Palmyra and Damascus. Sqn Ldr Blomfield now arrived at Aqir as Commanding Officer of this unit, which was reorganised from a three-flight to a two-flight basis, 'A' Flight flying the Mark IVs on operations while 'B' Flight used the Mark Is as trainers.

Sunday, 18 May 1941

On the 18th 'Kingcol' at last arrived at Habbaniya, having suffered a further strafing attack during the final stages of the march by two or three Bf 110s. In the afternoon Sgt Hemsted of 203 Squadron found a Bf 110 crash-landed east of Baghdad and strafed it. This may possibly have been one of the aircraft attacked by the two Gladiators on the previous day.

From Aqir two SAAF Marylands again set course for Syria, one flown by Lt Labat and one by Cdt Goumin (No 1617). One of these, probably that flown by Labat, was pursued by four MS 406s soon after midday, but without result. Three 84 Squadron Blenheims also departed Aqir to raid Rayak again, being intercepted by another trio of MS 406s from Groupe de Chasse I/7, only 30 minutes after the abortive attack on the Maryland. Sgt Chef Veillie attacked two of the bombers, while Lt de la Taille and Sous Lt Trulla went after the third. While they believed that they had all obtained hits before the bombers escaped, all actually returned unscathed.

On this date command of the Royal Air Force in Iraq passed to Air Vice-Marshal J.H. D'Albiac, Air Vice-Marshal Smart having unfortunately been injured in a motor accident. D'Albiac had recently returned from Greece, where he had commanded the Expeditionary Air Force, and had during the last few weeks been commanding the units in Palestine and Transjordan. He now arrived at Habbaniya where he was joined by Maj Gen Clark, the 'Habforce' commander, to find that Col Roberts had prepared an attack to be made on the Iraqi positions at Fallujah next morning.

Monday, 19 May 1941

Early on the morning of the 19th therefore, 57 sorties were flown against Iraqi troops at Fallujah by the Air Striking Force, and leaflets were then dropped calling on them to surrender. This brought no response, and further bombing attacks were undertaken throughout the morning, 134 sorties being made in all. A detachment of the 1st King's Own Royals went aboard Bombays of 216 Squadron and Valentias of Habbaniya's Communications Flight, and were landed in the enemy's rear at Notch Falls, moving to cut the Baghdad road. A number of the Air Striking Force's sorties were made in an effort to cut the telephone wires to the capital in support of these landings. In some cases the Audaxes flew through the wires, but in one instance a pilot landed his aircraft alongside, and while the air gunner gave him cover, stood on the top mainplane to cut the line with shears! He then produced an axe and hacked down the poles! At 1445 the garrison force, reinforced by 'Kingcol' units, advanced on Fallujah; after only minor resistance the position was taken with 300 prisoners. However, on this date Empire forces were ordered to be ready to move into Syria at short notice, if required.

A further attack was made on Damascus's Mezze airfield during the day, where one Ju 52/3m was destroyed, and an He 111 and a Ju 90 which had been damaged on the 15th were also hit again. On this occasion French aircraft were also hit, Potez 63-11s Nos 647 and 652 of Groupe de Reconnaissance II/39 being hit, as was a Potez 25TOE of Escadrille d'Observation 594 and two Potez 29 liaison aircraft. Three German airmen and a French soldier were wounded.

Tuesday, 20 May 1941

In an effort to recover the lost position at Fallujah, the Luftwaffe was thrown in, and on the 20th the fighters of 'A' Squadron were kept very busy. The first encounter occurred when three Gladiators drove off a Bf 110 attacking forward troops here; two Hurricanes then chased four Bf 110s west of Ramadi. During the same period four Gladiators undertook a standing patrol over a force-landed Audax; one of these, flown by Sgt Smith, was attacked by five Bf 110s and only just managed to escape after the aircraft had suffered some damage. The Germans thought that they had managed to shoot the biplane down, and its destruction was credited to Lt Martin Drewes. This was the first victory claimed by this future night fighter 'Experte', who was to end the war with a Knight's Cross with Oakleaves, and 52 aerial victories.

Seven more scrambles were made by Hurricanes during the day; two of these chased Bf 110s which were strafing in the Fallujah area again, each British pilot getting in a burst, while at 1615 two other Hurricane pilots saw three He 111s and claimed damage to two of them. A strafe of Habbaniya by six Bf 110s destroyed a Blenheim of 84 Squadron, together with a DC-2 and two Valentias of 31 Squadron; two more Blenheims were damaged. A return visit to Rashid by six Blenheims escorted by three Gladiators and two Hurricanes was made. By the close of the day the nine available British fighters had flown no less than 26 sorties.

Leutnant Martin Drewes (left) and his radio operator in Iraq, in front of their Bf 110C. Drewes, who claimed his first victory in Iraq, was later to become a very successful night fighter pilot. *(via K. Ries)*

Monday, 19 to Wednesday, 21 May 1941

Meanwhile on the 19th three pilots from 208 Squadron at Gaza had been sent to Amman on attachment to 112 Squadron for a few days. On arrival they were sent with two of the latter unit's own pilots to Lydda to collect five Hurricanes on loan from 80 Squadron (112 Squadron had no aircraft of its own at this point, having just returned from Crete). Flying back to Amman, the five pilots — Flt Lt J.F. Fraser and Flg Off H.P. Cochrane of 112, Flt Lt L.G. Burnard, Flg Off Stephenson and Plt Off B.A.B. Attwood of 208 — took off early next morning (20th) to attack the French airfield at Mezze, just outside Damascus. On the run-in they missed the target, but on the return flight they found it, and at once attacked a Ju 52/3m and a Bf 110 which had just landed. Flt Lt Fraser claimed the former badly damaged; six French aircraft and 50 vehicles were also claimed strafed, as was the Bf 110; two of the Hurricanes were struck by small arms fire. The French reported that both German aircraft were damaged, the Ju 52/3m subsequently being burnt out, while two French aircraft were also damaged. The Hurricanes later undertook a 'flagwaving' flight over the Palestinian towns of Nablus, Jenin and Haifa on 21 May, but were then handed back to 80 Squadron, the 208 Squadron pilots returning to their own unit next day.

Two further long-range Hurricanes arrived in Iraq from Egypt on the 21st, Flg Off J.G. Sandison and another pilot landing at Habbaniya to join 'A' Squadron.

Thursday, 22 May 1941

In the early hours of the 22nd the Iraqis made an unusually determined attempt to retake Fallujah, supported by light tanks. By daybreak they had driven back the two companies of the 1st King's Own Royals and levies, who were holding the area. The levies swiftly counter-attacked and drove them out again, but a later attack made some progress before being stopped and completely repelled by 'Kingcol' troops of the 1st Essex Regiment, rushed up to the area. During these actions the Iraqis suffered heavy casualties, but inflicted quite severe losses on the British force.

The Air Striking Force flew 56 sorties over Fallujah in support of the army, also attacking a convoy of 40 vehicles that was moving up to reinforce the Iraqi attack. One Audax flown by Flg Off L.I. Dremas, a Greek pilot, was shot down and force-landed; the air gunner dismounted his Lewis gun and took two pans of ammunition, the two men then running for friendly lines, firing as they went. They were joined by some levies, and made their way to the rear under fire, several of the levies being shot on the way by snipers. As Dremas spoke no English, the young airman gunner had to take charge of the party and bring it back to safety.

During the day 203 Squadron's Blenheim fighters made several strafing attacks on lorry convoys, but in the evening Flg Off Lane-Sansom made for Mosul. He was attacked by an aircraft which he reported to be a Bf 109, but shook it off in the gathering gloom and bombed the airfield in the dark, setting one aircraft on fire. Earlier two Hurricanes had attacked the same target, the destruction of at least two aircraft on the ground being claimed. However, one of the Hurricanes piloted by Flt Lt Sir R.A. MacRobert failed to return.

In Syria the French reported that an Armée de l'Air reconnaissance Potez 63-11 of GR II/39 was attacked without result by two British fighters whilst on a reconnaissance between Merjayoun and H-4. Three more RAF aircraft flew high-altitude reconnaissances over Aleppo airfield.

Three weeks had now expired since the first shots had been fired. The current week had opened with the damaging attack by the three He 111s of KG 4 on Habbaniya, which managed in one fell blow to do more damage than the whole Iraqi Air Force had achieved before its effective demise. Added to this was the destruction of six more operational aircraft, so it had been a rather more expensive week for the British air forces. However, at least five German aircraft had been totally destroyed and others damaged, reducing considerably the striking power of this component.

On the ground the eventual arrival of 'Habforce' at Habbaniya had allowed an attack to be launched on the main Iraqi positions at Fallujah, ably supported by the increasingly efficient Air Striking Force. The substantial reinforcement of 'A' Fighter Squadron with Hurricanes prevented any disastrous consequences when the Luftwaffe contingent was finally thrown in in strength on 19 May in an effort to save the Iraqis from defeat. Despite all efforts of the German aircrews, the Fallujah position was taken by the British Imperial forces, and a determined counter-attack had been beaten off.

Following only a brief appearance over Syria, the remaining Tomahawks of 250 Squadron now departed for Egypt. While the strength of the RAF bombers in Palestine continued to grow, an increasing number of sorties were devoted to reconnaissance over, and bombing attacks on, the French airfields in Syria. Exact Luftwaffe serviceable strength on 22 May is not known, but already their operational elements at Mosul and Rashid were considerably weakened. The RAF Order of Battle was now substantially altered:

	Habbaniya
'A' Squadron	13 Gladiators
	five Hurricanes
'B', 'C', and 'D' Squadrons	All remaining serviceable Oxfords, Audaxes and Gordons
84 Squadron (detachment)	seven Blenheim IVs
203 Squadron (detachment)	seven Blenheim IVFs
	Transjordan
208 Squadron (detachment)	Lysanders at H-4
	Palestine
11 Squadron	Blenheim Is and IVs at Aqir
84 Squadron	Blenheim IVs at Aqir
211 Squadron	Blenheim IVs at Aqir
216 Squadron	five Bombays at Lydda
	two Valentias at Lydda
	Southern Iraq
244 Squadron	Vincents at Shaibah
31 Squadron	six Valentias at Shaibah
	three Douglas DC-2s at Shaibah
	three A-W Atalantas at Shaibah
814 Squadron	Swordfish on HMS *Hermes*

Friday, 23 May 1941

The fourth week of the campaign began badly when the fighters suffered another loss. Flg Off Sandison was on a reconnaissance in a Gladiator when his oil tank was holed by ground fire and he had to force-land on the Fallujah Plain. However he managed to evade capture and walk through hostile lines, subsequently being picked up by friendly troops. The detachment of 84 Squadron at Habbaniya was now joined there by the rest of the Squadron from Aqir.

At this stage, however, more help for the Iraqis was on the way. The French had been considerably more hostile to the idea of Italian aircraft staging through Syria than had been the case with the Germans, and they had prevaricated for some time. Now agreement had at last been reached, and 12 Fiat CR 42 biplane fighters of the 155ª Squadriglia, 3° Gruppo, 6° Stormo CT, left Italy for Iraq under the leadership of Capitano Francesco Sforza. First stop was Greece, but as the formation landed at Valona one CR 42 crashed. The other 11, after refuelling, flew on to the island of Rhodes.

Saturday, 24 May 1941

Meanwhile the supply of arms to the Iraqis by the French authorities in Syria was clearly one item which might prolong hostilities. Indeed the first trainload had reached Mosul on 13 May, accompanied personally by Dr Rudolf Rahn of the German Foreign Office, a prime mover in persuading the French to despatch the shipment. To counter this threat, the British now undertook an unorthodox step. On the 24th Flt Lt Bartlett of 216 Squadron flew Valentia K2803 from Heliopolis to Habbaniya, where he took aboard a party of 13 sappers. Taking off again, he flew to a point in Syrian territory west of Campaniya, where he landed close to an important bridge on the Aleppo–Mosul line, in the north-east corner of the country. Over the next 45 minutes the sappers successfully demolished this structure. As the aircraft took off again, an armoured car arrived and opened fire, but did no damage; Bartlett was subsequently awarded the DFC.

In the afternoon a Blenheim IV of 211 Squadron on a reconnaissance over the Homs area of Syria was chased by Morane 406s, but escaped; two other Blenheims attacked a Ju 52/3m on Nerab landing ground, near Aleppo, leaving this on fire.

Sunday, 25 May 1941
Three Blenheims from 84 Squadron bombed Mosul on the 25th, while three more dropped leaflets on Iraqi troops in the Fallujah area. At Aqir 11 Squadron took over eight of 84's old Blenheims, which had been left behind due to unserviceability when the Squadron had moved to Habbaniya. Six more were obtained from 211 Squadron, only three of which were serviceable. At Gaza 'C' Flight of 208 Squadron took over four new Hurricanes for tactical recon-naissance duties.

Monday, 26 to Tuesday, 27 May 1941
On the 26th two Blenheims, one from 203 Squadron flown by Flg Off Lane-Sansom, and one from 84 Squadron flown by Flg Off Goudge, went to Kirkuk on a strafing sortie, but found no Bf 110s there. They did however see an He 111 crash-landed on a landing ground ten miles south of Baghdad, and this was shot up by Goudge. Next day two 84 Squadron Blenheims bombed and strafed Kirkuk, while two others strafed an aircraft identified as a Dornier, on the ground north of Habbaniya — this was probably the crash-landed Bf 110 which had already been shot up some days earlier.

During the previous day the 11 CR 42s of the Italian 155ª Squadriglia had arrived at Aleppo from Rhodes, remaining there overnight. Now they flew on to Mosul, and thence to Kirkuk, from where they at once undertook the first of a number of strafing attacks on British forces moving from Fallujah to Baghdad.

The French in Syria were by now thoroughly alarmed by the continued British air attacks, and the authorities in France ordered in reinforcements. Indeed, RAF activities were being stepped up, two Blenheims bombing and strafing Palmyra airfield on the 26th, doing slight damage to stores and installations, while on the 27th one bomber over Aleppo caused very much greater damage. Consequently some local reorganisation was undertaken, four MS 406s of GC I/7 moving to Aleppo's Nerab satellite landing ground for the defence of the airfield complex there.

Wednesday, 28 May 1941
On the 28th the French fighters intercepted Blenheim V5818 of 211 Squadron over Aleppo, and this was shot down by Sous Lt Vuillemin; the bomber, which

Dewoitine D 520 fighters of Groupe de Chasse III/6 are seen here at Brindisi, Italy, on 25 May 1941, on their way to Syria. No 382 ('25') and No 52 ('29') were aircraft of the unit's 6 escadrille. *(C-J. Ehrengardt)*

had left Aqir at 0730, was being piloted on a reconnaissance sortie by Sgt David, who was killed with all his crew. During the evening the Moranes at Nerab were again in the air, this time escorting in four 'Iraqi–German' Ju 52/3ms; the rear gunners in the transports opened fire on the fighters, not ceasing until their aircraft had landed. Their aim was poor, however, and no damage was done to any of the French aircraft. Further British attacks were made on Deir ez Zor, Palmyra and Rayak on this date, installations at the latter base being seriously damaged.

In the course of the day the first French reinforcements arrived in the shape of 24 Dewoitine D 520 fighters of GC III/6 from Algeria. These had left their base four days earlier, flying round the north coast of the Mediterranean, as had the Italian CR 42s. En route two fighters had been forced to try and land in Turkey, but one crashed and the pilot was killed; the other pilot was interned. At Aqir 11 Squadron was becoming operational, and one Blenheim flew a photographic reconnaissance over Beirut.

In Iraq the pressure was maintained, the advance from Fallujah continuing; the main force, led by Brigadier Kingstone, took the direct route to Baghdad, while a diversionary force under Col A.H. Ferguson made for a new ferry over the Euphrates at Sin el Dhibban well to the north. They were to proceed from this direction in an endeavour to outflank any defences on the road to the capital. This latter force was held up, but the main force, which received nearly all the air support, made good progress. Sqn Ldr Pike of 203 Squadron attacked Kirkuk airfield again, dropping his bombs near a Bf 110, then strafing two monoplanes on the ground near Fallujah. He reported seeing a Bf 109 taking off from Kirkuk, but this aircraft — whatever it was — did not close on its own.

Thursday, 29 May 1941

The main column of Empire troops reached the Iraqi stronghold of Khan Nuquta on the 29th, and the Audaxes of the Air Striking Force were ordered to attack this. One such attack at 1000 was made by three Audaxes escorted by

The only known photo of a Fiat CR 42 of the Regia Aeronautica's 155ª Squadriglia, painted with Iraqi markings. This unit arrived at Kirkuk on 28 May 1941.

two Gladiators; this formation was intercepted by two CR 42s of the 155ª Squadriglia, flown by Tenente De Merich and Sottotenente Valentini. Flt Lt Webster of 208 Squadron was piloting one of the Audaxes, with Sgt Payne as his gunner, and he observed the Italian fighters make an attack on one of the Gladiators. Immediately following this, they attacked his Audax; Payne was slightly wounded and the pilot was obliged to force-land the aircraft in a damaged condition. At this point, Wg Cdr Wightman in Gladiator N5777 dived to the attack and shot down Valentini's CR 42, the pilot baling out and becoming a prisoner. (Ten De Merich was later to be killed over Malta in 1942, while flying a Reggianne Re 2001 fighter — see *Malta: the Spitfire Year, 1942*.)

Following this engagement, heavy attacks were immediately organised on the rest of the Italian aircraft at their base at Kirkuk, albeit without effect. Meanwhile, reinforcements for 'Habforce' now arrived when a battalion of the Gurkha Rifles was flown into Habbaniya from Basra during the day.

Friday, 30 May 1941

'Habforce' with 1,200 men, eight guns and a few RAF armoured cars now awaited outside Baghdad, faced by an Iraqi division in the capital and another force behind them at Ramadi, to the west of Habbaniya. However, the air was the decisive factor, and on the 30th a Hurricane and three Gladiators escorted bombers to Khadiman without opposition, while others flew reconnaissance and strafing missions. In Baghdad Rashid Ali and his supporters decided all was lost and fled. The mayor of the city requested a truce and terms; the end in Iraq was virtually at hand, and before the close of the day 203 Squadron left Habbaniya to return to its ground echelon at Kabrit.

Saturday, 31 May 1941

Next day most of the personnel of 94 Squadron also left Habbaniya, returning to Ismailia; the Hurricanes and Gladiators were all left behind. All operations by the Air Striking Force now ceased. An armistice was signed, rioting and looting then breaking out in Baghdad. On this date a Blenheim of 84 Squadron, flown by Sgt Gordon, went missing whilst on a reconnaissance sortie from Habbaniya — no cause for its loss was discovered. Another Blenheim, this one from 211 Squadron, undertook a sortie into Syria, but was intercepted by Lt de la Taille and Sgt Chef Veillie of GC I/7 near Aleppo. Plt Off J.G.M. Hooper managed to evade these attackers, jettisoning his bombs over some mountains as he did so.

Following the conclusion of hostilities, the Italians were to prove more successful than the Germans in extricating themselves from the debacle. Warned on 30 May to be ready to leave Kirkuk in a hurry, they had packed up that night, and were ready to leave early next morning. Apart from the fight with the Audaxes and Gladiators on the 29th, they had recorded several other brushes with British aircraft, identified as Gladiators and 'Superfuries', and thought they might have shot down two more, but had been unable to obtain any confirmation. Two CR 42s had been damaged — one having suffered only a single bullet through the fuel tank — but neither were flyable, and they were both burnt before the Squadriglia departed.

Some of the ground staff went aboard an S 79 which had accompanied the unit as a transport, the rest piling into two small buses. The whole unit moved off together early on the 31st, across the border into Syria, the fighters covering both the S 79 and the vehicles on the journey to Aleppo. Here they were ordered by a German officer to disperse their aircraft at the southern end of the airfield. Strong headwinds prevented the unit's early return to Rhodes, and it was 5 June before it was finally able to take off, following a British air raid which caused some slight splinter damage to several aircraft. The flight then took three hours, 40 minutes. On arrival on Rhodes the aircraft were repainted in Italian markings and the unit was renumbered 164ᵃ Squadriglia. It was later to join 162ᵃ and 163ᵃ Squadriglie to form the 161° Gruppo Autonomo (Rodi) for the air defence of the island.

Fliegerführer Irak had suffered much more severely, losing all the original 14 Bf 110s and five He 111s, as well as the various transport aircraft destroyed here and on the Syrian airfields; only the surviving personnel managed to escape to Syria to tell their sorry tale. Although only a minor involvement, it was the first defeat suffered by the Luftwaffe in the Mediterranean and Middle East area.

He 111H-6 5J+AC is inspected by British personnel after it had been abandoned due to damage, as the German contingent withdrew.

A British airman inspects the tail of 5J+GM, another abandoned 4/KG 4 He 111H-6, on which he is able to identify the Luftwaffe swastika, despite the efforts that were made to paint this over.

SECTION III · SYRIA

Chapter Seven

THE FRATRICIDAL CAMPAIGN IN
SYRIA AND THE LEBANON

The Syrian and Lebanese territories of the old Turkish colonial empire had been placed under French mandate by the Treaty of Versailles in 1919 (to the detriment of the British, who considered this area to be indispensable for the defence of the Suez Canal). As already detailed, the use of Syrian airfields as staging bases for German and Italian aircraft heading for Iraq had not been well received by the British authorities. Syria had seen years of turmoil not dissimilar to those in Iraq, as the indigenous population pressed the French for early self-government. Resentment regarding the activities of the Jews in neighbouring Palestine also simmered beneath the surface.

Following the Franco–German Armistice of June 1940, the French in Syria rapidly fell in behind the Vichy government. Numbers of those who disagreed, together with a force of Poles who had made their way through south-eastern Europe following the fall of their own country, had crossed into Palestine at that point to continue the struggle. The British government, with problems enough to cope with, decided to take no action towards Syria or the Lebanon as long as they did not become bases for hostile activity against countries within the British sphere of influence.

Concern that Syria was becoming a hotbed of subversive activities was soon worrying the Middle East Command, providing ready fuel for Général Charles de Gaulle and his Free French, who had claimed from the start that Syria was ripe for takeover by their faction. In October 1940 de Gaulle sent Général Georges Catroux to Egypt to commence a propaganda campaign; however, the following month his efforts were negated by the arrival as High Commissioner of the pro-Vichy Général Henri Dentz. Thereafter, Free French efforts at influence faded away in their effectiveness, despite the arrival in the area during April 1941 of de Gaulle himself.

British concern regarding both the situation in Syria and Vichy attitudes generally was matched by worries that the Free French might precipitate unwelcome involvements if not closely controlled. After the loss of Greece and Crete, worries regarding a potential German paratroop landing in Syria brought consideration of a possible need to send assistance to Dentz, if he decided to resist. No approach was possible, however, as it was deemed most undesirable to advise this untrusted and potentially hostile commander of the current critical weakness of the British forces in the area. Almost immediately, the situation in Iraq put paid to any such eventuality in any event.

The use of Syrian airfields by the Germans had resulted in permission being given in mid-May for attacks on Luftwaffe aircraft on Syrian soil, whilst on 16 May it was learned that Turkish forces were being moved up to their frontier with Syria, obviously also in anticipation of a German move into that country. Anxious to co-operate with the Turks, the Chiefs of Staff in London ordered the Commanders-in-Chief in the Middle East to prepare plans for the formation of the largest possible force to be ready to advance into Syria at the earliest possible date. Meanwhile, on 18 May Général Catroux advised General Wavell that he had learned of Vichy plans to withdraw troops into the Lebanon and pass Syria over to German control. This move, he considered, would temporarily leave the road to Damascus open, and he asked Wavell to allow an immediate advance over the border. Wavell declined. Catroux protested that German pressure, together with his own speeches, had brought attitudes in Syria to a point where little opposition to such a move was likely. Wavell remained unenthusiastic to the blandishments of both London and Catroux, since his own forces remained so weak. Although reinforcements were now beginning to arrive from East Africa, and from England, he was preparing for the first offensive to be launched from Egypt towards Libya since the arrival of General Erwin Rommel and his Afrika Korps. He would need every available man, gun, tank and aircraft for that undertaking. He was, however, overruled by the Chiefs of Staff, and ultimately by the Prime Minister, Winston Churchill, and was ordered to prepare for an advance into Syria under the codename Operation 'Exporter'. 7th Australian Division (less one brigade which was garrisoning the invested port of Tobruk) was ordered to Palestine. Lt Gen Sir Henry Maitland Wilson, commander in Palestine and Transjordan, was to run the operation, the principal objectives of which were to secure the airfields at Damascus, Beirut and Rayak.

On 25 May the plan for 'Exporter' was sent to London, proposing that the Australians, together with Free French troops and part of the 1st Cavalry Division, should form the basis of the force to be employed. Wavell remained a dissenting voice, considering this force to be insufficient. He felt that it was unlikely to be able to do more than take the initial airfield objectives and then launch some raids towards Tripoli and Homs. The French, he advised, would be likely to establish themselves further north around Aleppo and Mosul, and then counter-attack southwards. Again, he was overruled.

Turkish support failed to materialise, when on 2 June their government refused a proposal to join in an occupation, and following this, the Imperial Defence Committee in London reached the decision that Syria was of more direct importance to the Allied cause than Cyprus. Consequently, the force committed to the operation grew, and during the first week in June came to comprise:

7th Australian Infantry Division — two brigades.
Two cavalry regiments, one horsed, and one — a composite regiment — mechanised.
5th Indian Infantry Brigade Group (newly arrived from Eritrea).
A weak Free French force under Général Legentilhomme, com-

prising six battalions, one battery of artillery and a few tanks.
One squadron of armoured cars; one light and one heavy anti-aircraft regiment; one field regiment, Royal Artillery.
'C' Battalion, Special Service Brigade, available on Cyprus.

To support this force, particularly on its left flank of advance up the Lebanese coast, was 15th Cruiser Squadron under the command of Vice-Admiral E.L.S. King. This force comprised the cruisers HMS *Phoebe*, *Ajax* and *Coventry*, the landing ship HMS *Glengyle*, and eight destroyers. Available for air cover and support, under the command of Air Commodore L.O. Brown, a limited force was to be put together from what was available.

This Allied force was to advance on three fronts, with Beirut, the centre of government in the country, as the main objective. On the right, inland, one column was to head through Deraa to Damascus. This attack would be made initially by 5th Indian Brigade (Brigadier W.L. Lloyd), but upon reaching Deraa, the Free French would pass through and deploy towards Damascus. In the centre a small force would head for Rayak via Merjayoun, but the main effort would be made up the coast by 7th Australian Division (Major General J.D. Lavarack), aided by a seaborne landing by the Special Service Brigade, and reinforced as necessary by elements of the Cavalry Division and 6th Division, their target being Beirut itself.

To face this threat, the Vichy authorities had available a force of some 32,000 men (6,000 of them Europeans), organised in eight infantry battalions, 11 battalions of special troops, six Groupes d'Escadrons de Cavalerie (each with two machine gun carriers and two tanks), nine batteries of field artillery, each with six guns of 65mm or 75mm calibre, six batteries with 105mm or 155mm guns, nine anti-aircraft batteries and one anti-tank battery, the latter with 21

Two of GC III/6's D 520s after arrival at Rayak. No 277 ('6') was flown by Sous Lieutenant Pierre Le Gloan, while No 329 ('9') was flown by Sergeant-Chef Mertzisen; both aircraft would be lost during the opening week of hostilities. *(C-J. Ehrengardt)*

Morane MS 406 fighters of the 1ere escadrille of Groupe de Chasse I/7 at their base at Estabel early in June 1941. *(C-J. Ehrengardt)*

anti-tank weapons of 47mm calibre. This force included about 100 Hotchkiss R-35 tanks, but the terrain was not well suited to their use.

There was also a small naval force, La Division Navale du Levant (Amiral Gouton), based in Beirut and Tripoli, with two large Fleet destroyers, *Guepard* and *Valmy*, three submarines, a patrol vessel, a minelayer and a sloop. This force was due to be reinforced by a third destroyer, *Vauquelin*, which left Marseilles on 8 June.

It was in the air, however, that the French were now greatly strengthened. The initial colonial force of Potez 25TOE biplanes had been increased by the arrival between 31 January and 5 March 1940 of Groupe de Chasse I/7 with 26 Morane 406 fighters. This unit had been followed by Groupe de Bombardement I/39 with 12 Martin 167F bombers, and by a training unit which was formed within the Groupe during September 1940, Escadrille 3/39, with six elderly Bloch MB 200 bombers. Groupe de Reconnaissance II/39 with Potez 63-11 twin-engined aircraft had also been sent in 1940, together with Groupe Aerienne d'Observation 583 from Oran, Algeria, which was similarly equipped. These units had joined five escadrilles d'observation, four with six Potez 25TOEs each, and one with only four; there was also a single Aeronavale (French naval air force) escadrille (19S) with Loire 130 single-engined flying boats.

One of the long-serving Potez 25TOE army co-operation biplanes (this one No 1510 of EO 595) of the Armée de l'Air, passes over a French colonial camel patrol. *(via C-J. Ehrengardt)*

The RAF's attacks on the Syrian airfields had resulted in reinforcement being sought. Consequently, as already mentioned, the potent Dewoitine D 520 fighters of Groupe de Chasse III/6 had arrived at Rayak on

28 May. Thus by the evening of 7 June 1941 the Armée de l'Air and Aeronavale had available the following force:

Base	Unit	Aircraft	Groupe Commander	Escadrille Commanders
Rayak	GC III/6	25 D 520		
	GB I/39	3 M-167F (detachment)		
	EO 592	6 Pz 25TOE		Lt Marozeau
Estabel	GC I/7	12 MS 406	Cdt Deschamps de Pas	Cne Dessalles
Madjaloun	GB I/39	10 M-167F	Cdt Ader	Cne Faure
				Lt Duparchy
	EB 3/39	6 MB 200		Cne Marin
Damascus–Mezze	GR II/39	12 Pz 63-11	Cdt Larroze	Cne Guignard
				Cne Forget
	EO 594	6 Pz 25TOE		Cne Capdaspe
				Couchet
Aleppo–Nerab	GC I/7	6 MS 406 (detachment)		Lt de la Taille
	GAO 583	5 Pz 63-11		Cne d'Argoubet
	EO 593	6 Pz 25TOE		Lt Poncet
Palmyra	EO 595	6 Pz 25TOE		Cne Lanson
Deir ez Zor	EO 596	4 Pz 25TOE		Lt Hercouet
Tripoli	Esc 19S	5 Loire 130		Lt de V. Brossier

Civil-registered Martin 167F G-BACF, which was used as a high-speed transport to carry General Bergeret and two adjutant-chefs to Beirut on 18 May. It was then handed to GB I/39 to provide spare parts, and was finally destroyed during a strafing attack on Madjaloun airfield by Hurricanes on 23 June. *(SHAA)*

3 RAAF Squadron's new Curtiss Tomahawk IIBs lined up at Jenin early in June. *(AWM)*

On 18 May a civil-registered Martin 167F, G-BACF, which had been converted as a high-speed VIP transport, had flown in from Tunis to Beirut, carrying the Secretaire d'Etat à l'Air, Général Bergeret. This aircraft had been handed to GB I/39 to break up for spares as necessary.

Unknown to the British, the Germans, disillusioned by the failure of their attempt to support Rashid Ali in Iraq, had given up all ideas of involvement in Syria. With their impending invasion of the Soviet Union (Operation 'Barbarossa') less than a month away, they now withdrew from the area.

Meanwhile the build-up of British air strength was getting under way. Initially, three Hurricanes from 80 Squadron, re-equipped following its return from Crete, moved to Haifa in Palestine on 2 June, while 3 RAAF Squadron, newly re-equipped with Curtiss Tomahawk IIb fighters following this unit's recent involvement in the retreat from Libya, moved to Jenin in the same area. This unit was still suffering considerable 'teething troubles' with its new aircraft.

Sunday, 1 to Monday, 2 June 1941
On 1 June 211 Squadron at Aqir handed eight Blenheim IVs to 11 Squadron and departed for the Sudan to become a training unit. Next day there was further French aerial reaction when one of 11 Squadron's newly received aircraft undertook an early morning photo-reconnaissance over the Palmyra–Aleppo area; it was chased out to sea by MS 406s. Here the pilot was unable to turn on his outer fuel tanks as the fuel cocks had jammed, and as a result he was obliged to force-land on a beach at Rouviani with both engines dead.

Tuesday, 3 June 1941
On 3 June three more Hurricanes from 80 Squadron flew to Cyprus to establish

an air defence of the island, being joined next day by a fourth. Meanwhile 'A' and 'C' Flights of 208 Squadron with tactical reconnaissance Hurricanes arrived at Haifa on the same day, and 'B' Flight (with Lysander IIs) flew to the landing ground at pumping station H-4 on the Iraq pipeline. A Hurricane from 'A' Flight would fly the unit's first operational reconnaissance in the area on the 5th.

Thursday, 5 June 1941

During the morning two Beaufighters of 272 Squadron and two of 252 Squadron arrived at Lydda, Palestine, from Egypt, together with a Maryland of 39 Squadron. Led by Sqn Ldr Fletcher, 272's Commanding Officer, these five aircraft left at 1500 to attack the Royal Dutch Shell fuel oil depot at Beirut. The 272 pair strafed first, then the Maryland bombed, and finally the 252 Squadron aircraft strafed. They then returned to Lydda to refuel, before flying back to Abu Sueir, Egypt, that night. Next day a lone Blenheim bombed from high altitude, but the results of these two attacks were to cause only minor damage to the installations.

Général Dentz had demanded the immediate departure of Axis aircraft from Syria by this time, the Germans complying at once, but the Italians acting rather more tardily for the reasons already specified (the high headwinds), the last of their aircraft not leaving for Rhodes until the 5th. During the morning of that day three Blenheims from 11 Squadron attacked Aleppo airfield, where several CR 42s and S 79s were reported seen on the ground; one aircraft and a hangar were reported to have received direct hits. Three MS 406s took off led by Adj Chef Georges Amarger, but were unable to intercept.

Frequently during the course of the campaign which was to follow, the French fighters would take off too late, sometimes even as the bombs were falling. A

warning network had been set up, but in the east and west it was operated by colonial troops who did not prove up to their task, while in the south the observer posts were rapidly to be overrun by the Allied advance when it began. The terrain also proved too restrictive to allow such a network to be effective; as a result the French fighter groupes were forced to institute standing patrols.

Following the departure of the last of the British aircraft carriers from the eastern Mediterranean following the damage inflicted on HMS *Formidable* during the Crete operations (see *Air War for Yugoslavia, Greece and Crete, 1940-1941*), a number of Fleet Air Arm units had become available for the Syrian venture, operating from land bases, mainly in support of 15th Cruiser Squadron. These would

Adjutant Chef Georges Amarger, a member of GC I/7's 2ᵉ escadrille, with MS 406 No 749. Amarger was to become the most successful of the Morane pilots in Syria. *(G. Amarger)*

include Swordfish and Albacore torpedo-bomber-reconnaissance biplanes drawn from 815, 826 and 829 Squadrons, Fulmar two-seat fighters of 803 Squadron, and 806 Squadron, which had exchanged its Fulmars for Hurricane Is borrowed from the RAF. The Allied force would also be joined by 'X' Flight from Habbaniya. This unit was formed there on 6 June with most of the remaining Gladiators. These were all well-used aircraft, which had seen service with either 33, 80, 112 or 3 RAAF Squadrons, apart from a few which had been flown in by 94 Squadron direct from Maintenance Unit in Egypt. Eight of these aircraft — K6110, '6141, '7914, '7947, '7954, '7978, and N5777 and '5780 — were flown to Amman in Transjordan next day under the command of Flg Off K.H.O. Young. His pilots included six of the former instructors who had formed the Fighter Flight at Habbaniya, Flg Offs Cleaver, Craigie and Jeffrey, Plt Off Watson, and Sgts Horsham and Appleby, plus two of the ex-94 Squadron NCOs, Sgts Buchanan and Dunwoodie.

Friday, 6 June 1941
During the 6th a Vichy M-167F dropped leaflets (written in French!) on Haifa airfield. As it flew up the correct approach path to the base, it was believed at the time that possibly it was flown by a Free French pilot who had defected to the Vichy authorities. On this date a second M-167F, flown by Cdt Ader, Commanding Officer of GB I/39, made a reconnaissance flight to Cyprus. During the day Flt Lt J. Lockhart and Flg Off G.H. Westlake of 80 Squadron reported intercepting and shooting down such an aircraft between Haifa and Beirut, their claim being supported by the Royal Navy. However no such loss was suffered by the French.

Saturday, 7 June 1941
Next day MS 406s led by Adj Chef Veillie intercepted a long-range Hurricane from 'A' Flight, 208 Squadron, in which Flg Off Holdsworth was undertaking a reconnaissance of all Syrian airfields. The French fighters attacked as he departed the Rayak area during the mid-afternoon, inflicting some damage to the tail of his aircraft.

With the arrival of 'X' Flight at Amman on the 7th, the Allied air forces now available for the imminent conflict were as listed on page 206.

Meanwhile on 6 June Lt Col Montrelay of the Vichy command had advised the US counsel in Beirut that all Germans had left Syria, and that any further attacks by British forces would constitute an act of war. Next evening two Bristol Bombays of 216 Squadron, operating from Heliopolis, Egypt, dropped leaflets over Syria and the Lebanon, advising of the intention of British and Free French forces to invade the country.

Sunday, 8 June 1941
In the early hours Operation 'Exporter' commenced, the Australians heading up the coast, while on the right the Indians secured Deraa. By nightfall they would have progressed 15 miles further north to Sheikh Meskine. In the centre Vichy forces withdrew rapidly from Quneitra (Kuneitra).

First operations by the air forces commenced early with an attack on the French base at Rayak by three Hurricanes of 80 Squadron. They had been despatched to strafe the Martin 167Fs of GB I/39, which had been reported there, but arrived to find the birds flown. Indeed most of the French unit had

Iraq

Habbaniya	203 Squadron	four Blenheim IVFs (detachment)	
Mosul	84 Squadron	three Blenheim IVs (detachment)	

Palestine

Aqir	11 Squadron	12 Blenheim IVs	
	80 Squadron	two Hurricanes (detachment)	
	208 Squadron	seven Hurricane Is	Sqn Ldr J.R. Wilson
Haifa	80 Squadron	six Hurricanes	Sqn Ldr E.G. Jones
Jenin	3 RAAF Squadron	12 Tomahawk IIbs	Sqn Ldr P. Jeffrey
Lydda	252/272 Squadron	three Beaufighter ICs	Sqn Ldr A.W. Fletcher
	803 Squadron (FAA)	six Fulmars	Lt J.M. Bruen

Transjordan

Amman	'X' Flight	eight Gladiators	Flg Off K.H.O. Young
H-4	203 Squadron	two Blenheim IVFs (detachment)	
	208 Squadron	two Lysander IIs (detachment)	

Cyprus

	80 Squadron	four Hurricanes (detachment)	
	815 Squadron (FAA)	six Swordfish	Lt Cdr F.M.A. Torrens-Spence

Egypt

Gaza	208 Squadron	three Hurricane Is (detachment) one Lysander II	
Aboukir	806 Squadron (FAA)	six Hurricane Is	

already moved to Madjaloun, as has already been indicated, but the trio still at Rayak were already in the air, bombing the columns approaching Quneitra. At Rayak two or three miscellaneous aircraft were reported to have been set on fire, but only a single Potez 25TOE of EO 592 was in fact damaged.

The Hurricanes were followed by five Tomahawks of 3 RAAF Squadron on their first operational sorties, and these were mistaken by the French ground spotters for D 520s, the ground defences being taken completely by surprise. Their attack proved more effective, one of GC III/6's D 520s, No 330, being destroyed and five more hit, two of them suffering serious damage.

Before the Tomahawks had arrived, GC III/6's most successful pilot of the

The first D 520 to be lost was Sgt Chef Mertzisen's No 329 ('9'), seen here being examined by Australian troops after crash-landing near Ezraa on 8 June. The pilot escaped on foot. Note the GC III/6 emblem on the tailfin. *(F.F. Smith)*

1940 campaign, Sous Lt Pierre Le Gloan, had led a 'patrouille double' of six D 520s to Damascus, from where ten sorties were to be flown during the day. At midday Le Gloan and Sgt Chef Mertzisen took off to escort a Pz 63-11 of GR II/39 on a reconnaissance over the Ezraa region. A motorised column was seen, and the two fighters swept down to strafe, but return fire struck Mertzisen's Dewoitine, and he crash-landed No 329, suffering multiple contusions. He managed to escape on foot, and was assisted back to his unit by the local Druze population. Meanwhile Le Gloan rejoined the Potez, and during the return flight spotted one of 208 Squadron's 'A' Flight Hurricanes (Z4364) engaged in a long-range reconnaissance of the Damascus–Quneitra–Deraa area in the hands of Flt Lt J.R. Aldis. Le Gloan attacked at once and shot the aircraft down over Damascus for his 12th personal victory of the war. Later that afternoon during a further escort sortie from Damascus–Mezze, Sgt Chef Ravily crashed on the edge of the airfield from 200 metres altitude while taking off in No 132, and was killed.

From Rayak at 1300 a 'patrouille simple' of two D 520s from GC III/6 had taken off for the coastal region, where they found Fulmars of 803 Squadron patrolling over the Royal Navy cruisers off Sidon. The French pilots took their opponents to be Hurricanes, and Lt Martin (No 331) reported that he was about to attack one, but was shot down, baling out over the coast to be captured by the advancing Australians. His wingman, Sous Lt Brondel, returned to report that his leader had been shot down by a fighter, but British records attributed the success to the anti-aircraft guns of the 15th Cruiser Squadron.

At 1532 the six D 520s of a full 'patrouille double', comprising the 6ᵉ Escadrille of GC III/6, took off for the same area, Cne Leon Richard leading Sous Lt Rivory and Sgt Michaux, followed by Lts Stenou and Boiries, and Sous Lt Satgé. Again six Fulmars were seen, and again identified as Hurricanes. The naval two-seaters proved no match for the Dewoitines, each patrouille claiming one shot down, although several of the French fighters were hit and slightly damaged by the gunfire from the ships below.

During the day 803 Squadron had suffered heavily, the leader of the second formation, Lt J.M. Christian, and his observer, Sub Lt N. Cullen, both being killed (in N1950), as were Pty Off (A) J.A. Gardner and Leading Airman H. Pickering (in N1956). A third Fulmar was lost, the observer, Leading Airman B.P. Dearnley, being rescued from the sea, as apparently was his pilot, while a fourth was so badly damaged that it had to be written off, and a fifth suffered less severe damage. It is possible that some of this execution had been achieved by Lt Martin before he was shot down during the earlier sortie.

As a consequence of these losses, the RAF was requested to provide additional fighter cover over the ships, and this was done at the expense of the troops on the ground. The first such was undertaken by Hurricanes of 80 Squadron, during which Plt Off Roald Dahl reported intercepting an aircraft at 1630, which he identified as a Potez 63, claiming to have set one engine on fire. He thought the aircraft then dived into the sea, and was credited with a 'probable'. No such loss is recorded by the French, and whilst two sections each of three M 167Fs attacked targets along the coast at Sheikh Meskine during the late afternoon, they reported no casualties or damage. At the end of the day three Blenheims bombed the radio station at Jedida, while three others again attacked the Shell depot to the east of Beirut. One was claimed shot down by the AA guns of the 24 RMC, but no loss actually occurred.

It had been planned to land the commandos of the Special Service Brigade on the coast at dawn, to secure a bridge over the Litani River for the Australians. HMS *Glengyle* attempted to approach the shore as planned, but the surf proved too heavy and she withdrew. The vessel returned that night, but the element of surprise was gone and the commandos met strong resistance from French colonial troops, suffering heavy losses and seeing the bridge blown.

Monday, 9 June 1941

On the right flank on the 9th, the Indians reached Sheikh Meskine, which was evacuated by the Vichy defenders under cover of air attack. Here the Free French Brigade passed through to take up the advance, pressing on to Kissoué, only some ten miles south of Damascus. Here, however, resistance stiffened, and attacks which were to follow on 11 and 12 June made no headway.

Much of the action in the air centred on the coast, where attacks on the 15th Cruiser Squadron were to be made by French bombers, while two of the Vichy Fleet destroyers sent out sorties to shell the Australians around the mouth of

Two of the six Bloch MB 200 bombers which equipped escadrille 3/39 of Groupe de Bombardement I/39 at the commencement of hostilities in Syria. *(via C-J. Ehrengardt)*

the Litani. British destroyers intervened, but in an exchange of fire with the larger and more powerful French warships, HMS *Janus* was badly damaged, and HMS *Jackal* was less severely hit.

While on patrol during the morning, Flg Off G.H. Westlake of 80 Squadron made a similar report to that of Dahl on the previous day, claiming to have probably shot down a Potez 63, although again no French loss of any kind is to be found. At 1420 three more of this unit's Hurricanes were off on patrol, where they had just arrived when the first major attack developed, six Martin 167Fs of GB I/39, the four Bloch MB 200s of EB 3/39, and six escorting D 520s from GC III/6 approaching. As they neared the ships at 1525, Flt Lt J. Lockhart, leader of the Hurricane section, spotted three of the MB 200s in vic formation, but failed to spot the escorting fighters which were above. He led an attack on the leading bomber, diving out of the sun from the port quarter and firing several long bursts, whereupon the bomber turned for Beirut and was last seen at 3,000 feet in a steep dive, followed by a large splash; a parachute was also seen nearby. While Lockhart's attack was under way, three of the escorting Dewoitines dived on the Hurricanes, Sous Lt Le Gloan at once attacking what he believed to be the formation leader, which he shot down in flames, the pilot baling out. Sgt Mequet attacked one of the others, while the third was seen continuing to attack the Blochs. The covering section then joined the fight to attack this aircraft, which dived away. Le Gloan half-turned and saw Mequet's Dewoitine behind a Hurricane, but the latter then broke away, out of ammunition, and Le Gloan took up the attack, sending this Hurricane down in flames also, again seeing the pilot bale out. His first victim had not been the formation leader, since Lockhart returned safely, and was also the pilot who had been seen attacking the bombers. Le Gloan had shot down Plt Offs Lynch and Crowther, both of whom were killed. EB 3/39 had actually lost two of its aircraft in this attack, one indeed crashing into the sea with the loss of three members of the crew (Adj de Riverleux de Varax, Adj Idier and Sgt Orgueil), while Sgt Seize baled out. A second Bloch, badly hit, crashed near Bir Hassen without injury to the crew.

What followed became more confused. Three more Hurricanes had taken off at 1540 to relieve Lockhart's patrol, while at precisely the same time three D 520s had scrambled from Rayak, led by Cne Richard, on receipt of Le Gloan's radioed report of the action. On approaching the area, the 80 Squadron pilots saw the Dewoitines at 12,000 feet and at once attacked, the aircraft then splitting up into a dogfight, the French pilots having been well on their guard. Flg Off Westlake attacked one and claimed to have shot it down into the sea. He and Sgt R.T. Wallace then got on the tail of another, firing several short bursts from 100 to 150 yards' range. The propeller appeared to stop, the aircraft seemed to burst into flames and fall into the sea. Cne Richard had fired at one Hurricane,

Bloch MB 200 No 2 survived the sortie of 9 June 1941, to see further service by night during the rest of the campaign. *(J. Mutin)*

Two pilots of GC III/6 who achieved some success over Syria. On the left is Sgt 'Achille' Ghesquiere, and on the right is Sgt 'Papichou' Michaux. *(A. Michaux)*

which dived seawards and disappeared from view, when his own aircraft was hit by a burst of fire which destroyed the electrical circuit, causing a burst of flame to appear, and he dived away — obviously the second aircraft attacked by Westlake and Wallace. However, Richard was not shot down; the flames went out, and he was able to join Sgt Michaux, who claimed to have shot down one of the aircraft that had been attacking his leader, and they returned to be credited with one victory apiece.

Meanwhile, the third Dewoitine (No 346), flown by Sous Lt Rivory, collided head-on with the third Hurricane, both Rivory and Sgt M.W. Bennett baling out to be picked up by the Royal Navy, Bennett suffering severe burns. On his return from captivity, Rivory later sought a share in each of the victories claimed by Richard and Michaux, which was refused as neither had made any mention of his involvement, while he reported that his fire had exploded a third opponent — obviously Bennett's Hurricane — which was credited to him. In practice it appears possible that his had been the aircraft first attacked by George Westlake, and that he had collided with Bennett as he dived away. Having witnessed two fighters crashing into the sea, the Navy subsequently confirmed both of the 80 Squadron claims, almost certainly believing that Bennett's Hurricane was a second Dewoitine! Westlake reported on return that the Hurricane appeared able to outclimb, outrun and outmanoeuvre the D 520s; he considered that the French pilots seemed to be good flyers and full of spirit, but poor shots!

During the day three Potez 25TOEs of EO 594, escorted by two GC I/7 MS 406s, attacked Allied columns on the Deraa–Damascus road, but both fighters were hit by ground fire. While taking off from Damascus for a similar escort sortie, another Morane, No 749, was crashed by Sous Lt Gimprel, and destroyed.

The Aeronavale Escadrille 19S undertook its first sorties, Loire 130 19S-6 in the hands of the Commanding Officer, Lt de V Brossier, flying a reconnaissance to Famagusta, Cyprus, at 1800, and dropping two bombs on a merchant vessel off Cape Greco. AA fire from the ship slightly damaged his aircraft. 84 Squadron moved its Blenheims from Habbaniya to Mosul, to undertake reconnaissances over eastern Syria; 'X' Flight also commenced operations from Amman, flying patrols over the Free French troops in the Sanamein–Kissoué area. GAO 583 left Aleppo for Rayak, where its Potez 63-11s were attached to GR II/39, the unit coming under Cdt Larroze's overall command.

Tuesday, 10 June 1941

By the 10th French resistance was stiffening everywhere and RAF support was requested by the land forces, 803 Squadron's remaining Fulmars re-commencing patrols over the Fleet in consequence. However, the 21st Australian Infantry Brigade got across the Litani River on a newly constructed pontoon bridge during the day, and overran the defenders locally, resuming the advance with the surviving commandos. They would reach Sidon late on the 12th. Meanwhile Merjayoun had been taken by the 25th Australian Infantry Brigade, a unit newly arrived in the Middle East, but here the French were found to be present in strength. A planned advance north up the Litani valley to Rayak was therefore postponed, and most of the Brigade moved to support the main 7th Division thrust by turning through Jezzine, to the immediate east of Sidon.

More French reinforcements arrived during the morning of the 10th, nine Loire et Olivier LeO 451 bombers of GB I/31 landing at Aleppo, with four Farman 222.2 transports of GT I/15 carrying the ground crews. Led by the Commanding Officer, Cdt Lauzin, the bombers had flown from Istres via Brindisi, Italy. Thirteen had left, but four had fallen by the wayside for a variety of reasons en route; three of these would soon arrive.

Over the front, M-167Fs of GB I/39 undertook a number of reconnaissance sorties over the Damascus–Deraa area. Two Tomahawks of 3 RAAF Squadron were scrambled to intercept the third of these, which was covering the Amman–Aqir–Haifa area, bringing the French aircraft well into Palestinian airspace.

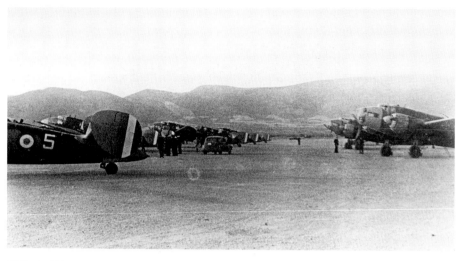

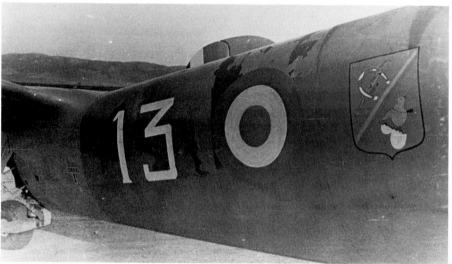

Fairey Swordfish L7646 'X' of 815 Squadron at Heliopolis. *(R.C. Sturtivant via A.S. Thomas)*

Before they could get into position to attack, the Martin was shot down by AA fire, Sous Lt Causson and his crew all being killed when No 88 crashed. Six more sorties were flown by this French unit to attack vehicles on the Deraa–Damascus road, and five against the British warships north of Sidon.

GR II/39 made five reconnaissances over southern Syria, but the unit's base at Damascus–Mezze was now considered to be too close to the fighting, and it withdrew to Baalbeck–La Colonne, where it was accompanied by EO 594, also Damascus-based. The Loire 130s were out throughout the day, 19S-2, 3 and 4 all making attacks on Allied merchant vessels, the two former aircraft both suffering some AA damage in return. That night three Bloch MB 200s of EB 3/39, accompanied by nine Pz 25TOEs from EO 593 and 594, bombed vehicles south of Sanamein, without loss or damage. In return three Swordfish of 815 Squadron, led by Lt F.M.A. Torrens-Spence, raided Beirut harbour, dropping six 250lb bombs on the destroyers there.

In further efforts to reinforce the Armée de l'Air, ten D 520s from GC I/2 and four MS 406s from a training school at Aulnot were released to be sent to Syria as reinforcements. The British were strengthened by the arrival at Lydda of six Albacores of 829 Squadron from HMS *Formidable*, while at Habbaniya another new unit commenced forming. This was to be known as 127 Squadron, commanded by Flt Lt J.M. Bodman, which received as initial equipment two long-range Hurricanes and four standard Mark Is. The latter included two (P3731 and V7370) which had reached Iraq from Malta, where they had served for many months, and were, to borrow a phrase, thoroughly 'clapped-out' (see

Opposite top: Loire et Olivier LeO 451 bombers of the 1ere escadrille of Groupe de Bombardement I/31 at Athens–Eleusis airfield en route to Syria on 9 June. Aircraft '5' is No 187, flown by Sous Lt Bornecque, which would be lost in an accident three days after arrival. *(Bundesarchiv). Opposite middle:* LeO 451 No 295 ('13') was flown by the commander of GB I/31, Commandant Lauzin. It carries the insignias of both of the Groupe's escadrilles. This aircraft would be destroyed in an accident on 11 June. *(Bundesarchiv). Opposite bottom:* Farman 223.3 — possibly No 4 — seen at Brindisi on its way to Syria, carrying personnel and supplies. Note the Junkers Ju 52/3m transports in the background. *(G.F. Ghergo)*

213

Malta: the Hurricane Years, 1940-41). The other pair, V7543 and V7654, were newer, the former having previously served with 94 Squadron, the latter being effectively new. Four Gladiators were also made available, three being ex-'A' Squadron Mark Is, K7899, '7907 and '8048, and one newly issued Mark II, N5857.

Wednesday, 11 June 1941

Efforts by the Armée de l'Air to interfere with the Allied advance were redoubled on the 11th, GC I/7 undertaking 21 strafing sorties against the Free French in the Kissoué region, one MS 406 being hit in the radiator. Later in the day this unit would be ordered to leave Estabel for Homs, as the former was now considered to be too exposed. This proved to be too far from the front to be practical, and six aircraft were detached back to Rayak, led by Cne Polikow.

GB I/39's M-167Fs undertook 11 sorties, including an attack by nine bombers on a column north of Ghabarheb on the Sheikh Meskine–Damascus road. Lt Duparchy's aircraft was hit by AA fire and he flew 200 kilometres to Palmyra on one engine.

At 1920 GB I/31 undertook its first mission, four LeO 451s taking off to bomb vehicles 25 kilometres south of Damascus. They were to have had an escort of D 520s, but arrived an hour late for the rendezvous. By the time the attack had been made, night was falling. Worried that they would not find their airfield again in the dark, Cdt Lauzin decided they would land at Damascus–Mezze, unaware that it had been abandoned due to the proximity of the advancing Allied forces, and had been rendered unusable with obstacles, etc. Consequently three of the bombers, Nos 189, 263 and 295, were destroyed in landing accidents.

Potez 63-11s and 25TOEs undertook various sorties during the day, and may have been involved in another difficult-to-resolve report. 80 Squadron's Plt Off Bill Vale, one of the top scorers of the Greek campaign (see *Air War for*

LeO 451 No 263 of GB I/31, one of three which crashed while landing in the dark at Damascus–Mezze airfield on 11 June 1941. *(C-J. Ehrengardt)*

Yugoslavia, Greece and Crete, 1940-41), apparently claimed the destruction of a Potez 63 whilst on patrol in Hurricane V6939 during the day. GR II/39's No 676, flown by Cne Forget, was indeed intercepted and hit by two bullets whilst on a reconnaissance of the Merjayoun–Sidon–Nagoura area. However, an account written afterwards indicates that Vale's victim had actually been a D 520, which had crashed with the death of the pilot on the coast near Haifa. No French fighters were lost or damaged in such circumstances on this date, but next day one was, although to AA fire. It is possible that the report of this wreck was subsequently incorrectly assumed to confirm Vale's claim.

Thursday, 12 June 1941

In an effort to assist the ground forces, even the tactical reconnaissance aircraft of 208 Squadron were ordered to undertake strafing sorties. At 0600 Flg Offs Holdsworth and Macrostie of 'A' Flight flew to Roshpina landing ground from where they were to carry out attacks on troops on the road north of Merjayoun. However, Macrostie's Hurricane was hit in the oil cooler by ground fire and he crash-landed on a hillslope, while Holdsworth returned with a damaged aircraft. (Macrostie was picked up safely next day by a Lysander from 'B' Flight from H-4.)

At much the same time three D 520s of GC III/6 escorted a Pz 63-11 of GAO 583 to strafe near Sanamein. Cdt Deschamps de Pas was ordered to take a patrouille from his GC I/7 to strafe 'small units of the British Fleet', but on arrival found these in fact to be the whole of the 15th Cruiser Squadron! He requested confirmation of his orders, which were at once changed and instead a GR II/39 Pz 63-11 was escorted to Deraa, where the Moranes strafed a camp and a concentration of vehicles. GC I/7 was now attached to the Groupement Mixte Nord, which had been formed under Lt Col Monniot, and which included GB I/31, based upon Homs, Nerab and Rayak.

GB I/39 undertook two reconnaissances, and five M-167Fs bombed vehicles north-east of Merjayoun, two of the bombers being hit by AA fire, one of them badly, the gunner being wounded.

At 1230 six Blenheims from 11 Squadron attacked French positions south of Kissoué, one of these bombers being damaged by AA. At around the same time, whilst on a patrol over the cruisers, Plt Off Vale of 80 Squadron suffered an engine failure, and force-landed at Tyr, writing off his Hurricane.

3 RAAF Squadron twice provided patrols over the cruisers on this date. On the second operation, which commenced at 1450, the eight Tomahawks intercepted eight Ju 88s which were attempting to bomb the ships, identifying these (incorrectly) as Italian-flown aircraft. Three of these were claimed shot down by Sqn Ldr Peter Jeffrey, Flt Lt J.R. Perrin and Flg Off J.W.H. Saunders, while two more were believed to have been damaged. These were in fact Luftwaffe machines of II/LG 1 from Crete; two of the German bombers actually failed to return, one from 4 Staffel (L1+DM) flown by Lt H. Dickjobst, and one of 5 Staffel, flown by Lt R. Bennewitz. These were the first victories obtained anywhere by aircraft of the Curtiss P-40 series.

At 1609 a 'patrouille double' from GC III/6, led by the 5ᵉ Escadrille commander, Cne Jacobi, a well-known French pilot, took off on a reconnaissance mission over Deraa and Hasbaya, looking for British troops and vehicles. Fire from a column of vehicles hit three of the fighters and Jacobi crashed to his death in No 229 six kilometres south of Sidon, on the coast. Sgt Coisneau

Capitaine Jacobi, a notable pre-war aerobatic pilot, and commander of the 5 escadrille of GC III/6, with his D 520 No 229 ('1'), at Brindisi on 25 May 1941, discussing his aircraft with Luftwaffe officers. He was shot down and killed by Australian AA fire on 12 June. *(Bundesarchiv)*

was wounded in the face, but managed to return, and Sgt Chef Monribot lost control of his damaged aircraft whilst trying to land back at Rayak, crashing No 284, but suffering no injury.

Six Hurricanes of 80 Squadron escorted Blenheims to bomb Rayak at 1800, on the way spotting two French aircraft which a pair of fighters broke off to pursue. These may have been Pz 63-11s of GAO 583, one of which Sgt R.T. Wallace reported attacking, causing the starboard engine to pour smoke; this may have been Sous Lt Tataux's aircraft. Wallace broke off when his Hurricane was hit by return fire. The second Potez, flown by Cne d'Argoubet, was not attacked, and the two French aircraft returned to base without further incident (see 13 June for further comment).

GB I/31 was out again, four LeO 451s attacking columns near Sanamein. Again the bombers returned at nightfall and Sous Lt Bornecque crashed No 187 at Rayak whilst attempting to land there. A Pz 63-11 of GR II/39, strafing near Kissoué, was hit by AA, Lt Torlois returning with one of the crew, Adj Bahout, wounded in one leg.

By night Swordfish of 815 Squadron attacked the port of Jounie, to the north of Beirut. Sub Lt A.S.D. Macaulay, DSC & Bar and Sub Lt P.A. Hall successfully torpedoed a tanker, which caught fire, while three other aircraft dropped six 250lb bombs without effect.

With the Australians at Sidon, still aided by the 15th Cruiser Squadron, Amiral Gouton requested Général Dentz to seek attack on the vessels by German Ju 87 Stuka dive-bombers. When this request was passed to Amiral Darlan, he sought to have an Aeronavale flotille specialising in maritime attack sent to Syria as an alternative.

Friday, 13 June 1941
The situation for the invaders was by no means as good as might have been hoped, for by this time 500 casualties had been sustained. The Australians

The cannoneer's dorsal position in the LeO 451 bomber, with the 20mm cannon elevated for use. *(C-J. Ehrengardt)*

pressed forward from Sidon towards Damour, but found the defences strong, and were brought to a halt. Little progress was being made in the centre around Merjayoun, and while the situation in the east was rather better, the 5th Indian Infantry Brigade having taken up the attack again from the stalled Free French, it was clear that, as Wavell had feared, the forces generally were not strong enough for the task. Any possibility of a collapse of resistance such as had been envisaged by the Free French had proved to be an illusion. Indeed, it was against the latter that the Vichy troops had fought with particular determination, clearly unwilling to submit to what they saw as a bunch of rebels and traitors. Consequently on this date Wavell decided to commit the 6th (British) Division of two Brigades from Egypt.

Early in the day Pz 63-11s from GAO 583 were out on reconnaissance, but on their return this unit was evacuated from Rayak to Baalbeck–La Colonne. At 1100 a Blenheim of 11 Squadron, flown by Plt Off Lea, commenced a photographic reconnaissance over the Beirut area. At the same time a patrouille of three D 520s began a patrol over the capital. Half an hour later the French pilots spotted the Blenheim approaching from the south, identifying it as a Martin in Free French colours. Lea tried to turn away, but the three fighters dived to attack, opening fire. Cne Richard, the formation leader, kept after his quarry, which fell away, engines smoking, to crash in a small valley ten kilometres north of the Litani, all the crew being killed.

GB I/31 was now moving to Qousseir, but four of its aircraft were led by Cne de Salaberry to attack the British cruisers off Sidon, escorted by four Moranes of GC I/7. Over Jezzine the French reported being attacked by Hurricanes, although MS 406 pilot Sous Lt Demoulin identified the two attackers as 'P-40s'. One LeO 451, flown by Lt Lecerf, was attacked by both, but the cannoneer, Sgt de Feligonde, hit one with his 20mm gun and it broke away, trailing black smoke. The second dived away, and Lecerf made for Rayak, landing with de Feligonde wounded. This action appears to fit very well the engagement reported by Sgt Wallace of 80 Squadron on the previous day, and the latter unit's account may well have been incorrectly dated. Twenty-one bombing sorties and three reconnaissances were flown by GB I/31 during the day, mainly against vehicles on the coast road near Sidon.

During the day 13 LeO 451s of GB I/12 and four Farman transports arrived at Aleppo–Nerab, having departed France on the 11th. They had been delayed when three aircraft were involved in an accident at Brindisi, where a Farman had collided with an Air France Dewoitine D 338 which was carrying some of the unit's equip-

LeO 451s of GB I/12 in flight. In the foreground is No 234 ('6') of the 2 escadrille, accompanied by No 409 ('5') of the 1ere escadrille. No 6's dorsal cannon is elevated. *(P. Riviere)*

ment. Next day the Groupe would begin moving to join GB I/31 at Qousseir.

EB 3/39 now returned to Rayak, where it joined with EO 592 to form Groupement de Nuit Marin; EO 593 and 594 formed the Groupement Faure (named after the new commander of EO 594).

Saturday, 14 June 1941

At 0627 on the 14th five Blenheims from 11 Squadron left to attack Aleppo airfield; three broke away to hit Rayak, where they surprised the Moranes of the Polikow detachment, three of which were slightly damaged. The bombers returned later, when during a second attack at 1330 MS 406 No 770 was destroyed in flames and a Pz 25TOE was also written off. Earlier at 0500 GAO 583 had commenced sending out Pz 63-11s on reconnaissances over the coastal area. Sous Lt Collonfiers' No 793 was hit in the oil tank by a bullet, forcing him to return. Departing at the same time, Sous Lt Tatraux returned from Kissoué with several holes in the fuselage.

Five LeO 451s of GB I/31 were off at 1755 to attack the cruisers, escorted by six D 520s led by Sous Lt Le Gloan. An 80 Squadron Hurricane had been sent off half an hour earlier on a reconnaissance over Beirut, but as Flg Off The Honourable David Coke approached his target, he received a request over the R/T to undertake an immediate patrol over the fleet. On arrival he saw four of the bombers in the act of unloading their cargo, but before he could attack, he was 'jumped' from out of the sun by three fighters which he took to be MS 406s. Turning, he climbed into the sun and attacked the rear aircraft from below, reporting that he saw strikes on the tail; the other two then attacked him, but at that point another Hurricane joined him.

Indeed, three more had taken off at 1810 for a patrol, arriving to see three

MS 406 No 770 of the 1ᵉ escadrille of GC I/7 was destroyed on the ground at Aleppo on 14 June. The aircraft carries high on the fuselage side, the plumed helmet of 'Chevalier Bayard', previously the insignia of the old SPA 15. On the tailfin is a stylised number 11. *(C-J. Ehrengardt)*

D 520 No 368 of GC III/6, flown by Sous Lt Brondel, flipped over whilst the pilot was attempting to force-land the badly damaged aircraft after an engagement with Hurricanes of 80 Squadron on 14 June 1941. *(C-J. Ehrengardt)*

D 520s. Flg Off P.T. Dowding at once got on the tail of the left-hand aircraft and opened fire, reporting that his opponent half-rolled and dived away pouring smoke. Four bombers were then spotted and Sgt Hancock, who had fallen behind, saw Coke alone and joined him, as already noted. He attacked, but the Dewoitines at once turned on him, a dogfight ensuing for ten minutes before they broke off; Hancock returned claiming one probable, while Dowding's victim was confirmed by the Navy to have crashed into the sea.

This was not the case, however. Le Gloan, Sous Lt Brondel and Sgt Chef Mertzisen had been involved in the fight, and Dowding's opponent had obviously been Brondel. The latter, his aircraft terribly damaged by his opponent's fire and the ships' AA, reached land, where he attempted a wheels-down landing, but the aircraft flipped on to its back, No 368 being a write-off. Le Gloan and Mertzisen returned with their aircraft showing numerous signs of this engagement, each claiming to have hit opponents, and each being credited with a 'probable' victory.

Blenheims again attacked Aleppo at 2000, Cne Dessalles leading three Moranes of GC I/7 in pursuit. Dessalles kept up the pursuit with an overheating engine, firing without effect. His aircraft was hit by return fire from one bomber, and he came down at Sfire, some distance south-east of Nerab airfield, his Morane (No 831) being destroyed, although he was unhurt. This was to be the only Morane lost as a direct result of aerial combat during the campaign.

More Armée de l'Air reinforcements arrived when the first seven LeO 451s of GB I/25 flew in to Aleppo, led by Cdt Lambert and accompanied by four D 338s of Air France with the groundcrews and equipment. On the same date 21 D 520s of GC II/3 reached Rhodes from Tunis, via Brindisi and Athens, flying on to Homs on the 15th. These were to be the last Armée de l'Air units to be despatched to the Levant, although certain Aeronavale units were still to arrive. That evening Vichy troops began an offensive in the Damascus sector against lines of communication, against Jezzine, and against the Merjayoun–Quneitra–Sidon area.

Top: Three GB I/25 LeO 451s, the nearest of which features a natural metal, uncamouflaged fuselage. This is No 346 ('22'), which carried the name 'Coquit'. *(C-J. Ehrengardt). Bottom:* D 520s of GC II/3 newly-arrived in Syria. *(J. Mutin)*

Thus ended the first full week of fighting, which had cost the French 12 aircraft in action against nine such losses to the British. However, the strength of the Armée de l'Air had grown considerably, whilst the RAF's strength remained almost unchanged. In this improved situation the French now counter-attacked in the west, the Allied inferiority in tanks and armoured cars causing them to be driven out of Quneitra. Having made good progress at Kissoué, 5th Indian Infantry Brigade despatched the 1st Royal Fusiliers to Quneitra on the 16th, but they were overrun by a much bigger force. 16th Infantry Brigade, the first element of 6th Division to arrive from Egypt, would then advance on Quneitra from Sanamein, and retake it. Further east a Vichy force sallied out from the Jebel Druse, driving out the Transjordan Frontier Force detachment which was garrisoning Ezraa, next morning opening an attack on Sheikh Meskine. On the 17th a 'scratch' force under Major J.W. Hackett counterattacked fiercely, retaking Ezraa with some 160 Tunisian prisoners.

Meanwhile, on the 15th the garrison at Merjayoun had sent the greater part of its force to attack French units blocking the road to Rayak. Whilst they were gone, a Vichy attack captured Merjayoun and appeared to be in a position to press straight on south into Palestine. However, this force paused, and reserves from the 25th Australian Infantry Brigade at Jezzine were thrown into the gap, holding the line firm.

On the coast the Australians had launched an attack on Sidon coupled with an outflanking 'push' in the hills to the east, the town falling to them during the evening of the 14th. Repeated counter-attacks followed at Jezzine.

Sunday, 15 June 1941

Early on this second Sunday, Flg Off Macrostie of 'A' Flight, 208 Squadron, commenced a tactical reconnaissance in Hurricane 2626 over Quatana, Damascus and Kissoué. In the latter area he was shot down and killed in error by Allied AA fire.

By now 'X' Flight had begun making use of an advanced landing ground at Mafraq, to which six Gladiators flew each morning at daybreak for their scheduled patrol activity. On this morning the six were all on patrol over Kissoué at 8,000 feet when they entered the same airspace as a 'patrouille double' from GC III/6, which had taken off at 0803 to patrol over the Ezraa–Soueida area, led by Sous Lt Le Gloan. At 0945 three of the Gladiators were spotted below, Le Gloan leading Cne de Rivals-Mazeres and Sgt Chef Mertzisen down in a dive on them, at once shooting down K7947, which crashed straight into the ground east of Ezraa, Flg Off J.N. Craigie being killed. A confusing engagement followed, during which Flg Off Jeffrey and Sgt Appleby each claimed a Dewoitine shot down. Sgt Chef Mertzisen's No 367 was badly hit and he came down in British-held territory at Sanamein. Cne de Rivals-Mazeres claimed

Sous Lt Pierre Le Gloan (front right) and his mechanic consider his crash-landed D 520 No 277 ('6') at Rayak, following his fraught engagement with 'X' Flight's Gladiators on 15 June. *(C. Iltis)*

Martin 167Fs of escadrille 7B, Flotille 4F, lined up ready to depart for Syria. The nearest aircraft, No 31, is 7B-6, whilst beyond can be seen 7B-2,4 and 5, and apparently 6B-4 and 6 of escadrille 6B, identified by the individual numbers being positioned lower on the tailfins. The individual aircraft numeral was repeated on the outside of the engine nacelles. *(C-J. Ehrengardt)*

another Gladiator, which he reported exploded on hitting the ground — he had probably fired at Craigie's aircraft, unaware that Le Gloan had already hit this. Le Gloan attacked a second, claiming a probable, but then ran out of ammunition. His No 277 was hit repeatedly, and he was pursued back towards Rayak by two Gladiators, crash-landing on the airfield with his fighter in write-off condition.

The second patrouille had meanwhile joined the fight, Sgt Chef Elmlinger and Sgt Mequet reporting a further victory between them, but incorrectly stating that the pilot had baled out. Either they or Le Gloan had hit Plt Off Watson's K7914, damaging it severely, causing him to fly directly back to Amman. The other four Gladiators landed safely at Mafraq. Sgt Chef Mertzisen escaped on foot, and aided by some Bedouin was back at Rayak by the evening of the 20th.

80 Squadron meanwhile spent the whole day over the 15th Cruiser Squadron, sections relieving each other on a regular basis. Towards the end of the afternoon six of the unit's Hurricanes intercepted nine Luftwaffe Ju 88s, again from II/LG 1, as these were dive-bombing the British vessels, their bombs again hitting the destroyer *Isis*, which was quite severely damaged, and which the fighters escorted into Haifa harbour later that evening. While the attack was under way Flg Off Dahl claimed to have shot down one bomber into the sea, but the Navy later reported that a second had crashed into the water near Cyprus and a third had force-landed in Syria. This was not correct however, LG 1 reporting that one bomber had been hard hit, and had force-landed in Turkey.

It was not only the Germans who had bombed the ships during the day. That morning the Aeronavale Escadrille 6B, equipped with M-167Fs, had arrived at Rayak from Sidi Ahmed, North Africa, led by Lt de V Ziegler. Ordered at once to attack, three of the bombers were off at 1840, each loaded with a single 225 kg bomb, and with an escort of seven D 520s from GC III/6. Six MS 406s from GC I/7 also patrolled in the area, and the naval bombers were joined in their attack by four LeO 451s of GB I/12. Lt de V Ortolan in 6B-3 obtained a direct hit on the destroyer *Ilex*, which he claimed to have sunk; it suffered damage, but did not go down. The British authorities remained a long time under the impression that this vessel had also been a victim of the German bombers. As

This Martin 167F of Aeronavale escadrille 6B demonstrates the dorsal turret modified by the French Navy to carry two, rather than a single machine gun. *(Bundesarchiv)*

the formation returned, four more LeOs from GB I/31 went out to repeat the attack at 1930, one being hit and damaged by AA.

GB I/39 was also active, over both land and sea, on reconnaissances and bombing attacks. About an hour after 80 Squadron's engagement with the Ju 88s, five of this unit's Martins raiding in the Deraa area were spotted by the pilots of seven 3 RAAF Squadron Tomahawks which were strafing in the Sheikh Meskine area. The Australians attacked at once, Sqn Ldr Jeffrey and Flg Off Peter Turnbull shooting down two of the bombers, No 111 crashing near Deraa, Lt Baron and two of his crew being wounded, although the fourth member remained unhurt; all were captured. No 118 crashed in flames, however, Sgt

A trio of GB I/25's LeO 451s in flight. The nearest aircraft, No 197 ('23') would be destroyed in an accident on 18 June. *(EC des Armées)*

Chef Tanchoux's crew all being killed. Over the fleet another M-167F was badly damaged by AA and a second slightly so. It is probable that the former was the aircraft reported by the Royal Navy as the Ju 88 which was believed to have force-landed in Syria. Indeed, the British believed all the attacks had been made by the Luftwaffe on this date. In consequence of the increased hostile air activity and the sorties by the French warships a few days previously, Admiral Cunningham, the Royal Navy's Commander-in-Chief, Mediterranean, ordered the 15th Cruiser Squadron to withdraw to Haifa, and to sally forth only when necessary, and under strong air cover. Thereafter Admiral King's force restricted itself to night and early morning attacks on coastal targets in support of 7th Australian Division.

At evening on this active Sunday, Flg Off Holdsworth of 208 Squadron's 'A' Flight sought to repeat the reconnaissance over Quatana, Damascus and Kissoué which Macrostie had failed to return from earlier in the day. After landing to refuel at Roshpina on his way north, he too was shot down by Allied AA as he attempted to drop a message. He force-landed, but was shot dead by Free French colonial troops as he left his aircraft.

GR II/39 undertook seven reconnaissance sorties during the day, but on one of these over Merjayoun at 1745, Cne Guignard failed to return in his Pz 63-11 No 653, the crew all being lost. The circumstances were not known, and while the aircraft may have fallen to AA fire, it is also possible that it was one of the Potez claimed on earlier dates by 80 Squadron, incorrectly recorded.

By night Martins of GB I/39 and Pz 25TOE aircraft of Groupement Faure bombed Deraa railway station, which was set on fire and burned for three days. To the north 14 LeO 451s (nine of GB I/12 and five of GB I/31) were attached to the command of a new Groupement Mixte Nord at Homs, under Cdt Fine.

Monday, 16 June 1941

In the early hours three Blenheims of 11 Squadron took off to undertake the unit's first night raid, attacking Rayak. With daylight, 'X' Flight resumed its patrol activities, but now in company with Tomahawks of 3 RAAF Squadron. It was the intention that these would deal with any escorting fighters whilst the Gladiators concentrated their attention on bombers.

French aircraft were out on various reconnaissances again, while two LeO 451s of GB I/12 and two of GB I/31, escorted by MS 406s, raided motor columns at Kafer Houn and Jezzine. A little later Lt Genty of I/12 flew a long recon- naissance to H-4, where he spotted 12 aircraft on the ground and numerous vehicles. A raid was organised, five of the unit's LeOs with three more from I/31 setting off at 1325. Due to a navigational error, they arrived over Platform 17, an unoccupied landing strip 20 kilometres east of H-4, where 50 200kg bombs were released fruitlessly. Meanwhile at 0800 a trio of Esc 6B Martins, escorted by nine of GC III/6's D 520s, had gone out after the cruisers near Damour. AA struck one bomber, which was damaged.

A trio of French destroyers, *Guepard*, *Valmy* and *Chevalier Paul*, were now on their way to Syria from Toulon, to reinforce the 3 DCT, but these had been spotted and reported by a Sunderland flying boat of 230 Squadron from Alexandria on the 15th. As they approached the Syrian coast early on the 16th, they were attacked by Swordfish of 815 Squadron from Cyprus when 25 miles off Lattaquie, where *Chevalier Paul* was torpedoed by Sub Lt D.A. Wise in L2818. Three further Swordfish then attacked, but that flown by Lt M.G.W. Clifford was shot down into the sea by AA from the other ships, he and his gunner, Sub Lt Winter, being captured. At 0415 a Loire 130 (19S-3) landed and picked up one badly wounded sailor, but the other 240 survivors, together with the two captured Fleet Air Arm officers, were brought in by the two surviving vessels. The attack had cost six dead and nine wounded.

Tuesday, 17 June 1941

Soon after midnight, 16/17 June, three Blenheims of 11 Squadron again took off, this time with Homs airfield as their target. As they sought to form up in the moonlight over their base, two collided, crashing in flames. Only the leading aircraft survived, continuing to its target, where bombs were dropped.

The French bombers resumed their attacks with daylight, seven LeO 451s from GBs I/12 and I/31 setting out from Qousseir at 0935 to bomb concentrations of vehicles near Merjayoun. They were escorted on this occasion by nine D 520s of GC II/3 on their first operational sorties over Syria. Early in the afternoon three of Escadrille 6B's Martins attacked a battery south of Kafer Houn, near Jezzine, while another, 6B-5, flew a reconnaissance sortie to Cyprus. GB I/25 made nine sorties during the day, five LeOs attacking a village south of Damascus, while four others raided Artouz, near Qatana. In the evening this unit moved to Homs. At 1835 the other LeO units were off again, ten GB I/12 and I/31 aircraft attacking Kissoué and destroying a bridge over the River Nar at Aouaj.

At 1905 Loire 130 19S-5, flown by Lt de V Simon, spotted the cargo vessel *Kirkland* east of Beirut, and bombed it without success. During the day another Pz 63-11 was lost; Cne Capdaspe-Coudet, ex-Commanding Officer of EO 594, now with GR II/39, failed to return from a reconnaissance over Kissoué in No 646. All three members of the crew were wounded and were captured, Capdaspe-Couchet dying that evening. It was believed that they had fallen to AA, but again theirs may have been one of the Potez claimed on other dates by 80 Squadron.

Sous Lt Leon Cuffaut of GC II/3 in D 520 No 358 ('23') on arrival at Aleppo. A narrow diagonal red band is painted along the fuselage side — denoting that the aircraft belongs to the 4e escadrille; 3e escadrille aircraft carried a blue band. *(L. Cuffaut)*

Martin 167F of Aeronavale escadrille 7B at Athens–Eleusis airfield on 16 June 1941, on its way to Syria. *(Bundesarchiv)*

The end of the day also saw the arrival of Escadrille 7B, the other element of Flotille 4F, with seven more Martin 167Fs. The unit had left Sidi Ahmed on the 14th, flying by way of Brindisi and Athens to Rayak, and thence to Madjaloun to join Escadrille 6B. Whilst led by Lt de V Lainé, the unit brought with it Capitaine de Corvette Huber, the Flotille commander.

Wednesday, 18 June 1941

On the ground the second phase of the invasion was now approaching its end. Quneitra and Ezraa had been retaken, but at Merjayoun the French defenders were still holding out.

On the 18th an important command change took place, General Lavarack with his 1st Australian Corps headquarters taking over command of the whole land front from Damascus to the sea. The Corps HQ had become available to Lavarack when he replaced General Blamey as Corps Commander on the appointment of the latter to the post of Deputy Commander-in-Chief, Middle East. 7th Australian Division now passed to Maj Gen A.S. Allen. At the same time Maj Gen J.F. Evetts, commander of the British 6th Division, took command, under Lavarack's overall control, of all troops in the Damascus–Deraa–Quneitra area, except for the Free French.

On the right flank Brigadier Lloyd decided to make a push for Damascus-Mezze airfield on the 18th, attacking late that day and capturing this objective by dawn next day. Counter-attacks followed on the 19th and the 20th, his force being virtually wiped out before help arrived. It was therefore in this area that much of the aerial activity continued.

At 0400 four Pz 25TOEs of EO 596 from Deir ez Zor bombed vehicles south-east of Abu Kemal, while at 0952 seven D 520s from GC III/6 set off to escort a Pz 63-11 of GAO 583 over the Quneitra–Sheikh Meskine–Kissoué area. They were led by Cne Rivals-Mazeres, but he was obliged to return early due to engine trouble, Sous Lt Le Gloan taking over the lead. In consequence the formation became somewhat confused, circling over the area while Le Gloan

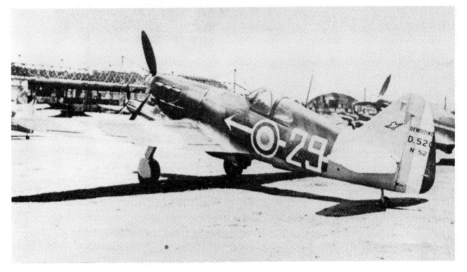

Top: The old Potez biplanes continued to give faithful service throughout the period of hostilities. Potez 25TOE No 2219 ('1') is flanked by a Potez 29 on the right; both were aircraft of EO 596, and are seen here at Deir ez Zor. *(C-J. Ehrengardt). Bottom:* D 520 No 52 ('29') was shot down by 'X' Flight Gladiators on 18 June, Sgt Roger Pimont crash-landing and becoming a prisoner. *(G.F. Ghergo)*

dived down to investigate a group of vehicles seen near Kissoué. At this point five 'X' Flight Gladiators appeared on the scene, led by Flg Off Young. Six had taken off, but one of these too had returned due to engine trouble. Enjoying the advantage of altitude, the British pilots dived on the unsuspecting French, who were at 8,000 feet, and at once Lt Boiries No 389 was shot down in flames, crashing near Abu Kemal. Sgt Pimont made the mistake of attempting to turn with the Gladiators, and his No 52 was also hit, causing him to crash-land, when he was captured. The three remaining Dewoitines became involved in a 15-minute dogfight during which again they found the biplanes to be too nimble for them, although their superior speed allowed them to depart, having been unable to inflict any damage whatsoever on their attackers. Le Gloan, meanwhile, had missed the whole engagement. One of the victories was credited to Flg Off Young, but the identity of the second victor was not disclosed.

At 1335 nine LeOs from GBs I/12 and I/31, covered by nine GC II/3 D 520s,

Top: The crew of LeO 451 No 241 ('10') of GB I/31, led by Cne Hugol. This aircraft was later passed to GB I/25. The dorsal cannon with its ammunition drum in place can be seen clearly. *(W. Anon). Bottom:* On arrival at Homs to take over from GC I/7, Adj Chef Marie Leblanc stood his GC II/3 D 520 on its nose; little damage was caused. *(SHAA)*

attacked vehicles on roads near Merjayoun, the bomber flown by Cne Guignard of I/12 being slightly damaged by AA. At 1720 11 M-167Fs of Flotille 4F were led to the Jezzine area by Cne Huber, while at 1830 eight LeO 451s and five of GB I/39's M-167Fs attacked Artouz village. This final raid was escorted by GC I/7 MS 406s, in one of which Adj Andre attacked a tank which he estimated to be of 30 tons weight, finding that he could make little impact with his 20mm cannon.

At this stage GC I/7 regrouped all its aircraft at Homs, the section at Aleppo-Nerab being replaced by aircraft of GC II/3. The three LeO 451 groupes and the Aeronavale Martins of Flot 4F were all now placed under the command of

Groupement Nord (Col Monniot), with headquarters at Homs. In order to keep GB I/39 at full strength, GR I/22 in France was now ordered to despatch most of its M-167Fs to Syria to reinforce this unit. Ten would be sent during the next few days, although two of these were to be lost en route.

GC III/6 was down to only eight serviceable D 520s by now, however. Next day reinforcement by five newly arrived aircraft and pilots was received, while hard work by ground crews made others serviceable by the 20th.

In Egypt the British offensive codenamed Operation 'Battleaxe' had come to an early standstill, and was abandoned on the 17th, which allowed more aid to be allocated for the forces in Syria. Wellingtons of 37, 38, 70 and 148 Squadrons in the Canal Zone were to commence attacks on Aleppo and Beirut, whilst several other squadrons were identified to move to Palestine. The first of these arrived on the 18th, or at least, a group of pilots from 260 Squadron who had reached Egypt without aircraft or ground crews reached Haifa to be attached to 80 Squadron. Next day these pilots would be flown to Abu Sueir in a Bombay of 216 Squadron to collect Hurricanes from the Maintenance Unit there, returning with these to Aqir that evening.

Thursday, 19 June 1941

The 19th proved to be a rather quiet day in the air, although on the ground the fighting around Mezze airfield was fierce. Several reconnaissance sorties were undertaken by Pz 63-11s of GAO 583, No 795, flown by Sous Lt Metz, being damaged by AA over Jezzine during one of these.

Ten of Flotille 4F's Martins were off in two groups to attack the Australians around Sidon at 1605, while seven Tomahawks of 3 RAAF Squadron escorted Blenheims on a leaflet raid over Masbaja and Merjayoun. Having seen their charges safely back into Allied territory, the Australians were ordered to the Sidon area, where four bombers of Escadrille 7B and three of 6B were seen and attacked, four being claimed damaged. Lt de V De Gail's 7B-3 at the rear of the formation suffered severe damage, while Ens de V Lacoste was unwise enough to leave the formation when his 6B-6 was hit. Fortunately for him, the Tomahawks were by now low on fuel, and departed for their base without pressing the attack further.

At the end of the afternoon four LeO 451s of GB I/25 and five M-167Fs of GB I/39 attacked Artouz again. Four of I/25's LeOs were then despatched to Qousseir, where three were handed to GB I/31 and the fourth to GB I/12.

By evening two Indian infantry battalions had taken Damascus–Mezze airfield, but here they found themselves isolated, and as already described, were to be engaged in two days of fighting which were to result in their being virtually wiped out as operational units.

Friday, 20 June 1941

During the next two days the RAF's units were concentrated on harassing the French forces retiring on Beirut, several aircraft being damaged by ground fire during this period. French operations were also restricted mainly to this front. During the afternoon of the 20th six LeO 451s from GB I/12 and three from GB I/31 bombed a village called Mouaddamiye, four miles south-east of Damascus, under a defensive umbrella provided by 11 D 520s of GC II/3, which strafed after the bombers had departed. Five more LeOs returned at evening to repeat the attack, this time escorted by a trio of GC I/7 MS 406s. By night

Potez 650 transports of GT II/15. The aircraft seen to the right, beyond that in the immediate foreground, was No 15. *(SHAA)*

Mouaddamiye would be the target for six Pz 25TOEs from Groupement Faure.

Elsewhere during the day Lt Ancel flew M-167F No 67 of GB I/39 over the Jezzine area on a reconnaissance, but here the aircraft was shot down by fire from the Bofors guns of the Australian 2/31 Battery, and the British 170th LAA Battery. Ancel and the observer, Lt Duparchy, were both killed, a third member of the crew dying of his injuries, whilst a fourth baled out and was captured. A further reconnaissance into Iraq reported many vehicles and troops 15 miles inside Iraqi territory — this was 'Habforce', preparing to move from H-3 towards Palmyra and Abu Kemal in a convoy of some 800 vehicles.

Due to the difficulties and dangers associated with attempting to despatch reinforcements by sea from Metropolitan France, an 'air bridge' was opened on the 20th, Farman transports from GT I/15, Potez 650s of GT II/15 and Amiot 143s of Groupement de Marche de la 38ᵉ Escadre, supported by 18 Air France Dewoitine D 338s, commencing regular flights to the area, arriving by night. During the night the Australian 2/3 Battalion, which had been held in reserve,

Dewoitine D 338 F-AQBS of Air-France, one of the aircraft which took part in the 'air bridge' operation, seeking to re-supply the forces in Syria from Metropolitan France.

Amiot 143 'T-3' of Groupement de Marche de la 38ᵉ Escadre.

attacked in the Barada Gorge, cutting the road between Beirut and Damascus, and maintaining this position despite French counter-attacks. Damascus then fell on the 21st to the Free French Brigade, which had reached the outskirts of the town, allowing Général Legentilhomme to arrive and take over as military governor. The fall of this objective had been due in the main to the efforts of the Indian units, who had lost 738 officers and men; 300 were later reported to be prisoners, most of them wounded.

Saturday, 21 June 1941

'Habforce' now began its advance towards Palmyra. This had been made possible by the arrival at Basra, in southern Iraq, of the 10th Indian Division to take over the garrisoning of that country, thereby freeing 'Habforce' to threaten the Vichy forces between Damascus and Homs. The advance followed two routes, the first moving west from Abu Kemal, and the second north from the Haifa–Baghdad road, near Rutbah.

Early on, an isolated fort some 40 miles from Palmyra was captured, providing firm warning to the Vichy command of this threat. Cne Tonon of GB I/12 reconnoitred, confirming that at least 150 vehicles were approaching Palmyra, and at once air attacks were ordered. Two hours later four LeO 451s went out from Qousseir, followed later in the afternoon by six more, which repeated the raid. Nine Moranes were led by Cne Dessalles to strafe near T-3, while GC II/3 despatched 26 sorties during the day, 17 of these also in the strafing role. Pz 25TOEs took up the attack as darkness fell. Meanwhile at Palmyra two companies of the Foreign Legion and a Light Desert Company prepared to undertake a resolute defence.

Early in the morning a reconnaissance M-167F (6B-6) from Flotille 4F had spotted British warships, reported as two cruisers and six destroyers, some 45 miles or so off Beirut, before the aircraft was driven off by four escorting fighters, damaged and with one of the crew wounded. On receipt of Ens de V Lacoste's report, nine Martins from the Flotille's two escadrilles were sent off to attack. At around the same time the destroyer *Vauquelin* arrived off Beirut on its journey from France, being escorted into port by a relay of fighters from

Martin 167F No 83 was the first reinforcement for GB I/39 to arrive from North Africa. It landed at Rayak on 21 June. *(ECPA)*

GC I/7 and II/3. The first of GR I/22's M-167Fs (No 83) also arrived at Madjaloun, and was attached to GB I/39.

Sunday, 22 June 1941

On the day upon which the world was shaken by the news of the German invasion of Russia, almost the whole of the French Air Force was turned upon 'Habforce', virtually bringing the columns to a standstill some 25 miles from Palmyra. With very little anti-aircraft artillery available, the columns lost a lot of their vehicles during these attacks, and it became very difficult to maintain their advance.

GC III/6 was retained to provide cover for *Vauquelin* in Beirut harbour, and GR II/39 was ordered to concentrate on patrols in the Damascus area, but otherwise units undertook the following sortie totals against 'Habforce' during the day:

GC I/7	30	GB I/12	3	Esc 6B	10
GC II/3	30	GB I/25	20	Esc 7B	12
		GB I/31	5		
		GB I/39	12		

'X' Flight moved its Gladiators to H-4 to join 'B' Flight of 208 Squadron in an attempt to provide support, but without sufficient aircraft to maintain standing patrols, there was little that could be done, and no interceptions took place.

Fire from 'Habforce' did achieve some results during the day. Pz 63-11 No 803 of GAO 583 was hit over the T-3 area, and damaged, crashing on return and being destroyed. A morning raid by Martins of Esc 6B saw Ens de V Gisbert's aircraft damaged, while during a further raid an hour later Ens de V Lacoste's Martin was badly damaged. Mid-afternoon three Esc 7B aircraft returned, and this time Lt de V De Gail's 7B-3 was damaged beyond repair. Whilst strafing, Morane No 818 of GC I/7 was shot down, Sous Lt Seinturier being killed.

LeO 451 of GBI/25 at Hama with locals. *(SHAA)*

During the day three Blenheims from 11 Squadron were led by Flg Off R.H. Moore in an attack on the *Vauquelin* in Beirut harbour. No fighters were encountered, but Moore's aircraft was hit and suffered serious damage from AA fire, the observer, Sgt Manley, being badly wounded. Nonetheless, the bombing was accurate, the destroyer being hit six times, five sailors being killed and 17 wounded.

Despite the almost universal dedication to duty within the Vichy forces, a 'Gaullist psychosis' was spreading, and on several occasions pilots were arrested upon landing at airfields other than their own on suspicion of being about to change sides!

That evening EB 3/39 and EOs 592, 593 and 594 were formed into a Groupement de Nuit at Abu Danne, incorporating the Groupement Faure, the new unit coming under the overall command of Cne Marin.

Monday, 23 June 1941

The 23rd marked the start of the final phase of the campaign, as the Vichy units were driven back to Merjayoun, and at the same time, shaken by the ferocity of the fighting at Mezze airfield, began to fall back everywhere — except at Palmyra.

With the early failure of Operation 'Battleaxe' in the Western Desert, which had been called off on 17 June after making little progress with heavy losses, more forces now became available to allow an early conclusion of the Syrian occupation. The ground party of 450 (RAAF) Squadron, as yet with no aircraft or pilots of its own service, arrived to join the air party of 260 Squadron, currently attached to 80 Squadron. This allowed a composite unit, 260/450 Squadron, to come into existence immediately, under the command of Sqn Ldr C.J. 'Mickey' Mount, DFC. A further section of Hurricanes from 33 Squadron joined 806 Squadron at Lydda to allow the fighter patrols to be maintained over 15th Cruiser Squadron, while Wg Cdr J.O. Willis led the 12 Blenheim IVs of 45 Squadron to Aqir during the morning, these undertaking a raid on a fort at Suweida that night.

Pilots of 260 Squadron with a Hurricane at Aqir. *(IWM)*

While for the time being little could be done to assist the hard-pressed 'Habforce' by direct fighter action, the increase in available strength did allow the RAF to commence an immediate series of attacks on the Vichy airfields in an effort to reduce their available aerial strength. Consequently at 1320 six Hurricanes from 80 Squadron took off to make a strafing attack on Rayak and Baalbeck–Talia airfields, covered by four more from 260/450 Squadron. The formation flew north, then turning south into the Bekaa Valley south of Qousseir, to approach Baalbeck first, achieving complete surprise. Five Martin 167Fs of GB I/39 had arrived from Madjaloun only ten minutes earlier, two of these being destroyed; No 40 was left in flames, while No 104 blew up when it started to burn. A third was damaged, and the other two suffered minor hits.

Hurricane I Z4172 'G' of 260/450 Squadron coming in to land at Aqir. *(via A.S. Thomas)*

Four more M-167Fs of Flotille 4F were about to take off for Palmyra, and all were hit, but none suffered severe damage. The same was not true of the Potez 63-11s of GR II/39, which suffered badly. Nos 649 and 650 of the 1ʳᵉ Escadrille were destroyed, while Nos 651 and 676 of the 2ᵉ Escadrille were damaged so badly as to be classed as being beyond repair, while two more were less severely damaged. It seems that one more of these was subsequently written off, as No 647 is also listed as destroyed during this attack. Another Pz 63-11, No 793 of GAO 583, was also damaged, as was this unit's 'hack' Bloch 81, OD-AAD, while Pz 25TOE No 918 of EO 593 was destroyed and a Farman 222-1 (No 7) of GT I/15 was damaged. It seems that before reaching Baalbeck, the Hurricanes had also attacked Merjayoun as they passed, for the abandoned Martin 167F, F-BACF, was reported destroyed here by such fighters on this date.

As soon as this attack had got under way, GC III/6 at Rayak was telephoned, and D 520s were scrambled in time to meet the Hurricanes as these swept in from the north to attack this airfield. The first four French pilots to get into the air reported first six, then eight Hurricanes at their own altitude, at once attacking, Sous Lt Le Gloan claiming to have shot down one which had broken away. The other pilots then engaged in a turning fight, Cne Richard, Sgt Chef Mertzisen and Sgt Coisneau claiming another shot down between them. At that point more D 520s arrived, Lt Stenou claiming one Hurricane, which crashed with the pilot still aboard, and then a second, shared with Sous Lt Satgé and Sgt Chef Maccia, from which the pilot baled out. Three of 260/450 Squadron's Hurricanes were lost, Plt Off F. Baldwin being killed in Z4353, Sgt G.J. Black (Z4537) being reported a PoW, while Plt Off T. Livingstone (Z6984) was wounded. A fourth aircraft, Z4608, was badly damaged, and Plt Off O.V. Hanbury was slightly wounded. Sgt Hindle of this unit claimed a D 520 damaged during an attack on Rayak on 24 June, but since no such engagement was reported by GC III/6 on that date, it is assumed that this related to the attack

Damaged outer wing panel of a Hurricane following a sortie over Syria. *(IWM)*

on the 23rd, indicating that one of the 260 Squadron pilots may have been flying an 80 Squadron aircraft. Certainly one D 520 was indeed damaged during this engagement, Sgt Michaux crash-landing.

A slight confusion now arises. At 1455 a patrouille from GC III/6 intercepted an aircraft apparently identified as a Hurricane over the sea near Damour. Sgt Chef Monribot and Sgt Coisneau fired copious amounts of ammunition at this intruder, and it disappeared from view. A parachute was then seen over the sea, and was presumed to be from their victim, and they were credited with a fifth victory for the unit on this date. In fact at precisely this time, a Blenheim from 45 Squadron, flown by Plt Off Champion, was attacked by two fighters whilst on a reconnaissance to Beirut, and was damaged, later crashing as it landed. It seems very likely that this was Monribot's and Coisneau's target, and that they had subsequently seen one of the Hurricane pilots from the Rayak engagement baling out (possibly Livingstone).

At 1720 a dozen Tomahawks of 3 RAAF Squadron set off to attack Qousseir airfield (identified as 'El Asir, in the Kousseir area'), where a Martin 167F was claimed destroyed in flames. This was actually LeO 451 No 240 of GB I/31, which had been badly damaged in an accident on the 16th, and abandoned. The other birds had flown, the bombers of GB I/12 and I/31 having been withdrawn to Abu Danne earlier on this date.

Nine D 520s were again scrambled from Rayak by GC III/6 to intercept at 1834, but as they headed up the Bekaa Valley, they were surprised by the Tomahawks, which dived on them. Sous Lt Le Gloan's aircraft was hit and began to burn, and he at once retreated as rapidly as possible. Four more Dewoitines became engaged in a turning fight with the Australians to the south of Zahle, Cne Richard claiming one shot down. The Tomahawks proved superior in performance at this altitude however, and gained the upper hand, Flg Off Bothwell shooting down Lt Stenou in No 382 and Sgt Savinel in No 370; Stenou, credited with two victories in 1940 and three to date over Syria, crashed in flames in the Zahle area, while Savinel came down between Ablah and Malakaa; both were killed. Bothwell also claimed a probable (probably Le Gloan's aircraft), and Flg Off L.E.S. Knowles reported shooting the wingtip off one, claiming this damaged. Two Tomahawks were damaged, Flg Off P.St.G.B. Turnbull crashing AK463 on return to Jenin (possibly Richard's victim). The second aircraft hit was Sgt F.B. Reid's AK370, which had the starboard mainplane badly damaged by two 20mm cannon shells.

Attacks on 'Habforce' continued throughout the day; on one sortie Lt de la Taille's section of MS 406s from GC I/7, which had moved to Aleppo–Nerab airfield, approached a motorised column reported on the Aleppo–Palmyra axis to discover that it was in fact a Bedouin caravan! Instead the French pilots strafed some 100 to 200 vehicles near Pumping Station T-3.

Tuesday, 24 June 1941

Elements of 25th Australian Infantry Brigade and 6th Division now invested Merjayoun, while the Free French Brigade began moving north towards Nebeck, from where Homs might be threatened. The security of all the airfields in the Bekaa Valley was thereby put at risk, particularly that at Rayak.

During the day 80 and 260/450 Squadrons again despatched Hurricanes to the Baalbeck airfields at midday, where reportedly some 24 bombers were seen, several being claimed damaged or destroyed. It was on this occasion that Sgt

Seen en route to Syria, with Luftwaffe personnel in the foreground, is D 520 No 370 ('33') in which Lt Marcel Stenou was to be shot down and killed on 23 June; he fell victim to the Tomahawk flown by Flg Off R. Bothwell of 3 RAAF Squadron. *(Bundesarchiv)*

Hindle apparently reported seeing a D 520 taking off and attacked this, seeing hits, before his own aircraft was attacked by another and he was driven off. The attack was not so effective on this occasion, Farman 222.1s No 7 and 8 of GT I/15 suffering damage (No 7 for the second time), but that was about the extent of the success achieved. Both these transport aircraft appear to have been written off next day.

'Habforce' remained the main focus for French attention, LeO 451s of GB I/12 and I/31 making eight sorties, while GB I/25 accomplished seven. Three of the latter were directed against tanks near T-3, but here LeO No 413 was hit in the left engine by AA, crashing in flames 20 miles south-east of T-4 with the loss of the whole of Sous Lt Lerat's crew.

Seven Aeronavale M-167Fs, led by Lt de V Ziegler, attacked 300 vehicles south-east of Palmyra during the evening, one of the Martins suffering AA damage.

Wednesday, 25 June 1941

Following violent protests and representations by the harassed 'Habforce', on this date eight Tomahawks from 3 RAAF Squadron were despatched to give some cover. After refuelling at H-4, these took off at 1330 to patrol towards Palmyra, one returning early. Meanwhile six LeO 451s, three from GB I/12 and three from GB I/31, had set off to attack the columns again. East of Joufa the two formations separated, GB I/31's aircraft returning, whilst those from I/12 reconnoitred Saba Biar, between Damascus and Palmyra. Ten minutes later the

Whilst the Allies lost far fewer aircraft in accidents than did the French, they were not immune. These two 3 RAAF Squadron Tomahawks have suffered a collision during take-off from Aqir, and have both obviously suffered some severe damage. *(F.F. Smith)*

Tomahawks appeared, their pilots incorrectly identifying the French formation as comprising four Potez 63s. Flg Offs J.F. Jackson and J.H.W. Saunders, and Sgt A.C. Cameron claimed one shot down each, while Flg Off Jewell reported setting the starboard engine of one alight, which he last saw losing height. This was later confirmed to have come down, and he was credited with a victory, but as only three LeOs were present, he had obviously attacked one of the bombers shot down by one of the other three Australian pilots. None of the GB I/12 formation returned, aircraft '12' (No 373), Lt Goumin, '10' (No 344), Lt Simon, and '2' (No 27), Adj Chef Orliac, all being lost and five of the 12 men aboard being killed.

During the day two M-167Fs from Escadrille 7B, led by Lt de V Lainé, had set out to bomb an observatory near Palmyra which had fallen into British hands during the previous evening. During the night this had been retaken by the French, who waved white flags to indicate their presence to the bomber crews as they approached. Despite this, one bombed before the situation was appreciated.

During the day the LeOs of the three units so equipped had undertaken 23 sorties in total. However a fourth aircraft of this type was lost when Cne Lassale of GB I/25 crashed accidentally on return from a raid on Merjayoun, writing off No 3004. The day was also marked by a loss for the Vichy naval forces when the British submarine HMS *Parthian* sank its opposite number, the *Souffleur*, off Beirut.

Thursday, 26 June 1941
At 0600 two D 520s of GC II/3 went on a reconnaissance, flown by Cne Bordier and Menu, during which the former in No 97 was shot down and killed by AA fire. Sometime later nine Tomahawks from H-4 swept in to strafe Homs airfield, where they caught most of the rest of GC II/3 on the ground. Believing the Dewoitines to be Morane 406s, the Australian pilots claimed four destroyed on

Two views of the remains of GC II/3's D 520 No 327 ('22') following 3 RAAF Squadron's devastatingly successful attack on Homs airfield on 26 June. The unit's 'greyhound' insignia can be seen on the tailfin. *(SHAA)*

fire and six damaged. They had been even more successful than they believed, five D 520s — '30' (No 208), '22' (No 327), '23' (No 358) and Nos 290 and 342 — all being destroyed, while six more were badly damaged, and 11 others to a lesser extent, all this being achieved in ten seconds. An exploding ammunition case killed three mechanics, while Sous Lt Gimprel of GC I/7 was also killed. The 3 RAAF Squadron aircraft swept on down to Rayak, where D 520 No 314 of GC III/6 was destroyed and two more of the unit's fighters were damaged, while three Pz 25TOEs of the Groupement Marin were destroyed and a fourth damaged. Motor vehicles were then shot up, but at this stage AA fire struck Sgt Baillie's aircraft, and he force-landed north of Lake Tiberius.

Following this disastrous attack for the French fighters, the three Groupes de Chasse were ordered to move all surviving aircraft to Aleppo–Nerab, where they were to be supplied with new aircraft from France. Here GC III/6 was to escort

Top: D 520 No 314 of GC III/6, destroyed on the ground at Rayak during 3 RAAF Squadron's strafing attack on 26 June. *(Musée de l'Air). Below:* Tomahawk IIB AK366 of 3 RAAF Squadron, in which Sgt M.J. Baillie was shot down by fire from 10ᵉ Batterie of the 1ᵉʳᵉ RAML during the morning of 26 June; he force-landed near Lake Tiberius. *(F.F. Smith)*

Aeronavale M-167Fs and strafe in the Palmyra area during the next few days.

Over the main front at 1030, Lt Guillot of GAO 583, artillery spotting near Jezzine in his Pz 63-11, was attacked by three fighters, but escaped into cloud. During the day LeO 451s undertook 15 sorties over the Palmyra–Joufa area, while GB I/39 managed a single reconnaissance to Abu Kemal. Flotille 4F sent Martin 6B-2 on reconnaissance to Cyprus, where six Swordfish were spotted on the ground at Nicosia.

Early in the evening six 80 Squadron Hurricanes and six from 260/450 Squadron from Haifa attacked Rayak, nine of these fighters strafing. The British pilots reported seeing nine D 520s and MS 406s, and ten other aircraft, claiming three fighters and a Potez 63 in flames. Since all serviceable aircraft had already been withdrawn to Aleppo, they are believed to have attacked those already rendered beyond repair by the Australians earlier in the day.

Friday, 27 June 1941

The new British tactics were bearing fruit rapidly. On this date French aerial

Farman 223-3 No 4 of GT II/15. *(Bundesarchiv)*

activity was greatly reduced to 45 sorties, including 18 escorts to bombers by fighters, and four reconnaissances. Only 23 offensive flights could be launched. Early in the day Escadrille 6B Martins bombed British warships off Sidon and Beirut, while at 1345 nine D 520s of GC III/6 escorted two GT I/15 Farmans carrying ammunition to T-4 for the Palmyra garrison.

At 1330 four 45 Squadron Blenheims attacked artillery positions and vehicles north-east of Damascus, but Sgt Bullock's bomber was hit by AA, and the radio operator was badly wounded. Bullock at once landed at nearby Mezze airfield for urgent medical assistance, but the wounded man died later.

Five Martins, two of Esc 6B and three of Esc 7B, were led by Cne de Corvette Huber to attack the warships off Damour again at 1515, covered by nine GC III/6 D 520s. Two of the bombers returned early, and during the attack one, 7B-6, was damaged by AA. On return one D 520 (No 321) crashed while landing, and was destroyed.

On this date 'X' Flight despatched three worn Gladiators to 102 MU as no longer suitable for operations, leaving the little unit with only three aircraft. This was too few to maintain any further patrols over 'Habforce', and these ceased, apart from such as the Australians of 3 RAAF could fit in between their other duties.

Evening brought the third week of the campaign to a close, with the balance suddenly altered. During the first two weeks the French had lost 21 aircraft in action, and the RAF 11. In the past seven days, at a cost of three Hurricanes and two Tomahawks, 24 more French machines had been destroyed, including nine D 520s, five Pz 63-11s, four LeO 451s and three M-167Fs. The disposition of forces was now:

French

Homs	GC II/3	three D 520s (all damaged)
	GC I/7	one MS 406 (damaged)
Baalbeck–La Colonne	GR II/39	five Pz 63-11s
	GAO 583	four Pz 63-11s
Madjaloun	GB I/39	eight M-167Fs
	Flotille 4F	11 M-167Fs
Rayak	GT II/15	one F 223-3
Beirut	GT II/15	one Pz 650
Hama	GB I/25	10 LeO 451s
Aleppo–Nerab	GC II/3	10 D 520s
	GC III/6	13 D 520s
	GC I/7	12 MS 406s
	GB I/12	eight LeO 451s
	GB I/31	nine LeO 451s
	EO 596	some Pz 25TOEs
	GT I/15	five F 222s
	GT II/15	four Pz 650s
Abu Danne	Groupement Marin	three MB 200s
		some Pz 25TOEs
Palmyra	EO 595	some Pz 25TOEs
Deir ez Zor	EO 596	some Pz 25TOEs
Tripoli	Esc 19S	five Loire 130s

British

Iraq

Mosul	84 Squadron	six Blenheim IVs

Palestine

Aqir	11 Squadron	12 Blenheim IVs
	45 Squadron	11 Blenheim IVs
	80 Squadron	two Hurricanes
	260/450 Squadron	six Hurricane Is
Haifa	80 Squadron	six Hurricanes
Jenin	3 RAAF Squadron	12 Tomahawk IIBs
Lydda	33/806 Squadron	six Hurricane Is
	272 Squadron	three Beaufighter ICs
	829 Squadron	six Albacores
Ramleh	208 Squadron	nine Hurricane Is
		two Hurricane PR Is
		three Lysander IIs

Transjordan

H-4	'X' Flight	three Gladiators

Cyprus

	80 Squadron	four Hurricanes
	252 Squadron	three Beaufighter ICs
	815 Squadron	five Swordfish
	826 Squadron	five Albacores

Egypt

	37 Squadron ⎫	
	38 Squadron ⎬	Wellington
	70 Squadron ⎭	

Top: 3 RAAF Squadron's Tomahawks in flight over mountainous terrain. It was nine of these aircraft which wiped out the Aeronavale formation on 28 June 1941. *(AWM). Bottom:* A quartette of Flotille 4F M 167F bombers in flight, 7B-3 in the foreground. *(C-J. Ehrengardt)*

Saturday, 28 June 1941

Despite the non-availability of 'X' Flight over the 'Habforce' columns, probably the greatest Allied aerial successes of the campaign occurred on the 28th. Nine 3 RAAF Squadron Tomahawks flew up to Damascus–Mezze where they refuelled, taking off again at 1015 to escort Blenheims on a raid. At 1010 meanwhile, six Martin 167Fs of Flotille 4F had taken off, one section of two being sent to bomb troops south-east of Palmyra, while the other four as a second section headed for a British concentration near Mohammed Ben Ali, to the north of the oasis. The sections were:

1   7B-5 (No 274) Ens de V Massicot (pilot), Lt de V Lainé (observer)
     7B-4 OE Le Friant
2   6B-3 Lt de V Ziegler
     6B-4 Ens de V Playe
     6B-6 Ens de V Lacoste
     7B-6 (No 31) Lt de V De Gail

Top: Personnel of escadrille 7B with M 167F No 21 (7B-6). On 28 June many of these men would lose their lives to the 3 RAAF Squadron pilots. *(C-J.Ehrengardt). Bottom:* The pilots of 3 RAAF Squadron at Roshpina with one of their Tomahawks. L to r: Sgts R.K. Wilson, Parker, D. Scott and G.E. Hiller, Flg Offs W.G. Kloster, P.St.G.B. Turnbull, Flt Lt J.R. Perrin, Sqn Ldr P. Jeffrey, Sgt A.C. Cameron, Flt Lt A.C. Rawlinson, Medical Officer (at rear), Flg Offs J.H.W. Saunders, W.E. Jewell, L.E.S. Knowles and T. Trimble. *(IWM)*

The Blenheims having completed their attack, the Australians' attention was caught by the explosions of bombs dropped by the Aeronavale aircraft, all six being seen bombing in pairs. In the execution which followed, all the bombers were shot down, 6B-3, 6B-4, 6B-6 and 7B-4 all crashing with total loss of life. PM Sarrotte, the pilot of 7B-6, held the aircraft in the air long enough for the crew to bale out, he and SM Gueret surviving. From 7B-5, Lt de V Lainé and Ens de V Massicot survived, though both were badly injured. They were found by Bedouins and carried to T-4 next day; six officers and 14 airmen had died. The Tomahawks returned to Damascus without damage, victories being credited to Flt Lt A.C. Rawlinson (three), Flg Off Turnbull (two) and Sgt Wilson. After refuelling, the formation took off to return to Jenin, but Sgt Randall's AK436 suffered an engine failure, and he crashed to his death. The remains of the Aeronavale units were taken over by Lt de V Ortolan (Esc 6B) and Lt de V Le Saint (Esc 7B), but between them they now had only five aircraft. Cne Huber despatched an SOS for reinforcements, but none would arrive. Some days later GB I/39 would pass over No 119 to bring 6B up to three aircraft.

During the day GB I/39 despatched M-167F No 115 on a reconnaissance over the Damascus–Quneitra area, but this was hit by AA and actually touched the ground. Adj Chef Lamarque somehow managed to retain control, and flew his damaged bomber back to Madjaloun.

The fighters were now so weakened that for the time being GC II/3 and III/6 were having to operate as a composite unit, three from each groupe undertaking a strafing attack on the columns near Palmyra during the day, while the three LeO 451 groupes managed 21 sorties over the same area.

Sunday, 29 June 1941

On an early reconnaissance in the Nebeck area, Pz 63-11 No 211 of GAO 583 was shot down by AA with the loss of Sous Lt Pouey and his crew. A little later a 'patrouille double' from GC I/7, led by Lt de la Taille, was detached to Deir ez Zor for operations, three Moranes taking off at 0830 to escort five LeO 451s from GB I/12 and I/31 over Abu Kemal. Three more were off at 1000 to strafe, one being hit by ground fire. As Adj Dufour attempted to crash-land No 785, he crashed and was killed.

Soon after midday six D 520s from GC II/3 and three from GC III/6 set off to escort seven LeOs of GB I/25 to the Palmyra area, where three of the Dewoitines also strafed. Palmyra was the target for ten 45 Squadron Blenheims, which bombed accurately.

Towards the end of the day GB I/39 was ordered to move its Martins to Qousseir, as Madjaloun was now considered to be too vulnerable to attack. However, an hour after they had arrived at their new base, eight Tomahawks from 3 RAAF Squadron swept in to strafe, and three of the unit's bombers — Nos 83, 221 and 229 — were destroyed in flames, a fourth being damaged, as were a Farman and a D 338. A hangar, an ammunition depot and a fuel storage tank were all destroyed as well.

Just as this attack was under way, M-167F No 126 arrived, having taken medical supplies to T-4. It was at once pursued by Flg Offs Arthur and Knowles, who chased it for 30 minutes before the latter finally managed to shoot it down into the sea some 20 to 30 miles west of Beirut, Sous Lt Lefroid and his crew perishing.

During the day GB I/31 moved to Abu Danne to allow some dispersal from the crowded Aleppo–Nerab, while from Habbaniya, the new 127 Squadron despatched four Hurricanes and four Gladiators to Haditha, at Station K-3 on the pipeline, for forthcoming operations.

By now, however, the Allied advance had again virtually come to a halt. Merjayoun had again been taken on the 24th by the Australians, aided by 2nd Battalion, The King's Own Regiment. 23rd Infantry Brigade then began to take over this area, allowing the Australians to move back to the coast for the advance on Beirut. 16th Infantry Brigade (less 2nd King's Own) from 6th Division, moved up from Palestine to support the attack on Damour. On the collapse of resistance here, the Brigade advanced on towards Zahle to try and take Rayak and cut off the forces at Merjayoun. Strong resistance was encountered in the mountainous approaches, and the 5,000 feet Jebel Mazar had to be taken, which involved several days of hard fighting.

Meanwhile, the exploitation from Damascus had failed, and had been called off. With 4th Cavalry Brigade Group still held at Palmyra, both by air attack and by the determined resistance of the defenders, the Arab Legion took Saba Biar to the south, which allowed a shorter supply line to 'Habforce' from this direction.

In an effort to get things moving again, Air Vice-Marshal Arthur Tedder ordered an attack to be made on the Residency of the Vichy High Commissioner in Beirut, and during the 29th this was undertaken by four Blenheims of 11 Squadron, led by Sqn Ldr Bocking, three direct hits being achieved with 250lb bombs. This attack would be repeated on subsequent days. That night six Wellingtons from 37 Squadron launched their first attack on Beirut, bombing the port facilities.

Monday, 30 June 1941

Despite recent losses, the Armée de l'Air sought to continue the pressure on 'Habforce', where the most effect might still be achieved, and where a British breakthrough must signal the beginning of the end. At 0450 seven LeO 451s of GB I/25, led by Cdt Lambert and escorted by six D 520s of GC III/6, bombed concentrations in the area, returning for a second such attack at 1140, this time covered by seven Dewoitines from both GCs. During the day GB I/12, reduced now to only five serviceable aircraft, managed only a single sortie, in company with two launched by GB I/31.

From Mosul Blenheims of 84 Squadron now launched three raids on the Aleppo airfields, at 1400, 1625 and 2100. An Air France D 338, F-ARIA, was destroyed during one of these. Further south ten Hurricanes from 260/450 Squadron, having refuelled at Damascus, took off to attack Madjaloun, which they reached at 1445. Martin No 122 of GB I/39, already damaged by the Australians, was destroyed in flames, and two Aeronavale aircraft were slightly damaged (6B-2 and 7B-1).

Tuesday, 1 July 1941

On the previous day the 127 Squadron detachment had moved on from Haditha to Pumping Station T-1, and now at 0525, commenced patrols over the area as a brigade from 10th Indian Division began moving up the Euphrates towards Aleppo, to pose a further new threat to the French from the north.

On this same date the Arab Legion undertook a reconnaissance near Sukhine, some 40 miles north-east of Palmyra, where they encountered the 2nd Light Desert Company (2ᵉ Groupe Leger du Desert Français) from Deir ez Zor. At once, the Arab force launched a mechanised cavalry charge, which routed the French, killing 11, while five officers and 75 men were captured, all for the loss of one killed and one wounded.

LeO 451s from GB I/25 undertook raids in the Palmyra area at 0600 and 1745, on both occasions escorted by D 520s from the two groupes, whilst LeOs from the other GBs attacked columns moving between Abu Kemal and Deir ez Zor. GC I/7 now moved to Tell-Arane, joined by GC II/3.

Further south during the early morning seven Tomahawks, now operating from Roshpina, attacked Baalbeck at 0930, where several Pz 63-11s were strafed. No 671 of GR II/39 was irreparably damaged, while No 793 of GAO

583 was also badly hit, but was capable of being repaired in three days. No 795 was also hit, and two Pz 25TOEs of EO 594 were destroyed.

At 1600 three GC II/3 D 520s took off on a mission over the Deir ez Zor area. Cne Boillot was obliged to return after 20 minutes, the other two continuing to the target area. Here they encountered the four Hurricanes of 127 Squadron, which attacked, Flt Lt Cremin claiming damage to one of the French fighters. He had hit that flown by Sgt Chef Killy (whose son, Jean-Claude, was later to become famous as a champion Olympic skier). Killy was wounded in the arm, and was also hit by fragments of plexiglass from the cockpit. He managed to return to Aleppo and crash-landed on the airfield. Twenty minutes later the other D 520 (No 343), which had been flown by Cdt Morlot, suddenly caught fire and burnt out, one of the ground crew suffering serious burns while attempting to extinguish the flames.

During the evening three Blenheims from 84 Squadron again attacked Aleppo, strafing the airfield and gaining hits on two LeOs of GB I/12 and one of GB I/31. The British aircraft had flown up to the Turkish frontier from Mosul, before turning to attack their target, leading the French to believe that they were operating from an airfield within that country. Other Blenheims from 45 Squadron undertook their third attack on Palmyra, again with great accuracy.

French efforts to get troop reinforcements into Syria had met much delay. Finally negotiations with the German Armistice Commission had proved fruitful, but by 27 June only a single battalion had left France for Salonika. The problem remained how they were to be got from there to Syria, since the Turkish authorities objected strongly to the prospect of allowing passage through their territory. Hope that German transport aircraft might be made available had been negated by the opening of Operation 'Barbarossa', so that only the sea route remained a possibility in the time available.

Consequently the troops went aboard the transports *Saint-Didier* and *Oued-Yquem*, setting sail down the Turkish coast. To support them, the destroyers in Beirut harbour sortied out on 1 July. To cover their departure, three Aeronavale M-167Fs flew from Madjaloun to Rayak during the afternoon, taking off from there at 0250 on the 2nd to raid Haifa, led by Cne Huber in 7B-2. During the same night three Wellingtons from 38 Squadron and two from 37 Squadron bombed Beirut.

Wednesday, 2 July 1941

In the north the first objective for 10th Indian Division had been confirmed as Deir ez Zor, 20th Indian Infantry Brigade Group heading towards Mosul as a feint, while 21st Brigade Group moved through Abu Kemal. 17th Brigade safe-guarded the railway line in the extreme north-east corner of Syria.

The move up the Euphrates by 21st Brigade had been delayed by a dust storm, but by the evening of the 1st, the troops had been under shellfire from Deir ez Zor. On the 2nd, meanwhile, the courageous and outnumbered garrison at Palmyra at last surrendered, as did the post at T-3; 187 prisoners were taken, including 48 men of the Armée de l'Air. During the same day Nebeck also fell, and on 6 July units of 4th Cavalry Brigade would make contact with British armoured cars working with the Free French Brigade, advancing from here. Next day these forces entered Furglus, only some 20 miles from Homs.

Meanwhile, at 0640 on the 2nd LeO 451s of GB I/12 and I/31, preparing for a mission at Abu Danne, were attacked by four Blenheims of 84 Squadron, No

LeO 451 No 142 ('3') of GB I/31 was destroyed during an attack by Blenheims of 84 Squadron on Abu Danne airfield during the early hours of 2 July 1941. It was the only aircraft lost by the unit to enemy action. *(W. Anon)*

142 of I/31 being destroyed by fire which caused its bombs to explode; a number of other bombers were damaged during this attack, the two groupes being left with four serviceable aircraft between them.

Three of GB I/25's LeOs were escorted to bomb Palmyra by six D 520s of GC II/3 and four of GC III/6, following which the bombers returned alone and the fighters spread out on patrol. Lt Patin, Adj Chef Leblanc and Sgt Hurtin of GC II/3 headed for Deir ez Zor, where they spotted some Hurricanes of 127 Squadron and the 84 Squadron Blenheims on their way back from attacking Abu Danne. They at once attacked the Hurricanes head-on, Le Blanc and Hurtin jointly claiming one shot down, although none was actually lost. Patin then attacked the Blenheims, shooting down two; Sgt Batch crash-landed 80 miles north of Deir ez Zor in Z5629, while Flt Lt Williams force-landed near the town, he and his crew being captured.

During the day GB I/25 LeOs made two further attacks on the Palmyra area, their escorts also strafing. It was considered that with only four serviceable aircraft available, GBs I/12 and I/31 could no longer operate effectively, and the two groupes were now ordered to pass their remaining aircraft to GB I/25 at Hama for the time being. In the event, one GB I/31 aircraft and two from I/12 were flown over to this airfield.

Seven Tomahawks from 3 RAAF Squadron were despatched to Tripoli, previously spared such attack, and strafed the base of Escadrille 19S, damaging one Loire 130.

The Aeronavale Martins again headed for Haifa at 2250, four making the attack. In bad weather Cne de Corvette Huber in 6B-1 made three runs over the target, during the last of which the aircraft was critically hit by AA fire, he and his crew baling out to become prisoners. The others returned to Madjaloun, where Lt de V Ortolan took over command of the Flotille.

Thursday, 3 July 1941

The 3rd saw 21st Indian Brigade launch their assault on Deir ez Zor, which fell by evening to a frontal and flanking attack. Nine guns and over 100 prisoners were taken — the rest of 2ᵉ Groupe Leger du Desert Français. A small column from 17th Brigade headed along the railway from Tel Kotchek in the far north-east, taking the town of El Haseke against only light opposition. On the main front 7th Australian Division, reinforced to three full brigades by 6th Infantry Division, prepared to attack Damour and Beirut. The area was held by five well-established French battalions, supported by artillery and dug in behind the River Damour, 12 miles south of Beirut. To support these actions, 3 RAAF and 45 Squadrons were transferred to 7th Australian Division's direct control, 45 Squadron moving to Muquibila to be ready to offer immediate close support.

The Deir ez Zor area had now become the main focus of French aerial attention, and at 0930 four LeOs, from GB I/12 and I/31, which had now been repaired after the damage suffered during the previous day, were escorted by nine D 520s to attack vehicle concentrations on the right bank of the Euphrates.

It appears that a Beaufighter from Cyprus flown by Plt Off Lee then left that island at 1030 to strafe the Esc 19S base at Tripoli, the pilot claiming to have damaged five of the little flying boats. None was reported damaged on this date however, and it is possible that this sortie was recorded erroneously, relating in fact to 7 July.

At 1250 ten Hurricanes from 260/450 Squadron attacked an airfield south-west of Hama, where 12 bombers were seen, two being claimed destroyed and eight probably damaged. It was indeed Hama airfield which they had hit, GB I/25 losing several aircraft during this attack. The 1ᵉʳᵉ Escadrille had two destroyed, one in flames, and two others slightly damaged, while the 2ᵉ Escadrille had two damaged beyond repair and four others to a lesser extent. Amongst those written off were Nos 291, 416 and 442. A further loss was suffered when Lt Collongues of GAO 583 crashed one of the few remaining Pz 63-11s, aircraft '1' (No 792), on return from a reconnaissance north of Sidon.

On their second mission of the day over Deir ez Zor, a trio of GB I/12 LeO 451s were escorted by three D 520s of GC III/6 and five of GC II/3. Two

Potez 63-11 No 792 ('1') was the aircraft normally flown by Cne d'Argoubet, commanding officer of GAO 583. It was destroyed in an accidental crash whilst being flown by another pilot on 3 July. *(J. Mutin)*

One of the tired Morane MS 406s despatched from France as reinforcements for GC I/7 during early July. *(J. Hallade)*

Hurricanes of 127 Squadron were making their third patrol of the day over the area, and these spotted the bombers, attacking at once. Lt Legrand of GC III/6 saw one of these firing on the LeOs, and immediately attacked this with his wingmen, Sgt Chef Maccia and Sgt Ghesquière, the trio shooting it down in flames; this is believed to have been V7543, flown by Flt Sgt Adams.

A few minutes later a second Hurricane was seen attacking the bombers, although the crews of the latter aircraft reported two. Sgt Rolland, the dorsal cannoneer in Cne Pinteaux's aircraft, claimed that he had shot one down before the D 520s could get in position to attack. A second, although it must actually have been the same aircraft, was seen to collide with Lt Bardollet's '13' (No 202), following which it crashed. This Hurricane, which appears to have been hit by Rolland and then collided with the other LeO, was V7654, flown by Wt Off Pitcher; both RAF pilots brought down in this action were killed. Bardollet managed to fly his damaged bomber back to Abu Danne and land. Strangely, the French reported that these Hurricanes were carrying American markings, and a protest was lodged with the US ambassador in Madrid!

Later in the evening a further raid was made on the area by three LeOs of GB I/25, but no British fighters were seen on this occasion. That night Wellingtons from 37, 38 and 70 Squadrons bombed Beirut and Aleppo, AA damaging one bomber from the first of these units.

So ended the fourth week of operations, during which the French had lost a further 21 aircraft at a cost to the British of four. Reinforcements from France and repairs to damaged machines had somewhat ameliorated the situation, GC II/3 and III/6 now having some 23 D 520s available, while GC I/7 had 13 MS 406s. Amongst the bomber units the three LeO 451-equipped groupes disposed 30 of these aircraft, although only nine M-167Fs — GB I/39 and Flotille 4F — and five Pz 63-11s remained. Escadrille 19S was down to three Loire 130s, two having been destroyed in various attacks.

Friday, 4 July 1941
At this late stage, more reinforcements for the French air units arrived. Six

12 D 520s of the Aeronavale escadrille 1AC, lined up at Tafaroui, North Africa, prior to departure for Syria, where they arrived on 4 July. *(C-J. Ehrengardt)*

Morane 406s, relics of the Battle of France in 1940, had departed that country; one crashed at Rome, and one was left behind unserviceable at Eleusis, but four now arrived at Rayak. However, on arrival at Aleppo, to where they were despatched later in the day, one caught fire and crashed, killing Adj Chef Landry (ex-GC I/2). Five D 520s also arrived at Aleppo, two aircraft and four pilots joining GC III/6, while the three other fighters were handed to GC II/3.

This was not all, for during the day Escadrille 1AC, an Aeronavale fighter unit, also equipped with D 520s, arrived from Morocco with a dozen more of these aircraft, led by Lt de V Pirel. This unit, part of Flotille de Chasse 1F, moved to Madjaloun. At Tripoli six Late 298 floatplane torpedo-bombers of Escadrille 1T also arrived on this date.

Earlier in the day a lone Blenheim from 45 Squadron undertook a strategic reconnaissance over the Homs–Aleppo area, where it was intercepted by three MS 406s of GC I/7, led by Lt de la Taille. He and Sous Lt Demoulin pursued

Late 298s of escadrille 1T in flight, led by Lieutenant de Vaisseau P. Jourdain. *(P. Jourdain)*

the aircraft as it undertook violent evasive actions, the French pilots returning to claim a 'probable' — but the Blenheim had in fact escaped them, returning without damage. A little later another of these aircraft, this time T2189 of 84 Squadron flown by Plt Off Ryan, appeared from the north to photograph Aleppo. Two more Moranes, this time flown by Adj Chef Amarger and Sous Lt Fabre, intercepted, and Amarger was able to get a telling burst into the left engine, which exploded into flames. Another burst, and it crashed, Ryan baling out, wounded, to become a prisoner. He was the only survivor.

At 0750 four more Blenheims raided Hama, where LeO 451 No 401 of GB I/25 caught fire and blew up. Later in the day ten Hurricanes of 260/450 Squadron shot up Baalbeck and Madjaloun. At the former they fired on a reported five bombers; Pz 63-11 No 795 of GAO 583, already badly damaged on the 1st, was hit again, while two more of GR II/39's aircraft were damaged, as was Pz 29 No 56. At Madjaloun two Aeronavale M-167Fs were slightly damaged, as was a D 338 of Air France.

During the day 14 sorties were made by the three LeO 451 groupes, all attacking in the Deir ez Zor area. Late in the afternoon No 324 of GB I/12 was hit by AA, Sous Lt Laurent's crew baling out about ten miles from the Euphrates where they were picked up by Arabs friendly to the British, and became prisoners. Two Aeronavale Martins reconnoitred Cyprus, Ens de V Granry in 7B-1 strafing Nicosia airfield without apparent result.

By now the first of the transport vessels carrying reinforcements to the area by sea, the steamer *Saint-Didier*, was sailing down the Turkish coast, having reached the Gulf of Adalia. Here at 0700 it was attacked by a Fleet Air Arm Albacore of 829 Squadron from Cyprus, which launched a torpedo without success. At 1250 a further attack was made, followed by three more 45 minutes later. All torpedos were evaded by turning into the attacks, but the vessel then hove-to 400 yards off the port of Adalia. Here at 1700 four more Albacores attacked. The first torpedo missed, and hit a jetty in the port, drawing a diplomatic protest from the Turkish government. However, the other three torpedos struck the vessel, which sank with the loss of 52 of those aboard, 18 more being injured. The survivors were rescued by the Turks and interned. Following this, the second steamer, the *Oued-Yquem*, was ordered to turn back, arriving off Rhodes four days later.

Saturday, 5 July 1941

10th Indian Division continued its advance in the north, 21st Brigade pushing on 75 miles up the Euphrates to Raqqa, from where they threatened Aleppo and its airfields. Part of the force then swung northwards, ultimately reaching Jerablus on the Turkish frontier.

On this side of the country LeO 451s managed 22 sorties without mishap during the day, under escort by D 520s, while GB I/39 Martins undertook reconnaissances over Nebeck, Palmyra and on the approaches to Aleppo.

127 Squadron was involved in standing patrols over the Deir ez Zor area throughout the day, the last of these commencing at about 1700 hours. At this time a dozen Dewoitines from both groupes were providing cover for LeOs bombing columns on the right bank of the Euphrates, between Sabkha and Dibsi. Two turned back early, but in the target area a 'patrouille double' from GC III/6 spotted the British fighters, which they identified as five unidentified types covered by three Hurricanes. This was a gross overestimate, for the

With parachutes and flying helmets already on over their overalls, four pilots of GC III/6's 5^e escadrille await take-off. L to r: Sgt Chefs Monribot and Mertzisen, Sous Lt Le Gloan and Sgt Louis Coisneau. *(A. Michaux)*

formation actually comprised two Hurricanes and a single Gladiator.

Some confusion again arises from the reports of the action, for the British unit recorded that newly promoted Sqn Ldr Bodman and Flt Lt Cremin, both flying ex-Malta Hurricanes, dived on the French fighters, which turned on them, while the French pilots reported that, leaving the Gladiator to the GC II/3 fighters, they dived on the Hurricanes. Whichever is correct, Sous Lt Le Gloan and Sgt Chef Mertzisen quickly cut out one of the Hurricanes, which is believed to have been Bodman's V7370, and shot it down about ten miles north-east of Deir ez Zor. Cne Richard and Sgt Chef Loi pursued the other, Le Gloan then joining them in shooting this down too; this was Cremin's P3731. The GC II/3 pilots failed to spot the Gladiator. The two RAF pilots survived, Cremin returning on foot next day, while Bodman, who had been slightly wounded, reached Allied territory on the 7th.

During the day two Aeronavale M-167Fs again headed for Cyprus, Lt de V Ortolan bombing a small boat while PM Kervarec strafed a reported eight Beaufighters at Nicosia. The British later admitted the loss of a Hurricane and an Albacore during attacks on the island on 4 and 5 July.

On the main front Blenheims of 45 Squadron attacked targets facing 7th Australian Division at evening, as the latter prepared to launch a new offensive. These attacks were followed up by four Wellingtons from 37 and 70 Squadrons, while by night other Wellingtons from 38 Squadron raided Beirut again.

Sunday, 6 July 1941

At midnight on 5/6 July the Australians commenced their attack, crossing the

River Damour at El Aliqa under a bombardment by 60 guns. Heavy fighting throughout the day would achieve only partial success, however.

To the east on this date armoured cars of the Household Cavalry, patrolling from Palmyra, met patrols coming up from Damascus. Indian forces from Deir ez Zor outflanked the French defences and captured one of the outlying airfields near Aleppo, seizing nine aircraft and other materials, while a number of forts on the frontier with Turkey were also taken. French records do not indicate what the aircraft captured on this date were, but it is presumed that the older types being operated by Groupement Marin were involved, since little mention is made of these after this date.

Late on the 5th the Hurricanes of 260/450 Squadron had flown to Damascus where they stayed overnight, taking off at first light for another surprise attack on Baalbeck. Little was to be found on the airfield here, although an ambulance was destroyed. They then headed on down the valley in line abreast to attack Madjaloun. Here four Aeronavale M-167Fs were just about to take off, to protect the reported incoming shipping (the demise of the *Saint-Didier* and recall of the *Oued-Yquem* had not yet been reported to them). Three of the bombers were damaged to varying degrees, leaving the ill-fated Flotille 4F with virtually no serviceable aircraft.

Six D 520s of Escadrille 1AC had already taken off to escort the Martins, and these sought to intercept the marauding Hurricanes, Premier Maître Benezet believing that he had probably shot one down; he had in fact inflicted only slight damage on Sgt Patterson's aircraft, which reached base safely. Sgt T.W. Wilmot's Z4629 was also slightly damaged during this action.

At 0940 Flg Off Waymark of 208 Squadron's 'C' Flight set off on a recon-naissance over Damour, but he too was intercepted by the French naval fighters, and was claimed shot down by Ens de V Du Merle. Again, his Hurricane had only been damaged, and he returned unharmed. Elsewhere, LeO 451s under-took 17 sorties, escorted by Armée de l'Air D 520s, while one of the Late 298 floatplanes of Escadrille 1T on a reconnaissance towards Cyprus encountered a Fleet Air Arm biplane, apparently either a Swordfish or Albacore. There was an exchange of fire, and the British aircraft withdrew, the French gaining the impression that they had hit it.

While strafing one of the 10th Indian Division columns near Raqqa, Sgt Sudan's GC I/7 Morane was hit and damaged by ground fire. During the day GAO 583 flew out five Pz 63-11s to Athens, the first French aircraft to be evacuated; they would not return. GC II/3 moved back to Tell Arane, while on the Allied side of the lines, 127 Squadron moved up to a rough landing strip at Takoume Guenoc, 15 miles south of Meyadine. That night during further RAF bombing raids, Pz 650 No 13 of GT II/15 was destroyed at Aleppo.

Monday, 7 July 1941

On the 7th the village of Furglus, only about 35 miles from Homs, fell to 'Habforce'. It was on the main front that most aerial activity occurred on this date, as this became once more the focus of attention, the Australians now steadily closing on Beirut.

First, however, five of GC III/6's Dewoitines set off at 0600 to strafe columns north-west of Raqqa. Cne Rivals-Mazeres' aircraft was hit by AA fire and he was obliged to force-land No 302 in the open desert near Abu Hareira and walk back some 20 miles. The possibility of salvaging the aircraft was given up on

No 302 ('30') was the D 520 force-landed in the open desert by Cne de Rivals–Mazeres on 7 July, and subsequently abandoned by GC III/6. It is seen here at Brindisi, on its way to Syria, with a Farman 222 transport in the background at right. *(G.F. Ghergo)*

the 9th, when it was declared a write-off. At 1240 three D 520s of GC II/3, three of GC III/6 and six of Escadrille 1AC provided cover for 14 LeO 451s, seven of these from GB I/25, attacking nine British warships in the Damour area, while three from GB I/12 and four from GB I/31 bombed troop concentrations on the coast near Damour.

In the afternoon the sole serviceable Aeronavale Martin, 6B-1, flew another reconnaissance to Cyprus and bombed a vessel in Famagusta harbour without effect. Escadrille 1AC strafed 10th Indian Division troops near Raqqa.

While the French attack on the vessels of 15th Cruiser Division had avoided interception, German bombers were not so fortunate. Late in the afternoon Ju 88s from II/LG 1 again flew from Crete to attack the British vessels but again found Hurricanes of 80 Squadron on patrol. Sgts Hancock, Mason and Casbolt each claimed one such bomber damaged; one aircraft of 5/LG 1 returned suffering fifty per cent damage, while a second from 6/LG 1 reached its base trailing black smoke, with Gefr H. Lipka badly wounded.

As evening approached, Beaufighters from Cyprus swept in to strafe the Aeronavale floatplane base at Tripoli, damaging two Loire 130s, but failing to hit any of the more potent Late 298s.

With the increase of night bombing occasioned by the availability of the Delta-based Wellingtons, GC I/7 was now ordered to commence operations in the hours of darkness in an attempt to counter this new threat. Shortly after midnight Adj Chef Amarger intercepted two bombers, which in the darkness he identified as Blenheims. They were in fact Wellingtons of 70 Squadron, the first flown by Plt Off Barton, who identified his target as Nacuda, making two passes and claiming three aircraft destroyed on the ground here. This appears actually to have been Abu Danne, where a GB I/12 LeO 451 was illuminated by bomb flashes, but was not actually hit. In the second bomber, piloted by Plt Off Duigan, the crew reported being attacked by three fighters while making four passes over the target. As a result, they were forced to jettison the bombs, while the rear turret was damaged during one of the attacks. Operating the guns manually, Sgt Morris, who had been wounded, claimed one fighter shot down, one probable and one damaged, for which he would subsequently be awarded a DFM. No French aircraft were actually damaged, but the Wellington (W5660) certainly was, crashing on return to base. Amarger was credited with a confirmed victory.

Tuesday, 8 July 1941

With the Damascus–Palmyra road now open to supplies for the Allied forces, it was clear that resistance could not continue for much longer. After its activities on the 7th, GC III/6 had moved to Mousilimiye, north of Aleppo, from where it flew a strafing operation in the Raqqa area in the morning, and then escorted LeO 451s to bomb 15th Cruiser Squadron during the afternoon. At 2000 the unit was ordered to prepare to withdraw to Athens, the D 520s to be flown out, while pilots for whom no aircraft were available and ground crews would leave at midnight in a D 338. They were not alone, for the remaining LeOs of GB I/12 and I/31 were also ordered to be ready to head for Athens, as were the few remaining aircraft of the Groupement de Nuit with the range to cross the Mediterranean.

Despite this, reinforcements continued to arrive. Five M-167Fs from GR I/22 reached Aleppo on this date, No 78 being passed to Groupement Nord for reconnaissance, while GB I/39 moved the rest to Madjaloun. Two Pz 63-11s also arrived, allocated one each to GR II/39 and GAO 583, whose other aircraft had already left! The first of these, No 828, was an ex-GR I/14 aircraft. The intention now was that only GC II/3, GB I/25 and the Aeronavale units should remain, but GC I/7 was obliged to stay as most of their Moranes lacked the range to cross the sea to Greece (those that had arrived as reinforcements had been modified to incorporate additional tankage for the flight).

127 Squadron now moved forward again, this time to Deir ez Zor, where it was brought back up to strength with five more Hurricanes.

Wednesday, 9 July 1941

Heavy fighting had continued on the coast throughout the 8th, but now

Potez 63-11 No 828 reached Syria on 8 July as a reinforcement for GR II/39. An ex-GR I/14 aircraft, it was too late to be used, and was abandoned to the British. *(F.F. Smith)*

Loire et Olivier LeO 257bis 1E-4 of Aeronavale escadrille 1E, one of three such aircraft which arrived at Aleppo on 9 July 1941. Within minutes of their arrival, all had been destroyed or rendered unserviceable by strafing Hurricanes of 260/450 Squadron. *(SHAA)*

the defences began to crumble. During the 9th Damour at last fell to the Australians, and the French began to withdraw. In the north 10th Indian Division troops were again subjected to air attack at Raqqa by GB I/25 LeO 451s, and at night were assaulted by a band of insurgents led by Fawzi Qawakji, an old opponent of the British in Palestine, whose involvement was rapidly dealt with by the experienced Indian troops.

At this very late stage, Aeronavale Escadrille 1E arrived at Aleppo at 1100, equipped with a trio of elderly LeO H-257bis biplane bombers, led by Lt de V Clavel. What the rationale had been behind the despatch of these antiquities at this time has not been discovered, but it was intended that they would be used to bomb the pumping stations on the oil pipeline, leaving Flotille 4F's Martins free to concentrate on naval targets.

They had only been on the ground about an hour when ten Hurricanes of 260/450 Squadron appeared overhead. These had refuelled at Damascus and Palmyra, before undertaking their midday attack. In moments H-257bis 1E-6 was on fire, 1E-4 and 1E-5 both suffering damage. M-167F No 63 of GB I/39 was also damaged, as was the newly arrived No 78. The High Commissioner's Pz 540TOE transport, No 242, was abandoned as a result of the damage it suffered, while Farman 222.1 No 10 of GT I/15 and 223.3 No 2 of Air France were also damaged. Sgt Chef Villeneau of EO 592 was killed during the strafing.

At 1800 the combined remnants of GR II/39 and GAO 583 despatched Sous Lt Metz in Pz 63-11 No 817 on the unit's last sortie of the campaign, on a reconnaissance over the Damour area. He was followed 20 minutes later by four Aeronavale Martins, escorted by five of Escadrille 1AC's D 520s, to attack to north and south of the town. During a further night raid, another of GT II/15's Pz 650s, No 5, was destroyed at Rayak.

Thursday, 10 July 1941

During the night, on the right of the main front 6th Division found that the forces facing them were thinning out, and 16th Infantry Brigade commenced an attack astride the Damascus–Beirut road. Hard fighting continued to be

This reinforcement D 520, No 369, was issued to the 5ᵉ escadrille of GC III/6, and was one of the 14 aircraft flown out of Syria early on 10 July 1941. *(J. Mutin)*

experienced here however, and both sides rapidly became exhausted. During the day the Australians would overcome the last sustained defence in the Khalde area, only five miles from Beirut.

At 0530 on the 10th the exodus began, 14 GC III/6 D 520s leaving Mousilimiye, following eight GB I/31 LeO 451s, which had departed some hours earlier. In the afternoon seven more LeOs of GB I/12 departed from Abu Danne, although on the way to Greece '3' (No 450) would force-land on the Turkish coast, where Sous Lt Roquefort and his crew were interned. Seven Martin 167Fs of GB I/39 also left, but one of these would also fail to get home, No 186 crashing on Corfu on the 14th.

Aeronavale aircraft also now began to depart, three of Escadrille 1AC's D 520s leaving during the day, as did three Loire 130s of Escadrille 19S from Tripoli. At 1430 Martin 7B-1 (No 202) had also left Madjaloun for Athens. However, one of the fuel tanks had been damaged during the strafing attack on 6 July, and 40 miles south of Cyprus the right engine stopped. Ens de V Granry was obliged to return and land at Beirut, where the aircraft was abandoned.

At 0815 six Tomahawks of 3 RAAF Squadron strafed Hama airfield, setting fire to two of GB I/25's LeO 451s, and damaging two more. Earlier in the morning three of the French unit's aircraft had bombed drinking water tanks at T-4, a target that would be visited by four more during the afternoon. It seems that Pz 63-11s of GR II/39 and GAO 583 were also strafed at Hama, the former unit reporting the attacks as occurring in the morning, the latter in the afternoon. Whichever is correct, No 688 of GR II/39 was destroyed, as well as

Ensign de Vaisseau Granry of Flotille 4F attempted to fly Martin 167F No 202 (7B-1) from Madjaloun to Athens on 10 July. Due to earlier battle damage, the right engine failed and he was obliged to return and land at Beirut, where the aircraft was abandoned. *(IWM)*

GB I/25's LeO No 364. Seven more Tomahawks took off at 1025 to cover a dozen Blenheims of 45 Squadron which were to attack an ammunition dump near Hamana, just south of Beirut. Five minutes later M-167Fs 6B-1, 7B-2 and 6B-2 took off from Madjaloun to bomb vehicles in the Khalde region, covered by five D 520s of Esc 1AC. The Blenheims arrived over their target, which was hit repeatedly, many large explosions being seen. However, these were also seen by the French naval fighter pilots, who identified the British bombers as 15 Marylands, at once attacking these from head-on and below. In moments three Blenheims were shot down, a fourth so badly damaged that it crash-landed on return, and six others damaged to a lesser extent.

Looking down on the craggy, scrub-covered terrain, the Australians failed to spot this attack until the stricken Blenheims were falling, but they then dived to the attack, claiming all five French fighters shot down. These were credited, two to Flg Off Turnbull, and one each to Flg Off J.F. Jackson, Plt Off Lane and Sgt Hiller. It is notoriously difficult to judge results in a diving attack such as this, and French losses were nowhere near as severe as believed. Perhaps also the Australian pilots felt guilty at having failed to protect the bombers from this attack, and subconsciously were anxious to confirm that they had exacted full payment for the French success. Premier Maître Ancyon was shot down at once, critically wounded; he would die a few days later. PM Goffeny was pursued by a Tomahawk, but believed that his pursuer had crashed into a mountain whilst trying to follow his evasive manoeuvres; however, his own aircraft, No 75, had been set on fire and he baled out of it over the Bekaa Valley. Returning with only slight wounds, he claimed, and was credited with, the aircraft which he believed he had caused to crash. In fact the Australians suffered no such loss.

These were the only losses suffered by the French, the other three pilots returning to claim four bombers shot down, two by Ens de V Du Merle, one by PM Benezet, and one which Lt de V Pirel had shared with Goffeny, before the latter's engagement with the Tomahawk. Blenheim losses included V5967, from which Flt Sgt Wilton-Jones baled out to become a prisoner; however, the other two members of his crew were lost, Sgt Wimhurst having been killed during the attack, and Sgt Lowe's parachute failing to open. The full crews of Sgt Hardy (V6433) and Sgt Cawthen (V5926) were lost; T2049 was the aircraft which crash-landed. All the missing crews were recent arrivals from the UK.

One reconnaissance was flown during the day by Sgt Chef Gein of GR I/22 in Martin No 78 (now repaired), during which he covered Homs, Nebeck, Palmyra, Deir ez Zor and Raqqa. He would fly this aircraft out to Athens two days later. At 2000 British fighters strafed Aleppo airfield, where Martin No 63 of GB I/39 was badly damaged (it would be written off next day), and the Aeronavale's 6B-1 and 6B-2 were also hit.

Friday, 11 July 1941

At dawn 12 D 520s of GC II/3, off at 0500 whilst it was still dark, swept in to strafe Palmyra airfield, where the Lysanders of 'B' Flight, 208 Squadron, and the Gladiators of 'X' Flight had arrived on the 9th. One Lysander was burnt out and one damaged, while two Gladiators were also badly damaged. The French pilots returned, claiming to have destroyed 15 aircraft!

During the morning six Tomahawks flew up to Palmyra, where they were joined by six Hurricanes from 80 Squadron and six from 260/450 Squadron. All

Lt Lèté of GC II/3 crash-landed this D 520, No 332 ('1') near Hama after shooting down Flg Off F. Fisher's 3 RAAF Squadron Tomahawk, when he was himself attacked by Flg Off R. Gibbes. *(Lèté)*

were to refuel and prepare for an attack on the Aleppo airfields in the early afternoon. Off at 1200, they headed for their targets just as nine D 520s of GC II/3 set off to escort three LeO 451s on their final sorties to the Damour and Khalde areas. Lt Lèté in No 332 encountered some engine trouble and fell behind the rest of the formation. Thus flying alone, he spotted three of the Australian Tomahawks and attacked at once, shooting down Flg Off F. Fisher.

Lt Lèté of GC II/3, posing with a local and his goat by D 520 No 38 ('3'), was one of only two French pilots to shoot down a Tomahawk during the campaign. *(Lèté)*

This is believed to be the Tomahawk crash-landed near Yafour on 11 July by Flg Off L.E.S. Knowles of 3 RAAF Squadron after it was hit by fire from DCA Batterie 1015/421 over the Jebel Mazar area. *(F.F. Smith)*

Immediately, Flg Off R. Gibbes turned on to his tail, reporting that the Dewoitine crashed in flames. In fact Lèté managed to crash-land near Hama, and survived. It was believed that Fisher had lost his life, but he returned later, having been hidden from French troops in an Arab village until after the conclusion of hostilities.

The rest of the two formations each completed their missions, oblivious of this engagement. After the bombing, the Dewoitines flew back to Mousilimiye and the LeOs to Hama. Meanwhile the Tomahawks and Hurricanes reached Aleppo, the latter attacking Abu Danne where two suffered damage from AA fire. Various claims were submitted, but the serious damage occurred at Hama, which the Australians attacked last on their way back to Palmyra. Here the rest of GB I/25's LeO 451s not away on the raid were caught. No 253 caught fire and blew up, Nos 308, 343 and 396 then being damaged beyond repair, and five others slightly damaged. One Tomahawk was claimed shot down by DCA Battery 1055/421 in the Hama area, but no loss was suffered.

While this attack was under way, six more Tomahawks had left Jenin to attack vehicles and guns in the Djebel Manzar area where 16th Infantry Brigade was being held up. One Tomahawk was hit by fire from DCA Battery 1015/421, Flg Off Knowles crash-landing near Yafour, some ten miles from Damascus.

This was to be the final operation undertaken by the Allied air forces, for the fighting was about to cease. During the evening of the 11th Général Dentz, having received Allied terms for an armistice, radioed a request that hostilities should cease at midnight. Already 33/806 Squadron was leaving Lydda for Amriya, its role completed, while the French prepared to evacuate the last of their units. Hostilities ceased at 0001 on 12 July.

Saturday, 12 July 1941

Word of the armistice did not reach all units at once, and with morning six MS 406s of GC I/7 reconnoitred the Jerablus area, while five others, led by Lt de la Taille, strafed vehicles near Raqqa.

It was the end, however, for at 0800 the last four M-167Fs of Flotille 4F left for Rhodes, followed by four D 520s of Escadrille 1AC, and the Late 298s of Escadrille 1T. Thirteen D 520s of GC II/3 and the remaining LeO 451s of GB I/25 followed, heading for Athens.

During the day Dentz's representatives discussed and agreed the draft convention, which would be completed and signed at Acre on the 14th by General Maitland Wilson and Général de Verdilhac. The terms allowed the

occupation of the country and the handing over intact of ships, aircraft, naval and air establishments, and the release of prisoners. Because the Vichy government refused emphatically to deal with the Free French 'rebels', Général Catroux was not a signatory, although as now appointed the Delegue Général de la France, he would assume control of the civil administration.

Contrary to Général de Gaulle's wishes, the British government also insisted that all Frenchmen should be given the choice of repatriation or of joining the Free French. In the event 5,668 out of 37,736 decided to stay. In total, over 37,000 civil and military persons were shipped out to Metropolitan France. Some British prisoners had been sent from Syria during the fighting however, and to ensure that all were returned safely, Général Dentz and 29 senior officers were detained until this had been achieved.

During this sad campaign, British casualties, including prisoners, had totalled 3,300, to which were added 1,300 Free French. Vichy had suffered 6,000 casualties, including a number who had deserted to de Gaulle's cause during the fighting, but this total included some 1,000 killed.

With Syria in Allied hands and all prisoners of war returned from Metropolitan France, Général Henri Dentz, Vichy Govenor of Syria and the Lebanon, was allowed to return home on 10 September 1941. He is seen here disembarking at Marseille. *(ECPA)*

During the final week of action, a further 17 French aircraft had been destroyed, while British losses totalled 11. In the air French fighter pilots had claimed 34 confirmed victories and six probables, and bomber crews one more, compared with actual British losses in combat of about 27. The Allied fighter pilots had made 37 claims against the French compared with actual losses in these engagements of 26. Amongst the French pilots Sous Lt Pierre Le Gloan had been credited with seven victories (two of them shared) and two probables, Cne Leon Richard with six (three shared), whilst Lt Marcel Stenou had claimed three (two shared) and Ens de V Du Merle three. Four German bombers had also been added to the Allied totals, plus one claim by a bomber gunner. Here Flg Off Peter Turnbull of 3 RAAF Squadron had been the most successful pilot with five claims, followed by Flt Lt Alan Rawlinson of the same unit with three, and Plt Off Bill Vale of 80 Squadron with a similar total.

Honours in the air were therefore fairly equal. It was during the damaging attacks on their airfields that the French had suffered so badly. Apart from the

Sous Lt Pierre Le Gloan, top-scoring pilot of the campaign (right) stands in front of his D 520, '6', with Sous Lt Leon Cuffaut of GC II/3. *(C-J. Ehrengardt)*

one attack on Palmyra late in the campaign, no real effort had been made to reciprocate such attacks, and this omission had cost the French dear.

234 French aircraft had either been based in Syria at the commencement of hostilities, or had been sent out with their units by the Armée de l'Air and Aeronavale; 39 more had been despatched as reinforcements, bringing the overall total to 273. From this total, 26 had been lost in combat, 16 more to anti-aircraft fire, and 45 on the ground during attacks on their airfields. Added to this, 20 more had been destroyed in accidents, 54 were abandoned due to damage, or because they lacked the range necessary to be evacuated, while five others had been written off to other causes — a total of 169. Thirty more, not included in the 273 which reached the country, were lost while flying to or from the area between 24 May and 30 August. By contrast, the British units had lost 27 in combat, four to AA fire and three on the ground to hostile strafing or bombing (plus two in Cyprus), while three had been destroyed in accidents and four to other causes — a total of 41.

Against this background, it is interesting to note the comparative strengths of

Most successful fighter pilot over Syria on the Allies side was Flg Off Peter St.G.B. Turnbull (left) of 3 RAAF Squadron, seen here in front of one of the unit Tomahawks with Flg Off J.H.W. Saunders. *(AWM)*

the two air forces at various points throughout the campaign. These were as follows:

Date	8 June	14 June	20 June	27 June	3 July
Fighters	43/54*	33/47	51/55	39/45	36/63
Bombers	13/24	35/15	52/15	46/41	39/40
All modern aircraft	73/73	84/65	117/75	94/97	80/120

*In each case the figures are presented French/British.

French aircraft lost during the campaign can be quite accurately identified in regard to most of the main types, and these are shown in Figure 1. A summary

Top: Australian and RAF troops pose with the Morane MS 406s of GC I/7, left in Syria at Aleppo–Nerab due to their lack of range. *(AWM). Bottom:* Australian troops with a two-pounder anti-tank gun in front of the remains of Dewoitine D 338 F-AQBO (No 15) and F-ARIA, both of which suddenly went up in flames on 15 July 1941 at Aleppo-Nerab airfield. *(AWM)*

of losses can be found in Figure 2. Aircraft left behind at the end of the campaign included 11 Morane 406s, two D 520s, two LeO 451s, six Potez 63-11s, five Dewoitine D 338s, two Farman 223.3s, and one each Martin 167F, Farman 222.1 and Potez 650. On 15 July two of the D 338s at Aleppo–Nerab,

Top: RAF and Australian personnel, together with two French officers, prepare for the symbolic burning of Pz 63-11 No 310 and a pair of MS 406s. *(AWM). Below:* Potez 63-11 No 310 is already well alight, as one of the blazing Moranes collapses. *(AWM)*

F-AQBO and F-ARIA, suddenly went up in flames, while on the 24th British forces staged a symbolic destruction by fire there of Pz 63-11 No 310 and two MS 406s (one of them No 587).

Figure 1

KNOWN FRENCH AIRCRAFT LOSSES DURING THE CAMPAIGN IN SYRIA

Dewoitine D 520

Unit	Air Combat	AA Fire	Ground Strafing	Accident	Abandoned	Other Causes
GC II/3	332(11.7)	97(26.6)	208(26.6)	276(21.6)	38(12.7)	343(1.7)
			290(26.6)	395(16.6)	397(12.7)	
			327(26.6)			
			342(26.6)			
			358(26.6)			
GC III/6	52(18.6)	229(12.6)	314(26.6)	132(8.6)	302(9.7)	
	277(15.6)	284(12.6)	330(8.6)	321(27.6)		
	346(9.6)	329(8.6)		357(15.6)		
	367(15.6)	331(8.6)				
	368(14.6)					
	370(23.6)					
	382(23.6)					
	389(18.6)					

Loire et Olivier LeO 451

Unit	Air Combat	AA Fire	Ground Strafing	Accident	Abandoned	Other Causes
GB I/12	217(25.6)	324(4.7)		240(16.6)	207(29.6)	
	344(25.6)					
	373(25.6)					
GB I/25		413(24.6)	253(11.7)	197(18.6)	343(11.7)	
			291(3.7)	3004(25.6)	396(11.7)	
			308(11.7)			
			364(10.7)			
			401(4.7)			
			416(3.7)			
			442(3.7)			
GB I/31			142(2.7)	187(12.6)		220(9.7)
				189(11.6)		
				263(11.6)		
				278(13.6)		
				295(11.6)		

Martin M-167F

Unit	Air Combat	AA Fire	Ground Strafing	Accident	Abandoned	Other Causes
GB I/39	111(15.6)	67(20.6)	40(23.6)			119(4.7)
	118(15.6)	88(10.6)	63(11.7)			
	126(29.6)		83(29.6)			
			104(23.6)			
			122(30.6)			
			221(29.6)			
			229(29.6)			
Esc 6B	6B-3(28.6)	6B-1(2.7)				
	6B-4(28.6)					
	6B-6(28.6)					
Esc 7B	7B-4(28.6)	7B-3(22.6)				7B-1(10.7)
	7B-5(28.6)					
	7B-6(28.6)					

Potez 63-11						
GR II/39		646(12.6)	647(23.6)	667(10.6)	648(12.7)	
		653(15.6)	649(23.6)	828(12.7)	652(12.7)	
			650(23.6)			
			651(23.6)			
			668(10.7)			
			671(1.7)			
			676(23.6)			
GAO 583		211(29.6)		792(3.7)	793(9.7)	
				803(22.6)	795(12.7)	
					817(12.7)	
					310(12.7)	
Morane MS 406						
GC I/7	831(14.6)	785(29.6)	770(14.6)	204(4.7)	213(12.7)	
		818(22.6)		749(9.6)	587(12.7)	
					667(12.7)	
					741(12.7)	
					762(12.7)	
					784(12.7)	
					805(12.7)	
					807(12.7)	
					825(19.6)	
					829(12.7)	
					830(12.7)	
					835(12.7)	
Farman 222.1						
GT I/15			7(25.6)	18(25.6)	10(12.7)	
			8(25.6)			
Potez 650						
GT II/15			13(6.7)		5(12.7)	
Farman 223.3						
GT II/15					4(12.7)	
Air France					F-BAFM(15.7)	
Dewoitine D 338						
Air France					F-AQBD(12.7)	
					F-AQBS(12.7)	
					F-ARIE(12.7)	
					F-AQBO(15.7)	
					F-ARIA(15.7)	
Totals	22	16	33	18	36	3

And other types of which complete details are not available

D 520s						
(Esc 1AC)	2					
Bloch MB 200						
Esc 3/39	2			1		3
Potez 29TOE			7		18	
Loire 130			2			
LeO 257bis			3			

Figure 2

SUMMARY OF FRENCH LOSSES IN THE SYRIAN CAMPAIGN

	Aircraft employed			Losses						Total
				To Enemy			Other Causes			
Type	Initial	Reinf'mt	Total	Combat	AA	Ground	Acc.	Aband	Other	
D 520	59	12	71	11	5	7	5	5	1	34
MS 406	18	4	22	1	2	1	2	12	2	20
LeO 451	33	11	44	3	2	8	9	3	—	25
M-167F	24	9	33	9	4	7	—	1	—	21
Pz 63-11	17	3	20	—	3	7	2	8	—	20
MB 200	6	—	6	2	—	—	1	3	—	6
Pz 25TOE	25	—	25	—	—	7	—	18	—	25
Lo 130	5	—	5	—	—	2	—	—	—	2
Late 298	6	—	6	—	—	—	—	—	—	—
LeO 257	3	—	3	—	—	3	—	—	—	3
F 222	10	—	10	—	—	2	1	1	—	4
F 223	4	—	4	—	—	—	—	2	—	2
F 224	1	—	1	—	—	—	—	—	—	—
Pz 650	5	—	5	—	—	1	—	1	—	1
D 338	18	—	18	—	—	—	—	3	2	5
Totals	**234**	**39**	**273**	**26**	**16**	**45**	**20**	**57**	**5**	**169**

Figure 3

ARRIVALS OF FRENCH REINFORCEMENTS

	June						July			Total
Type	17th	19th	21st	23rd	28th	29th	30th	4th	8th	
D 520		5			2			5		12
MS 406								4		4
LeO 451	1	5				1	4			11
M-167F			1	1			1		5	8
Pz 63-11							1		2	3
Totals	**1**	**10**	**1**	**1**	**2**	**1**	**6**	**9**	**7**	**38**

Place Names in Syria Used in Text, with Alternative Spelling

N.B. Since spelling of many place names in Syria and the Lebanon differed considerably in French and British accounts, the form of spelling employed here is given in the left-hand column, with any alternative spelling to the right:

Beirut	Beyrouth
Sidon	Saida
Rayak	Rayack
Jezzine	Djezzine
Sheikh Meskine	Cheikh Meskine
Quneitra	Qouneitra or Kuneitra
Damascus	Damas
Furglus	Forglus
Palmyra	Palmyre
Aleppo	Alep
Abu Kemal	Abou Kemal
Jerablus	Djerablus
Haditha	Hadita
Qusaybah	El Quaim
Rutbah	Routba
El Haseke	Hassetdu

Ranks (with abbreviations used in the text)

Armée de l'Air	**Aeronavale**
Sergeant (Sgt)	Sous Maître (SM)
Sergeant Chef (Sgt Chef)	Quartière Maître (QM)
Adjutant (Adj)	Premier Maître (PM)
Sous Lieutenant (Sous Lt)	Ensigne de Vaisseau (Ens de V)
Lieutenant (Lt)	Lieutenant de Vaisseau (Lt de V)
Capitaine (Cne)	Capitaine de Corvette (Cne de Corvette)
Commandant (Cdt)	Osserver Engineur (OE)
Lieutenant Colonel (Lt Col)	
Colonel (Col)	

SECTION IV · IRAN

Chapter Eight

ABADAN, OIL AND THE IVANS

Following the conclusion of hostilities over Syria, 'X' Flight and 127 Squadron both at once returned to Habbaniya, where they were disbanded, the personnel and aircraft being amalgamated to form a new 261 Squadron. On 10 August this unit moved to Shaibah in southern Iraq, where command passed to a famous fighter pilot of the First Libyan campaign, Sqn Ldr E.M. 'Imshi' Mason DFC, who had also seen action over Malta earlier in the year, where he had been shot down and wounded (see *Malta: the Hurricane Years, 1940-41*).

Iran had now become a problem requiring a solution also. Located immediately east of Iraq, this nation's oil-producing areas were situated close to the head of the Persian Gulf, the refineries at Abadan being located on the estuary of the River Tigris, just a few miles over the border from Basra. Following the German invasion of the Soviet Union however, the main importance of the country to the Allies became the route it offered to send supplies, and possibly an expeditionary force, into southern Russia via the Caucasus.

Since 1939 there had been a considerable number of German nationals working in Iran, always offering the potential for de-stabilisation of the situation here to the disadvantage of the British. Following the conclusion of operations in Iraq during May 1941, many more Germans had entered Iran, obtaining important positions with the railway operators and in government service, all of which threatened the unfettered use of the communications throughout the country which the British and Russians were anxious to secure.

This was a situation most unsatisfactory to the Chiefs of Staff, and to the new Commander-in-Chief, Middle East. In consequence of a lack of complete confidence in General Wavell by the Prime Minister, he had exchanged posts with the Commander-in-Chief, India, General Sir Claude Auchinleck, who had arrived to take over his new role at the start of July, just as the campaign in Syria was drawing to its conclusion. However it was Wavell, whose Indian responsibilities included the area of the Persian Gulf, who would be called upon once more to resolve the matter.

Action in concert with the Soviet Union was proposed, and on 17 August a joint Anglo–Soviet Note was delivered to the Iranian government, demanding the expulsion of Axis personnel from the country forthwith. This brought an unsatisfactory response, and Wavell was at once ordered to arrange for the southern oilfields to be occupied around Abadan and Ahwaz at the head of the

Gulf, and at Khanikin, just inside the Iraqi border to the north-east of Baghdad. He was then to obtain control of communications through the country, aided by the Russians.

The operation, codenamed 'Y', was entrusted to Lt Gen E.P. Quinan, the commander of troops in Iraq. Occupation of the southern oil-producing area was to be undertaken by 8th Indian Division, while Royal Navy, Royal Indian Navy and Royal Australian Navy vessels joined to deal with five German and three Italian merchant vessels known to have taken shelter in the harbour at Bandar Shahpur. To the north elements of 10th Indian Division moved from north-east Syria to take part; 2nd Indian and 9th (British) Armoured Brigades would advance across the frontier to Shahabad, 80 miles east of Baghdad. These brigades were 'armoured' in name only, 2nd Brigade fielding but a single British regiment of light tanks, all other units being mechanised at this stage, rather than armoured. As back-up in case of severe resistance or German intervention, 5th Indian Division was moved from the Western Desert to Iraq, while 6th (British) Division in Syria was also put on readiness.

Operation 'Y' commenced on 25 August, and 261 Squadron provided the fighter support for the British element of this venture. The total RAF component for the operation was based at Shaibah, and included 11 and 84 Squadrons with Blenheim IVs, 244 Squadron with Vincents and 'A' Flight of 31 Squadron with Valentia transports. Theoretically the Iranian Air Force was a fairly formidable opponent for such a small force, comprising four air regiments. In fact these could muster between them only six squadrons, all with obsolescent equipment, and based as follows:

> 1st Air Regiment (three squadrons) at Tehran–Gila Murgha airfield
> 2nd Air Regiment (one squadron) at Tabriz
> 3rd Air Regiment (one squadron) at Meshed
> 4th Air Regiment (one squadron) at Ahwaz
> Air Detachment at Abadan

This force was equipped almost entirely with biplanes of Hawker manufacture, including Fury fighters with Bristol Mercury radial engines, and Pegasus-powered Audaxes, plus a few Hinds. Fifty-six Audaxes had originally been purchased by Iran, and 26 were still operational, most of them with the 4th Regiment at Ahwaz, near Abadan. A few Hurricanes had been ordered from Britain, but the outbreak of war had caused an embargo to be placed on the supply of these. Ten Curtiss Hawk 75A-9 fighters had been acquired from the United States, but these had only just been delivered and were still packed unassembled in their delivery crates.

Operation 'Y' lasted only a few days. On Monday, 25 August 31 Squadron's six Valentias flew a company of troops to Haft Kel to protect the oilfields there and to escort British and Indian women and children from the main fields at Masjid-i-Suleiman to safety. Two Valentias (K1312 and K3611) crashed while landing, but no casualties were suffered. A naval force, including the aircraft carrier HMS *Hermes*, landed two Indian infantry companies from Basra at Bandar Shahpur, and these occupied the Naft-i-Shah oilfields in the face of only light opposition; the Abadan refineries were also taken after a little infantry skirmishing. Of the Axis merchant vessels hiding here, all but one were captured, the eighth vessel being run ashore and wrecked by her own crew.

Royal Iranian Air Force Hawker biplanes. The Audax flies in the foreground, with the Fury beyond. Note the air-cooled radial engines fitted to both these aircraft. *(Flight International)*

261 Squadron's Hurricanes and Gladiators flew patrols and offensive reconnaissances throughout the day, totalling 55 sorties. They strafed Ahwaz airfield three times; on the first occasion Hurricane pilots saw three Audaxes with their engines running and machine gunned them. During the morning Blenheims from 84 Squadron made two raids, the second of these on Ahwaz, escorted by Hurricanes. Vincents of 244 Squadron completed ten reconnaissance sorties over the advancing troops.

Iranian Curtiss Hawk 75A-9. Most of these newly-delivered aircraft were still in their packing cases in August 1941, and were too late to see service during the Anglo-Russian occupation. *(G. Beauchamp)*

The fighters were very active again on Tuesday, 26 August, making 11 strafing sorties against Ahwaz airfield. At 0830 Sqn Ldr Mason and Sgt Hitching encountered an Iranian Audax which had taken off from this base, and this was at once shot down. Seven more sorties were flown by 244 Squadron's Vincents, but one of these elderly biplanes was intercepted by another of 261 Squadron's Hurricanes, the pilot mistaking it for an Iranian machine and shooting it down, Fortunately no one was killed, but the pilot, Flg Off F.G. Woolley DFC, who had accomplished a most daring rescue of a downed crew early in the Iraqi campaign, was wounded. The crew burned the aircraft and reached Allied troops safely on foot.

The Blenheims of 11 Squadron were also active, but only to drop leaflets. 84 Squadron was not called upon until the evening, when its aircraft bombed positions in Pai Tak Pass, believed to be strongly held. This seemed to do the trick and the Iranians withdrew during the night.

Wednesday, 27 August 1941

The next morning British troops advanced through the pass until held up by defences above the village of Zibiri on the Kermanshah road. No bombing was undertaken on this date, 11 Squadron again dropping leaflets while 84 Squadron undertook a few photo-reconnaissance sorties.

Thursday, 28 August 1941

On the morning of the 28th 84 Squadron was in action again however, making three attacks on Ahwaz airfield and one on troop concentrations in the Zibiri area. The ground forces were about to follow up this raid with an attack when a white flag appeared, and all fighting ceased forthwith. Terms were agreed the next day, and the troops then moved on to occupy the refinery at Kermanshah.

Operation 'Y' had cost the British 22 killed and 42 wounded. Later, forces were sent to Hamadan, and a detachment to Senna where the first contact was made with Russian forces from the north. Other Russian formations were contacted just south of Kazin on 31 August and at Sunbulagh on 7 September. The only other Allied air loss of the operation occurred two days later when a Vincent crashed at Mulla Abdulla during a reconnaissance. On 10 September another Vincent landed alongside, salvaging all worthwhile parts, the residue being burnt.

Despite these operations, the Iranians refused to surrender Axis nationals to the Allies, and on 17 September Anglo–Russian forces moved into Tehran, the capital, where they met in considerable harmony. A month later, on 17 October, they held a combined parade in the city, then withdrew, the Soviets to Kazarin and Pahlevi, the British to Sultanabad and Hamadan. They left Tehran under the control of the son of the old Shah, whose father had abdicated in his favour. He was to reign until 1979.

Meanwhile 'X' Flight had been re-formed at Abadan with all 261 Squadron's remaining Gladiators, and there it was to remain with 244 Squadron as the air component of the occupation forces until late 1942, when it returned to Iraq to be disbanded. It seems that its pilots, and possibly some of the Gladiators, went to 123 Squadron, which had recently arrived in the Middle East from the United Kingdom, without aircraft. At the end of the year the remaining Gladiators, including K7907, K7928 and K7989 were passed to the re-formed Iraqi Air Force. The 'X' Flight pilots remained with 123 Squadron to fly Hurricanes.

261 Squadron had moved back to Iraq, going to Mosul while 11 and 84 Squadrons went to Habbaniya. The two bomber units then moved to Egypt later in the year to take part in the great Operation 'Crusader' offensive in the Libyan desert, which commenced in November 1941.

Early in 1942, following the Japanese attack in the Far East, 261 Squadron was transferred aboard the aircraft carrier HMS *Indomitable* to Ceylon, still with some of the original Habbaniya Fighter Flight ex-instructors on its establishment. In Ceylon 261 was again joined by 11 Squadron, and by the Fleet Air Arm fighter squadrons, 803 and 806, while 84 Squadron, together with 211 Squadron, went to reinforce the East Indies, and 45 Squadron to Burma. The further activities of all these units, and of HMS *Hermes*, are recounted in *Bloody Shambles, Volumes 1 and 2*. All the RAF units mentioned saw much service during the later campaigns in Burma.

SECTION V · MADAGASCAR

Chapter Nine

SECURING THE INDIAN OCEAN

In April 1942 the fortunes of the Allied nations in the Far East were at low ebb, not least those of the British Commonwealth. The Philippines and Dutch East Indies, Malaya, Singapore and Burma had all fallen to the victorious Japanese forces. Only in New Guinea were Australian and US troops still fighting back, and there too the position was parlous. The exhausted remnants of the British forces from Burma had staggered into India after a long and gruelling retreat, and only the onset of the monsoon, coupled with the overstretched supply lines of the Japanese Army, would prevent their ultimate annihilation.

The US Pacific battle fleet lay at the bottom of Pearl Harbor, the British capital ships *Prince of Wales* and *Repulse* had also gone beneath the waves. At the start of April the immensely powerful Japanese Carrier Fleet had steamed through the Indian Ocean, sinking a record tonnage of merchant shipping and inflicting heavy air attacks on the naval bases at Colombo and China Bay in Ceylon, also sinking the small aircraft carrier HMS *Hermes* together with two heavy cruisers and a number of other naval vessels. Only by avoiding a daylight confrontation had the British Eastern Fleet ensured that it too was not swept from the face of the globe.

As the enemy carriers sailed back towards the Pacific for their next major mission — the support of landings in south-western New Guinea, which would culminate in the first major Japanese setback of the war during the Battle of the Coral Sea — the British turned their thoughts towards the island of Madagascar, against which action had been planned before the Japanese attack on Ceylon had materialised.

Situated off the south-east coast of Africa, Madagascar was an island of considerable size, measuring over 1,000 miles north to south, and being nearly 400 miles wide at its widest point. It was also a French colony, and in the hands of the Vichy administration. It must be recalled that it was the decision of the Vichy government to allow Japanese forces to occupy French Indo-China which had provided the bases from which they could attack southern China, and from where in more recent months, the attacks on Thailand, Malaya and Borneo had been launched.

Madagascar was well situated to provide a base from which an enemy might strike at the main Allied sea routes round the Cape of Good Hope to India and Ceylon, and to the Middle East via the Red Sea. It was feared that the French might be persuaded to allow the Japanese to install facilities there for the servicing of submarines operating in the Indian Ocean, both their own and German, or for other more elaborate and even more dangerous purposes.

Clearly it was desirable that the island be occupied to prevent such an eventuality but the forces then available to Britain would not allow this to be accomplished. However, plans were formulated for the capture of the main port of Diego Suarez, its naval base of Antsirane, and the surrounding territory. Operation 'Ironclad' was therefore to be put into effect with this limited objective in mind.

Diego Suarez is situated on the extreme northern tip of the island, almost parallel with the southern border of the British territory of Tanganyika (now the independent Republic of Tanzania). Of roughly the same size and shape as Scapa Flow, it has one of the largest anchorages in the world, and could with ease have provided accommodation for the ships of every navy in the world at that time, all at once. It was also easily defensible in its own right, separately from the rest of the island.

The French garrison had enjoyed the support of only a few old Potez 25TOE army co-operation biplanes until 1941, but in January of that year the Vichy government decided to provide a more potent air arm, and Escadrille 565 was formed which was eventually to receive Morane 406 fighters. The Escadrille did not in fact come into being other than on paper until 1 July 1941, when it was set up with 13 pilots under Capitaine Leonetti at Diego-Arrachart, an airfield about six or seven miles south of Diego Suarez town. The base was poorly equipped and until the arrival of their Moranes, the pilots flew communication, reconnaissance and training sorties in the Potez 25TOEs and some Caudron Pelicans.

On 23 July seven Potez 63-11 twin-engined reconnaissance-bombers arrived by sea aboard the SS *Bangkok*, and were sent to Escadrille 555 at Ivato-Tananarive in the south-centre of the island. One of these had been destroyed in an accident on 16 October 1941 shortly after the first Moranes finally arrived. In February 1942 the two escadrilles were merged to form the Groupe Aerien Mixte under Cne Leonetti, the whole unit being based initially at Ivato. There the Moranes remained under Leonetti's operational control, while Cne Bache commanded the Potez types. A few examples of each type were then sent up to Diego-Arrachart on constant alert, under the local command of Lt Rossigneux. The number of Moranes sent to the island is not known, but is believed to have been over 20. This then was the strength and disposition of the French air arm facing the British in May 1942.

On the ground the French were distinctly weak in real terms, although quite strong in numbers. Their forces lacked heavy equipment, adequate artillery support, armoured vehicles, etc. Indeed, the greater part of the army was composed of Senegalese and local Malagaches under French officers. The local islanders were an easygoing and peace-loving people, not aggressive by nature.

To make the landings the British had gathered the 29th Independent Brigade Group, 5 Commando, and the 17th Infantry Brigade from the 5th Division. These forces were shipped from the United Kingdom to South Africa in the first instance, the point of departure for the venture being Durban. Vice-Admiral E.N. Syfret's 'Force F' was to provide naval and air support, the latter being in the hands of carrier units, since the employment of land-based units from East Africa on the scale necessary was at that time impracticable.

The first part of the force left Durban on 25 April 1942 in a slow convoy, escorted by the cruiser *Devonshire*, two destroyers and a number of corvettes and minesweepers. Three days later the rest of the force departed in a fast convoy comprising assault ships, the battleship *Ramillies*, cruiser *Hermione*, six destroyers, and the aircraft carrier *Illustrious*. Admiral Syfret was aboard *Ramillies*, as was Major-General R.G. Sturges, CB, RM, the land forces commander.

HMS *Illustrious* was newly arrived in the East, following repairs carried out in the USA as a result of damage inflicted by dive-bombers near Malta in January the previous year. This was to be her first major operation since that time, and for it she had embarked the following Air Group:

881 Squadron	12 Grumman Martlet IIIs	Lt Cdr J.C. Cockburn
882 Squadron	8 Grumman Martlets ⎫ 1 Fairey Fulmar NF I ⎭	Lt Cdr H.J.F. Lane
810 Squadron ⎱ 829 Squadron ⎰	20 Fairey Swordfish	Lt R.N. Everett Lt W.F.M. Griffiths

The convoys sailed north up the African coast, passing to the west of Madagascar up the Mozambique Channel. On 3 May they were joined by a further carrier, HMS *Indomitable*, and two escorting destroyers. *Indomitable* was part of Admiral Somerville's Eastern Fleet, based on Ceylon, and carried the flag of Rear-Admiral D.W. Boyd, Commander Aircraft Carriers in that fleet. It was intended that *Illustrious*'s aircraft would deal with any naval opposition to the landings, while *Indomitable*'s air group would neutralise the French airfields and provide support for the invading ground forces. For this purpose *Indomitable* had on board:

800 Squadron	8 Fairey Fulmars	Lt Cdr J.M. Bruen
806 Squadron	4 Fairey Fulmars	Lt Cdr J.N. Garnett
880 Squadron	9 Hawker Sea Hurricanes	Lt Cdr J.E.C. Judd
827 Squadron ⎱ 831 Squadron ⎰	24 Fairey Albacores	Lt Cdr P.G.O. Sydney-Turner Lt Cdr P.L. Mortimer

A degree of support was also to be provided by land-based units of the South African Air Force. Three Coastal Flights in the Dominion which had been involved in anti-submarine patrols, 32, 36 and 37 equipped with Avro Ansons, began receiving more modern aircraft during April, and at the end of the month were all despatched to East Africa to co-operate in the Madagascar enterprise. Amalgamated for administrative purposes into 20 Squadron, SAAF, they were to carry out photographic reconnaissance sorties, and bomb French airfields and defences if necessary. 32 Flight had received a number of Martin Marylands for this purpose, while 36 and 37 Flights were each now equipped with Bristol Beauforts.

Meanwhile Eastern Fleet, which included the carrier *Formidable*, cruised through the central Indian Ocean to provide distant cover in case of any Japanese interference. In fact, the Japanese carrier forces were at this moment becoming involved in the Coral Sea battle to the north of Australia, and the only recorded interference during this stage of the operation was from a Kawanishi H6K 'Mavis' flying boat, which carried out a reconnaissance over the

Indian Ocean from its base at Port Blair in the Andaman Islands.

All was now ready for Operation 'Ironclad' to be launched. At noon on 4 May the capital ships and six escorting destroyers moved to a covering position to the west of Cap d'Amer on the northern tip of Madagascar. Secrecy had still been maintained, and the French had no inkling of their presence.

The prime objective at Diego Suarez was the Antsirane naval base and its airfield of Arrachart. The sea approach to the harbour was through a channel known as the Oronjia Pass, which was known to be strongly defended. It was vital therefore that troops should storm and capture this area in order that shipping might enter the base in safety.

Tuesday, 5 May 1942

During the night of 4/5 May the transports, led by a minesweeper, approached the western coastline and anchored before dawn. Assault craft carrying men of 5 Commando and the East Lancashires headed inshore into Courier Bay. Although minesweepers inadvertently detonated two mines, complete surprise was achieved, and the troops were able to head straight across the Andrakoka Peninsula. Other troops from 29th Brigade went ashore in Ambararata Bay without any opposition, although an additional landing which was then made at Basse Point did encounter some limited skirmishing.

Just before dawn the RN carriers launched their initial strikes, while the cruiser *Hermione* created a diversion off the east coast, to which position she had sailed during the night. *Illustrious* launched three strikes, each of six Swordfish, to attack shipping in Diego Suarez Bay just before 0400, while Albacores from *Indomitable* set course to bomb Arrachart airfield. Fighters followed from both carriers to patrol over airfield and beaches, and to attack French 75 mm artillery batteries.

The first six Swordfish, all carrying torpedoes, attacked the French sloop *D'Entrecasteaux* without result, and then torpedoed the armed merchant cruiser *Bougainville*, which blew up. The second flight, this one carrying depth charges, sank the submarine *Beveziers*, while the third group of Swordfish dropped leaflets and a copy of an ultimatum to the Governor, then bombed a gun battery and *D'Entrecasteaux*. The leading aircraft of this flight, flown by Lt R.N. Everett, was hit in the engine by AA fire during the last bombing run, and force-landed in the sea near a beach. Everett and his crew became prisoners, although they were released a few days later when the French capitulated.

Meanwhile the Albacores and escorting Martlets attacked Arrachart airfield at low level, setting the hangars on fire. Here a large part of the Groupe Aerien Mixte was taken by surprise, five Morane 406s being destroyed and two more damaged, while two Potez 63-11s, '4' (No 328) and '6' (No 372), were also hit. A stray bullet struck the detachment commander, Lt Rossigneux, who was killed.

Immediately the news of the British landings had been digested, the aircraft of the Groupe Aerien Mixte at Ivato were flown up to Anivorano, 50 miles south of Diego Suarez. From there over the next few days many sorties were to be flown, the Potez 63-11s bombing vehicles, while Moranes gave top cover and made occasional strafing attacks.

Initially two Moranes — No 842, flown by Lt Laurent and No 436 flown by Sgt Ehret — strafed beaches in Courier Bay. From a sortie to the mouth of the Ambre River at 1700, however, Sgt Ehret failed to return, his disappearance

Grumman Martlet II of 881 Squadron receives the signal to take off from *Illustrious. (Imperial War Museum)*

being something of a mystery, as no claims for the destruction of his aircraft were submitted.

Further sorties over Diego Suarez were made by bombers from the carriers to drop leaflets calling for an immediate surrender, but this demand was refused. The 9th Brigade column was now fast closing on Antsirane, spearheaded by Bren gun carriers, but short of the objective a grave error of judgement was made. A French officer had been captured and was sent into the town with a letter calling on the French to surrender. Until this point the defenders had been unsure where the British would strike, but now they were enabled to prepare defences which were able to bring the British advance to a halt. Five light tanks broke through and ran far ahead without supporting infantry. This was asking for trouble which was not long in coming. Heavy fire disabled four of the AFVs, and although the surviving crews fought a desperate hand-to-hand battle around their wrecked vehicles, all were captured.

These French defensive positions at Col de Bonne Nouvelle were strong, based on two solid forts commanding the narrowest part of the Antsirane peninsula. Despite the arrival of seven more British tanks during the afternoon, little further progress had been made when night fell.

Throughout the day troops continued to disembark with their equipment from the transports. During the morning it was seen that the sloop *D'Entrecasteaux* had got under way. She was bombed by a Swordfish which gained a direct hit, the bomb penetrating the platform deck and exploding, whereupon the stricken vessel was at once beached. Three more Swordfish then flew off to complete her destruction.

During the day Martlets and Fulmars flew tactical reconnaissance sorties on behalf of the army, but little was seen. A Pz 63-11 was lost by the French with its crew (Lt Schlienger, Sgt Chef Besset and Adj Chef Joffard), but again its disappearance was not explained, and again no British claim was made. It is possible that this aircraft was brought down by ground fire.

Wednesday, 6 May 1942
Next morning at dawn a frontal attack on the Col de Bonne Nouvelle defences by 29th Brigade failed, but reinforcements were now moving up from 17th Brigade, while further back-up units were coming ashore. At 0600 patrolling

Fairey Fulmar of 800 Squadron, with long range 'slipper' tank beneath its fuselage, takes off from HMS *Indomitable*. These aircraft were used for tactical reconnaissance over the northern end of Madagascar and for seaward search, watching for possible Japanese intervention. *(Imperial War Museum)*

Martlets from 881 Squadron encountered three Potez 63-11s approaching, two heading for the transports while the other made for the beach. The fighters attacked, Lt Bird and Sub Lt J. Waller shooting down one, while Lt C. C. Tomkinson despatched another; the third fled. No 232 went down in flames, the gunner, Sgt Loriette, having been killed by the first burst. Adj Dietsch remained at the controls to allow Lt Héloise, the observer, to bale out, but paid with his life for this unselfish act; Héloise survived with wounds. No 567 crashed north of Diego-Arrachart and blew up; Lt Harmant, the observer, died although Adj de Balathier-Lantage and Sgt Buffet survived, wounded, to be taken prisoner. They were later shipped to the African mainland.

After the failure of the dawn assault, Albacores bombed the French defences during the days, while Swordfish from *Illustrious* dropped dummy parachutists to the south-west to create a diversion and draw off some of the defenders. A patrolling Swordfish flown by Sub Lt (A) F.H. Alexander sank the submarine *Le Heros* with depth charges, then led a corvette to the scene to pick up the French crew.

A further attack on the French defences was launched in the evening, but this time it had been planned that a destroyer should fight its way into Antsirane harbour and land a party of marines to create a real diversion. While a Swordfish spotted for cruisers and destroyers bombarding the batteries commanding Oronjia Pass, HMS *Anthony* steamed through at top speed and landed the marines successfully. The renewed assault at Col de Bonne Nouvelle continued during the night, the positions being taken by 0300 on 7 May.

Thursday, 7 May 1942

As dawn broke on this latter date preparations began for a further attack if the French did not now surrender, and patrolling Martlets from 881 Squadron were again involved in combat — this time for the first and only time over Madagascar against opposing fighters. Three Moranes, led by Cne Leonetti, with Cne Bernache-Assollant and Lt Laurent, were undertaking a reconnaissance over the area. The Royal Navy pilots spotted the first two Moranes approaching from the south-west, and the leader at once dived to attack head-on. His Martlet was

Morane 406 No 842 of Escadrille 565 — one of those shot down by Royal Navy Martlets of 881 Squadron on 7 May 1942 near Diego Suarez and crash-landed by Lt Laurent. *(A. van der Bijl via K. Smy)*

hit in the engine and wings by the French fighter's 20 mm cannon shells, and he was obliged to carry out a force-landing in the sea alongside the coast; he had been shot down by Cne Leonetti. Getting out of his aircraft, he made his way to the shore and eventually managed to return to his ship, having been reported missing for two days.

Close-up of the tail of Morane 406 No 842. Note the unit badge (a stylised eagle's head), red and yellow recognition stripes on the fin, and the presence of several bullet holes. *(A. van der Bijl via K. Smy)*

Meanwhile the pilot of the second Martlet, Sub Lt J.A. Lyon, reported that he saw two more Moranes following him as he dived to engage the first pair, and turning on these, he claimed one shot down. Either he had engaged only the third aircraft, or it had been joined by one of the other two, for no more than three French fighters were in the air at this time.

A second section of Martlets was providing top cover, and seeing the dogfight below, they dived down to give assistance, Lt Tomkinson claiming one Morane shot down and Sub Lt (A) Waller a second; he then joined Sub Lt Lyon in an attack on the last Morane, which was also claimed shot down. All three Moranes were indeed lost, Cne Assollant being killed in No 995, while Cne Leonetti baled out of No 993 with only minor wounds, and returned to his unit. Lt Laurent was to crash-land No 842, suffering only some cuts and bruises. This was the last engagement of the operations in the air.

Fairey Albacores of 827 Squadron from HMS *Indomitable* disembarked on Port Reitz airfield near Mombasa, Kenya, after Operation 'Ironclad'. *(via G. Wallace/D. Brown)*

At 1040 the British warships opened a ten-minute barrage on Diego Suarez, following which a white flag was flown in the town. Minesweepers worked all day to clear the channel, and by 1700 naval vessels were in harbour. The following morning the convoys and the rest of 'Force F' sailed in, while at the Residency in the town the surrender terms were accepted by the Vichy authorities. At Arrachart airfield two damaged Morane 406s were burned, the French forces then withdrawing to the south.

The three days had been disastrous for the Groupe Aerien Mixte. Twelve Moranes had been lost, five on the ground plus the two damaged aircraft that had been burned, four in combat (one on the 5th and three on the 7th), and one in an accident on the 6th. Additionally, four or five Pz 63-11s had been destroyed, three of them in the air. It was hoped that two Moranes, Nos 706 and 815, could be kept serviceable by 'cannibalisation' from other aircraft.

Operation 'Ironclad' had been the first amphibious landing of the war for the British — indeed the first since that at the Dardanelles during World War I. The three days of fighting had not been cheap in terms of casualties, over 100 British troops being killed and nearly 300 wounded, while French losses were reported at more than 150 dead and 500 wounded.

In the air the Fleet Air Arm had completed 309 sorties, 130 of them patrols over the Fleet, the town, the landing ship anchorage, and the troops on the ground. Apart from the Martlet and the Swordfish already mentioned, a Fulmar was shot down by ground fire, and another was destroyed in an operational accident. While Sea Hurricanes from *Indomitable* had made one strafing attack on Arrachart airfield, claiming a single small biplane destroyed, they and the Fulmars had been employed mainly on ground-attack sorties in support of the army, leaving the patrolling almost entirely in the hands of the superior Martlets.

The ground echelon and equipment of 20 SAAF Squadron were flown to Madagascar by a dozen SAAF Lockheed Lodestar transports, which were also used to maintain supplies throughout the campaign. Lodestar No 245 is seen here at Diego Suarez; it was formerly ZS-ATF, c/n 243. *(D. Becker)*

Immediately following the occupation of the northern end of Madagascar, an Air Component was organised. 20 SAAF Squadron flew its aircraft over to Arrachart from Lindi on 12 May, the ground echelon and support personnel being carried by twelve SAAF Lockheed Lodestars. 20 Squadron at this stage had on hand twenty-two aircraft: six Marylands with 32 Flight and sixteen Beauforts with 36 and 37 Flights. Unfortunately the unit was informed initially that its presence would be required for only four weeks, and in consequence no major spares were brought over, and no arrangements made for their delivery. In the event the Squadron was to remain for six months!

Following the South Africans into captured bases on Madagascar came two

Aircraft of 20 SAAF Squadron on an airfield in Northern Rhodesia en route to Madagascar. In the foreground are three Bristol Beauforts, with a single Martin Maryland beyond. *(A. van der Bijl via K. Smy)*

RAF Westland Lysanders of 1433 Flight over Madagascar. Aircraft are (left to right): V9606, V9499, V9350 and V9728. *(Imperial War Museum)*

Royal Navy squadrons, 795 with Fairey Fulmars and 796 with Albacore torpedo-bombers. With the withdrawal of the carrier task force, command of the forces on the island passed from Admiral Syfret to Maj Gen R.C. Sturges, the land forces commander. On 29 May six Westland Lysanders were delivered by sea, and were assembled at Arrachart to equip 1433 Flight, RAF, which arrived to carry out army co-operation duties.

While the Lysanders were arriving, however, an unidentified aircraft flew over Diego Suarez, and fearing an aircraft or submarine attack at dawn next day, the battleship *Ramillies* raised steam preparatory to getting under way. Next morning Royal Navy aircraft flew patrols, but nothing was seen until 2025 that evening, when torpedoes suddenly struck *Ramillies* and a tanker, which latter sank almost at once. The battleship, although damaged, was subsequently able to reach South Africa under her own power for repairs. The attack had been made by Japanese submarines which had sailed from Malaya for this purpose. Field Marshal Jan Smuts, the South African Premier, was already pressing for the occupation of the island's other two major ports, Majunga on the north-west coast, and Tamatave on the east coast. Shortage of troops and the critical situation on the Indian frontier with Burma led the British authorities to seek talks with the Vichy administration in an effort to prevent the necessity for such action.

Despite its size, Madagascar had just three major highways, all radiating from the capital of Tananarive, to Majunga, Tamatave and Fianarantsoa; these roads were unmetalled, but were nonetheless of sound all-weather construction. The island also boasted 543 miles of railway track, the most important stretch being that from Tananarive to Tamatave.

Diego Suarez in the north was virtually cut off from the rest of the island, and could easily be held on its own. It possessed a fine harbour, and with Mombasa in East Africa, and Colombo in Ceylon, formed a most important base for the defence of the Indian Ocean. However, should the rest of Madagascar fall into Japanese hands, it would enable them to cut the Allies'

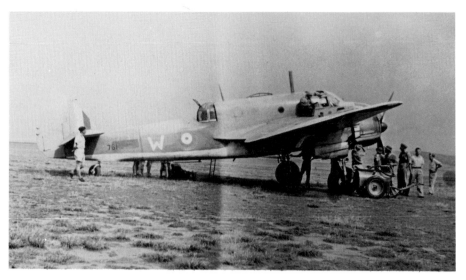

SAAF Bristol Beaufort 761 'W' at Arrachart shortly after arriving from Kenya.

lines of communication between Egypt, India, Iran and East Africa. Many airfields were available in southern Madagascar, which if in Allied hands could provide excellent bases for anti-submarine aircraft on long-distance patrols. A Japanese presence on the rest of the island could well require more troops to defend Diego Suarez than would be required to garrison the whole island should it be seized forthwith.

Already there were rumours that Japanese submarines were refuelling at Majunga, adding to the pressure for a decision to be taken on the future of the Vichy part of the island. By June the garrison at Diego Suarez was made up of the 7th South African Brigade, and a brigade of the King's African Rifles. On 1 July control of operations passed to Lt Gen Sir William Platt, GOC-in-C, East Africa Command, and two days later troops of the King's African Rifles landed with speed and secrecy at Dzaudzi on Mayotte Island in the Comore group, to the west of Diego Suarez. They captured it with no loss of life on either side.

By mid-July it was clear that the Vichy authorities were prevaricating in an attempt to drag out the talks into the autumnal rainy season, when no operations would be able to take place. Consequently on 19 July, with the position in India much stabilised, the British Prime Minister gave the green light for operations to be planned for the occupation of the rest of Madagascar. Landings in the south were out of the question, so poor were the ports there and the communications from them. To press a major force south from Diego Suarez was also out of the question; the 350 miles to Majunga contained more than 300 bridges and culverts, and comprised only one poor track, which in places virtually petered away to nothing.

To reach Tananarive it would be necessary to land forces at either Majunga or Tamatave; it was thought that once the capital was captured, the French would capitulate. While sufficient troops were now being made available for the operation, landing craft and transports would be required, and these had to be despatched in secret to East Africa in time to allow training for seaborne landings to take place. They also had to be returned to the United Kingdom in time to take part in Operation 'Torch', the landings in French North Africa, at

SAAF 'brass' arriving at Arrachart. Behind is a Fairey Fulmar of 795 Squadron, RN (probably the only one ever illustrated), with an RAF Lysander of 1433 Flight to the left. *(SAAF via D. Becker)*

that time planned for mid-October 1942. It looked as if insufficient time would be available, but finally the operation was fixed for early September.

During the period June–August, aircraft of 20 SAAF Squadron flew a number of tactical and photographic reconnaissances and a 200 square mile photo mosaic of the Majunga area was prepared; another was made of the Diego Suarez–Majunga road, while a third was prepared of the Tamatave area. Anti-submarine patrols were also flown over the Indian Ocean and Mozambique Channel, and on one of these two unidentified submarines were sighted in Ampasindara Bay, but no attack was made. Four Beauforts crashed on landing

Line-up of Beauforts of 20 SAAF Squadron, on Arrachart airfield. These aircraft had previously formed the equipment of 36 and 37 Flights which, together with 32 Flight's Marylands, were combined to form 20 Squadron in July 1942. *(D. Becker)*

due to engine failures during this period, but otherwise it proved uneventful, save on one photographic mission.

On this occasion a Maryland was hit by French AA fire and had to force-land in Vichy territory; a number of local Malagache troops with a French officer attempted to take the crew prisoner, but using the gunner's Vickers 'K' gun from the dorsal turret of the aircraft, the South Africans turned the tables and captured this Vichy patrol. They then made their way to the coast where they were subsequently taken off by boats from a British destroyer and returned to Diego Suarez with their prisoners.

Preparatory to the forthcoming operations, in August a report on the air position was completed. As the French were believed to have an effective force of only four Morane 406s and three Potez 63-11s, it was decided that the balance was favourable to the Allied elements, and plans were accordingly put in hand. In fact, the French fighter strength was down to no more than two serviceable Moranes.

At the start of September control of the Air Component passed to the AOC of 207 Group (East Africa), which was now a part of Middle East Air Command, RAF. In consequence on 4 September 20 SAAF Squadron ceased to be under the direct control of Defence Headquarters, Pretoria, and was renumbered 16 SAAF Squadron, its official duties changing from that of a Union Coastal squadron to that of a bomber squadron. It was informed that as soon as the forthcoming operations were completed, it was to return to the African mainland to re-equip with Bristol Bisleys (Blenheim Vs). At this stage problems of unserviceability, and the unfortunate crashes already mentioned which had resulted from this, had reduced the establishment to five Marylands and seven Beauforts.

By September the RN aircraft carrier situation in the Indian Ocean had deteriorated considerably, and Eastern Fleet had only one such vessel under its command, *Illustrious*. *Indomitable* had left in July to take part in Operation 'Pedestal', the famous August 1942 Malta convoy, and when this ship was damaged during that operation, *Formidable* was at once ordered to take her place in the Mediterranean. The Madagascar invasion convoy and the landings were thus to be covered only by aircraft from *Illustrious*, which accompanied the force. Aircraft available for this operation included twelve Martlets of 881 Squadron, six Fulmars of 806 Squadron and eighteen Swordfish of 810 and 829 Squadrons.

The main assault was to begin on 10 September, when British troops of 29th Brigade were to be launched at Majunga to secure the port and its environs. Immediately this was done, 22nd East African Brigade was to be landed and, joined by one and a half troops of South African Marmon-Herrington Mark III armoured cars, was to push on at once towards Tananarive. At the same time units of 7th South African Brigade from Diego Suarez were to push southwards from Beramanje, the furthest south so far penetrated, to clean up another part of the island and draw off Vichy forces from the capital.

To create a diversion to these two major moves, a small commando force was to land at the village of Morondava, 600 miles to the south, to create a lot of noise and confusion in an effort to persuade the French that the main landings were being made there. At the earliest possible moment, 29th Brigade would re-embark at Majunga, and would be carried round to the east of the island to land at Tamatave and approach the capital from that direction.

The first landing craft went in just before dawn on 10 September at Ampozony, to the north of Majunga, troops of the East Lancashire Regiment and the Royal Welch Fusiliers going ashore at once. At dawn Swordfish from *Illustrious* appeared over the port and circled, making mock diving attacks, but dropping no bombs at this stage. Following a difficult climb up some cliffs, the infantry got through, and after some brief skirmishing, captured the main airfield and entered the town which swiftly surrendered. While this was going on vessels of the main force sailed into the mouth of the Betsiboka River, men of the South Lancashire Regiment and the 5th Commando storming the harbour which was quickly taken.

Without delay the East African Rifles, the South African armoured cars, and a detachment of engineers set off at top speed down the road towards Tananarive in an attempt to capture important bridges at miles 99 and 131 on the 400-mile route to the capital. Meeting virtually no opposition, they captured the first bridge at 1600 that day, and by dawn the next morning were on the northern approaches to the Betsiboka Bridge at mile 131.

This bridge had been blown, however, but it was swiftly discovered that the job had been botched, and the central span, although sagging into the river, was not broken. Indeed at the centre it was beneath only three feet of water and could be crossed by most vehicles with reasonable ease. Realising their error, the French despatched a single Potez 63-11, flown by Cne Baché, to bomb the bridge, this attack being made at 0730 on Friday the 11th without success. It was to be the last French aircraft to be seen in the air for several days.

One of the initial objectives taken on the 10th had been the airfield at Majunga, from which air support could be provided close to the front. Consequently support personnel accompanied the invasion force, and on the 11th the Air Component was ordered to fly down to this new base. Owing to a misunderstanding they arrived before the support parties had left the ships and before Majunga North had been officially occupied, but no opposition was offered, and all aircraft landed safely.

All four units of the Component now came under the command of Colonel S.A. Melville, SAAF, and the Lysanders of 1433 Flight were placed under the direct control of 22 Brigade for tactical reconnaissance and close support during the advance. The arrival of the Component released *Illustrious*, and operations began at once.

Early on 12 September two Marylands took off to fly an offensive reconnaissance over the road from the Betsiboka Bridge to Tananarive. Motor vehicles on this road were bombed and strafed in an effort to delay the despatch of French troops to the Majunga area, but much anti-aircraft fire was encountered, SAAF Maryland 1681 being hit and returning to base with one engine stopped and the observer dead.

After the Betsiboka Bridge, the advance began to slow up as roadblocks were met in increasing numbers, though most of these were not defended and no mines had been laid. The advancing troops also found the road cratered in several places, and a number of bridges had been rendered impassable; often this had been done merely by removing some of the wooden planking providing the surface, and as this had generally been hidden nearby, the planks were soon restored.

Not until 16 September was the first serious opposition met, when a company of Nyasalanders, supported by armoured cars, 25-pounder guns and mortars

Sagging but unbroken, the Betsiboka Bridge was attacked several times by SAAF Beauforts and Marylands and by RN Albacores during the advance on Tananarive in late September 1942. *(A. van der Bijl via K. Smy)*

encountered a bridge over the Mamokomita river at Andriba, and a roadblock defended by a company of Senegalese troops. In a brief but sharp fight the position was taken, but one British platoon commander and four Askaris were killed, another officer and eight men being wounded.

M. Annet, the Vichy Governor, now requested an armistice, and consequently a Maryland was despatched to the French airfield at Ivato on the 17th to collect the French plenipotentiaries. On landing it became unserviceable, and a second aircraft had to be sent while Armée de l'Air mechanics carried out repairs to the first. Terms similar to those offered earlier in the year were set before the French, but after protracted discussions they were rejected, and next day the delegates were flown back to Ivato.

While the operations of 22nd East African Brigade had been proceeding slowly towards Tananarive, from the north 7th South African Brigade had covered the first 80 miles from Sokarang fairly easily. However, from Beramanje to Miromandia were 150 miles of burnt bridges, collapsed culverts and persistent mosquitoes, and it was not until the 18th that the latter village was reached. At Jojohely on the 14th there had been a brief skirmish between French machine gunners and South African armoured cars, but the French had swiftly surrendered.

For mile after mile the South African engineers with the column advancing on Majunga from the north constructed temporary bridges, but at Miromandia they halted. Since the advance towards Tananarive was progressing so well from Majunga, there was no need for the South African combat troops to continue their southward move, and they now turned back for Diego Suarez. The engineers continued southwards to complete the route to Majunga, and on 22 September were to meet a small force of the King's African Rifles at Antsohihy, this latter formation having struck off northwards from the Majunga–Tananarive road to make contact with them.

Other elements of 7th SA Brigade had advanced to Vohemar on the east coast, arriving there on the 11th, and moving on southwards to Antalaha, where they would halt on the 20th.

The commando force which had landed at Morondava on the 10th had met no resistance, and the French had surrendered at once, the commandos moving inland to Mahabo by the 11th, halting a few miles east of that town as they did not possess sufficient reserves to advance any further.

At dawn on 18 September the invasion fleet that had sailed around the north of the island from Majunga, anchored off Tamatave and aircraft were launched from *Illustrious* to patrol over the port while an ultimatum was delivered. At 0730 a boat was sent in under a white flag, but machine guns opened up from the jetty and the boat withdrew at once. At 0750 an RN destroyer opened fire on the beach at Tannio Point, a cruiser and other vessels also firing for three minutes. A flag of truce was then hoisted by the French, and the landing craft went in. The South Lancashires landed north of Tannio Point, to the north of the town, and the Royal Welch Fusiliers went ashore to the south of the port. Immediately afterwards three destroyers rushed into the harbour, landing more South Lancashires and men of 5th Commando on the jetty.

The invaders found the defences deserted and swiftly entered the town without loss of life. All but 80 French troops had left the port the previous day, taking with them their 65mm guns and machine guns.

By sheer chance a train was just entering the station as the town was captured, and after quickly checking it for booby traps, it was turned round and steamed for Brickaville, some 50 miles down the coast, with the South Lancashires aboard. This speedy advance caught the French unprepared, and not until two miles from Brickaville was the train brought to a halt by two blown bridges over a river. A slight skirmish followed, and Brickaville fell, the commandos then following up and passing through at once to continue the advance towards Tananarive.

Saturday, 19 to Sunday, 20 September 1942

On this same date 1433 Flight moved its Lysanders forward to Marosipoy to maintain contact with 22nd East African Brigade, and French resistance now stiffened in front of Tananarive, the Air Component beginning a more active period. It is estimated that by this time the strength of the Groupe Aerien Mixte stood at two serviceable Moranes, one Pz 63-11, one or two Pz 25TOEs, a Phrygane, and a Pz 29, all at Fianarantsoa. On Monday the 20th a Maryland undertook a strategic reconnaissance along the railway line from Antisirabe to Tananarive, looking for a suitable spot to cut the line and so prevent the French from moving supplies away southwards. The crew spotted a bridge across the Betsiboka River south of the capital, and selected this as the best target, bombing it but missing.

Three Beauforts were then launched after the same objective, but achieved no better results. Next day the Albacores of 796 Squadron took a hand, three of these aircraft making a dive-bombing attack; again no hits were scored, so the three Beauforts tried again — once more with no luck! The attempt was then given up.

Monday, 21 September 1942

Meanwhile on the ground 22nd East African Brigade were now close to

Tananarive, but were faced by strong positions at Mahitsy, two miles wide and held in depth on high ground. The African troops made wide outflanking movements and attacked the position at night on the 21st, becoming involved in some hard fighting during a two-day battle. Finally the French abandoned their positions as the Africans' attack gained ground bit by bit; 45 prisoners were taken, a 75mm and two 65mm guns were captured, together with two mortars and some machine guns.

Tananarive lay only 30 miles ahead now, but another force still faced the advance, occupying another strong position at Ahidatrino. There, however, as the 22nd Brigade column approached on the 23 September, the Malagache troops fled before a shot had been fired; the Senegalese, who made up the rest of the defence, held on for only half an hour before they too retreated. By 1700 African infantry and South African amoured cars had entered the capital.

Tuesday, 22 September 1942
A Maryland reconnoitred over 29th Brigade on the 22nd, as this formation advanced across the island from Brickaville, and on the 23rd 1433 Flight's Lysanders had a busy day, flying seven sorties in support of 22nd Brigade, strafing gun positions and strong-points at Ahidatrino during the brief battle there. With the occupation of Tananarive, a SAAF advance party at once moved on to Ivato airfield, although it was not to be ready to receive aircraft for four more days. By a stroke of luck, however, the French had carelessly left behind aerial photographs of the other Madagascan airfields and landing grounds — a windfall which was soon to be put to good use.

Thursday, 24 September 1942
From Tananarive King's African Rifles units at once moved east to meet the spearheads of 29th Brigade from Brickaville, the two columns meeting at Moramanga on 24 September. A victory parade was laid on in Tananarive, but still the French did not capitulate, retreating to Fianarantsoa, the only remaining town of any size on the island still in their hands. Allied troops pressed south from Tananarive in pursuit of them, but now met an incredible plethora of roadblocks: in one stretch of two and a half kilometres were 29 stone walls, the broadest being 18 feet across, and in one stretch of only half a mile 800 trees had been felled across the road.

Friday, 25 September 1942
South African Marylands were again active on the 25th, aircraft Nos 1663 and 1671 making an attack on a fort three miles north of Behenjy on the Tananarive–Antisirabe road shortly after dawn; sixteen 250lb bombs were dropped on the target. During the day one FAA Fulmar of 795 Squadron was reported lost in uncertain circumstances. On the 28th and 29th Lt Toulouse of the GAM flew reconnaissances north of Antisirabe in Morane No 815, the first sign of French aerial resistance being reported on the 30th when he strafed troops and vehicles in this forward area. A Maryland crew was briefed to find which airfield he had come from, and No 1680, using Ivato as a forward refuelling base, made a reconnaissance of the various landing grounds south of Tananarive; nothing was seen however. The search was continued for a week without success, despite the fact that both the Morane and a Potez 63-11 were seen by the ground forces during this period.

Tananarive, the capital of Madagascar, fell on 23 September 1942. Seen during the victory parade held shortly afterwards is one of the South African Marmon-Herrington armoured cars which had spear-headed the advance on the city. *(Imperial War Museum)*

Some 80 miles from the capital at Gare de Sambaina, a group of 600 Malagache troops were encountered by the ground forces on 30 September, but these were not prepared to do more than skirmish briefly, and two days later, on 2 October, Tanganyikan soldiers entered Antisirabe, a highland health resort, without meeting further resistance: one hour after the Africans' entry into the town, the French declared it open. Despite the many roadblocks, the French had refrained from damaging the railway from Tananarive to Antisirabe, and this was captured intact.

Meanwhile, on 29 September South African forces landed at Tulear in the far south-west, and began moving northwards, while another small force landed at Fort Dauphin in the south-east. These landings were reconnoitred by Cne Baché in a Pz 25TOE and Sgt Chef du Courtin in one of the Moranes. Several flights had been made to check this area during the preceding days. These flights were followed on 3 October by similar reconnaissances by the Pz 63-11, escorted again by a Morane, this time flown by Sgt Chef Largeau.

Saturday, 3 October 1942
The major part of the Air Component moved forward on 3 October, 1433 Flight going to Antisirabe, the other units settling at Ivato; four Albacores remained at Majunga for anti-submarine patrols.

Tuesday, 6 to Wednesday, 7 October 1942
On the 6th Sgt Chef Largeau was out again in one of the Moranes, strafing a column of Bren carriers near Antinchi. In response to this an offensive sweep was launched from Ivato on the 7th over all airfields in range, and during this a Potez 63-11 was seen in the air; two Fulmars at once gave chase, but the French

aircraft was able to outrun them and escape. The two Marylands engaged in the sweep dropped their bombs on a hangar at Ihosy, and on return an analysis of sightings and reconnaissance reports indicated that this was indeed the operational base from which the French aircraft were coming.

Thursday, 8 October 1942

Next day three Beauforts took off to bomb the airfield, but on their approach run to the target spotted three Potez 25TOE biplanes, one Potez 63-11 and one Morane 406 hidden in the bush a mile to the south-west of the airfield. These were all strafed by the Beauforts before the bombers went on to bomb the main target; the Morane appeared to have its tail on fire.

Not having any code in which to wireless their base of their find, the radio operator of one SAAF aircraft reported in Afrikaans 'Vier Fliegtuie op Ihosy in Bosse Ooste Kout'. A photograph was taken by the crew of one Beaufort on which all five aircraft were visible. On return of the formation to Ivato, a Maryland was at once sent for a repeat attack, but on arrival it was noted that the Morane had been removed. Indeed, the Morane had been hit in the fuselage, and one Pz 25TOE had been set on fire, the French having been caught by surprise on this occasion. As soon as the Beauforts had departed, the Morane and the Pz 63-11 had been moved into the hangar with one Pz 25TOE and one Pz 29, the other aircraft having been dispersed as best as possible.

The remaining aircraft that could be seen were therefore bombed, and a wing was seen to be blown off one Pz 25TOE. Attacks on Ihosy were repeated during the next two days, the hangar finally receiving a direct hit on the 10th, which destroyed the Pz 63-11 and the Pz 29. After the armistice, the two Potez aircraft and two civil machines were discovered here, all damaged beyond repair. However, Morane No 815 still survived intact, and Sgt Chef Largeau would again fly a reconnaissance in this on the 12th, covering the Ihosy–Sakaraha area.

At Ivato meanwhile, 16 SAAF Squadron was reorganised, 32, 36 and 37 Flights being abolished and replaced by two normal squadron flights — 'A' with Marylands and 'B' with Beauforts. By 10 October, 1433 Flight had only two Lysanders left serviceable; during operations the unit had lost one aircraft to French ground fire, one member of the crew being killed. To ensure sufficient support for the ground forces, therefore, the RAF Flight was relieved by three Fulmars and five Albacores, and moved back to the main Component base at Ivato. The Royal Navy aircraft then undertook daily tactical reconnaissance and ground-attack sorties throughout the rest of the campaign. On one occasion a Fulmar strafed a convoy of cars in which the Vichy Governor and his staff were evacuating Fianarantsoa.

16 SAAF Squadron had at last received an adequate supply of spares, and now became markedly more active, undertaking a much-increased programme of bombing during the closing weeks of fighting. On the 12th four Beauforts bombed Ihosy, and on the 15th two Marylands attacked troops in positions in hills south of Ambositra. These positions had been chosen by the French for their main stand. At Ambositra a Malagache platoon had already fought to the last, the stiffest fight since Andriba, but after the heaviest bombardment of the campaign (by sixteen guns) had been carried out, they surrendered to the African infantry as the latter moved in.

Five miles south of Ambositra was a U-shaped line of hills with the prongs pointing northwards and the road running between them. Well entrenched along the crests, the French waited for several days for the British forces to arrive and be trapped. At dawn on 19 October an artillery barrage broke on their positions, but still there was no sign of 22nd East African Brigade on the road. Suddenly the French were attacked from the rear at many points by the King's African Rifles, who had successfully outflanked them, and with all their positions facing north and north-east, the French were quickly surrounded and captured, their commander, Colonel Metras, and his headquarters being some of the first to be taken.

This operation cost the French 40 dead and many prisoners, the British forces suffering no casualties. The attack had also been undertaken without the support of 29th Brigade, which had been withdrawn the previous day to be shipped to Durban in South Africa for rest, due to a high incidence of malaria.

The defenders were now down to some six companies, and for the first time British forces enjoyed numerical superiority. 22nd Brigade pushed on fast, reaching Ankorona before dark on the 19th. Vichy forces fell back to defensive positions in front of Fianarantsoa, but at dawn next morning Tanganyikan infantry attacked them frontally, while Kenyans, closely supported by South African armoured cars, outflanked them, attacking from the rear and again capturing the commanding Colonel. 200 prisoners were taken and the French army now swiftly melted away as the Malagache elements deserted in droves.

Despite the attacks on Ihosy, the last Morane was still at large, and had carried out attacks on the South Africans from Tulear, who reached Sakaraha on 21 October, the limit of their advance. On this date the Groupe Aerien Mixte was officially disbanded and became the Corps France de l'Air. By this time only one aircraft — a Phrygane — was left serviceable, and this was to make its final sortie next day in the hands of Cne Baché. It was spotted and pursued by a Fulmar, but he had little difficulty in avoiding this by employing the light aircraft's greatly superior manoeuvrability. On the same day two Marylands returned to Ihosy to ensure that no further Armée de l'Air activity was in the offing, and to bomb the airfield again. Next day three Beauforts and a Maryland bombed positions north of Alakamisy, where the French were making their final stand. This attack was repeated on the 24th by two Beauforts and two Marylands, and further assaults were made in the course of the next few days. Propaganda leaflets were also dropped.

From Fianarantsoa one column of African infantry moved eastwards towards Manakara on the coast, reaching the village on 2 November. Four days later, in the early hours of 6 November, an armistice was at last signed at Ambalavao, a few miles south of Fianarantsoa, before a final advance to Ihosy was made. The whole island now came fully under Allied control, and the ex-Governor was flown to Tamatave in a Maryland. 22nd East African Brigade had advanced 650 miles in eight weeks in the face of over 3,000 roadblocks. They had fought five major and a number of minor engagements during which an army of about 6,000 men had been defeated.

As operations ceased a number of replacement Lysanders arrived for 1433 Flight. This unit was to remain as the island's sole air garrison as, immediately after the armistice, 795 and 796 Squadrons flew to East Africa, with 16 SAAF Squadron not far behind; the Marylands were flown to the Union for disposal, while the rest of the Squadron also moved to East Africa to exchange the surviving Beauforts for the promised Bisleys.

During the period 12 May to 6 November 1942 the Air Component undertook

230 operational sorties. Apart from the casualties already mentioned, the observer of one Albacore was killed by ground fire, and six aircraft were damaged beyond repair by enemy action of this kind; three more were slightly damaged. It is thought that the former figure was considerably affected by the difficulty in obtaining spares, and that had facilities for repair been better, fewer aircraft would have been written off.

Operational sorties were as follows:

16 SAAF Squadron	
(Marylands)	33 sorties
(Beauforts)	34 sorties
1433 Flight	
(Lysanders)	29 sorties
795 Squadron	
(Fulmars)	45 sorties
796 Squadron	
(Albacores)	89 sorties
Total	230 sorties
Totalling 591 individual operational flights.	

N.B. Of the sorties flown by 796 Squadron, 25 were anti-submarine patrols undertaken from Majunga.

Within days, on Sunday, 8 November 1942, the Vichy air forces would yet again find themselves in action against their former allies when Anglo–American forces landed in Algeria and Morocco at the commencement of Operation 'Torch'. It would prove to be the last such occasion however, for within weeks the French would be firmly back within the Allied camp. The full account of those events can be found in *Fighters over Tunisia*, which it is hoped will be republished in updated form in the future.

(N.B. Personnel listed in this index who have also appeared in other volumes in this series are identified by a series of letters in brackets after their names, as follows:

AWYGC — *Air War for Yugoslavia, Greece and Crete, 1940-1941*
MHY — *Malta: the Hurricane Years, 1940-1941*
MSY — *Malta: the Spitfire Year, 1942*
FOT — *Fighters over Tunisia*
FE — *Fledgling Eagles*
BS I or BS II — *Bloody Shambles Vols I and II*

Personnel — British Commonwealth

Personnel — French

Personnel — Italian

Tellurio, Serg Magg 410ª Sq CT 46
Tieghi, Serg Magg Athos 410ª Sq CT 87
Titi, Sottoten 29° Gr BT 69, *70*, 70-1
Tominello, Serg Magg 413ª Sq CT 123
Trezzani, Gen 36

Valentini, Sottoten 155ª Sq CT 195

Valenza, Sottoten MAS 213 140
Veronese, Sottoten Alberto 410 Sq CT
    35, 49, *49*, 50, *51*, 54, 87, 108, 116,
    118, 141, 162
Via, Col Francesco Cdr, Diredawa 78
Violetti, Serg Magg Piero 10ª Sq, 28°
    Gr BT 33

Visintini, Cap Mario 412ª Sq CT 21, 32,
    63, *75*, *83*, 84, 111, 162
Volpe, Serg Magg 410ª Sq CT 54

Zoino, Serg Magg Ugo 411ª Sq CT 68-9
Zucconi, Capt Tito 29° Gr BT 69, 71

Personnel — German

Bennewitz, Lt R. 5/LG 1 215
Blomberg, Maj Axel von Luftwaffe
    Liaison Officer, Iraq 180-1
Bob, Ofw 4/ZG 76 180
Brandstetter, Ofw 4/ZG 76 180

Dickjobst, Lt H. 4/LG 1 215
Drewes, Lt Martin 4/ZG 76 180, 189,
    190

Eisenach, Lt 4/ZG 76 180

Fischer, Uffz I/ZG 26 187
Froehling, Lt 4/ZG 76 180

Graubner, Olt 4/KG 4 180, 185-6
Guretzki, Uffz 4/KG 4 180, 186

Hennies, Uffz 4/ZG 76 180
Herget, Olt Wilhelm 4/ZG 76 180
Hobein, Olt 4/ZG 76 180

Junck, Oberst Werner Luftwaffe Cdr,
    Iraq 180

Lipka, Gefr H. 6/LG 1 255

Neureiter, Ofw 4/ZG 76 180

Oertel, Ofw 4/KG 4 180

Piwarz, Ofw 4/ZG 76 180
Prinz, Fw 4/KG 4 180, 186

Rahn, Dr Rudolf Foreign Minister 192

Rommel, Gen Erwin Cdr, Afrika
    Korps 143, 199
Rother, Hpt Harry Transport pilot 180

Schmidt, Olt 4/KG 4 180
Schwanhäuser, Hpt 4/KG 4 180, 185

Thomas, Ofw 4/KG 4 180, 186

Weber, Uffz 4/KG 4 180
Wenke, Uffz 4/ZG 76 180
Woerner, Lt I/ZG 26 180, 187
Wolf, Lt Lothar 4/KG 4 180

Ziegler, Uffz 4/ZG 76 180

Personnel — Other Nationalities

Dremas, Flg Off L.C. (Greek)
    Habbaniya 191

Fawzi Qawukji Arab guerilla leader
    257

Gilliaert, Maj Gen (Belgian) Cdr,
    Belgian Forces, East Africa 154

Illah, Emir Abdul Regent of Iraq 164
Iraq, King of 164

Jerusalem, Mufti of 164, 166

Rashid Ali el Ghailani Iraqi Prime
    Minister 164, 166, 181, 195, 203

Roosevelt, Franklin D. US President 147

Places

Abadan, Iran 271-2
Abalti, Ethiopia 153
Ablah, Syria 236
Aboukir, Egypt 206
Abu-Danne, Syria 233, 236, 242, 245,
    247-8, *248*, 250, 255, 258, 261
Abu Hareira, Syria 254
Abu Kemal, Syria 226-7, 230-1, 240,
    245, 246-7, 270
Abu Sueir, Egypt 38, 44, 204, 229
Acico Bay, Eritrea 30
Acre, Palestine 261
Adadleh, British Somaliland 51
Adalia, Gulf of, Turkey 252
Adama, Ethiopia 134, 137
Adarte, Eritrea 81
Addis Ababa, Ethiopia 5, 10, 11, 22,
    25, 30, 35, 37, 39, 40, 45, 48, *49*, *50*,
    53, 54-5, 56, 58, 63, 66, *76*, 83, 87,
    119, 129-32, 134-8, 140, *141*, 141-2,
    143, *144*, 145-7, 150, 153-5, 162
Aden 4, 13, *13*, 18, 19, *19*, 20-4, 28, 30,
    34, 36-41, 44, 45-6, 48-9, *50*, 52,
    54-60, 62-3, 65, 67-8, 71, 78, 80, 93,
    110, 116-7, 127, 129/ 131, 134-5, 137,
    139, 149, 152, 154, 164
Adi Ugri, Ethiopia 100, 102, 109, 117,
    142
Adowa, Ethiopia 134
Ad Teclesan, Eritrea 135-7
Afmadu, Italian Somaliland 21-2, 65,
    89, 100, 104, 106, 110, 113
Agara, Ethiopia 150

Agordat, Eritrea 11, 36, 41, 57, 81, 94-
    9, 101, 103-4, 108, 110-11, 116-7,
    128, 131, *132*
Ahidatrino, Madagascar 292
Ahwaz, Iran 271-4
Aicota district, Eritrea 97, 99
Aiscia, Ethiopia 58, 158, 162
Aksum, Ethiopia 157
Alakamisy, Madagascar 295
Aleppo, Syria 177, 184, 187, 191, 193,
    195-6, 202-4, 211, 215, 217-9, *225*,
    228-9, 236, 239, 240, 242, 245-7, 250-
    2, 254, 256-7, *257*, 259-61, 265, *265*,
    270
Alexandria, Egypt 139, 180, 224
Algato, Ethiopia 151, 153
Aligabe, Kenya 104-6, 109
Alomata, Ethiopia 68, 109, 120, 146,
    148-9, 155-7, 159, 160
Amawa, Iraq 187
Amba Alagi, Ethiopia 147, 150-2
Ambalavao, Madagascar 295
Ambararata Bay, Madagascar 279
Ambazzo, Ethiopia 160, 161
Ambre River, Madagascar 279
Ambositra, Madagascar 194
Amman, Transjordan 190, 205-6, 211,
    222
Amanamit, Ethiopia 94
Ampasindara Bay, Madagascar 287
Ampozony, Madagascar 289
Amriya, Egypt 180, 261
Ancober, Ethiopia 6

Andrakoka Peninsula, Madagascar 279
Andriba, Madagascar 290, 294
Anivorano, Madagascar 279
Ankorone, Madagascar 295
Antalaha, Madagascar 291
Antinichi, Madagascar 295
Antsirabe, Madagascar 291-3
Antsirane, Madagascar 277, 279, 280-1
Antsohoky, Madagascar 290
Aouaj, Syria 225
Aqir, Palestine 166, 168, 171-2, 178-9,
    182, *183*, 183-4, 192-4, 203, 206, 211,
    229, 233, *234*, *238*, 242
Archer's Post, Kenya 51, 61, 63, 72, 88,
    92
Aroma, Sudan *83*, 84, 95
Arrachart, Diego Suarez, Madagascar
    277, 279, 281, 284-5, *286*, *287*
Artouz, Syria 225, 228-9
Aselle, Ethiopia 142
Asmara, Eritrea 5, 10, 17-19, 28, 32,
    37, 42, 57, 61, 87, 95, 98, 101, 108-
    10, 112, 114, 116, 120-22, 130-1, 133,
    136, 137-8, 142-3, 147, 152, 159
Asosa, Ethiopia 26
Assab, Eritrea 6, 10, 11, 17, *18*, 18, 19,
    20, 22, 26-32, *29*, 34, 36-7, 40, 57-8,
    63, 65, 109, 146
Athens, Greece 180, *213/214*, 219, *226*,
    226, 254, 256, 258, *258*, 259, 261
Atbara, Sudan 57, 84
Auascia, Eritrea 97
Aulnot, France 213

Air Force Units

Part One — Commonwealth

Part Two — Regia Aeronautica

Part Three — Armée de l' Air

Part Four — Luftwaffe

Part Five — Other Air Forces

ii) Naval Units

Part One — British Commonwealth

308